SWEATSHOPS AT SEA

Sweatshops at Sea

MERCHANT SEAMEN IN THE WORLD'S FIRST GLOBALIZED INDUSTRY, FROM 1812 TO THE PRESENT

Leon Fink

The University of North Carolina CHAPEL HILL

This book was published with the assistance of the Thornton H. Brooks Fund of the University of North Carolina Press.

 Set in Minion Pro by Tseng Information Systems, Inc.
Manufactured in the United States of America

The paper in this book meets the guidelines for permanence and durability of the Committee on Production Guidelines for Book Longevity of the Council on Library Resources. The University of North Carolina Press has been a member of the Green Press Initiative since 2003.

Library of Congress Cataloging-in-Publication Data
Fink, Leon, 1948–
Sweatshops at sea : merchant seamen in the world's first globalized industry, from 1812 to the present / Leon Fink.
p. cm.
Includes bibliographical references and index.
ISBN 978-0-8078-3450-3 (cloth : alk. paper)
1. Merchant mariners—History. 2. Merchant marine—History. I. Title.
HD8039.S4F56 2011
387.5—dc22
2010037736

15 14 13 12 11 5 4 3 2 1

To the SS *Newberry Library*—including its wise officers, scholarly passengers, and cheerful proletariat of the stacks—for providing me a comfortable berth and stimulating company throughout the journey of this book

Contents

Introduction 1

PART I. MASTERED AND COMMANDED

1. The Nation's Property 9
Nineteenth-Century Sailors and the Political Economy of the Atlantic World

2. Liberty before the Mast 35
Defining Free Labor in Law and Literature

PART II. STRATEGIES OF REFORM

3. Wave of Reform 67
The Sailor's Friend and the Drift toward a Welfare State

4. The Nationalist Solution 93
The La Follette Act of 1915 and the Janus Face of Progressive Reform

5. Workers of the Sea, Unite? 117
The Internationalist Legacy of the Pre–World War I Years

PART III. A WORLD FIT FOR SEAFARERS?

6. A Sea of Difference 145
The International Labor Organization and the Search for Common Standards, 1919–1946

7. Cooperation and Cash 171
Labor's Opportunity in a Post-Deregulatory Era

Notes 203 *Works Cited* 241 *Acknowledgments* 259 *Index* 261

Figures

1.1. *Boarding the "Chesapeake"* 15

1.2. *Impressment of American Seamen* 17

2.1. *Flogging on a Man-of-War* 46

2.2. *The Sailor's Farewell* 58

3.1. Plimsoll line 69

3.2. The coffin ships 72

3.3. *A Tribute to Samuel Plimsoll* 91

4.1. "Unskilled Seamen at Work" 96

4.2. U.S. Progressive reformers 99

5.1. "In Mid-Ocean during the Seamen's Strike" 126

5.2. An exoticized view of Indian seamen 134

6.1. Yank in *The Hairy Ape* 147

6.2. Albert Thomas and shipowners 151

6.3. American Merchant Marine Memorial 165

7.1. ITF flag-of-convenience inspection 192

7.2. Filipino sailors on Greek freighter 199

Introduction

This is not a book about pirates, but let's begin with pirates. In April 2009, most Americans were startled to learn that a U.S. flagged merchant ship, the *Maersk Alabama*, had been attacked by Somali pirates off the Horn of Africa and equally relieved when the destroyer USS *Bainbridge*, which happened to be patrolling in the area, arrived to rescue the captain and literally blow up his captors. A sporadic and generally marginal phenomenon across two centuries, the incidence of oceanic piracy has picked up in recent years due to the juncture of rising Asian exports (especially for transshipment through the Suez Canal and the Molucca Straits) and the number of "failed states" around the Indian Ocean.

Still, the story of the *Maersk* was exceptional, and the Somalis in this case were particularly unlucky thieves. One sequestered U.S. captain drew more attention than the hundreds of other pirate captives, either previously ransomed or at the time still in Somali custody. The difference between the *Maersk Alabama* and the Somalis' other targets, however, was not just that they had picked on the most powerful nation in the world but that they were suddenly confronting a "nation" at all. Unlike the corsairs of the early-nineteenth-century "Barbary Wars," to whom they are sometimes compared on the superficial grounds of their being both poor Muslims feeding off nearby oceanic traffic, today's pirates are stateless actors generally operating in a medium of weak or even fictive states. Oceanic piracy, in short, no longer triggers "war talk" in powerful capitals because those capitals are seldom directly involved. The industries of most contemporary global powers (the United States included) no longer use their own ships or seafarers when engaging in world commerce. Long without a competitive oceangoing merchant fleet, for example, the United States has sought since World War I to maintain only a minimal seagoing presence by governmental subsidy. In the latest version of this principle, the Maritime Security Program subsidizes some sixty U.S.-flag vessels (including, as it happens, the *Maersk Alabama*) in foreign commerce, with the proviso that they can be summoned in event of emergency by the secretary of defense. Instead of engaging superpowers like Great Britain, which long famously "ruled the waves," or the United States, which in the aftermath of each of two world wars dominated global tonnage, latter-day oceanic marauders face relatively stateless targets. Ships filled with poor nationals from the Philippines, Indonesia, and China regularly sail today under flags of virtual nonentities like the Marshall Islands, Panama, and Liberia in ferrying the world's goods.

This is a roundabout way of saying that much has changed in the maritime world over the past two hundred years. In exploring that world, this volume asks, Who sails? Who governs the shipping world—both ships and seafarers? And under what rules? As we will observe, the seas served as an extension of political principles and laws that generally prevailed in the world's commercial centers—but with a twist. Those who made up the workforce of the merchant marine (or what the British call the merchant navy) were often regarded as a breed apart and thus in need of special legislative or other legal administration. We are generally sensitive today to how "global" or international virtually all commerce has become—as have virtually all our economic problems. Yet, if recent economic activity has generally moved in this global direction—so much so that many call our times the "era of globalization"—the shipping industry, including its labor relations, has always been so.

This is a book about the laws and labor relations of ordinary seamen plying the waters of an Atlantic-based trading system over the past two hundred years. It is, perhaps, less a social history than a political history of seafaring, for the seafarers themselves are as often the objects as the subjects of the story. It is also necessarily, and perhaps arbitrarily, selective in its geographic focus. For the nineteenth century, it concentrates on the world's dominant sea power, Great Britain, and its chief challenger, the United States; then, in concert with shifting trade patterns and the rise of international institutions of governance, both the geographic and political focus determinedly widen for the twentieth century. As an intrinsic part of the nation-building and empire-building process of the nineteenth century, recruitment and regulation of a seafaring labor force emerged as a high priority and a vexing problem for both the British and the Americans. When sea workers themselves, through their trade unions, emerged as powerful agents by the end of the century, governance of the shipping industry took on still more complex dimensions. Among the complications, the mixture of peoples composing the seagoing labor force recurringly injected citizenship and immigration issues into maritime labor discussions. Given smoldering conflicts between workers and employers as well as among governments themselves, the twentieth century witnessed repeated attempts to bring order to the industrial relations of the shipping world through a variety of international agreements and transnational agencies. The very artery of international commerce, merchant shipping continually served as a site of regulatory enforcement, whether applied by individual states, an organized world community, or labor-management consent through collective bargaining agreements.

The changing topical (not to mention geographical and chronological) focus of my story dictates an equally eclectic range of sources. One continuing strand involves the legislative record, as reported in the *Congressional Record* (and its antecedents) and the *Hansard Parliamentary Debates*. In addition to select U.S. Supreme Court cases, the other lawmaking proceedings that were indispensable to my research are those of the International Labor Organization in Geneva. Not surprisingly, union records and newspapers—particularly those of the U.S. Sailors' Union of the Pacific, the U.S. International Longshore and Warehouse Union, the British National Union of Seamen, the International Transport Workers' Federation, and present-day Filipino mariners—also play a constitutive role. Then, of course, there is the rich, near-limitless literature on shipping and seafaring compiled by generations of maritime historians and other specialists. Like a scavenger on the beach, I have pillaged the accumulated scholarly record (with due deference in footnotes and bibliography, I hope) for all it was worth. Finally, I have been lucky enough to meet (or otherwise converse at long distance) with a select group of related experts and actors in the subject explored below. None of them is any way responsible for my mistakes or oversights, but they have in every case enriched my understanding by welcoming me into their specialized and complex worlds.

I hope this study adds a novel angle to the well-established, rich field of maritime history. In hearkening, like many others, to the "call" of the sea, I hope not to exoticize my findings beyond their logical limits. To that end I am reminded of a recent passage concerning British oceanic explorations in the eighteenth century:

> A number of writers have stressed the symbolic, tropic, and political significance of the ship in the age of the revolution. For Michel Foucault, the ship was the "heterotopia *par excellence*," a chronotype that

moved through space, compressing, inventing and inverting terrestrial social relations and re-shaping the human imaginary. For Paul Gilroy, the linguistic and political hybridity of the ship constituted a "counter-culture of modernity" that enabled men and women to cross and transgress social, geographical and national boundaries. For Marcus Rediker and Peter Linebaugh, the ship, with its dangers, monotonies and tyrannies, its paradoxical imperatives of cooperation and coercion, was the engine of radical proletarian consciousness. And for Greg Dening, the ship was both a floating island and a "beach" where cultures were made to reveal themselves to each other.[1]

Notwithstanding the thrill of metaphorical excursions, our voyage will be a more prosaic (one is tempted to say grounded) one. Indeed, though I am precisely interested in the internationalist (hybrid, heterotopic, cooperative, and so on) *promise* of seagoing commerce, I do not think we can take those relations as a given or even, for most periods, as historical fact. Rather, we must look carefully at the actions not only of the seafarers themselves but of the land-based authorities, national and occasionally supranational, who composed the rules for the floating world.

Sweatshops at Sea proceeds in three stages. Part 1, "Mastered and Commanded," surveys the Atlantic world from the mercantilist controls still in place on sailing ships at the end of the Napoleonic Wars through the rise of a more "liberal" industrial capitalism powered by steam at the end of the century. Chapter 1 revisits the impressment controversy at the heart of the War of 1812, asking why this labor-centered issue should momentarily so roil international waters—as well as how and why the issue should quickly thereafter sink into historical oblivion. Sailors' citizenship, a key factor in the impressment dispute, also makes the first of many appearances—whether as a concern of governments, shipowners, or native workers themselves—as a contentious aspect of in maritime employment. Chapter 2 opens a wider canvas on the place of merchant seamen or "sailors" (a term that by the twentieth century was reserved in the United States—though less so in Great Britain—for the navy) in Anglo-American political culture. In particular, the peculiar degree of coercion applied in both the recruitment and management of the seagoing commercial labor force in two societies otherwise touting their commitment to individual liberties emerged as a cause célèbre for both American and British intellectuals. The seagoing norms of shanghaiing, whipping, crimps, and imprisonment for desertion wrestled for a century with the more market-driven incentives for labor control predominant in land-based industries.

In part 2, "Strategies of Reform," both the similarities and differences between maritime and mainland labor problems emerge in bold relief. I turn to the principal strategies employed for advancing sailor welfare as well as to spreading conflicts that emerged among seafarers of different ethnic, racial, and national backgrounds. In Britain, as related in chapter 3, the quixotic gentleman-reformer Samuel Plimsoll fashioned an influential new constituency for redress of grievances affecting both safety and worker welfare. Just as Lord Shaftesbury fought for factory reform and Henry Mayhew exposed urban poverty in Britain and just as Upton Sinclair and Robert La Follette would later rally the middle-class public to the cause of labor reform in the United States, so Plimsoll became the first great champion of sailor safety and welfare. Plimsoll's pioneering efforts in parliamentary agitprop and public exposé ultimately bore fruit in a combination of legislative action and sailor union organization. Chapter 4 tracks the outer limits of maritime reform evidenced within a single national polity. The far-reaching La Follette Act of 1915, brainchild of American seamen's leader Andrew Furuseth, aimed to abolish the sweatshop-like conditions of all seamen by unilateral action in U.S. ports. Yet, in a kind of dress rehearsal for latter-day struggles over globalization, American reformers, in defense of higher-paid native workers, also betrayed a racist disdain for would-be foreign—and especially Asian—competitors. The world's first global union, as we learn in chapter 5, followed a distinctly different path in confronting the challenge of the global labor competition. Quickly seizing on the inevitably international composition of the seagoing labor force, British sailor union leader Havelock Wilson set out to organize the seafarers of the world. The story winds from heady moments of seamen's self-government and dramatic examples of international worker solidarity to bitter wartime disillusionment and recourse to a regulatory regime of national corporatism.

In part 3, "A World Fit for Seafarers?," I look especially to the international, multilateral mechanisms of workplace regulation that first appeared in the early twentieth century. Even as unionized, "white" workers sought to shore up their positions vis-à-vis "colored" competitors in the world's merchant marine, so too did they seek to establish a safety and welfare floor for all maritime workers. The role of the big national unions is considered here as well as the early development of international agents, particularly the International Labor Organization (ILO), established in Geneva in

1919, and the International Transport Workers' Federation (ITF), a global union federation combining transportation workers on land, sea, and air, formed in London in 1896 and reconstituted after World War I. Chapter 6 balances the agonizingly slow, convention-setting process of interwar ILO internationalism against the protectionist instincts that increasingly held sway over Depression-era governments. In the post–World War II world, as I mentioned at the outset, the rise of low-tax, low-regulation "flags of convenience" employing low-wage, third-world crews for much of the world's waterborne commerce posed new challenges to existing international structures. Concentrating on the shifting strategy of the ITF's FOC "boycott" campaign, chapter 7 weighs the strengths and weaknesses of a new international regulatory regime. By the early twenty-first century, the ITF managed to erect an impressive inspection system at ports around the world through a combination of idealism and pragmatic deal-making among its many international confederates. Yet the new structure, in important ways, created an organization that resembled social service agencies more than democratic, worker-centered unions. Whether the new agreements will truly enfranchise their seafaring clients or simply attend to their needs from on-high remains to be seen. Either way, what happens on the world's waters is likely to tell us a great deal about the possibilities of humane governance in a globalized world economy.

PART I

Mastered and Commanded

1

The Nation's Property

NINETEENTH-CENTURY SAILORS AND THE POLITICAL ECONOMY OF THE ATLANTIC WORLD

In *The Wealth of Nations* (1776), Adam Smith famously anticipated a world in which a relatively unfettered marketplace would maximize production, trade, and wealth for all those who could participate in its self-regulating mechanism. Yet, even as he identified the welfare of "nations" with the expansion of "wealth"—both of which, he believed, required restraint from governmental interference—Smith allowed himself some wiggle room when it came to shipping and sea power. It was no accident, he suggested, that the "first civilized" nations were those, around the coast of the tame Mediterranean Sea, that had first succeeded in "the infant navigation of the world."[1] Maintaining access to that navigable world and, if possible, dominance in world trade, it followed, was a crucial mark of national power. In a much-debated section of his classic text, Smith allowed that the bedrock principle of free trade might be abridged "when some particular sort of industry is necessary for the defence of the country. The defence of Great Britain, for example, depends very much upon the number of its sailors and shipping. The act of navigation, therefore, very properly endeavors to give the sailors and shipping of Great Britain the monopoly of the trade of their own country."[2] Thus it was that he offered a qualified defense of the notoriously restrictive Navigation Acts. Originally conceived amid rising Dutch-English tensions of the mid-seventeenth century, the assemblage of acts stipulated that a British-flagged ship be British-owned and British-built, that the master and at least three-quarters of the crew be British subjects, and (in order to protect the imperial "triangular trade") that traffic between colonial ports be limited to British carriers. Smith did not directly contradict his general premise that free trade promised the greatest economic returns or his specific claim that the Navigation Acts distorted trade and dampened economic growth.[3] Rather, his "exception" depended on an allowance that, "as defence . . . is of much more importance than opulence, the act of navigation is, perhaps, the wisest of all the commercial regulations of England."[4]

The Smithian exception regarding national shipping and naval interests rested on long legs that convinced even an outwardly powerful and confident England to carefully nurture and regulate its maritime trades at least through the mid-nineteenth century. Both in symbol and fact, abolition of the British Navigation Acts in 1849 represented a key disjuncture (one is tempted to say "watershed") of economic policy, even as it invited a new era of re-regulation in British shipping. For, even absent an older mercantilist emphasis on a favorable national balance of trade, there remained (for latter-day policy makers, just as for Smith) the residual strategic considerations that the merchant marine, or commercial sea labor, constituted a "nursery" for the navy and national defense as well as a key economic lifeline that could not be allowed to be ceded to potentially hostile powers. Thus it was that labor issues resonated throughout the nineteenth century at the center of transatlantic political debates about trade and shipping. Recruitment, disciplining, and ultimately the welfare of seamen were seen to bear on both national strength and reputation. As the American *Niles Register* asserted in 1829, seamen constituted the "property of the nation."[5] Even after midcentury, this assumption carried equally abiding force within the liberal, free-trade-oriented policies of a world-dominant United Kingdom as it did within the more rigidly protectionist policies of Britain's biggest contemporary trade rival, the United States.[6]

Impressment and the War of 1812

The logic of mercantilism—a bundle of assumptions emphasizing the national accumulation of wealth, positive balance of trade, and control of shipping lanes—exhausted itself in what qualifies as one of the last armed conflicts of the premodern era. The War of 1812 is properly seen as a battle between a defensive, maritime-based empire on the British side (fending off both Spain and France in the extended French Revolutionary and Napoleonic Wars, 1793–1815) and the boisterous sovereignty of the United States. Not coincidentally, however, it was also a war explicitly fought over a labor issue—impressment. The theme of "Free Trade and Sailors' Rights" (as the

Americans saw it) versus the duty of military service for native-born subjects (as the British preferred) defined the stakes of national power and identity in a world that Adam Smith might still have recognized as his own. Not surprisingly, the new symbols of national identity that emerged for Americans from the war—"The Star-Spangled Banner," "Old Ironsides," as well as the immemorial injunction "Don't give up the ship!"—all derived from the insistence on freeing American shipping, and ipso facto the nation's sailors, from British domination.[7] Considerations of trade, nationalism, and citizenship all beckoned toward war in 1812, and each theme hinged in important respects on the status of merchant seamen.

That the condition and status of seamen should serve as a flashpoint of conflict between Great Britain and her former colony was no accident. As historians Jesse Lemisch and Gary Nash first documented, much of the American Revolutionary agitation derived from the conflicts and contentious labor forces of the late-eighteenth-century colonial ports.[8] Waterfront rebels played key roles in the Knowles anti-impressment riot of 1747 and then again in resistance to the Townshend Duties of 1767 as well as the Boston Massacre of 1770 (where two of five victims were sailors and a third a ropemaker). In addition, captive sailors in Britain's Mill and Forton prisons kept both their own and home spirits alive with their proclamation of an in-house republic.[9] Partly, the maritime presence in contemporary protests was a matter of sheer numbers. Though the figures are at best guesswork, Thomas Jefferson estimated in 1791 that 20,000 men were employed in the brand-new nation as merchant sailors or fishermen; by the era 1830–50, the seamen's number likely exceeded 100,000, or roughly half that employed by Great Britain in a period of population symmetry.[10] In the Revolutionary Era (at least through 1813), these American crews included substantial numbers of both foreign-born (about 10 to 15 percent) and African American sailors (again, perhaps as many as 15 percent by 1812). The latter most famously included Olaudah Equiano, an Igbo slave and sailor before his London abolitionist agitation; Frederick Douglass, a slave caulker in Baltimore who, disguised as a merchant sailor, slipped north to his freedom; and "King Dick," who judiciously ruled over 800 captured black privateers among a total of 5,000 seamen inside Britain's dismal Dartmoor Prison during the War of 1812.[11]

The emergent American Republic, moreover, found itself challenged on the seas in two fundamental respects. The first was the case of the "Barbary captives." Caught by privateers (or privately commissioned corsairs) while entering Mediterranean waters off the North African coast, "enslaved"

American merchantmen served as a major political embarrassment for the young Republic between 1785 and 1815. Counting themselves the "only victims" of American independence, more than 700 sailors languishing for as long as ten years in Algerine captivity haunted the popular imagination on two counts.[12] Not only did their presence in the petty Barbary city-states of Algiers, Tunis, and Tripoli mock the capacity of the nation to defend and rescue its own citizens, it also highlighted the hypocrisy of the United States as a slave-holding power in its own right. In taking up the cause of abolition near the end of his life, Benjamin Franklin thus openly linked the captivity of Africans by Americans with that of Americans by North Africans: both, he suggested, represented a betrayal of man's natural right to freedom.[13] In the popular culture, a more racist angle prevailed with plays and novels depicting virtuous, liberty-loving Americans as victimized by corrupt and bloodthirsty black Algerians. Lurid newspaper reports circulated of American prisoners with heads shaven and in rags led to work in chains by their barbarian captors.[14] The Barbary issue would not go away, in fact, until the abatement of the British threat allowed for a concentration of U.S. military and diplomatic strategy on the North African coast.

The nub of maritime conflict throughout this period rested on the practice of British impressment. More than merely symbolic, the issue constituted an undeniable political crisis in the United States. To be sure, estimates vary as to the actual number of American citizen-sailors seized by British ships. Historians commonly cite the roughly 6,000 petitions from aggrieved U.S. seamen that President Madison himself pointed to in 1812. While contemporary newspaper and congressional testimony differed wildly in assessing the extent of the phenomenon, a recent scholarly assessment accepts the figure of "approximately 10,000 American sailors impressed between 1793 and 1812."[15] Most humiliatingly for an infant nation, the United States could only watch as the Royal Navy regularly stopped U.S. ships on the high seas, searched them for so-called British deserters, and claimed the right to "impress" any allegedly British-born subject, whether naturalized as an American citizen or not. As Secretary of State James Monroe insisted at the peace talks of 1814, "This degrading practice . . . must cease, our flag must protect the crew, or the United States cannot consider themselves an independent Nation."[16]

For British officialdom, regular resort to impressment, a long-authorized albeit contentious practice, appeared throughout the Napoleonic Wars as a necessary emergency measure. Rooted in measures adopted by Oliver Cromwell to make war against the Dutch in the 1650s, impressment helped fashion what historians Peter Linebaugh and Marcus Rediker have labeled an "imperial hydrarchy" or "maritime state."[17] Perhaps at its most harsh in the 1690s, some three-fourths of those impressed reportedly died within two years, and the image of the "starving, often lame sailor in the seaport town became a permanent feature of European civilization."[18] As early as the seventeenth century, as Nicholas Rogers has demonstrated, Leveller protest in the English Civil War had likened impressment into the British navy as a form of "galley slavery" common to Turkey or Algiers. Repeatedly in the eighteenth century, sailor-reformers insisted that impressment violated Clause 39 of the Magna Carta, that there could be no arrest without a trial by jury. The *Somerset* case of 1772, which decided that no slave could be forcibly removed from Britain and sold into slavery again, raised the question of how seamen could similarly be forced to serve against their will. Such complaints, if not exactly answered, were trumped by a resort to the royal prerogative, as in Lord Walpole's 1740 rationale that "we must not only have ships but sailors."[19] Thus, despite persistent criticism, impressment continued to be regularly deployed in wartime, and those caught in its grip tended to escape only with help from social superiors. Though, in principle, every British-born or naturalized male subject was legally pressable, in practice the press gangs centered their attention on the most skilled, "able seamen" approaching land on inbound merchant ships.[20] As need arose, however, the "floating population" or, more specifically, "men of seafaring habits between the ages of 18 and 55" not specifically exempted (such as fishermen and apprentices) in port towns were liable to forced service.[21] Beginning in the 1770s, the Royal Navy began impressing all apprentices who were not carrying their indentures; by 1779, now facing the hostile forces of France, Spain, and Holland as well as the United States, press gangs proved ever less discriminate in their zeal.[22] Indeed, at the height of British recruiting problems in 1812, an estimated 15 percent of the Royal Navy deckhands were "foreigners," most of them simply seized off merchant ships in foreign ports.[23]

With the renewal of British-French hostilities in 1803—following a brief demobilization of sailors that had accompanied the Treaty of Amiens—Britain resumed the practice of stopping foreign vessels for inspection in order to impress any of the king's subjects aboard ship.[24] Such encounters especially stoked tensions with the Americans both because their nation's higher wage rates induced recruitment of many British seamen and because of the difficulty of ascertaining the true citizenship of any Anglo-American sailor.[25] Sailors in this era, as ever, it seems, were a young, mobile, and migrating lot: historian Paul A. Gilje, for example, relates the story of one John Blatchford, who signed on the Continental ship *Hancock* as a cabin boy in 1777 and returned to New Jersey six years later, having served under six flags and traveled halfway around the world.[26] Moreover, throughout the long period of Anglo-American tensions, numerous sailors switched not only flags but allegiance and citizenship, whether according to immediate self-interest or political principle.[27]

Such messy demographic reality in the maritime trade, however, ran directly afoul of British war imperatives, post-1805. Particularly following the *Essex* decision (1805) and Orders in Council (1807), which aimed especially to curtail promiscuous U.S. trading with France and her colonies, British impressment policy merged with a geopolitical attempt to maintain commercial hegemony in the Atlantic world.[28] In defense of the system's coercive features, British advocates repeatedly complained that the new nation offered all-too-easy employment and all-too-quick citizenship for deserting or refugee seamen. As protection against British impressment of legitimate American nationals, the U.S. government had begun issuing "certificates of citizenship" to American seamen in 1796. Bureaucratic controls, however, were lax. Unlike a latter day's concern for tight immigration restriction, "it is notoriously known," wrote a British pamphleteer in 1807, "that the channels of perjury are, as they have been for years, still open for the obtaining of certificates of American citizenship. It is only necessary for one sailor to get another to swear for him, that he was born in such a place, and a certificate is granted. . . . It has now arisen to that height, that men speaking most palpably the provincial dialects of England, Ireland, and Scotland, are to be seen thus protected. Is the British government tamely to acquiesce in this robbery of her seamen?"[29]

The issue was all the more strained because, under the principle of indefeasible nationality (formally maintained as late as 1870), expatriation *away* from British identity was not recognized: in short, "once a British subject, always a British subject."[30] The needs of the British fleet combined with its expansive legal claims, however, were exacted at the expense of U.S. sovereignty. Despite angry protests of the American government, post-1805, the cargoes of dozens of American merchant ships had been confiscated and virtually every vessel leaving the port of New York faced the indignity of an impressment search by British warships. War was nearly set off in 1807 in the *Chesapeake* affair. A patrolling British squadron, which had lost men to desertion, fired on the USS *Chesapeake* near Norfolk, Virginia, killing three

FIGURE 1.1. *Boarding the "Chesapeake"* by John Christian Schetsky (1778–1874). In an incident that stoked international tensions associated with impressment policy, the British warship *Leopard* in 1807 confronted the American frigate *Chesapeake* and demanded to search her crew for suspected British deserters. When the American captain refused, the British opened fire, killing three sailors and seizing four others as Royal Navy deserters. Quickly commemorated by Scottish marine artist John Christian Schetsky, the incident and others like it helped lead to the U.S. declaration of war in 1812. Private Collection/Bridgeman Art Library.

sailors and mortally wounding another, then boarded the wrecked vessel and impressed a British-born deserter, two African American freemen, and a white native of Maryland. The incident unleashed a tide of indignation across the young Republic.[31]

In the short term, however, the aggrieved Americans had few alternatives. Fearing a permanent and costly professional military on land or sea, the young nation simply had no effective defense beyond diplomacy against true sea powers. Already, the Federalists had been ridiculing President Jefferson's preference for small gunboats (which easily capsized or ran ashore in foul weather), taunting the Republican president by saying, "If our gunboats are no use on the water, may they at least be the best on earth!"[32] Jefferson's initial response was the Embargo Act of 1807, an unhappy experiment in commercial self-isolation, whose suspension in 1809 coincided with a steady clamor of war talk.

With rhetorical focus on the evils of impressment and other restrictions on its commerce, the United States declared war on Britain in June 1812.[33] Months later, in his second inaugural address, President Madison tried to rally support for the war by again invoking "the cruel sufferings" of "an important class of citizens" that "have found their way to every bosom not dead to the sympathies of human nature."[34] As if to underscore the president's message, the *Chesapeake* went bravely, if inauspiciously, back into battle from Boston Harbor with the banner "Free Trade and Sailors' Rights" emblazoned on its side.[35] A contemporary poem in the *New York Public Advertiser* highlighted the theme of "The Kidnapped Seamen":

> Sons of Freedom break your slumbers
> Hear a brother's piercing cries
> From amid your foe's deep thunders
> Hear his bitter griefs arise.

Surrounded by patriotic rhetoric placing themselves at the rising crux of international grievances, "most Jack Tars," Gilje fairly generalizes, "believed that the United States went to war with Great Britain in 1812 to protect their liberty."[36]

In truth, for both combatants, the impressment dispute was less about the rights or welfare of seamen than the prerogatives of government over its own citizens. While Britain effectively asserted the right to coerce the labor power of its errant seamen, the U.S. response focused less on abuses of individual sailor rights than on the allegedly unlawful jurisdiction of British patrols in stopping "neutral" U.S. ships at sea and/or seizing those sailors whom the United States claimed as American citizens. As exemplified in the *Chesapeake* affair and in the exchanges between the U.S. minister to Britain, James Monroe, and the British foreign minister, George Canning, national honor (and sovereignty) weighed considerably more heavily—on both sides—than the much-trumpeted theme of "seamen's rights." As Canning acknowledged fault for impressing sailors from a ship of war like the *Chesapeake* (such practice having been renounced in principle in favor of government-to-government negotiation), he stuck strongly to the "ancient prerogative" of impressment over "defecting" British subjects—the deprecatory classification for any non-serving seaman of British birth—off any

FIGURE 1.2. *Impressment of American Seamen.* In this wood engraving, a British officer is looking over a group of American seamen with the aim of impressing any alleged deserters, ca. 1810. Created for the American *Harper's Monthly* in April 1884, the image celebrates the War of 1812 as one fought for "free trade and sailors' rights." *Harper's Monthly*, Apr. 1884, p. 751.

merchant ship. In resisting British practice, Monroe did not directly challenge British principle. Rather, he pointed to the peculiar difficulty of fairly enforcing impressment in the U.S. case. "It would be easy to distinguish between an Englishman and a Spaniard, an Italian or a Swede; and the clear and irresistible Evidence of this National Character, and perhaps of his Desertion, would establish the British Claim to the Individual, and reconcile the Nation into whose Service he had entered to his Surrender." But the U.S. case was different, for "who is so skilful in Physiognomy as to distinguish between an American and an Englishman, especially among those whose Profession and whose Sea Terms are the same?" In vainly demanding reparations for the *Chesapeake* incident, the Americans accused the British not of any crime against seamen but of reneging on terms of independence agreed to at the end of the American Revolution.[37] Initially supporting the resulting Embargo Act, southern Democratic-Republicans (hereafter Republicans) like Senator John Pope of Kentucky self-consciously opted for sacrifice to the nationalist cause: "For what are the agricultural people now suffering, but to maintain our maritime rights: Sir, we are willing to discard all calculations of profit or loss, and make a common cause with our brethren of other States in defense of our national rights and independence."[38]

Citizenship itself in this early-nineteenth-century period possessed a significance in both the United States and Britain somewhat different from its modern-day meaning. Recent commentators have pointed to the lack of attention to national citizenship in U.S. laws until the Civil War era and particularly the "revolution" of the postwar 14th Amendment. Certainly, the contemporary invocation of citizenship with regard to the impressment controversy carried no claim to the larger rights-bearing agenda that we associate with citizenship claims in the aftermath of the 1960s social movements.[39] Sailors on neither side of the Atlantic, for example, were likely in a position to vote (in Britain for want of sufficient property, in the United States for lack of stable residency), let alone exercise larger civic influence, during the age of impressment. Yet, neither should we make too little of citizenship's importance, particularly as it concerned international relations. The pride and rights to which potential impressment victims appealed likely adhered to radical principles of American sovereignty even if not necessarily to "active participants in self-government."[40] As Aristide R. Zolberg has argued, a key tenet of the American Revolution was the rejection of "perpetual allegiance" (the European norm resting on birth, descent, and lifelong subjecthood) in favor of a "voluntaristic" loyalty of a nation's citizens (albeit limited to whites), thus validating both expatriation and naturalization.[41] Even an administratively weak state (as was certainly the U.S. federal government), by this rationale, had reason to demarcate its "citizens" from the control of others.

Yet, defense of national sovereignty and liberal citizenship claims by American leaders did not necessarily translate to unlimited support for its seagoing labor force. In 1806, for example, Secretary of State James Madison downplayed the numbers of British-born seamen who may have been naturalized since the treaty of 1785 (and thus, according to British logic, legally susceptible to impressment). "Very few, if any such naturalizations can take place," Madison privately explained to Monroe, "the law here requiring a preparatory residence of five years, with notice of intention to become a citizen entered of record two years before the last necessary formality, besides a regular proof of good moral character, conditions little likely to be complied with by ordinary sea-faring persons."[42] Already something of a class apart—conspicuous by their garb, gait, and unruly behavior, not to mention often interracial character—seamen could not automatically count on any national commitment to their immediate welfare. Even in the *Chesapeake* affair, as historian Robert E. Cray Jr. documents, "people focused on the men killed and honor compromised, not the sailors taken." Cray attributes the disparity to considerations of "class and race" as well as to public embarrassment at the sailors' "inglorious capture."[43]

Congressional debate over what was variously called the "Impressment" or "Seamen's Bill" (finally passed in February 1813) offers further clues as to the degree of contemporary conflation among Americans of maritime rights with national identity and citizenship issues.[44] Promulgated more as a measure to shore up domestic (and especially Federalist) political support for the war effort than as a serious diplomatic initiative, the bill ostensibly offered a sensible and moderate compromise to the impressment issue.[45] Offering a quid pro quo to any nation that would bar U.S. seamen from its ships (that is, we won't hire yours if you don't hire ours), the bill limited employment on U.S. ships to native-born or naturalized citizens, extended the requirement for naturalization to five continuous years of residency, and forbade foreign seamen to travel even as passengers on U.S. ships without a valid passport.[46] Each clause screamed America's disinterest in serving as a haven for foreign seamen—with the intended effect of eliminating any rationale for stopping and pressing U.S.-flagged ships at sea.

Politically, as historian J. C. A. Stagg demonstrated, the bill failed to achieve its intended unifying effect. The bill passed both houses of Congress in February 1813, to be quickly signed into law, but by margins "no larger than those obtained by the declaration of war eight months earlier."[47] In the end, the number of Federalists won over by the conciliatory language of the bill were outnumbered by Republicans who believed it went too far toward concession.[48] With little effect on the war's prosecution or outcome—where the United States was checked on both land and sea, yet escaped tangible setback due to Britain's own war weariness—the Impressment Bill has rightly been seen as one more barometer of internal wartime tensions.

Yet, debate on the Impressment Bill rippled beyond the response to impressment per se. Perhaps more than even those who took part realized, the wartime arguments also revealed an underlying ambivalence about immigration and who counted as full-fledged American citizens. Led by Tennessee Republican representative Felix Grundy, the bill's supporters readily mixed the promotion of peace (by categorically denying Britons sailing berths) with an economic-protectionist argument about American jobs. Pointing to an "overflowing population" along the East Coast either driven from employment or facing reduced wages due to the "swarms of foreign seamen [who] flock to the United States in search of a livelihood," Grundy argued that a U.S.-only labor force would ensure both a steady and loyal domestic labor market for seamen.[49] Already naturalized citizens by this proposal would have the full protection of the U.S. government, but not newer arrivals (who could not go to sea until they had completed the new, five-year domestic residency requirement, thus deterring any foreign sailor from continuing to practice his craft). As to the argument over whether the United States required foreign seamen at all, Republican representative (and future vice president) William R. King of North Carolina scoffed, "We want them not. . . . I regret that such a law as this . . . was not adopted for years past, thereby giving greater encouragement to the native seamen of our country, (than whom there are none superior) and preventing some of the points of collision which have unhappily arisen between this Government and others."[50]

To the president's critics (a curious combination of Republican War Hawks and antiwar Federalists), the bill's proposed division of protections for native versus immigrant seamen offered a convenient opening for a patriotic critique of the whole war's management.[51] The bill was thus assailed both strategically, as ineffectual wartime policy, and substantively, for undermining the constitutional protection of immigrant rights. Kentucky Republican Joseph Desha counseled against "humbling ourselves at the footstool of British corruption."[52] Similarly, Republican Adam Seybert of Pennsylvania insisted that now was no time to offer further submission to the power that by impressment had committed a "crime [that] in the great catalogue of human enormities, stands alone." Accommodation, the latter predicted, would only beget further indignities from Great Britain: "She [could then] naturalize any British subject hereafter." "Her claims to her artisans and manufacturers," warned Seybert, "are as strong as those in favor of her seamen." Industrious migrants from Birmingham, Manchester, or Leeds, he suggested, could conceivably be the next to feel the sting of British principle: "You can only maintain your ground by a manly resistance."[53]

The hottest disagreement, however, concerned immigrant citizenship rights. Any limitation on occupation by citizenship status, Seybert warned, carried grave legal implications. Except for eligibility for the presidency, he noted, the U.S. Constitution did not distinguish between "native and naturalized" citizens. The laws of Congress, therefore, "cannot deprive any particular species of citizens of the right of personal liberty or the locomotive faculty." To do so, Seybert asserted, would introduce the "abominable India gradation of *castes*" into the American political system.[54] Not only should would-be expatriates be able to travel anywhere to practice the occupation of their choice, Representative Desha added, but the United States should welcome all immigrants, with or without passports or official approval from their home governments: "We want citizens, sir, particularly mechanics and manufacturers, to enable us finally to become in reality independent of the conflicting European despots."[55]

Perhaps less predictably, Massachusetts representative Josiah Quincy III, who saw the bill as a sly attempt to reconcile opposing political interests around a war he, like other Federalists, detested, equally condemned any limitation on immigrant rights:

> Sir, what are the United States in respect to their composite character? Are they a simple homogeneous race of men? Did we all spring out of mushroom soil? Does each of us carry about him the marks of the grit and clay of his mother earth? Sir, the fact is altogether the reverse. The column of our American State is neither composed of flint nor of granite, but rather of a sort of pudding-stone; of a casual collection of distinct individuals, aggregated together, with no selection in the particulars, and little strength in the cement. In a nation thus constituted, it is now seriously proposed, as it is pretended, to turn all foreigners from its sea service, and to form, by a sort of parliamentary magic, in a moment, a new marine of pure and exclusive native citizens.[56]

In defending immigrant rights, Quincy seized the opportunity to hoist the Jeffersonian, Francophile Republicans by their own petard. "It is most extraordinary," he deadpanned, "that men, who have been all their lives long, perfect knight errants, in favor of distressed foreigners, who have set their spears in their rests, and gone tilting all over the world in defence of oppressed humanity; who have been inviting it to our shores with both hands, should turn round at once, and pretend to be about to send them all home again, and leave them to the mercy of ancient systems and of their former masters."[57]

Against the critics' onslaughts, the defenders of the bill held fast to the conviction that theirs was the moderate, prudent course of action. Yet, in downplaying the victimization of immigrant seafarers in the restrictive clauses of the 1813 legislation, the bill's advocates rather arbitrarily separated the victims of impressment into two categories. Maryland Republican Peter Little, for example, statistically compared the 1,530 foreign-born and legally naturalized citizens who had registered as American seamen from 1796 to 1812—that is, the class of people who might now be barred from sea service—with the much larger population (which he estimated at 15,000–20,000) of American seamen impressed into the British service. Potential discomfort to the former, he suggested, was nothing compared to the benefit of freeing the latter from subjugation. Protecting the interests of full-fledged American citizens, he insisted, surely came first: "Beyond our territorial limits I am not willing to extend my obligation to follow those to whom, as yet, I am not united as fellow citizens."[58]

The most disenchanted voice on behalf of the bill came from Maryland Federalist Charles Goldsborough, who refused to join Josiah Quincy in playing either to "sailors' rights" or American immigrant idealism. Hoping against hope that the measure would bring an early end to the war, Goldsborough denied any "*real obligation* to hazard the prosperity, the welfare, and the happiness of our own people by engaging in quixotic wars to absolve and shield them from the allegiance or obligations they may owe to the Government or Sovereign of the country of their nativity." This was particularly so of that "seafaring class . . . of wandering foreigners [who] may literally be said to be of no nation. Whatever oaths they may swallow, they imbibe no attachment with the allegiance they may so profess; they feel the sacredness of its obligations to no country. Interest is their impelling motive."[59] An act outwardly designed to protect U.S. sailors thus inwardly betrayed more ambivalent assumptions about America's floating proletariat.[60]

Formally, the impressment-induced limitation on the recruitment of the American merchant fleet lasted nearly a half century. In practice, erosion of the citizens-only principle happened sooner. The end of the Napoleonic Wars as well as the War of 1812 ushered in a new, more capital-intensive world of shipping. Bigger ships plying longer routes at higher risk across both the Atlantic and Pacific led at once to tighter discipline and less autonomy for the common seaman. In the circumstances, many young Americans turned away from the sea's adventure after a brief sojourn or avoided it altogether in favor of other commercial pursuits.[61] As early as 1828, for example, U.S. secretary of the navy Samuel Southard was complaining of the difficulty of attracting enough native-born citizens into the service: at least a quarter of the oceanic merchant force was foreign-born, and an even higher proportion in the navy itself.[62] In the circumstances of bustling world trade and increasingly amiable relations with Great Britain, Congress, encouraging maritime enrollment, in 1843 abolished the requirement for purchase of citizenship certificates imposed on sailors since

1796 and four years later shortened the residency clause for those awaiting citizenship.[63] Moreover, despite formal prescription on seafaring noncitizens, it remained notoriously easy to opt—and be readily accepted—for U.S. citizenship. Finally, in 1864, again under wartime pressures of recruitment, Congress repealed the nationality restrictions of the 1813 act, except for ships' officers, altogether.[64]

Liberal Individualism and the Rise of Free Trade

Though the official peace terms of the Treaty of Ghent that ended the War of 1812 said nothing about ending naval impressment, the British practice soon abated.[65] Impressment's damage to naval morale, its deleterious effects on the operation of the domestic merchant marine, and its polarization of political opinion all triggered a search for alternatives in a period made easier by the relative international calm, itself cushioned by British naval supremacy, following on the Napoleonic Wars.[66] Impressment became unnecessary (if never officially abolished) with the formation of a naval militia, a reserves system based on a registry of merchant seamen, and ultimately a larger, professional "standing navy."[67] Even Britain's mobilization for the Crimean War in the 1850s, the last in which the idea was seriously entertained, proceeded without resort to the once-common measure.[68]

At an ideological level, naval impressment among the British public went the way of chattel slavery as a form of coerced labor. By 1800, British commentators on the subject generally conceded that the practice was "wrong" and justifiable only for want of an alternative in a situation of "national emergency."[69] Such, for example, was the argument of Captain (and future admiral of the Royal Navy) Anselm John Griffiths in his 1825 volume, *Impressment Fully Considered with a View to Its Gradual Abolition*. Only absolute "necessity," Griffiths counseled his readers, could justify the subjection into the "degraded," "abject," and "marketable property of Crimps" of those who "by carrying the [Napoleonic] war into every country, every clime, every quarter of the globe . . . set you free."[70] It was fundamentally impressment, not the lure of higher wages, according to Griffiths, that accounted for a high desertion rate of British sailors to American ships. "Being impressed, a seaman deems himself a prisoner, *not on his parole*, and considering this forcible seizure as an act of injustice, he has no one feeling of moral honor to attach him to the service. Yet, so far as relates to *Liberty*, where in *fact*, was the difference between the Seaman and the Convict?"[71] Urging expansion of a peacetime navy as a first step toward gradual abolition of impressment, Griffiths concluded that the world's trajectory was toward voluntarism and individual liberty: "Compulsion subdues all the better feelings of our nature."[72] Although forced entrance into labor had once been common for a variety of workers, by the eighteenth century, as historian Robert J. Steinfeld has documented, the thrust of British master and servant law had changed to compelling performance only of agreements "voluntarily" entered. It was thus the "involuntary" nature of *the initiation of labor* via impressment that marked it as so egregious. By the 1820s, when even the indenture contract, once a major conduit for Anglo-American migrants, had been both popularly and legally tarred as a form of involuntary servitude, impressment stood out as an embarrassing anomaly in Western society.[73]

The transformation is well-marked, for example, in Elizabeth Gaskell's *Sylvia's Lovers* (1863). In a climactic moment within a romance set against the backdrop of the Napoleonic Wars, Sylvia—who has already lost her sailor-father to hanging following an anti-press-gang riot in their seaport town—learns that rather than a victim of drowning (the story told her by her deceptive husband), her original suitor, the honest sailor Charley Kinraid, has also been carried away by a press gang. As if highlighting the offensiveness not only of by-then-distant maritime practices like impressment but also of continuing remnants of physical coercion common to the maritime enterprise, Gaskell's omniscient narrator dryly declares, "Now all this tyranny (for I can use no other word) is marvelous to us; we cannot imagine how it is that a nation submitted to it for so long, even under any warlike enthusiasm, any panic of invasion, any amount of loyal subservience to the governing powers."[74]

Yet, there is an irony worth noting about the dissolution of the press gang. The same mechanism, the same rationale that on the high seas facilitated the canvassing of foreign ships for runaway British seamen, was also employed to interrupt the slave trade. Indeed, in retrospect, the villains and heroes of the campaigns for human freedom at sea—that is, slave captives and impressed seamen—were sometimes the same, only with reversed roles. James Stephen, for example, chief architect of the 1807 British slave-trade abolition act, also, as a member of the Privy Council, helped precipitate the War of 1812 with a legal justification for the Orders in Council. Stephen, in short, was determined to use British control of the high seas to prevent neutral as well as enemy ships from trafficking in human cargo.[75] Beginning in 1811, to make good on its abolition of the slave trade four years earlier, Great Britain sent warships to patrol the African coast. Using both economic and military muscle, the British wrested agreements from both Portuguese and Spanish (and, for a short time, even French) over their right to board and inspect suspicious-looking ships.

In principle, U.S. policy synchronized with that of the British, having outlawed slave importation in the same year and, in 1819, passed the Slave Trade Act, directing U.S. warships to suppress the trade as well as anointing Liberia as a haven for freed slaves.[76] Practice, however, was something else again. Not only were the U.S. Navy's antislavery squadrons undermanned (virtually withdrawing completely from the African coast, 1824–43), but the known resistance of U.S.-flagged ships to British search missions made them prime receptacles for illicit slave trafficking—to Brazil, Cuba, and ultimately the United States.[77] Having staked the nation's honor to the end of the press gang's attack on its seagoing citizens in 1812, American political leaders prioritized the issue of republican freedom in particular ways. As historian Calvin Lane reports, "When asked by the British Foreign Minister in 1822 if he could think of anything more atrocious than the slave trade, Secretary of State John Quincy Adams retorted: 'Yes. Admitting the right of search by foreign officers of our vessels upon the seas in time of peace; for that would be making slaves of ourselves.'"[78] For the American public, freedom from white slavery took clear precedence over any more-universal emancipation.

"Final supercession of the press-gang," shrewdly offered a 1914 British account of the subject, "was in essence, if not in name, the beginning of Free Trade."[79] Indeed, seaside labor practices offer a fair barometer of a larger "liberal" transformation—encompassing both an untangling of mercantilist restriction on commerce and an acceleration of rights-based sensibilities—in Western political culture. In Great Britain, in particular, the critique of impressment and physical punishment aboard ships, post-1815, fit neatly into a widening political democracy and protection of individual liberties. One by one, the building blocks of the liberal, democratic state were set in place: Catholic Emancipation (1829), the Reform Act (1832), insistence on individual autonomy and responsibility in the Abolition of Slavery Act (1833) and Poor Law Amendment Act (1834)—a process of what W. L. Burn called "ruthless clearance," famously crowned by a declaration of marketplace freedom in repeal of the Corn Laws (1846).[80] Repeal of the long-standing Navigation Acts in 1849 further consolidated a new era of free trade that would serve for a half century or more as a mantra of Victorian liberalism.[81] Indeed, economists increasingly viewed this "last" liberty as the fount of all the others: as Nassau William Senior put it in 1828, "The question of free trade is, next to the Reformation, next to the question of free religion, the most momentous that has ever been submitted to human decision."[82]

A shifting cultural climate is evident in the relish with which the liberal-par-excellence *Westminster Review* would sweep away any historical defense of the long-standing institution of coercive seagoing labor. Likening the defense of impressment to apologies of West Indian slave owners, *Review* author T. P. Thompson declared in 1834, "A free government is one where the working men and women are able to prevent their aristocracy from whipping them or their offspring; where a man can walk this way or that way at discretion, and follow his calling without having it announced to him that it is the pleasure of his betters that he should be taken away to do their work for less than it will be done for in the market." The difference between slavery (coercion) and freedom (voluntarism), demanded ascendant liberals, must now be asserted on all fronts by a would-be free and democratic citizenry. To modern, liberal Englishmen, impressment and flogging were now anathema: "They are a set of poor *niggers*, the common English, after all their bullying; that will allow themselves tamely to have personal slavery thrust down their proper throats. . . . If the thing be as good as they tell you, what need to force people into it? It is because it is *not* as good, that your enemies go about to cheat you into acquiescence in their using force."[83]

In the War of 1812, both combatant states had gone to war over an essentially mercantilistic definition of the relation of shipping and sea power to national welfare.[84] It mattered crucially to both Great Britain and the United States that their sailors be both sufficiently numerous and secure on the world's sea-lanes. Even as the British had seen impressment as a vital link in their maritime supremacy, so the Americans rested their national independence and republican character on expansion "across space" into new territories rather than "through time"—in the corruption-prone manner of more-densely populated European empires—a strategy, as historian Drew McCoy has explained, that depended on unmolested international trade.[85] Even for Republicans, who had disdained promotion of a national carrying trade as part of Old World corruption, self-government at sea offered a sudden, critical test of national power and perhaps even survival.[86] Yet, within only a few short decades, both the relationship between the two powers and their thinking about sea power had so changed as to render the past conflict almost anachronistic. Following the War of 1812, in short, both belligerents took advantage of an extended European peace to craft more open trade relations and ultimately a strong economic partnership. Immediately after the war, for example, the two powers cooperated, in the name of "free trade," in finally subduing "Barbary" privateering.[87] Reciprocal trade terms initially agreed to by treaty in 1815 and then opened further by termination of Britain's Navigation Acts in 1849 laid the groundwork for a sevenfold increase in mutual commercial exchanges by 1860.[88] In the process, the stakes tied to a national carrying trade manned by one's own loyal citizens had been substantially reduced, even as maritime commerce itself remained crucial to national prosperity.

Henceforth, merchant seamen, like gold or silver bullion, would tend to figure less as vital "national property" in and of themselves than as a means to an ever-wider network of international trade. Similarly, regulation of the merchant labor force would come to depend increasingly on considerations of labor discipline and worker welfare, even as reference to national security diminished (though without ever disappearing from the mix). Indeed, the mercantile marine offered the clearest test across the Atlantic world of how far governments were willing to trust their national fates to a free marketplace in both goods and labor.

Undoubtedly, the biggest step toward a more "liberal," global commercial order was taken by Great Britain in replacing its mercantilist structures with "free trade" principles, catalyzed legislatively in the years 1849–54. The Navigation Acts had, indeed, been far-reaching in their impact. Determined to deny East Indian or "lascar" sailors (needed since the early seventeenth century to complete East India Company crews on their return voyages) extended access to the mainland, the acts included West Indian and African colonial subjects but not lascars within their required "British" quotient. No foreigners, whatever, could serve in the "coastal trade" between U.K. ports. The acts, moreover, heavily favored British carriers: local port dues and taxes were assessed against foreign-owned ships, and traffic (with enumerated exceptions) between colonial ports in Africa, Asia, and the Americas as well as fishing rights and the coastal trade were limited to British ships.[89] Then, following an extended period of bilateral, "reciprocity" agreements, Her Majesty's Government under both Whig and Peelite leadership moved dramatically in the direction of laissez-faire with the scrapping of preferential treatment for the British fleet in the foreign trade (1849); repeal of the "manning clause," which had required that three-quarters of a crew be British (1853); and extension of coastal trade to open competition as well (1854).[90] Determined not to destabilize the industry, however, Parliament also moved swiftly to surround deregulation of trade with a measure of re-regulation, affecting both owners and seamen. As consolidated in the Merchant Shipping Act of 1854, new laws established exams and certificates of competency for ships' officers; a scale for shipboard accommodations, food, and medical supplies; local marine boards to oversee recruiting; a continuous discharge book established for each seaman; and harsher penalties for indiscipline or desertion by the crew.[91] The freer labor trafficking occasioned by the new legislation resulted, among other effects, in a quick tripling of the number of Asian seamen arriving in Britain.[92]

Within the development of liberal individualism, the establishment of British free-trade, free-employment policies may appear inexorable. Even a "Liberal" coalition of Whigs and Radicals under Lord John Russell, 1846–52, proceeded slowly, and with some back-pedaling, toward a free-trade regime.[93] As promulgated by Board of Trade president Henry Labouchere in the House of Commons and Liberal leaders Earl Granville and the Marquess of Lansdowne among the Lords, the case was made that competition would solidify both the industry and its labor pool. The more shipping, the more sailors, argued Lansdowne. "Whether they were employed in English ships or foreign ships, English seamen would always continue to be a more or less available resource for the naval and maritime power of this country."[94] Loosened from the nationalist, as well as mercantilist, instincts of wartime calculation, liberal statesmen thus reassigned sailors to their proper function in an industrializing economy: they were yet one more replaceable part.

Yet, there was no shortage of hand-wringing among the Opposition. Of these, old Tories and naval men, as well as some shipowner factions, bemoaned the move to free trade, free shipping (whereby ownership alone—regardless of place of construction—was sufficient to convey British "flag" status), and open manning. The Earl of Ellenborough, a confidant of the Duke of Wellington and British military strategist for India, believed that Britons were "sell[ing] their birthright for a mess of porridge" while acting on "principles more suitable to the diggers in California than to the once high-minded legislators of Great Britain."[95] Likewise, to Bishop Samuel Wilberforce (son of the famous abolitionist), the purely commercial calculus of free trade threatened to upset "the principles of high and universal humanity" upon which decades of antislavery agitation had been based.[96] The resolutely Tory *Quarterly Review* spared no ink in its denunciation of free trade policy: "It is in its very essence a mercenary, unsocial, demoralizing system, opposed to all generous actions, all kindly feelings. . . . It teaches competition and isolation instead of co-operation and brotherhood; it substitutes a vague and impracticable cosmopolitanism for a lofty and ennobling patriotism; it disregards the claims of humanity towards the poor, if opposed to the pecuniary interests of the rich. . . . Wealth is its end and aim, and Mammon its divinity."[97]

The future Tory prime minister Lord Stanley (Earl of Derby) labeled the new system "dangerous to the welfare of this country," while the Earl Talbot pointed to resistance from the "maritime population of the country."[98] Or, as one shipping journal versified:

> Patriots awake! Ye mariners arouse!
> Rally round the flag your leaders hoist
> Nail your unsullied colours to the mast;
> With dauntless valour and unshaken front,
> Your rights as free-born Englishmen defend!
> And ye shall yet victoriously ride out
> The battle and the storm, and England still
> Shall lead the mighty commerce of the world.
> Then be your watchwords in the sacred cause
> "Ships, England and the Navigation Laws!"[99]

Although the seamen themselves had no direct representation in Parliament in these years, the previous decades had demonstrated that they were not without means of asserting themselves in the public sphere. Most infamously, open mutiny over pay and conditions had broken out among navalmen at Spithead and the Nore, the latter ending in conviction for treason and a mass hanging in 1797.[100] Other issues, including impressment, had triggered smaller strikes by merchant seamen, especially by keelmen on coal barges along the northeast coast, in the course of the Napoleonic Wars. In particular, a strike in the same region by seamen in 1815 against the employment of foreigners on local ships most likely was not forgotten amid the legislative measures of 1849–54.[101] Some 3,000 seamen had sailed down the Thames as early as February 1848 to demonstrate against repeal of the Navigation Acts, and multiple petitions to the Home Office followed.[102] More strident, still, was the response to the 1850 legislation imposing harsher penalties for desertions and other disciplinary infractions as well as a one-shilling charge to accompany newly required registry tickets.

A "Penny Union" developed from Chartist remnants in several ports, and a strike and protests at Sutherland in 1851 produced a regional suspension of the worst regulations. Though the adoption of open-manning provisions, with their implied threat of worker replacement, broke up the budding union movement, a negative reaction "from below" was clearly manifest.[103]

Numerous parliamentary voices, moreover, took sympathetic note of the seamen's fears. Consigning the nation's merchant fleet to a "motley crew of men," argued Conservative admiral John Edward Walcott, who wished to re-apply the apprenticeship system for home-grown talent that had vanished with the Navigation Acts, would prove "unwise, impolitic, and unsafe."[104] Likewise, Liberal Henry Labouchere, who had pushed the early repeal legislation but was no longer part of the government by 1853, openly feared the reaction of seamen to extending open manning to coastal waterways.[105] More likely than direct action, warned Conservative Lord Colchester, was an evacuation of British seamen to U.S. citizenship. "There being no longer advantage to hail as Englishmen when this law is passed," Colchester quoted a resolution from a public meeting of seamen from the northern ports, "on the contrary, freedom from impressment or service in Her Majesty's Navy during war, may be secured by serving as foreigners during peace."[106] Liberal member of Parliament (MP) and retired naval captain George Scobell similarly reported on a meeting at Liverpool, where,

> when it was suggested that they should petition the House of Commons against [the manning clause], the answer was, "We have petitioned it long enough; we will now petition the President of the United States." . . . Much has been said about maintaining the dignity of the British flag, but Parliament was now about to entrust the keeping of that flag to a crew of foreigners. We refuse to admit foreigners into the House of Commons, or into our dockyards, or police, and yet we were ready to place them in the van of our protective power. . . . Why not have foreign militiamen as well as foreign seamen? The permission to employ foreign seamen was not limited to the foreign trade—it was extended to the coasting trade. Why, this was a suicidal act; it was downright madness.[107]

In the spirited parliamentary debates over repeal of the Navigation Acts, advocates of the new, more liberal trading order generally wasted fewer words than their antagonists. Amid a surge of prosperity, free-trade partisans pointed to results rather than to principle in their arguments. Critics of the open-manning provisions, scoffed Liberal Board of Trade president Edward Cardwell, were repeating the "same gloomy predictions" that had characterized arguments against repeal of the navigation laws, "all of which had been falsified by events." And he had official, government figures on his side. The past year, 1852, had seen the greatest number of British seamen in history employed; moreover, of these 190,000 sea workers, a mere 2,500 were foreign citizens. As for the resistance to extending the open labor market to the coastal trade, the Tory Henry Thomas Liddell, a former protectionist, wondered, "After they had swallowed the camel, [why] strain at the gnat?"[108] Government backers generally discounted the potential drain of sailors to America. Liddell claimed that in a period of full employment, even seamen who had gone to America were reportedly now returning "to enjoy the better market," and another former naval officer, Whig MP Sir George Pechell, insisted that there "need be no apprehension of 'Rule Britannia' being changed for 'Hail Columbia.'" Nor, the latter conjectured, would British shipmasters be tempted by lower-wage foreign labor. "They preferred to have [the British seaman] in their ships beyond all others, but more particularly beyond the Spaniard, who was always upon his knees in a storm, praying to some saint or other . . . while so far from the Lascar [Indian seamen] being ever likely to supplant the British sailor, it was notorious that he was a positive hindrance to the navigation of a ship."[109]

Conversion to a more liberal political economy, however, altered the very standards that had hitherto connected sea labor to national identity and citizenship. Both advocates and critics of the new measures henceforth applied a more purely economic yardstick to the seagoing labor force. What had once been taken for granted as the "nation's property" was now recognized as a more fungible asset. Establish the right conditions, the free traders claimed, and market incentives would ensure not only a booming economy but also an eager merchant navy, capable in an emergency of protecting the national security. Treat us as mere factors of production, the seamen appeared to reply, and our loyalty as citizens will equally go to the highest bidder. Still, such superficial adaptation to the logic of the free market was contradicted, on either side, by recurrent appeals to more primordial national and ethnic instincts: *they* (the non-British) are not really as good as *us*. Free-traders and anti–free traders could agree that, given the proper regulatory framework (about which of course they strenuously disagreed), "Hail Britannia" might long happily echo among most of those working before the mast.

The mast, itself, of course, would ultimately forfeit its place to steam power. Though conceptually framed by legislation, Britain's free-trade empire would depend for sustenance upon a happy juncture of technological innovation and a relatively peaceful world. The same conditions, alas, spelled a distinctly different outcome for the U.S. fleet on the high seas.

The utter triumph of the British and the precipitous decline of American shipping interests by the late nineteenth century could certainly not have been forecast at the time of the repeal of the Navigation Acts. In the 1830s, as an already rising world power, the United States was carrying 90 percent of its international trade in its own ships (a higher proportion than Britain itself), and it was still carrying half of its burgeoning trade by 1860, yet the figure would drop to a mere 9 percent by 1890.[110] America, indeed, is often said to have experienced a "golden era" of shipping, 1815–60, an era in which its barks and "clipper ships" pressed navigation by wood—with this raw material ever so more abundant in the New World compared to the Old—to new records in size and speed. Even the great British steamship owner of the late nineteenth century Sir Walter Runciman had sought service on a Yankee ship, attracted by their superior reputation in deep-sea navigation.[111]

Clearly, one source of the turnabout was technology, when the British were able to transfer their lead in the industrial application of steam power and iron construction to long-distance oceanic navigation. Given both a complacent overconfidence in relation to their sailing ships and an acute economic disadvantage when it came to alternatives, the Americans held onto their wooden ships even as the economic odds turned radically against them. In the 1860s, screw propulsion, the large iron hull, and the compound engine—all innovations in which the English had taken the lead—lent steam-driven ships an advantage in most seagoing runs, even as wooden sailing vessels competed gamely into the 1890s and indeed remained competitive on some long hauls until the opening of the Panama Canal in 1914. By 1870, the British, with three-quarters of their new ship construction in steam, were already carrying 45 percent of the world's commerce, or four times that of the United States, five times that of the French, and six times that of the Germans and Italians.[112] Yet, the peak of British sea hegemony would come over the next two decades, 1870–90, when the British share of world seagoing trade would reach a whopping 60 percent, a figure never before or after touched by any world power.[113] As sailor-author Frank T.

Bullen would exult in 1900, "The British Mercantile Marine is not only the greatest British industry, but . . . the most stupendous monument of human energy and enterprise that the world has ever seen."[114] Already lagging in metals engineering, American shipbuilders faced the added, ultimately impossible, burden of competing in the steamship trade with substantially higher material costs, accentuated by high protective tariffs, post-1861.[115]

Yet, U.S. public policy also undoubtedly collaborated in helping drive American ships from the sea. Acting like most other trading nations to protect its cabotage trade—that is, the transfer of goods between two points in the same country—from foreign competition, the United States, in the first session of the first Congress in 1789 (and further elaborated in 1792–93), limited the flying of the U.S. flag and protection by the navy to ships built and owned by U.S. citizens while also lending them preferential treatment in the coastwise trade via tonnage duties on foreign-owned craft.[116] In 1817, foreign flags were banned entirely from the cabotage trade, including a clause that at least two-thirds of the crew be composed of U.S. citizens—a preference later reinforced by the Jones Act (or sec. 27 of the Merchant Marine Act) of 1920, providing a framework that remains in place to this day.[117] Yet, while providing an enduring protective framework for domestic shipping, such legislation left the seagoing trade to the mercies of the global marketplace, a basic inconsistency of policy that historian John G. B. Hutchins euphemized as "a curious mixture of protectionism and free trade."[118]

American standing on the seas soon faced the adverse logic of both politics and the marketplace. Even as British steamships had begun to challenge U.S. clipper mastery in seamanship, Confederate raids on Union merchant ships (with a consequent eruption of insurance rates) began a wholesale move by U.S. merchants to neutral flags. Even after the Civil War, operating without subsidies but tied to higher-cost American materials, U.S. shipbuilders could never recover. As late as 1870, the total of U.S.-flagged traffic was only 20 percent less than Great Britain, yet less than 10 percent was carried in the foreign trade.[119] Through the end of the century, political debate stalemated between a shipowner lobby desiring a "free-ships" policy (whereby Americans could purchase ships abroad yet register them in the United States) and shipbuilders pushing for elimination of tariffs on building materials and/or direct, production subsidies—the latter proposal ultimately adopted only in the case of international mail delivery (packet boats). While each group appealed back to the national defense arguments of Adam Smith's day, their obvious self-interest tended to cancel each other out.[120] The result, little remarked on at the time or since, was that the "great leap forward" of the United States within the world economy was accomplished on the back of a foreign-flag (mainly British) carrying trade. America's industrial roll-out, like the more widely acknowledged capital that established its infrastructure, came with a British accent.[121] Transoceanic shipping, it is thus fair to say, was the first great American industry to be outsourced to foreign competition.

The yelps of commercial shippers, shipbuilders, and organized seamen regarding the decline of U.S. flag carriers did not attract effective attention until the crisis of World War I. As the belligerent European powers diverted their own ships to military support, the price of cotton shipped from a still-neutral U.S. port to Great Britain jumped from $2.50 to $60 a bale and wheat from five cents to sixty cents a bushel. The result, highlighted in the Shipping Act of 1916, was a binge of government-financed construction (though mostly too late for the war effort), followed by a massive sell-off of government property. A similar panic-followed-by-relaxation about trusting to the private maritime marketplace again gripped the nation during World War II, and even (albeit to a lesser extent) in both the Vietnam and Gulf War eras.[122] Try as they might, policy makers otherwise committed to market principles could never quite erase the image of merchant ships and their crew as the nation's property.

Though impressment was long gone, the memory of foreign trespass on American ships still stirred powerful emotions, as witnessed in the lead-up to the Spanish-American War of 1898. One Cuban revolutionary, Clemencia Arango, regularly slipped back and forth from the United States "to bring clothes, medicines, weapons, and messages" to her male comrades organizing on the island. Discovered and expelled from Cuba in 1897, she was searched by a police matron while aboard an American vessel, still docked in the Havana harbor, bound for New York City. When Richard Harding Davis of the sensationalist *New York Journal* got hold of the story, however, headlines screamed, "Does Our Flag Shield Women? Indignities Practiced by Spanish Officials on Board American Vessels" and "Refined Young Women Stripped and Searched by Brutal Spaniards While Under Our Flag." Notwithstanding the more nuanced details, the key issue here—as in the case of those earlier exposed to impressments—was the apparent affront to national honor and influence. Historically, the treatment of sailors and seamen paled in significance to the treatment of the flag itself.[123]

2

Liberty before the Mast

DEFINING FREE LABOR IN LAW AND LITERATURE

The sailor's freedom—or rather lack of it—exercised a peculiarly powerful hold on nineteenth-century imaginations across the Atlantic world. Images of the tyrannical captain applying the cat-o'-nine-tails, the drunken wastrel snatched from a seaside rooming house and dumped in a fetid foc's'l, or the runaway chained in a ship's hold awaiting criminal charges have long mixed fascination with discomfort in the landlocked reader. Though applied to what often appeared an exotic, separate world of its own, however, the drama of liberty versus license, rights versus authority, and independence versus dependency as enacted on the high seas, as writers of maritime fiction knew well, often touched themes affecting the home culture too. Perhaps it was a deep ambivalence toward those larger issues that accounts for the contradictory impulses enshrined in Anglo-American law in various efforts to "free," "reform," or "discipline" the seagoing labor force. Yet even as the seamen's symbolic presence figured prominently in these lively debates about their basic liberty and welfare, the seamen's own voices were scarcely heard.

For a brief few decades in the early to mid-nineteenth century, the issue of the sailor's freedom gained nationwide prominence in the United States. Likely reflecting differences in social class and political structures as well as the contrasting fortunes of their shipping industries, the "rights" of sailors undoubtedly figured more prominently as a public issue in the United States than in Great Britain. In the United States, the period witnessed a veritable literary battleground of liberty versus tyranny and dissipation versus redemption projected onto the seas. Given the heightened contemporary awareness of other forms of dependency (as witnessed by the antislavery, temperance, and women's rights movements), the continuing subjection of sailors might inevitably have raised hackles. Changes in the actual experience of sailoring, as we shall see, also figured into the controversy. Contemporary concern for seamen's conditions occurred even as U.S. economic and political focus was shifting away from the sea to inland challenges (in particular, economic development, slavery, and continental expansion), a shift marked by the precipitous decline of U.S. seafaring and shipping itself, post-1865.

As U.S. shipping waned across the century, so its British counterpart was waxing. Though initially the sailor's plight received a greater popular following in the United States, political reforms in this arena tended to occur first on the British side, where, not coincidentally, merchant shipping claimed a larger and more powerful role in the national political economy. From early on, in the British regulation of maritime labor, one detects many of the tensions that would long dog "liberal" reform thought and action: between social discipline and welfare, between the intellectual identification of problems and their political resolution, and, more generally, between top-down, administrative control and democratic empowerment. No fewer than eighty separate merchant shipping acts enacted by Parliament from 1840 to 1894 offer an abundant canvas for assessing the evolution of British social thought (some of which will be saved for the following chapter). Despite changing government norms and material conditions, merchant seamen remained in many respects a lower order among citizen-workers. So long as the seamen remained isolated and unorganized, both nations found ways to limit their freedom. By the end of the century, however, a more clamorous democracy had made itself felt in both the United States and Britain. Only then, as new forms of organization among seamen and their allies took hold, do we see a break in a long tradition of relative confinement and paternal rule.

Sailor Themes in Popular Culture

Just as during the War of 1812, sailors' "rights and liberties" remained for a few decades a touchstone of the quality and autonomy of American citizenship. For the same period, the canonical literary works of the young nation would regularly seize on the sailor's world as a kind of national character test. As literary critic Thomas Philbrick reminds us, "The primary frontier to most citizens of the new republic was the ocean."[1] Out of a spirit of maritime nationalism emerged the modern "sea novel"—often recognized as a stepping-stone to more sophisticated fictional forms—of which James Fenimore Cooper was the first American exemplar. His initial sea-based offering, *The Pilot* (1823), appropriately enough revolves around a patriotic plot set in Revolutionary times, wherein a fictional John Paul Jones sets out to capture a group of British notables in order to force a retraction of the policy of impressment.[2]

Yet, absent the foreign (read British) threat, Americans soon discovered that loss of self-government, and even tyranny, might emerge from more home-grown sources—and these too could be readily played out on a watery setting. Sweeping aside earlier romantic images from writers caught up in the adventures of a maritime officer class, such were the darker revelations, if not nightmare scenarios, implicit in the popular antebellum works of Richard Henry Dana Jr. and Herman Melville, who had both gone to sea in the late 1830s or early 1840s. In an important sense, these early sea-based fictions already documented the displacement of maritime occupations from work that naturally preoccupied a coastal population to adventures in a more exotic, transoceanic tableau.[3] However keen their perceptions, these "realist" writers were also likely projecting their values and sympathies onto the sailor populations with whom they could sympathize, if not fully identify. Dana's documentary exposé, *Two Years before the Mast* (1840), was written by a Harvard man who sought out a maritime adventure before returning to law school. Contrasting a tyrannical Captain Thompson (a possible forerunner to Simon Legree in Harriet Beecher Stowe's *Uncle Tom's Cabin*), given to regular flogging of his crew, with the more democratic, teacherly Captain Faucon, Dana nevertheless distances himself from the mental and political capacities of the crew. While allowing that "in no state prison are the convicts more regularly set to work, and more closely watched," and urging incremental reforms on behalf of the wretched seafarers, Dana cautions against an out-and-out prohibition of corporal punishment: "I have no fancies about equality on board ship."[4] In part a function of the absolute need for discipline in a place of constant danger, the necessary shipboard hierarchy that Dana imagines as inevitable "in the present state of mankind" is also a function of the fact, as he reports, that "more than three fourths of the seamen in our merchant vessels are foreigners."[5]

Equally a stranger to the society of the sea before his family's ill fortune interrupted his middle-class education, Melville, once resettled in Manhattan in the late 1840s, soon transformed his earlier maritime adventures into the stuff of human tragedy. While there is no shortage of exposé in his writings—where descriptions of the depredations of crimps (or infamous saloon recruiters) and the cat-o'-nine-tails provided useful grist for humanitarian reformers' mills—Melville maintains his own respectful distance from the sensibilities of the crew, even as he attacks their subjection to unwarranted authority. An alternately romantic and despairing view of working-class mariners contributes to the power of Melville's writings—particularly his subtle use of the sea to comment on America's social landscape. *Redburn: His First Voyage* (1849), for example, captures the paradox of a workforce at once indispensable to world commerce yet wretchedly self-corrupting and shunned by respectable society:

> They go and come round the globe; they are the true importers, and exporters of spices and silks; of fruits and wines and marbles . . . they are the *primum mobile* of all commerce; and in short, were they to emigrate in a body to man the navies of the moon, almost every thing would stop here on earth except its revolution on its axis, and the orators in the American Congress.
>
> And yet, what are sailors? What in your heart do you think of that fellow staggering along the dock? Do you not give him a wide berth, shun him, and account him but little above the brutes that perish? . . . It is useless to gainsay it; they are deemed almost the refuse and offscourings of the earth.[6]

Like the officer-apprentice Redburn, Melville's own experiences at sea occasioned insight and sympathy yet hardly identification with the common merchant sailor; if unfairly denigrated by the "better classes of people," they remained something of an exotic class-apart to the author (and thus his readers as well): "Consider that, with the majority of them, the very fact of their being sailors, argues a certain recklessness and sensualism of character, ignorance, and depravity; consider that they are generally friendless and alone in the world; or if they have friends and relatives, they are almost constantly beyond the reach of their good influences . . . consider all this, and the reflecting mind must very soon perceive that the case of sailors, as a class, is not a very promising one."[7]

Melville's *Moby Dick*, of course, is not only the recognized masterwork of the genre but a work that Marxist literary and social critic C. L. R. James, among others, properly extolled for its exploration of underlying social tensions within Western society. Despite his appreciation, however, James suggests that the male working class, in the form of the crew, ends up on the tragic periphery of Melville's cosmic tale, heroes who are never quite given their narrative due. To make his case, James points to an analytical feint in *Moby Dick*'s chapter 26: "If, then, to meanest mariners, and renegades and castaways, I shall hereafter ascribe high qualities, though dark; weave round them tragic graces; if even the most mournful, perchance the most abased, among them all, shall at times lift himself to the exalted mounts; if I shall touch that workman's arm with some ethereal light; if I shall spread a rainbow over his disastrous set of sun; then against all mortal critics bear me out in it, thou just Spirit of Equality, which hast spread one royal mantle of humanity over all my kind." Emphasizing Melville's romantically positive portraits of the South Sea Island and African harpooners—who, according to James, stand in for the polyglot labor force that dug canals, built railroads, and worked the American fishing fleet—James posits an author who "intends to make the crew the real heroes of his book, but . . . is afraid of criticism." Even if the latter statement goes unverified, James is surely right that Melville, in the end, sticks with the characters he knows best, and, as James says, thus "drops the meanest mariners, renegades and castaways, and goes back to the officers."[8] As a certifiably exotic class, merchant seamen, it seems, even in the hands of their most sympathetic contemporary commentator, cannot quite claim the character development of their more fully American, perhaps more morally complex, social betters.[9]

The exotic element captured during the golden age of American maritime fiction may help explain both the appeal and restricted life span of the genre. As Daniel Vickers has argued, the complexity of social relations highlighted in the works of Cooper, Dana, and Melville took place during the sunset of the native-born presence among seafarers and not long before the precipitous decline of the United States altogether as a world shipping power. Thus, even as better ships and peaceful relations with Britain sparked an upsurge in foreign trade in the post-1820 years and offered the promise of longer voyages to adventuresome young seamen, the American (and especially New England) romance with seafaring proved short-lived. Outside the fishing and coastal trade, Vickers estimates that two-thirds of the U.S. fleet was already foreign-born by 1839.[10] Indeed, the violent drama of seaboard relations captured by Dana and Melville partly stemmed from shipowner and master attempts to control a larger, more heterogeneous labor force and impose new disciplinary standards on longer, transoceanic voyages.[11] In a kind of chicken-and-egg syndrome, historians suggest, the exceptional "hard driving" by American "bucko mates" and captains led native sons to flee saltwater service, and the resulting demographic imbalance only accelerated the process.[12] The mid-nineteenth-century American fleet, as Elmo Paul Hohman noted in his classic 1956 study, witnessed "at once the highest development of sailing-ship design and operation and the lowest degradation of seagoing labor."[13]

By the time of the Civil War, seafaring had notably diminished as part of the national identity. Not only did popular writing of the new era focus inland and westward, but the most striking exception also underscored association of the sea with foreign territory. Edward Everett Hale's fictional patriotic tale *The Man Without a Country* (1863), which sold 500,000 copies by 1875, concerns the travail of Philip Nolan, who, having cursed his country when apprehended as a confederate of the Aaron Burr treason plot in 1817, is consigned to lifelong imprisonment on a navy ship where he is "never to hear the name of the United States again." The appeal of the story rests in the pathos—and unavailing regret—of a man who comes to appreciate that which he can no longer have: "Youngster [Nolan tells the narrator], let that show you what it is to be without a family, without a home, and without a country. . . . Remember, boy, that behind all these men you have to do with, behind officers, and government, and people even, there is the Country Herself, your Country, and that you belong to Her as you belong to your own mother. Stand by Her, boy, as you would stand by your mother if those devils there had got hold of her today!"[14]

Meant (and appreciated) at the time as a paean to the federal Union in wartime, the watery location of Nolan's estrangement from his country is, nevertheless, telling. The imagined community of the United States, whether as nation or empire, was now a decidedly land-centered construct. Home was where the hearth was. By contrast, the British equivalent to Philip Nolan would never have been considered "stateless" or homeless so long as he was safely berthed on one of Her Majesty's ships. As John Ruskin analogized in his inaugural Slade Lecture at Oxford in 1870, British settlers in faraway colonies "are no more to consider themselves . . . disfranchised from their native land, than the sailors of her fleets do, because they float on distant waves." With the Union Jack flying securely in ports all over the world, British national and imperial identity, far more than in the American case, was intimately bound up with the security and prosperity arranged by trade and a robust, seagoing presence.[15]

Although the maritime world suffused early-nineteenth-century British literature even as it did its American counterpart, the differences in perspective are significant. Rather than explore the exoticism of the merchant seaman, British fiction more neatly connected the maritime world to the mainsprings of national interest. The Royal Navy, and in particular the officer class, assumed the leading role. Reverberations from the battles of the Nile and Trafalgar in the Napoleonic Wars echoed for years in the popular imagination, where Admiral Lord Nelson also served as a quintessential exemplar of national gentlemanly attributes. The open and honest midshipman William Price in Jane Austen's *Mansfield Park* (1814) thus contrasts with the decadence and hypocrisy of those around him, and even a monarch's stature (in this case William IV, 1830–37) could be enhanced by an accolade as "the Sailor King."[16] On the popular stage as well, "nautical melodrama" maintained its attraction throughout the century. In 1804, for example, Sadler's Wells, calling itself the Aquatic Theatre, "installed on its stage a water-tank, fed by the New River, that measured approximately a hundred by a forty and two feet," upon which it displayed "lavish marine entertainments and spectacles for about an eleven-year period."[17]

Rather than a setting for the isolated soul-searching of alienated (Captain Ahab) or utterly estranged (Philip Nolan) individual characters, British writers commonly presented the sea world—whether the navy or the merchant marine—in comparatively positive, comfortable, even nostalgic terms. With particular reference to Charles Dickens's *Dombey and Son* (1848), a novel that captures the pathos of a changing commercial world, biographer Peter Ackroyd thus draws attention to the "connection Dickens generally makes between sailors and neatness or cleanliness; as if life on board ship was for him the epitome of the safe, private, and carefully arranged world to which he was always drawn."[18] Dickens directly identified with the earlier nautical melodramas in his 1856 story *The Wreck of the Golden Mary*, as coauthored with the young writer Wilkie Collins. "I am the Captain of the *Golden Mary*: Mr. Collins is the Mate," Dickens would write. In the story, as critic Anthea Trodd describes, the authors "[rebut] a charge of cannibalism recently brought against an elite group from [the British seafaring] community by asserting the incomparable gifts for leadership, fidelity, and self-sacrifice found among British Tars."[19] The popular nineteenth-century expression of orderliness, "ship shape and Bristol fashion," suggests that Dickens was in good company.[20]

Like Dickens, author Elizabeth Gaskell juxtaposed the essential worthiness of seafaring life and characters (albeit described from afar) with an indictment of materialism and hypocrisy of the rising bourgeois order on land. In *North and South* (1855), the protagonist's caring older brother Frederick is forced to live as a fugitive in Spain, following a mutiny to protest flogging and other physical violence inflicted by a tyrannical nineteenth-century captain. Similarly, in *Sylvia's Lovers* (1863), the Napoleonic Wars provide a setting to contrast the honest sailor Charley Kinraid with the devious shop assistant Philip Hepburn, his chief rival for Sylvia's affections.[21]

Such presentation tended to avoid more dissonant images of the common seaman's life, as evident in the figure of "Jolly Jack Tar" who made frequent appearance on the melodramatic stage. "Sailor-actor" Thomas Potter Cooke was reportedly "known and idolized for his nautical parts, which he performed by the dozen: Union Jack, Ben Brace, Tom Tackle, Jack Stedfast, Bob Stay, Jack Junk, Mat Merriton, Bill Bluff, Harry Bowline [and] Ben Billow."[22] Most commonly, notes literary critic John Peck, the sailor as portrayed in British maritime fiction "is cheerful, brave, and contented, not the kind of person who is likely to indulge in political agitation."[23] Typical of the dominant mode was the work of Captain William N. Glascock, whose naval sketches from the 1830s are "full of the honest qualities of good seamanhood."[24]

To be sure, the grievances of ordinary sailors—which most famously spilled out in the 1797 mutinies at Spithead and the Nore—did provoke popular sympathy. Playwright Douglas Jerrold thus stood out for his heroizing of rebel seamen, including mutineer Richard Parker, in his rendition of *The Mutiny at the Nore* (1830). In response to the law-and-order talk of a landlubbing clerk, Parker's confrere Jack Adams pleads for the audience's compassion: "I know that every sailor there (though there may be something to complain of, and they've gone on the wrong tack to remedy it) has done old England service; I know that many a brave heart there has watched, fought, bled, for his country; has spent years upon the salt sea in storms and peril; has had the waves beating over him and the shots flying about him, whilst you, and such as you, have been scratching your sixpences together, taking your grog with the curtains drawn, the doors listed, your feet upon your fender, and your wife and children alongside of you."[25] As critic Trodd convincingly reasons, "Awareness of both the sailor's usefulness and his capacity for disruption augmented public anxieties about Britain's dependence on seamen, and, in turn, deepened the need for reassuring myths about them."[26] Though capable of political inflection, the British sea story remained more moralistic than "realistic" until Joseph Conrad, at the end of the century, presented a much starker and more nuanced view of British maritime work and social life.

"Wards of the Admiralty"

Even as contrasting elements of national identity played out in Anglo-American maritime fiction, the essential similarity of Atlantic seamen's political status is more apparent when we turn to the public record. The issues surrounding impressment—the subject of the previous chapter—formed only the tip of public concern regarding that class that was in both countries considered part of the "nation's property." All in all, a rigid standard of legal discipline governed both British and American seamen, at once limiting their freedoms but also guaranteeing them certain protections unafforded to other domestic occupations. Similarly, assumptions about the group character and behavior of mariners were deeply rooted in Anglo-American statutes as well as in the British common law. Finally, in both societies, the growing rights-consciousness of the nineteenth century rendered the coercions surrounding the seafarer increasingly controversial.

The peculiar status of seamen in the eyes of the state was of venerable origin. Regulation of the merchant seaman began as early as the stipulation in the laws of ancient Rhodes (900 B.C.) that bound the sailor in a serflike contract to his ship and in the subsequent Rolls of Oléron, a set of late-medieval codes that elaborated duties, wages, and punishment in untoward events ranging from sickness to insubordination to shipwreck.[27] Much of the early legal inheritance transferred into British practice—as in the law of 1729 that at once established the modern-day signing of ship's articles and defined the crime of "desertion" (with a punishment of up to thirty days' hard labor for leaving a ship's service during the life of a contract)—and into generally derivative American laws of 1790 and 1792 as well.[28] As late as 1779, it is worth noting, Virginia statutes were still invoking "the laws of Oléron and the Rhodian and Imperial Laws" as relevant precedent.[29] Similarly extending ancient custom, in 1798, the U.S. federal government established the beginnings of a chain of hospitals for disabled seamen that would "constitute the largest federal health care program until the social insurance systems of the twentieth century."[30]

The special regulatory regime established for Anglo-American sailors doubly assumed both the importance and weakness of this occupational group. As a matter of law, the question of freedom was also always bound up with a distinctly paternalistic presumption in the treatment of merchant seamen. Particularly influential in setting legal precedent on both sides of the Atlantic was Lord Stowell (William Scott), who sat on the British High Court of Admiralty for thirty years beginning in 1798. Concerned that seamen, left to themselves, would be regularly disadvantaged when dealing with wealthy merchant shipowners, Stowell, in 1822, invoked admiralty authority over a party who "is easy and careless, illiterate and unthinking [and has] no such resources, in his own intelligence and experience in habits of business, as can enable him to take accurate measures of postponed payments, with proper estimate of profit and loss." A year later, positively citing Stowell's opinion, U.S. Supreme Court justice Joseph Story (of later *Amistad* fame), in a case reaffirming the legitimacy of the federal marine hospital system, formally christened seamen "wards of the admiralty" while further characterizing them as "generally poor and friendless . . . they are unprotected and need counsel . . . they are thoughtless and require indulgence . . . they are credulous and complying; and are easily overreached."[31]

For all their formal similarity in treatment, however, an important difference in context likely affected popular perception of the sailor class in Britain as compared to the young United States. In the post-revolutionary context of American "free-labor" thought, the treatment of seamen, clinging to Anglo (and even more ancient) precedent, constituted an anomalous social category. Whereas other white workers were experiencing the rapid elimination of coercive contracts (enforceable through criminal sanction)—with indenture effectively ended by 1830—seamen's employment stood out precisely for its relative unfreedom.[32] It was thus little coincidence that the administrative apparatus for arresting runaway seamen, as detailed in one of the early acts of the First Congress of the United States in 1790—including the right of any justice of the peace to apprehend the deserter and place him in jail as well as impose punishment on "any person [who] shall harbor or secrete" the fugitive—would serve as a prototype for the nation's first Fugitive Slave Law of 1793. (As we shall see, this was not the last time that the legal fate of seamen and slaves would be intertwined.) Still, it should be noted that at a post-revolutionary moment in which the country was celebrating the heightened status of the ordinary free white worker (while also moving in the North to eradicate slavery), the penalty for desertion was initially reduced from the British standard of jail time to monetary damages.[33] The very poignancy of American writing about seamen's lives in the early to mid-nineteenth century may thus be partly explained by the peculiar mix of freedom and coercion that still clung to this one among many "free"-labor occupations. While British seamen were no different than miners or textile workers in their subjection to the rigid penalties of master and servant laws (until 1875 for the others, until 1880 for seamen), American seamen stood out for the contrast between their lives and at least northern labor norms. No wonder they made good copy for middle-class readers.

Campaigns against Sailor Abuse

Eventually, reports of the extreme treatment of sailors stirred growing dissent on both sides of the Atlantic. Of the wide range of post-impressment issues, "flogging" and its association with the slavemaster's whip touched off the biggest storm. Though focused on abuse in the navies of both the United States and Britain, agitation as well as legislative remedies spilled out into the civilian arena of maritime operations.

In a world of nominally free laborers, reports of shipboard flogging—the punishment of choice by masters determined to maintain discipline over ever-larger work crews—inevitably engendered public discomfort. Once generally accepted as part of master-servant relations, physical punishment as an inducement to labor had become anathema on land. Greater respect for personal autonomy had outlawed the beating of adult servants in eighteenth-century Britain; even for imprisoned servants, whipping had largely disappeared by the early nineteenth century. In America, the corporal punishments regularly meted out to indentured laborers in colonial times likewise largely vanished with the Revolution in a "new order of things" that proscribed physical compulsion even against juvenile servants.[34]

So it was that the legal and customary "exception" still carved out for sailors struck a popular nerve. Indicative were accounts like that of John Randolph of Roanoke, Virginia, who traveled on an American man-of-war to take up his duties as ambassador to Russia in 1830: Randolph reported that he saw more flogging on his single voyage than had taken place on his own plantation of five hundred slaves across ten years.[35] A more graphic narrative of victimization was relayed by Jacksonian radical William Leggett, who nurtured a lifelong hatred for tyranny rooted in navy experience and court-martial for insubordinate behavior.[36] Leggett's 1834 tale, "Brought to the Gangway," tells the story of a young sailor who, daring to stand up to the false accusations of an officer with a penchant to "flog first, and report afterwards," suffers a brutal whipping before tackling his oppressor in a final, drowning embrace.[37] By 1835, a larger domestic movement against corporal punishment was reflected in lawful penalties for unjustified beating of the crew. Dana's *Two Years before the Mast* and Melville's *Redburn* and

FIGURE 2.1. *Flogging on a Man-of-War*, woodcut, ca. 1850. This illustration for Herman Melville's *White Jacket* (1850) of the flogging of a nineteen-year-old mizzen-top man (with two other young sailors awaiting their punishments) on a U.S. naval ship—based on Melville's own Pacific voyage of 1843–44—helped stoke a humanitarian campaign against such physical punishment. The quotation under the woodcut's caption is from the narrative: "Again, and again, and again; and at every blow, higher and higher rose the long, purple bars on the prisoner's back. But he only bowed over his head, and stood still." From Henry Howe, *Life and Death on the Ocean: A Collection of Extraordinary Adventures* (New York: Tuttle, 1855).

White-Jacket, or The World in a Man-of-War (1850) further stirred public revulsion and helped prompt ultimate legislative redress in 1850.[38] In Britain, a similar pattern of reform agitation against flogging gained persuasive parliamentary advocates like William Cobbett and Joseph Hume. Cobbett himself had been sentenced to two years in prison in 1810 for his printed attack on the vicious flogging of army mutineers at Ely in 1809: "Five hundred lashes each! Aye, that is right! Flog them! Flog! Flog! Flog! They deserve a flogging at every meal time. Lash them daily! Lash them duly!"[39] As historian E. P. Thompson summarized, "Next to the press-gang, flogging was perhaps the most hated of the institutions of Old England."[40]

To an important degree, the campaigns against flogging derived from a larger vector of transatlantic, evangelical-centered reform linking sailors to other unfortunate subjects. The British Bible Society began proselytizing among sailors in London as early as 1790, and a Mariners' Church was established in New York in 1821. Bethel societies (or Methodist meeting centers for sailors) multiplied on both sides of the Atlantic—the American Seamen's Friend Society boasted nearly one hundred local auxiliaries by the mid-1840s—aimed initially at self-reformation and temperance but inevitably also addressing the mistreatment of their sailor flock.[41] Directly boarding ships in port for meetings with the crew, the evangelicals quickly appreciated the link between the "evil" of brothels and groghouses and the larger toll of violence aboard ships, both naval and mercantile. Ardent spirits, argued the American *Sailor's Magazine*, rendered sailors so disorderly that the lash often followed the daily grog ration. As a purported "solution" to bad behavior, however, corporal punishment only further infantilized its victim, depriving him, be he plantation slave or free sailor, of the "last vestige of self-respect."[42] A spate of first-person testimonies by reformed alcoholics in the 1830s and 1840s mixed sometimes lurid accounts of debauchery with an effective appeal to limit the exercise of violence against woebegone sailors and seamen.[43]

It was just such reform logic among evangelicals that alarmed a conservative temperament like that of James Fenimore Cooper. "It is seldom," counseled Cooper in his revised 1849 preface to *The Pilot* at a time of both anti-flogging campaigns and his own defense of landlords' rights amid anti-rent campaigns in New York, "that any institution, practice, or system, is improved by the blind interference of those who know nothing about it. Better would it be to trust to the experience of those who have long governed turbulent men, than to the impulsive experiments of those who rarely regard more than one side of a question." Moreover, Cooper knew exactly who was keeping the social pot boiling. "There is an uneasy desire," he continued, "among a vast many well-disposed persons to get the fruits of the Christian Faith, without troubling themselves about the Faith itself. This is done under the sanction of Peace Societies, Temperance and Moral Reform Societies, in which the end is too often mistaken for the means."[44] Though, to such eyes, social improvement (including the end of flogging) had better be left to voluntary measures, evangelical activists saw no contradiction in calling both individual and community to moral account at one and the same time.[45]

As it happened, the evangelical campaigns against slavery and sailor abuse overlapped in the case of one famous American family. James Garrison, elder brother of radical abolitionist William Lloyd Garrison and an unrestrained alcoholic since age fourteen, disappeared from his New England home for over two decades. In September 1839, an unexpected summons from the Charleston Navy Yard reunited the editor of *The Liberator* with his long-lost brother, now a "weather-beaten sailor," "wretched, with shaking hands, the drunkard's splotched face, and a gaunt frame bent nearly double with a spinal complaint." He had been whipped on several occasions for drunkenness and once placed in double irons for twenty-eight days.[46] As William Lloyd Garrison's biographer describes the irony, "while Lloyd had made his name protesting the lash, James had suffered under it, enduring abuse in the merchant marine and the U.S. Navy that, in its physical cruelty and denial of rights, rivaled anything that Garrison had published in *The Liberator* about slavery."[47] Though William Lloyd encouraged his brother to commit his sad account to paper, the editor chose not to publish it in his antislavery organ. Simple embarrassment may explain such reticence, but one wonders also if such a tale of near–"white slavery" may also have been thought to divert *The Liberator*'s readers from the cause at hand.

The race theme affected the pace and politics of anti-flogging regulation on both sides of the Atlantic. "Rather than argue against flogging in general," suggests one recent historian, British naval reform proponents "chose to agitate specifically against the practice of flogging the 'true British seaman' on the grounds that this individual experienced flogging *differently* from a non-British individual such as a black slave."[48] Thus, whereas Cobbett's exposé of whipping might excite general consternation, an 1814 report of similar treatment visited on migrating lascar seamen (in this case by their native Indian supervisors or *serangs*) in London triggered a different response. Rather than prosecute the *serangs* or directly legislate against flogging, Parliament moved only to tighten the limitation of movement and enforced repatriation of the lascars themselves.[49] Delayed by such association of the naval occupations with a more exotic, imperial world, British anti-flogging agitation gave primacy to efforts directed at the army until the adoption of "professional" codes of supervisory conduct in the Naval Discipline Acts of 1860–66.[50]

In a pattern distinct from the British one, the U.S. anti-flogging measure, included in a naval appropriation act passed a mere nine days after narrow agreement on the Compromise of 1850 (focused on the territorial legacy of the Mexican-American War), inevitably joined the larger sectional debate about slavery. The shadow of the lash used on plantation field hands was ever-present in U.S. discussions of this maritime reform. Whig senator John Parker Hale of New Hampshire, a strong antislavery advocate, opened discussion on the measure by suggesting that flogging created more disciplinary problems than it solved. Surely, he suggested, "when we have done so much to heal the 'bleeding wounds' of a violated Constitution, the Senate of the United States will not consent that the bleeding wounds of the lacerated backs of the white citizens of this republic shall be longer submitted to this brutalizing punishment." Hannibal Hamlin of Maine (who, six years later, would bolt from the Democrats and then serve as Lincoln's running mate in 1860) went further: opposition to flogging, he insisted, came from "all creeds in religion, all parties in politics. . . . They look upon it, as I do, as being a reproach that any man should stand up, at this stage of the world, and demand corporal punishment at this day."[51] Defenders of flogging pointed to the lack of desirable alternatives. Conscious of the contemporary rise of the prison system, Democratic congressman Abraham Venable of North Carolina argued, "You must substitute some punishment, and the only one left is confinement. The lazy and the worthless sailor would not object to this, and in the gale and the storm good and true sailors have all the duty to perform. The bad ones are never better pleased than when they have nothing to do—imprisonment is to them an escape from work."[52] As an alternative to an outright ban, some defenders of the traditional discipline proposed instead to abolish the liquor allotment and/or ban liquor entirely on board ship. Such a remedy (which did not pass), however, struck Representative Isaac E. Morse of Louisiana as worse than the disease. His intervention, again, suggested that the issue of sailor punishment invoked larger divisions about workplace authority in an era of contention between free and coercive labor (not to mention, perhaps, a differing view of the physical effects of spirituous beverages): "If the sailors are thus to be exempted on the one hand from the punishment of a breach of the rules of the service, and, on the other, to be deprived of all stimulus to exertion, what is to become of the vessel in a crisis of difficulty and danger? Was the captain to call his sailors on deck as a sort of town meeting and consult with them whether he ought to take in sail in the fury of a storm?"[53]

Like the compromise measure on new territories, the naval bill's razor-thin margin in the Senate—26 to 24—directly testified to the nation's larger sectional polarization. As historian Harold D. Langley has documented, of the twenty-six votes to abolish flogging, twenty-four came from the North and the other two from border states. The overwhelmingly southern opposition, for example, included that of Jefferson Davis.[54] Southern resistance, ironically, also accounts for the bill's extension to the merchant marine, where flogging was less common but not unknown, as well as to the navy.[55]

In a failed ploy to derail the bill, which he opposed, Florida senator David Yulee successfully inserted the words "and on board vessels of commerce" after the word "navy."[56]

Though never reversed, the flogging ban caused initial consternation within the U.S. Navy itself. Within months of the passage of the restrictive legislation, the secretary of the navy submitted a report to the Senate, documenting widespread complaints of "insubordination and serious irregularities among the seamen of the navy, tending to show that the power to restrain bad men is lost to the service, and that no substitute for flogging has been found." The most notorious incident concerned the arrival of the U.S. frigate *Brandywine* at New York in December 1850, where reportedly more than half the crew (nearly 300 men) "left the ship in violation of orders, evincing entire indifference to regulations and to the authority placed over them." Among the "substitutes" for flogging initially proposed by the service lay a mixture of carrots and sticks: on the one hand, better pay, more careful recruiting, and good-conduct discharges that would ensure priority of future employment; on the other hand, bad conduct discharges, "accompanied by a mark on some part of the person, usually covered by their clothes, of the letter B, in indelible ink, to be inflicted by a sentence of a summary court-martial." Such physical identifiers could not be considered cruel, argued the secretary, "as few sailors are without marks [that is, tattoos] made in that way."[57] Once the navy's attempt to restore flogging failed, Congress in 1855 and again in 1862 established new guideposts for naval discipline. A system of summary courts-martial for minor offenses included the sentencing of guilty men to solitary confinement, with or without leg irons and/or a diet of bread and water for a limited time.[58]

African Americans at Sea

Though sailors were sometimes likened to slaves in the minds of reformers, the racial connections to maritime employment and regulation proved more complex. Despite certain parallels in the mistreatment of slaves and sailors and notwithstanding the horrors of the Middle Passage, the sea often represented a realm of relative freedom for African Americans. The latter theme is notable, for example, in the two paradigmatic slave narratives of Olaudah Equiano and Frederick Douglass. Equiano, whether or not he directly experienced the Middle Passage, spent considerable time as a seaman, first as a slave of a British naval officer, then as a freeman as a hairdresser and steward, and finally as a colonizer to both Central America and Sierra

Leone. Without romanticizing the sea, Equiano, as literary scholar Elizabeth Schultz summarized, found there "the respect of his fellows and the dignity of work." Late in life, as he put it in his *Narrative*, he still "thought of visiting old ocean again."[59] After sustaining a severe beating from a group of white ship's carpenter apprentices on the Baltimore docks, Douglass, a slave, took advantage of his own maritime knowledge to secure free black sailor's papers and journey north (via train) to New Bedford, where, again working as a dock laborer, he saw "the nearest approach to freedom and equality that I had ever seen."[60]

Perhaps it is not surprising, then, that free blacks took so readily to maritime occupations. "Relatively high wages, stable employment, and personal fulfillment," according to one study, explains the disproportionate presence of black mariners in northern U.S. port cities; by 1825, "blacks occupied nearly one-fifth of all berths aboard foreign-bound vessels leaving Philadelphia and New York" and likely one-quarter from Providence and Boston. Even in smaller New England ports like Salem, where their employment was restricted to the position of ship's cook or steward, seafaring remained the "most popular form of black employment" through 1840.[61]

The very image of freedom that the ship at sea inspired in the enslaved Douglass panicked southern slave owners and their political defenders. Most tangibly, such fears led, in the aftermath of the aborted slave insurrection of Charleston's skilled free-black sailor and carpenter Denmark Vesey—with its plan to ferry escaped slaves to Haiti—to the restrictive South Carolina Negro Seamen's Act in 1822. According to this act, and similar legislation subsequently passed in five other southern coastal states, free Negro sailors were effectively quarantined once they arrived in a southern port, with their custodial expenses charged against the offending ship itself. Failure to comply with the quarantine, the law stipulated, mandated enslavement, though this was subsequently moderated to mere whipping. With enforcement particularly strict in South Carolina and New Orleans, an estimated 10,000 black sailors were victimized by such legislation.[62]

Political dispute over the Negro Seamen's Acts quickly escalated from a domestic argument over free black sailors into a larger diplomatic incident, with both national and international repercussions. On the international front, both France and Great Britain complained repeatedly and vociferously that its treaty laws with the United States had been abrogated whenever its normal commerce in southern ports was interrupted by the seizure of Negro crew members.[63] British authorities pursued two cases with particular verve. In 1822, Secretary of State John Quincy Adams, after applying informal pressure to state officials, had assured the British minister in Washington, Stratford Canning, that British subjects would experience no further cause for complaint from the state's seamen's laws. In 1823, however, at the behest of the South Carolina Association—a group of prominent citizens determined to enforce the black codes—freeman Henry Elkison was taken from his ship in Charleston and lodged in prison. Despite a ruling from U.S. Supreme Court justice William Johnson (a native of South Carolina) that invoked the interstate commerce clause (art. 1, sec. 8) to find in favor of federal jurisdiction in the matter, no effective action was taken to reverse the state initiatives.[64]

The issue festered among the states and between southern states and their international trading partners for decades. A protest petition from Boston's major merchants and shipowners triggered hearings and a pointed exchange with southern defenders of the Negro Seamen's Acts in 1843. Citing the constitutional authority variously of the aforementioned "commerce clause," the "supremacy clause" (art. 6) regarding federal enforcement of treaty rights, and the "privilege and immunity" clause (art. 4, sec. 2) that "citizens of each state shall be entitled to all privileges and immunities of citizens of the several States," a majority report of the House Commerce Committee backed the petitioners, proposing override legislation to counter the state-based legislation. The police power of individual states, the committee majority argued, can never justify the arbitrary seizure—"charged with no crime and infected with no contagion"—of an entire class of people recognized with citizenship rights in another state. "For some of the stations on board both of our sail ships and steamboats," explained the report, "colored mariners are thought to possess peculiar qualifications. They are very generally employed as firemen, laborers, stewards, and cooks. The memorialists state that it is frequently *necessary* to employ them. The abduction of persons so employed immediately on the arrival of a vessel in port, and their detention at a heavy expense until the very moment of its departure, cannot be less an injury to their employers than it is an outrage on themselves."[65]

Until the Civil War, however, the South effectively defended its exclusion of free black seamen. By a vote of 86 to 59, the U.S. House of Representatives tabled the Commerce Committee's recommendation in 1843. Moreover, the Boston petitioners' alternative strategy to institute civil suits in the offending states with the hope of testing the acts before the Supreme Court never came to fruition. In two celebrated cases, agents seeking to bring suits on behalf of quarantined seamen in South Carolina and Louisiana were threatened with mob violence and driven back to Massachusetts.[66] In the course of the 1843 debates, southern lawmakers, supported by President Andrew Jackson's attorney general, John Macpherson Berrien, had stoutly defended their actions as matters of constitutional principle. Offering the minority report of the Commerce Committee, North Carolina Whig Kenneth Rayner subtly challenged the northern petitioners' defense of Negro seamen as "citizens" entitled to "all the rights and privileges . . . of the highest class of society." First, countered Rayner, "the term citizens, as used in the Constitution, has no specific or definite meaning, only so far as qualified by the regulations which the respective States may have adopted in defining their 'privileges and immunities.'" Second, he noted with ample illustration, free blacks were already disqualified from several rights of full citizenship across the northern as well as the southern states. Suffrage, militia service, and rights to intermarriage with whites were regularly barred to blacks. Rayner thus dismissed the claims of Negro sailors—they were not citizens but (and here he quoted from noted jurist James Kent) "essentially a degraded caste, of inferior rank and station in society."[67] Even those opposed to the South Carolina legislation as a breach of federal jurisdiction could not gainsay such arguments. Former attorney general Wirt, for example, had himself ruled in 1821 that free Negroes in Virginia did not constitute "citizens," in the sense of having the right, under U.S. shipping law, to "command vessels" in the foreign or coasting trade.[68]

Perhaps more fundamentally, the southerners defended the Negro Seamen's Acts as a form of state police power vested in the "reserve" clause of the Constitution's Tenth Amendment. Comparing the acts to state quarantine legislation, Berrien asked rhetorically, would it be fair to the southern states "to withhold from them the power of protecting themselves as they may against the introduction among their colored people of that moral contagion, compared with which physical pestilence, in the utmost imaginable extent of its horrors, would be light and trifling?"[69] Anticipating his state's advocacy of nullification (or selective enforcement) of federal tariffs in 1832 and ultimate secession in 1860, South Carolina governor John L. Wilson declared allegiance to the Negro Seamen's Act in 1824 in no uncertain terms: "[If] an appeal to . . . the right of self-government be disregarded . . . there would be more glory in forming a rampart with our bodies than to be . . . the slaves of a great consolidated Government."[70]

Southern defense of the Negro Seamen's Acts carried long historical coattails. When he replaced Berrien as Jackson's attorney general in 1832, Roger B. Taney more than concurred with his predecessor's constitutional defense of the restrictive acts. In an official, advisory opinion, Taney went further, denying Negroes, free or slave, any rights under the Constitution: "The African race," wrote Taney, "are everywhere a degraded class, and exercise no political influence."[71] Unpublished at the time, Taney resurrected the substance of this opinion as chief justice of the Supreme Court within his momentous *Dred Scott* decision of 1857. Even as a freeman, read the decision, Scott had no standing to bring suit as a citizen in a federal court; by the logic of the Constitution he was, whether emancipated or not, rather part of "a subordinate and inferior class of beings."[72]

Paternalism versus the Right to Quit

Leaving aside the question of race, how free were any seamen as a class of workers? In the Atlantic world of the mid- to late nineteenth century, controversy around this question tended to gather around one central feature of the sea worker's enterprise: his inability to quit (on penalty of criminal, usually physical punishment) within the life of his contract. As slavery defender George Fitzhugh noted in 1854, "Abolish negro slavery, and how much slavery still remains? Soldiers and sailors in Europe enlist for life: here, for five years. Are they not slaves who have not only sold their liberties, but their lives also? And they are worse treated than domestic slaves. No domestic affection and self-interest extend their aegis over them. No kind mistress, like a guardian angel, provides for them in health, tends them in sickness, and soothes their dying pillow."[73]

Compared to most landlocked occupations, the degree of compulsion at work for seamen was undoubtedly severe. Still, Fitzhugh did not acknowledge a key aspect of the sailor's lot. Though admittedly no equivalent to the slave mistress of Fitzhugh's imagination, the government itself played the role of guardian over the seamen's welfare. Part coercive, part protective, the government's role on both sides of the Atlantic ultimately figured mightily in defining the character of the seamen's experience at work as well as in shaping seamen unionism and seamen politics. To be sure, the seamen's own constituency, together with its broader-based labor allies, would ultimately also figure in the mix.

Even before any appreciable sailor-based reform effort was manifest, the foundations for widespread political regulation and governance of maritime occupations had been laid by landmark legislation affecting both shipowners and seamen. If by no means entirely to the seamen's liking, the British Merchant Shipping Acts of 1850, 1854, and 1867 (which effectively replaced or revised features of the earlier Navigation Acts) and the American Shipping Commissioners' Act of 1872 (largely an imitation of its British counterparts) set the parameters of the seamen's liberty, welfare, and "slavery" for decades to come.

The mid-Victorian legislation on both sides of the Atlantic amounted, as David M. Williams summarized the 1867 act, to "a strange mixture of protective paternalism and rigid, sometimes harsh supervision."[74] In a manner at once sentimental and condescending, New York representative Fernando Wood (who had himself parlayed a large shipowning interest into a political career as a Tammany Hall boss and two fractious terms as mayor of New York City, 1854–57 and 1860–62) thus entered discussion of the 1872 bill: "It is said—and there is great truth in the statement—that the sailors now have none to care for them; that they pursue lives of toil, of trial, and of danger, for a compensation which is almost nothing; and that their feet no sooner touch the soil than they become the victims of those who stand ready to prey upon them; who take from them fraudulently and sometimes violently their hard earnings, and then destroy, as far as possible, their moral, mental, and physical powers, in order to hold absolute control over them until they again ship to go upon the perilous deep."[75]

Resting, as Williams suggests, on a simultaneous concern and contempt for the sailor class as self-governing subjects, their legislative guardians served up an elaborate grid of controls on the seafaring occupation. On the one hand, for example, the Merchant Shipping Act of 1854 (a consolidation of previously prevailing codes that took up a fifth of the national statute book for the year) specified the variety and amount of food a captain must supply his crew and even required weighing scales to ensure compliance with the legislated standards. To the same end, the original draft of the U.S. act of 1872 allotted seamen daily rations of meat, potatoes, peas, flour, rice, and coffee or tea, even as an amendment specified that "for potatoes onions may be substituted."[76] The British Merchant Shipping Amendment Act of 1867, likewise, expanded the seaman's minimal sleeping space to twelve feet and sought to guarantee him privy access.[77] Even such attempts to "improve" the seaman's condition, however, were usually accompanied by unmistakable condescension. Thus, the clause in the 1867 act enforcing the provision of lime juice against scurvy specified that a refusal to drink the ration be regarded as "disobedience of orders" and entered in the ship's log.[78] As in the control of prostitutes in port towns under the Contagious Disease Acts of the 1860s, attitudes implicit in legislation directed at sailor subjects ranged from seeing them as innocents at risk to degenerate misfits.[79]

Although generally similar in tone, legislative arguments on the separate sides of the Atlantic were also clearly inflected by what we might call different "stages of state formation." The British, for example, were self-consciously straining to dispose of what were seen as the unnecessary and costly remains of a mercantilist state regime in favor of a free trade empire. To take but one example, despite expressed fears about the rise of foreign sailors in the British fleet, there was little sentiment in Parliament for going back to the Navigation Act–era institutionalization of an apprentice program for young sailors once the compulsory carriage of apprenticeships was abandoned in 1849.[80] The Americans, on the other hand, still betrayed post–Civil War confidence in building up the capacity of the federal government.[81] Thus, the newly established "shipping commissioners" were specifically invested with "facilitating apprenticeships" for boys age twelve and older. To be sure, the indentured (and thus "unfree") nature of apprenticeship required special U.S. handling. As the elderly Massachusetts congressman Samuel Hooper admonished the 1872 bill's sponsor, fellow Republican Omar Conger of Michigan, who had originally fixed the end of the apprenticeship term at twenty-one years of age, "A boy who has been on board ship from the age of twelve to that of eighteen is very often an able seaman. To extend the apprenticeship beyond that time would be to make him almost a slave." Conger quickly accepted Hooper's revision.[82]

The limits of consensus for government protections from either national side were, perhaps, best revealed in ineffectual efforts to end "crimping." The crimp (or boardinghouse boss) was notorious for running up the sailor's debt while in port and then mortgaging the often drunken victim's debt to the next voyage. The local shipping offices established by the British Mercantile Marine Act of 1850 were supposed to replace such "exploitative" middlemen with an "honest" commercial exchange between shipmaster and crew, brokered only by the government referee. In practice, however, the crimp (often a former sailor himself) was both better situated and better ensconced in sailor culture—having extended board, shelter, and credit during periods of unemployment or shore leave—than either employers or government officials.[83] Thus, despite anti-crimp measures like the establishment of seamen's savings banks and harsh penalties on outsiders who boarded ships before they had docked, sailor-town saloons long remained the prime source of both British and American sailor recruitment. An enduring source of crimp control was the long-established advance note offered the sailor when he registered for a voyage. Often signed over to the crimp to pay for accumulated boardinghouse debts, the advance note was further attacked by some shipowners as a prime goad to desertion (that is, once even partially paid, why continue to work?). Yet, for decades, no action was taken against the note. As the chief spokesman of Her Majesty's Government explained in 1854, despite "regret" about the "improvidence into which seamen were but too frequently led," a sailor was not "to be treated like a child or a minor, as one who could not be entrusted with his own resources" or "placed under restrictions from which every landsman was free, in making his own contracts."[84] Both the U.S. Shipping Commissioners' Act and the subsequent Dingley Act (1884) did attempt to protect the sailor's family by limiting payment of advance notes or subsequent allotments "to the seaman himself or to his wife or mother." Just as on the British side, however, the commercial interests of the crimps forced a relaxation of the prescriptions as early as 1886.[85]

Together, the midcentury legislative measures served further to highlight the peculiar and ambivalent status that merchant seamen occupied in the Anglo-American social structure. All male and overwhelmingly young, rough in dress and speech as well as "reckless and improvident," seafarers on the one hand fit a hypermasculine ideal of independence and adventurousness.[86] How indeed could such men be treated as children or minors? On the other hand, as historian Lisa Norling suggests, their very "incompleteness" as solitary male figures in a political universe built on "household" (male and female) stability shaped the seaman's image as both a pathetic and potentially dangerous subject. Even the married seaman—separated for extended periods from his family and frequently leaving them on the public dole—could not realize the nineteenth-century provider ideal.[87] However exaggerated, the image of Jack Tar—"footloose, careless, and fancy-free"—took powerful hold in the larger culture, helping to confirm "the prejudices of a class convinced of the seafarer's social and moral inferiority."[88] Cut off from civilizing, female influences, the lowly seaman would need to be "domesticated" by a surrounding apparatus of both employer and state-based controls. A seaman's governance began with his signing of the articles of agreement. More than any other class of worker in the nineteenth century, the seaman's contract partook of the basic qualities of the marriage contract—service (to the master) in exchange for protection or basic welfare.[89]

By far the most coercive aspect of the paternalist labor codes was the

FIGURE 2.2. Henry Corbould, *The Sailor's Farewell*, 1848. The English genre artist and book illustrator Henry Corbould turned his attention in an undocumented moment in the early to mid-nineteenth century to a well-worked, transatlantic romantic theme, the "Sailor's Farewell." With the implied subject returning to a ship ready for sail, the focus here falls on his family, emphasizing the danger, uncertainty, and even foreboding attached to the seaman's occupation as well as his expected role as sturdy family provider. Courtesy of Christie's.

treatment of desertion—or withdrawal from work during the life of a contract—the penalties for which were only slowly and incrementally updated across the century. Curiously, on the British side (as alluded to in chapter 1), the very loosening of mercantilist market controls occasioned rising concern regarding seamen's conduct. Typical was a Maltese marine official's warning in 1849 of the "recklessness of sailors, their ignorance and credibility, their want of forethought added to habits of dissipation which render them liable to every species of loss and robbery." Thus Henry Labouchere, who shepherded the repeal of the Navigation Acts through Parliament, also oversaw the Mercantile Marine Act of 1850 that, in deference to shipowner demands, lengthened the imprisonment penalties for desertion.[90] Incorporating the new disciplinary standard, the mammoth Merchant Shipping

Act of 1854 devoted twenty-one clauses to sailor discipline, specifying capture without warrant and then forfeiture of wages and up to twelve weeks of imprisonment on land "with or without hard labour" for desertion. To further bolster the ship's command structure, the act authorized up to ten weeks of the same treatment for any "Absence without Leave at any Time within Twenty-four Hours of the Ship's sailing from any Port either at the Commencement or during the Progress of any Voyage."[91] Though a month at hard labor may have been the more standard sentence, the maximum exaction was not uncommon.[92] Reflecting deep-seated mistrust regarding seamen's loyalty and character, draconian treatment of seamen's breach of contract (lightened for other workers in the Employers and Workmen Act of 1875) continued until the category of "desertion" was finally abolished from British law in 1970.[93]

Though the U.S. Congress had originally privileged monetary damages over corporal punishment in the case of desertion, such principled difference with British practice did not abide for long. Selective state laws had always taken a tougher line: Maryland, for example, as Richard B. Morris documented, regularly arrested deserting seamen, both before and after the Thirteenth Amendment formally abolished "involuntary servitude" in 1865.[94] Whatever initial anomaly existed between the United States and Britain, it was formally erased when the U.S. Shipping Commissioners' Act of 1872 added punishment by imprisonment to a maritime regulatory act that virtually mimicked the British wording of 1854.[95] The 1872 legislation offers a compelling example of what historian Amy Dru Stanley calls the "legends of contract freedom" that dominated American political thinking in the post–Civil War years.[96] As with the treatment of freedmen, vagrants, and wives, Republican legislators, fresh from the triumph over slavery, extended the doctrine of contract enforcement to merchant shipping. At the center of the new legislation, a new set of public officials, the shipping commissioners, were charged with overseeing and enforcing the traditional articles of agreement between a master or shipowner and his seamen. Tightening a whole set of disciplinary codes, the act extended imprisonment for desertion to not more than three months and also established a one-month sentence for "refusal to proceed to sea." Moreover, masters, owners, shipping commissioners, and local constables were permitted to apprehend and detain any absconding suspect "without first procuring a warrant" in the pursuit of ultimate justice.[97] Though the law would shortly be seen by organized-sailor representatives as the source of "the most drastic evils of maritime usage," the labor provisions sailed through Congress without dissent.[98] Massachusetts congressman Benjamin F. Butler, for example, a Radical Republican and former Union general who had backed the eight-hour day, greenback financing of the debt, and women suffrage—and who ironically had easily bested erstwhile maritime reformer Richard Henry Dana Jr. in the congressional election of 1868 by calling him "an aristocrat of the snobbiest sort"—was a vocal advocate of the 1872 bill.[99] When it came to seamen's conduct, Butler personally advanced the punishment clause for "assaulting any master or mate" from six months to two years.[100] Likely influenced both by his concern for discipline as a field commander and his experience in controlling "uppity" ex-slaves on Louisiana's wartime sugar plantations, Butler's coercive reflex was a further sign that seamen occupied the boundary waters of free-labor status.[101]

To be sure, the onerous legal penalties for quitting within the term of a seaman's contract by no means eliminated the practice of desertion. As Matthew Taylor Rafferty discovered in his study of New York federal and district court records, 1790–1861, desertions in the U.S. merchant fleet occurred on "almost every journey."[102] British desertions, especially to North America, rose dramatically in the 1840s, due both to a general American labor shortage and a boom in soft-wood shipbuilding with a consequent need for new crews to deliver them to European buyers. In Quebec alone, reported desertions of British and colonial seamen approached 20 percent of the total seamen in port.[103] Nor did Britain's midcentury legislation seem to matter. Another major survey, this one of some 54,000 British and Canadian crew members who sailed from St. John, New Brunswick, in the years 1863–1914, reported that 23 percent (and this was likely an understatement) deserted at intermediate ports of call, including an astronomical 49 percent on trips to New York City.[104] As historian Eric Sager points out, an able-bodied seaman from Liverpool "arrived in the United States to find that unskilled general laborers on shore were earning more than he was."[105] Neither higher wages (with an average 20 percent boost paid for trips to British North America than elsewhere) nor (for American seamen) the restrictive clauses of the 1872 legislation could staunch the flow.[106] Despite its legal excoriation, therefore, desertion proved an ineradicable part of Atlantic world shipping. Moreover, as Marcus Rediker demonstrated for the eighteenth century, desertion "was used in complex and ingenious ways." Escape from brutal officers, assertion of the seaman's autonomy, as well as the attraction of higher wages all made for options within what Rediker neatly labeled "the sprawling nature of the international labor market."[107] It was not just sailor agency, however, that contributed to the institutionalization of desertion. Crimps regularly offered inducements to "jump ship" in order that they could bargain with masters over subsequent contracts, while, on extended layovers in port, masters themselves might induce the same actions in order to reduce costs.[108]

Even as prosecutions for desertion declined by the end of the nineteenth century (with the act initially decriminalized in Great Britain in 1880, then formally recriminalized in 1894, as discussed in chapter 3), this symbol of the seaman's relative "unfreedom" as compared to any other group of ostensibly free laborers weighed heavily, especially in the self-consciously republican United States. Not surprisingly, therefore, the political impact of the rise of sailor unionism centered precisely on the elimination of these classic criminal sanctions for quitting work. The Sailors' Union of the Pacific, established in 1891 from a merger of two earlier West Coast maritime unions, within a year formed the nucleus of a nationwide federation of regional organizations, the International Seamen's Union. Directed by its secretary and leading strategist, Andrew Furuseth, the new union's legislative committee worked closely with San Francisco Democratic congressman and former judge James Maguire on a host of reform proposals. Named for its sponsor, the Maguire Act of February 1895 formally abolished imprisonment for desertion in the U.S. coastal trade.[109]

Unfortunately, the protection of seamen in U.S. ports imagined by Maguire Act supporters was rudely undermined by the *Arago* case, 1895–98. A group of American sailors who had shipped on the Chile-bound U.S. barkentine *Arago* from San Francisco in May 1895 grew dissatisfied with conditions on board and, relying on the logic of the Maguire Act, departed the voyage at the first port of call, in Astoria, Oregon. On complaint of the ship's captain, however, they were seized, imprisoned, and returned against their will to the *Arago* by U.S. marshals, and then, still refusing to work, imprisoned again when the ship returned to San Francisco. In January 1897, an extended legal challenge mounted by the seamen's union terminated with a Supreme Court decision (*Robertson v. Baldwin*) that not merely refused the men protection from the Maguire Act (on grounds that they had signed up for an international, not a "coastal," voyage) but also resurrected some of the oldest restrictions on sailor freedoms.[110] Denying the defendants protection from the Thirteenth Amendment (which the sailors' counsel, Representative Maguire, had sought to invoke), the majority opinion, delivered by Justice Henry Billings Brown, grouped seafaring among "services which have from time immemorial been treated as exceptional." Noting that "nearly all maritime nations" had made provisions for criminal punishment "for desertion, or absence without leave during the life of the shipping articles," the ruling self-consciously confirmed the practice of both the U.S. Congress and the British Parliament in treating seamen "as deficient in that full and intelligent responsibility for their acts which is accredited to ordinary adults, and as needing the protection of the law in the same sense which minors and wards are entitled to the protection of their parents and guardians. . . . The ancient characterization of seamen as 'wards of the admiralty' is even more accurate now than it was formerly."[111]

In a stinging dissent, Justice John Harlan attacked the *Robertson* decision as a basic abrogation of American liberties. First, he reaffirmed the reach of the prohibition of "involuntary servitude" in American law and took particular aim at the seamen's initial imprisonment, without a judicial proceeding, on board the *Arago*. Involuntary servitude in the United States, noted Harlan, "can only exist lawfully as a punishment for crime of which the party shall have been duly convicted. . . . It would by no means follow that government could, by force applied in advance of due conviction of some crime, compel a freeman to render personal services in respect of the private business of another." Second, Harlan fairly ridiculed the Court's resort to precedent: "The court refers to the laws of the ancient Rhodians, which are supposed to have antedated the Christian era. But those laws, whatever they may have been, were enacted at a time when no account was taken of man as man, when human life and human liberty were regarded as of little value, and when the powers of Government were employed to gratify the ambition and the pleasures of despotic rulers rather than promote the welfare of the people." Finally, Harlan challenged the psychology used to justify the peculiar confinement of seamen. "I am unable to understand," said Harlan, "how the necessity for the protection of seamen against those who take advantage of them can be made the basis of legislation compelling them, against their will, and by force, to render personal service for others engaged in private business. Their supposed helpless condition is thus made the excuse for imposing upon them burdens that could not be imposed upon other classes without depriving them of rights that inhere in personal freedom."[112] Following Harlan's logic, seamen's advocates immediately labeled *Robertson* the "Second Dred Scott Decision." Though likely unaware of the relation of the first *Dred Scott* decision to the prior treatment of Negro seamen, seamen's union counsel William Macarthur would explain in 1899: "In both cases the rule of personal liberty has been taken exception to—in the case of the negro on account of his color; in that of the seaman because of his calling."[113]

Robertson v. Baldwin carried an extended impact, only partly affecting the seamen themselves. In the post-Reconstruction South of the 1880s, in particular, state legislatures had also imposed criminal sanctions to punish breaches in agricultural labor contracts. Until *Robertson*, however, as Robert J. Steinfeld has documented, in order to avoid direct conflict with the Thirteenth Amendment and anti-peonage law, the state legislation subtly hid its intentions behind an "anti-fraud" rationale. Now, for years to come, "such subtlety would be unnecessary"; several southern states invoked *Robertson* in defense of contract labor laws on land.[114]

For American seamen themselves, the legal horizons were actually much brighter. Only months after the *Robertson* decision and under heavy union pressure, Congress passed the White Act. This act geographically extended the sailor's immunity from imprisonment for desertion under the Maguire Act from U.S. ports to those foreign parts participating in the "domestic trade" (Canada, West Indies, Mexico) and also reduced the term of imprisonment for desertion in a foreign port from three months to not more than one month. The national political consensus was clearly moving in Justice Harlan's direction.[115] Even as employers rarely sought the criminal punishment applied in the *Arago* case, U.S. law soon incorporated the principle of complete repeal of penal sanctions demanded by the seamen's union. Indeed, support for the principle would prove capacious enough to hide under its folds a whole new round of seamen's reform legislation.

PART II

Strategies of Reform

3

Wave of Reform

THE SAILOR'S FRIEND AND THE DRIFT TOWARD A WELFARE STATE

Perhaps never did the plight of the ordinary seaman command more attention from the British public than in the mid-1870s. To be sure, evidence of the problem abounded. Since 1830, some 20 percent of the nation's seamen regularly died at sea, and in some passages of the coal trade, the casualty rate of ships reached an astounding 70 percent. Nor did the men themselves have much recourse. In 1870–72 alone, 1,628 sailors were sent to jail for refusing to go to sea in ships they feared "unworthy."[1] Yet, although social causes have multiple and complex triggers, so too do they sometimes depend on the power of a single reformer to bring their message into crystalline focus. The names William Wilberforce and William Lloyd Garrison are thus inextricably associated with the campaigns against the slave trade and the evil of slavery more generally. Less well-known but equally passionate representatives of nineteenth-century reform currents include Richard Martin (or "Humanity Dick") and Henry Berghe, who organized the British and American branches, respectively, of the Society for the Protection of Animals; Josephine Butler, who campaigned for repeal of the coercive Contagious Diseases Act; and journalist W. T. Stead, who championed a crackdown on child prostitution.[2] In the realm of maritime reform, and certainly maritime safety, no one in the English-speaking world figured more prominently than Samuel Plimsoll. More than anyone else, Plimsoll's tireless advocacy, initially as member of Parliament and subsequently as the unofficial "Sailor's Friend," galvanized public attention so as to make regulatory reform politically desirable if not inevitable. Like other reform movements outwardly associated with the energies of extraordinary personae, so too the cause of maritime reform not only outpaced its progenitor but ultimately took a direction he would not have recognized. Tied all along to deeper currents in the relation of state and society, regulation of the merchant marine proved both harbinger and extreme example of the breakdown of classical, individual-rights-oriented liberalism by a new liberalism fundamentally defined by the arrival of the twentieth century's "representative/interventionist state."[3]

Something of the contemporary impact of Plimsoll's agitation on the popular conscience is suggested by a few particulars. Plimsoll published *Our Seamen: An Appeal*, his clarion call to action regarding the dangerous condition of oceangoing ships, in 1872. Within a year, despite being sanctioned by Parliament for disorderly behavior (an infraction he would commit again, to be upbraided by Prime Minister Benjamin Disraeli himself in 1875), his agitation forced the appointment of a Royal Commission on Unseaworthy Ships, and by 1876, his chief proposed solution for overloaded ships, the load line (an indication on the outside of a vessel indicating how low it may safely rest in the water when fully loaded) received initial legal approval, even as its exact position was not fixed by law until 1894. Within his own lifetime, the characteristic load line mark on the side of a ship, a circle with a horizontal line through the middle, was widely known as the "Plimsoll line." Indirectly, Plimsoll also proved a worldwide legislator, as the United States and other countries gradually adopted their own load line standards, ultimately universally codified by an international convention in 1930.[4]

This legislative legacy only begins to suggest Plimsoll's popular impact. In the course of his campaign, Plimsoll drew huge crowds in rallies around Britain. Newspapers and music halls soon sang his praises. Popular vocalist Fred Albert himself penned "A Cheer for Plimsoll" in 1876:

> There was a time when greed and crime did cruelly prevail,
> And rotten ships were sent on trips to founder in the gale;
> When worthless cargoes, well insured, would to the bottom go,
> And sailors' lives were sacrificed, that men might wealthy grow.
>
> Full many a boat, that scarce could float, was sent to dare the wave,
> Till Plimsoll wrote his book of note, our seamen's lives to save;
> His enemies then tried to prove the pictures false he drew,
> But with English pluck to his task he stuck, that task he deem'd so true.

FIGURE 3.1. Plimsoll line. Clearly visible on the hull of the Scottish steamship MV *Kyles*, the now-universal Plimsoll line also indicates the slightly varied load limits for freshwater (F) and winter seawater (W) traffic. The *Kyles*, now in the Clydebuilt museum at Braehead, Renfrew, Scotland—and as such the oldest floating Clydebuilt vessel in the United Kingdom—was originally launched in 1872 and thus likely would have sailed at least four years before the line was added. © Mr. George Gallagher (George.Gallagher@Gmail.com)

In the same period, composer John Guest also raised "a British cheer for Plimsoll":

'Tis not for gold he labors
A nobler aim has he
The widow and the orphan
And the sailor out to sea.
Their dangers and distresses
His heart of pity moves
His singleness of purpose
Day by day he proves.

Oh shame upon the wretches
Who, to increase their gain
Send men in rotten vessels

To perish on the main;
Then let us do our duty,
Not resting till we save,
By honest legislation
Poor Jack upon the waves.[5]

No one showed more appreciation for Plimsoll's efforts than the merchant seamen themselves. When the National Amalgamated Sailors' and Firemen's Union of Great Britain and Ireland was established in 1887, Plimsoll presided (as he would for the next five years) as ceremonial president. At the union's annual conference in Sunderland in 1888, he was reportedly "met by a brass band and hauled round decorated streets in a carriage by seamen."[6] Two years later, for his knowing sympathy with the work-life at sea, he was publicly presented with a model of a ship carved out of a piece of salt beef given to a sailor for his dinner.[7]

Even the commercial world took note. Just as the Plimsoll line appeared to protect ships from perils of the deep, so, as early as 1876, did the rubber band above a rubber sole protect the canvas top of "plimsolls"—the original British name for sneakers or tennis shoes—from inundation.[8] And Plimsoll references grew yet more metaphorical when an 1897 American newspaper referred to an indulgent sailor "who had taken on more cargo than his Plimsoll line justified, and was not quite able to keep steerage away."[9] In his day, Plimsoll clearly emerged as something of a household word—and not only in England. Across the seas, legislator Sam Smith was hailed as the "Plimsoll of Australia," and in the United States as well he did not lack for disciples.[10]

Plimsoll's story intrigues both on account of the authority and appeal of a single individual and because it opens out on a broader view of late-nineteenth-century maritime reform politics, a history in which Plimsoll figures as a kind of tripwire to a more self-consciously Labour-oriented campaign. Three questions focus my inquiry: How did a single-minded maritime reformer manage to situate himself effectively in the House of Commons? How does Plimsoll-era maritime reform connect to larger debates within contemporary Western liberalism? And what significance did the passage from charismatic, middle-class leadership to trade unionism carry for maritime reform?

The first question is at once the easiest and most difficult to answer. Though generally sympathetic to the sufferings of the working classes, Plimsoll did not arrive in Parliament in 1868 as a seamen's agitator; he was converted. Exactly why, however—in the absence of private correspondence—seems impossible to say. The eighth child of a peripatetic tax collector from Plymouth, Plimsoll, born in Bristol in 1824 and educated in Sheffield, had led an up-and-down life as an aspiring coal merchant, entrepreneur, and inventor. A failed attempt to circumvent the established coal delivery system for the Great Northern Railway forced him into bankruptcy (as well as suspension from his Congregationalist church) at age thirty, and he never forgot the ensuing period of privation when he lived among the unemployed in a cheap London lodging-house maintained by the efforts of the philanthropic Lord Shaftesbury. Soon after, however, he would return to Sheffield, marry a coal company owner's stepdaughter in a Methodist chapel, succeed with several patents, and happily assume the title of "gentleman" while establishing his wife and an adopted niece (a natural daughter had died at birth) on a comfortable estate. Like most self-made men, a political Liberal in the individual-rights tradition of William Gladstone, Plimsoll first stood for a parliamentary seat in the East Midland district of Derby in 1865 and succeeded there in 1868. Like several other "advanced Liberal manufacturers" who entered Parliament in this era, Plimsoll would make his public reputation as a healer of class divisions. To a degree, he had always shown sympathy for laboring causes—supporting moves for a broader suffrage, paying fines for trade union demonstrators, opening his estate to the South Yorkshire Miners' Association, and offering his maiden speech in Commons on trade union legalization—and perhaps it was only his own family's economic interests that restrained him from becoming the miners' all-out champion.[11]

Instead, Plimsoll turned to a virtual constituency far removed from the landlocked district in the center of the country that he formally represented. But for a harrowing sea voyage in a storm (during which his wife feared he had drowned) and his own memories of the Bristol docks, Plimsoll's attachment to the cause of the merchant seamen seems to have been occasioned by an accidental meeting with a reform-minded steamship company owner and director of insurance companies, James Hall. Concerned about rising maritime losses, which his own business had led him to analyze, Hall had begun to publicly advocate for better training of sea-

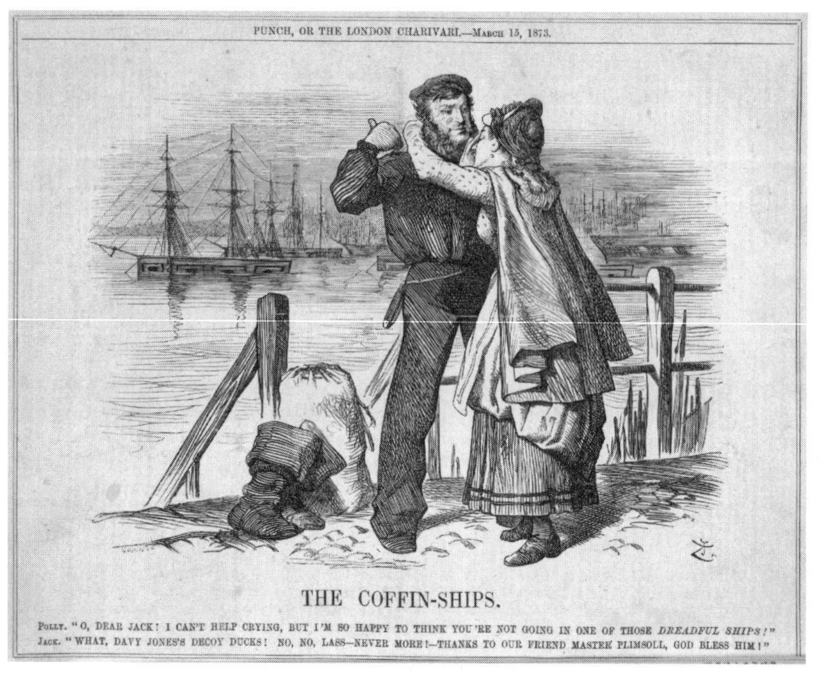

FIGURE 3.2. The coffin ships. Samuel Plimsoll gave legislative voice to a growing British alarm by 1870 of the loss of merchant seamen in ships unfit to sail, hence "coffin ships." From John Tenniel, "The Coffin-Ships," *Punch Magazine* (1873).

men, inspection of ships, and especially load limits. Listening to Hall at the Annual Meeting of Associated Chambers of Commerce in London in February 1870, Plimsoll came away shocked and outraged by the litany of abuses cited by the shipowner. Soon, he had met personally with Hall, obtained copies of his investigations, and pressed Lloyds of London (which, as early as 1835, had required a load line on selected ships) for their own information on the cause of shipwrecks. Almost immediately, he adopted the cause of the seamen, as victimized by overloading and "coffin ships" (unseaworthy vessels supposedly sent to their doom by owners eager to collect insurance money), as his own. A tame version of desired reforms passed in the Merchant Shipping Act of 1871. Allowing for a safety inspection of a suspected coffin ship on the demands of five seamen, it made the men themselves liable for fines and imprisonment in the event of a false alarm.[12] Plimsoll, however, had only just begun. A trip to visit relatives in the United States and Canada furthered his understanding of comparative shipping practices and reforms. Then, in 1872, Plimsoll used his own considerable fortune to publish and distribute *Our Seamen*, an overstuffed pamphlet of one hundred pages, largely repackaging (without attribution) Hall's research, which irrevocably set his course.[13]

Plimsoll rested his proposed state intervention on two converging streams of reform thought. Generally speaking, Plimsoll's work followed a pattern of investigative journalism (what Americans would three decades later call "muckracking"), pioneered in England at midcentury by Henry Mayhew and his discovery of the "poor" that was ultimately collected as *London Labour and the London Poor* in 1861–62. With roots in more official, and drier, accounts like those of the Poor Law Report in 1834 and Edwin Chadwick's Sanitary Report of 1842, Mayhew combined a careful assemblage of "facts" with lurid accounts of pitiful victims of the new system of manufacturing. The genre would influence an entire generation of public advocates and writers, including Christian socialist Charles Kingsley and novelist Charles Dickens.[14] Like many contemporary novelists, Plimsoll undoubtedly drew on a late-eighteenth-century tradition of humanitarian "sympathy" that trusted to "fellow-feeling" as a God-given instinct triggering immediate, empathetic identification with any class of sufferers. As several recent works have demonstrated, a doctrine first defined in rationalist philosophical circles expanded via evangelical Christian moralism and both marketplace and psychological individualism into a bulwark of Anglo-American support for slaves, children, animals, and sailors too in the nineteenth century.[15] In hindsight, Plimsoll might well be seen as harnessing this tradition of moral sympathy to the scientific rationalism of a new age.

Though neither a practiced writer nor an original thinker, Plimsoll drew power from the uncomplicated directness of his expression. His own obviously disinterested and initially quite distant relation to the seamen whose welfare he championed only added to his appeal. Even a parliamentary opponent in 1873 called *Our Seamen* a "remarkable" book, written "in the most simple, idiomatic, and racy English."[16] With far-fetched gentility, Plimsoll dedicated the book "to the lady, gracious and kind, who, seeing a labourer working in the rain, sent him her rug to wrap about his shoulders." "I have no idea of writing a book," he then began:

> I don't know how to do it, and fear I could not succeed if I tried. . . . I will suppose myself to be writing to an individual, and to be saying all I could think of to induce him to lend his utmost aid in remedying the great evil which we all deplore; and I will write, so far as I can, just as I would speak to him if he were now sitting by my side. If he

were so sitting, there are sundry papers I should like to show him in confirmation of my statements and opinions, so that he might know for himself how absolutely true they are. I cannot quite do this in your case, but very nearly; I can have them photographed, and then *you* will see them as really and truly as if they were held to a glass and you were looking at their reflection in it.[17]

Inveigling the reader, as fellow citizen, to join him in a commonsense inquiry, Plimsoll proceeded to penetrate the most abstruse aspects of shipping economics and insurance policies with meticulous, clear, and seemingly undeniable logic. The urgency of the matter, he suggested, was evident in the very statistics of the government's Board of Trade that had thus far turned a deaf ear to regulatory reform. *Our Seamen* cited the astounding (and unchallenged) statistic of 17,000 wrecks (more than half in colliers) from 1861 to 1871, on average five per day, with over 6,500 lives lost on the English coast alone.[18] The main remedies he proposed—a maximum load line; compulsory annual survey, or inspection; and "no re-christening of ships" (to prevent subterfuge of inspections)—were simple and, Plimsoll argued, almost self-evident. "No special knowledge," he assured his readers, "is needed here, and you who never saw a ship, or don't know a ship from a barque, or a brig from a schooner or brigantine, you are just as able to express an opinion, *and, better than that, your will on this point*."[19]

His argument in favor of government inspection of ships rather than trusting to the private insurance companies or the sailors themselves—presumably the two classes with the greatest self-interest at stake in a ship's seaworthiness—is a case in point. Instead of dealing with a single company (as was the case with someone seeking home insurance), Plimsoll took pains to point out, the shipowner applied to an insurance broker, who in turn reached out to multiple underwriters in setting the terms of risk. Once owner and broker agreed, "the broker then [wrote] out a slip like this [copy appended to Plimsoll's text], and send[t] a clerk with it into Lloyd's underwriters' room."

In this case the person applying to the broker wishes to ensure the steam ship *Sunshine* for £5500, for a voyage from the Clyde to Hong-Kong, and he and the firm of brokers consider that 70s. per £100 is an adequate premium for the risk, and these particulars, and the date of the transaction and name of the firm, are all noted on the slip, above the double line I have drawn across it. This slip is then sent into the room by the hand of one of his clerks. The clerk goes from table to table, and submits his slip to first one, then another; some decline it, others append their initials as accepting, and write also . . . the amounts which they are willing to insure. . . . The particulars of the slip are then formally set forth in a policy of insurance, and each of the persons who have agreed to insure then formally subscribe or *underwrite* the body of the policy (hence the term "underwriters"), and receives from the broker 3½ per cent on the respective amounts they had thus guaranteed to the owners of the ship in the event of her being lost. . . . In this case the whole of the sum insured is £5500, and the risk is divided amongst forty-five subscribers (underwriters), not one of whom loses more than £150, while twenty-five only lose £100, in the event of the loss of the ship.[20]

Being so carefully apprised of the nature of the maritime insurance business, the reader could understand why the individual underwriter was in no position to challenge a claim from a powerful shipowner. The former had neither the means nor incentive to proceed. "As a matter of fact," Plimsoll hammered the point home, "almost all claims, no matter how founded in fraud, are thus paid, and it is the rarest thing in the world (it does not occur once in 50,000 cases) that a claim is disputed."[21]

With similar persistence, Plimsoll also demonstrated why the seamen themselves could not be relied upon to avoid disaster. After all, should they not simply refuse to sail in unsafe ships? "Well," he calmly advanced his argument, "you have to consider their circumstances before you can form a sound opinion on this point. The sailor is not given to calculating too nicely all probable dangers any more than other working men; indeed, it may be safely said that if working men did thus stay to calculate their chances of safety, half the work of the world would remain undone":

The simple fact is that working men have no choice, their own needs are pressing, their wives and children look to them for bread; while they hesitate (if they do hesitate) they hunger, and so, as each man thinks all men mortal but himself, he goes to work and takes his chances. Seamen, too, are far more unprotected than other men, and this is especially so in the case of overloading (so great a cause of disaster), for their articles are signed beforehand, they have no voice in the matter of loading; and if they refuse to sail for any cause, they can be, as they have been, and as they are, sent to gaol for periods of three weeks to three months; and men have, to my own knowledge, gone to sea and to death in spite of tearful entreaties of wife and sister . . . owing to the almost invincible repugnance of respectable men . . . to the contamination, the degradation of a common gaol.[22]

As a polemicist, Plimsoll combined genteel solicitude and veiled threat. He thus claimed to "hate to appeal to class feelings or prejudices, but class jealously can only be allayed by justice, not by ignoring murderous wrong. . . . I ask, seriously and sadly, can any one doubt that if these brave men had been pigs or sheep, the Legislature had long since been compelled by powerful advocates to stop such losses!" But clearly, Plimsoll did not trust to the power of middle-class sympathy alone. Invoking the power of the press "on behalf of the oppressed," Plimsoll, writing within popular memory of the radical Chartist agitation of the late 1830s for political democracy that he himself had witnessed, argued that "Parliament will act readily enough if people out of doors make it a prominent question; and, as thoroughly am I satisfied on this point, that I begin to doubt whether I was right in trying to get into Parliament with the object of getting this done. It seems to me at least doubtful whether I should not have done better to have endeavored to rouse people out of doors to the urgency of the matter. . . . For, if the working men of Sheffield, Leeds, Birmingham, and Manchester only demand justice for these poor men, the thing is done."[23] To add force to his point, Plimsoll distributed a copy of his book to each delegate at the 1873 Trades Union Congress (TUC).

Nor did Plimsoll shy from jousting with opponents in high places. In a typical exchange with critics, he responded to a Board of Trade argument that government intervention "would entirely destroy the shipowner's responsibility" by quoting shipowner James Hall, who "[knew] of no case where a ship-owner has been held responsible for sending his ship to sea in an unseaworthy condition." Then, as if unable to restrain himself, the author of *Our Seamen* scoffed: "To talk, therefore, of destroying responsibility is nonsense. There is none, and therefore you can no more destroy it than you can steal a keyhole."[24] Similarly, when the owners of a ship, which Plimsoll had requested be detained by inspectors, demanded an "apology for injury," Plimsoll responded that the "only compensation due to your clients and all other ship owners who load unseaworthy vessels to sea with men a thousand times better than themselves on board, is, in my opinion, a halter apiece and the offices of the hangman."[25]

Such blunt, unbridled advocacy in print and in Commons touched off a political firestorm of reaction and counter-reaction. From the beginning of his agitation, Plimsoll had made no shortage of enemies in high places. Shipowners, Board of Trade officials, and other centers of respectable opinion bristled at Plimsoll's insinuations of faultfinding and quickly counterpunched. "Who would have thought that bad weather could have produced a land hero?" sneered a pamphlet labeled *The Plimsoll Sensation: A Reply* within months of *Our Seamen*'s publication. No new laws were needed, argued author John Glover, just better application of already-existing laws against the industry's few "bad men." Parliamentary critics easily poked holes in Plimsoll's documentation: he had, for example, likely exaggerated the number of wrecks and in three different instances offered significantly different estimates of the proportion of preventable losses.[26] More significantly, the official report of the Royal Commission on Unseaworthy Ships, the first result of Plimsoll's agitation under the Liberal Gladstone administration in 1873, denied the value of surveying or compulsory classification, Plimsoll's major legislative demands. Accusing Plimsoll of numerous "misstatements and exaggerations," the commissioners claimed that he failed to account for the responsibility and carelessness of the crews themselves: "They are often deficient in thrift, in sobriety, in discipline, and in that self-control which education is intended to promote."[27]

Educated opinion—on both sides of the contemporary political aisle—was generally skeptical of the man now popularly dubbed the "Sailor's Friend." Not surprisingly, perhaps, the Tory-identified *Quarterly Review* dismissed *Our Seamen* as "not the work of a man who has spent time, care, and thought on mastering a difficult subject"; Plimsoll's logic, it argued, would lead decidedly to excessive government interference in the shipping trade in the form of "over legislation."[28] For his style as much as his substance, however, Plimsoll equally offended the *Westminster Review*, the residual voice of nineteenth-century philosophical radicalism in the tradition of Jeremy Bentham and John Stuart Mill. While backhandedly congratulating Plimsoll for shining a light on an arena of "rascality" common "more or less in all trades," this paragon of rational reform thought took the reformer to task for "exciting popular feeling" at the expense of "mature judgment": "As regards his agitation, nothing would so much tend to enhance its value as his leaving it."[29] A writer in the staid *Shipping Gazette* pronounced simply, "Plimsollism is another word for terrorism."[30]

Emotional and seemingly uncontrolled, Plimsoll appeared at first to rise destructively to the bait of his critics. In 1873, he barely escaped official censure of the House (even as a civil case for defamation of character was opened against him in the courts) for having identified shipowner MPs among the "greatest sinners in the Trade."[31] Again, in February 1875, when Conservative prime minister Benjamin Disraeli opted to delay even a watered-down maritime reform bill, Plimsoll angrily took the floor. Entreating the prime minister "not to consign some thousands of living men to an undeserved and sudden death," Plimsoll assailed a class of "ship-knackers" and "villain" shipowners, pointedly including among them East India merchant Edward Bates, Conservative MP for Plymouth, then refused amid the ensuing uproar to withdraw the "slander."[32] For his outburst, Plimsoll was officially reprimanded, and the House adjourned for a week to allow the offending member to gather his senses and apologize. "This is not the House of the People," cried Plimsoll, and "thousands of sailors will find a watery grave in consequence of the conduct of the House."[33]

The normally shrewd Disraeli (who had been seriously ill and who appeared outwardly old and feeble, even falling asleep in cabinet meetings in this period) initially miscalculated in the case of Plimsoll and his cause. Mass meetings followed across the country, and even the Working Men's Conservative Association in Liverpool rallied in Plimsoll's defense. An official Plimsoll and Seamen's Fund Committee, formed to help pay his legal bills, was chaired by eminent education and child labor reformer Anthony Ashley Cooper, the Earl of Shaftesbury. The influential Christian socialist, Liberal MP, and popular author Thomas Hughes served as vice chairman.[34] Plimsoll had also gained the tireless support of TUC secretary George Howell—who now served, in effect, as the organizer of the Plimsoll defense committee—as well as other trade union leaders.[35] Having connected to Plimsoll as early as 1871, Howell criss-crossed the country in favor of Plimsoll's reform bill.

Attracting land-based workingmen as well as middle-class sympathizers, the Plimsoll agitation swelled into the beginnings of a mass movement. A newspaper account of a Liverpool meeting organized by Howell is telling. Dismissing Plimsoll as a "nervous, excitable man" of weak judgment, local shipowner W. J. Lamport (who had previously authored a stinging rebuttal of *Our Seamen*) warned the meeting attendees to consider well "before they interfered with the shipping interest and drove capital into other countries. (a voice from the gallery—'Where will it go to?'—hear, hear). A workman in the hall arose and said he could not sit there in silence and let a merchant prince like Mr. Lamport talk in the way he did when it was well known how he paid his workingmen and sailors. He said other things far less complimentary respecting Mr. Lamport's relations with his employees, and all that he said was endorsed by very hearty applause." At the end of the meeting, a mast-maker proposed a resolution in support of the Plimsoll bill, which was seconded by a sail-maker, and "cheers given for Mr. Plimsoll."[36] Howell, himself a sober Methodist-turned-craft-unionist as well as a leader of the trade union Liberal-Labour (or "Lib-Lab") effort to gain parliamentary influence by official alliance with the Liberal Party, would remember the Plimsoll committee mobilization, with its multiple rallies and distribution of a million copies of *Our Seamen*, as a phenomenon "never before invoked in the cause of any sector of the working-class."[37] At its height, the Plimsoll agitation threatened to surround the House of Commons with the widows of lost seamen until the reform program was carried. A tangible sign of Plimsoll's political effect was the newfound advocacy of Birmingham mayor Joseph Chamberlain, who added maritime reform to a growing radical-reform portfolio.[38] In the midst of the furor, Disraeli confessed, "The Plimsollites, in and out of Parliament, are at me; now cajoling, now the reign of terror." At one point, the prime minister estimated that "1000 constables [were] hid in the bowers of Whitehall Gardens and about" to protect him from possible mob violence.[39] Analyzing the British agitation, a *New York Times* observer speculated that Plimsoll must have "pre-arranged" his parliamentary uproar, for nothing had served his cause better than his own rebuke.[40]

For his part, Disraeli quickly readjusted his political antennae. Soon after Parliament reconvened, he recalled and steered the temporary Unseaworthy Ships Bill of 1875 (subsequently incorporated into the Merchant Shipping Act of 1876) to passage. Its most significant measures included the first requirement for a load line on seagoing British ships (although leaving their application to the shipowners themselves); inspection (this time with no penalty for self-reporting by a quorum of one-quarter of the ship's crew), detention, and prosecution of unseaworthy ships; and a variety of deck cargo restrictions.[41] As both shipowners and shipmasters (captains) expressed alarm over what they regarded as an increasing loss of control over the industry, Disraeli reassured them with smaller measures, offering a Court of Appeals review of a ship survey and reaffirming the legality of physical restraint for "troublemakers on board ship."[42] The new law had an immediate effect on seamen's lives. Of the 832 ships detained by the Board of Trade between 1876 and 1883, only 13 were found to be safe enough to proceed immediately to sea.[43] As the *London Times* explained of the Plimsoll-Disraeli dispute, "[Disraeli] so mistook the people's will, that he misapprehended its purport, until an 'inspired idiot' arose to tell him what it demanded. Mr. Plimsoll has been King during the past fortnight and Mr. Disraeli has been the humble henchman. The Prime Minister knew the power of sections of the House of Commons; he knew nothing of the strength of popular impulse."[44] For his part, once Plimsoll succumbed to Shaftesbury's counsel and humbly apologized in Commons, Disraeli made the most of the moment. Acknowledging that Plimsoll's emotions, however overwrought, had been directed by a "good cause," Disraeli blithely explained that "a popular breeze was needed to pass the measure."[45] Just as he had done a decade before with respect to suffrage extension (the 1867 Reform Act first gave a substantial portion of the male working class the vote), so Disraeli retained his political skills with respect to maritime reform. His advisers, for one, believed that his actions "checked" the mass movement building around Plimsoll and stopped what might have been a successful Liberal move to dissolve the government on the issue. A member of the inner cabinet, Lord Derby, the foreign secretary, felt that in recovering from the Plimsoll affair, his boss had been "at his best lately."[46]

Unassuaged by his partial legislative success, Plimsoll maintained a determined drumbeat for further reform. When he discovered that the required inspections of grain cargo were largely unenforced even after passage of the Unseaworthy Ships Bill of 1875, Plimsoll pinned the blame on his favorite adversary, the hidebound Board of Trade. On a tour of Black Sea ports, he denounced Board of Trade instructions to consular officials as "miserable, wretched and impotent" and swung at the sitting Board of Trade president, Charles Adderley, as a "model utterance of ignorance seated in the chair of authority, too proud to consult with men having the requisite knowledge and too tenacious of power to admit any want of ability."[47]

Plimsoll's political impact continued when the Liberals were restored to power in 1880, but now from a new angle. Uncomfortable with formalistic parliamentary mores and suffering health problems, Plimsoll shocked contemporaries following the general election by resigning his seat and allowing a restored Prime Minister Gladstone to appoint Sir William Harcourt (who had been upset in the election) as home secretary in his stead.[48] Still, this was hardly the end of Plimsoll as maritime reformer. He immediately concentrated his personal attentions on fellow manufacturer and legendary reform mayor of Birmingham, Joseph Chamberlain, the new president of the Board of Trade. Soon the Chamberlain-endorsed Merchant Seamen Act of 1880 advanced the reform cause on two fronts: it attacked the "crimp" system by outlawing the advance note and fining outsiders who boarded ships without permission, and it eliminated imprisonment for desertion in port. Incorporating seamen into the Employers and Workmen Act of 1875, the law finally made a seaman's violation of contract—like that of other workers—liable to civil rather than criminal prosecution.[49] Moved by statistics that an astounding 36,000 British merchant seamen (or one in six who shipped out) had perished at sea over a twelve-year period, Chamberlain sought to go further in 1884 with a measure against over-insurance. By this time, however, shipowners and associated commercial interests had dug in. As a businessman himself, Chamberlain's Plimsoll-like self-righteousness seemed particularly to inflame parliamentary conservatives. Tory shipowner David MacIver from Birkenhead, for example, gasped that Chamberlain had "slandered" a merchant class that, after all, had done "a great deal more than screw-making [a reference to Chamberlain's family firm] in Birmingham."[50] When the bill went down, Chamberlain bitterly commented about his parliamentary opponents, "It is not the 'black sheep' who are the worst; it is the smug self-righteous ship owner [who] like the Slaveowners of the South . . . were blinded to the misery & suffering caused by the practices to which custom & law had so long lent their sanction."[51] Merchant shipping reform might thus be seen as a down payment on Chamberlain's famous "Radical Programme" of 1885 that would include land and housing reform and higher taxes on the rich. Unfortunately for the larger social reform cause, Chamberlain's imperialist opposition to Irish Home Rule and personal estrangement from party leader Gladstone soon led Chamberlain off the Liberal reservation entirely and into a Liberal Unionist formation in alliance with the Conservative Party that formed a government but for two years between 1886 and 1902.[52]

Liberalism and Maritime Reform

The debate sparked by Plimsoll-era legislative maneuvers revealed important shifts in nineteenth-century British liberal political thought. Effectively, Plimsoll and his supporters were challenging the generally anti-statist, anti-regulatory turn taken by British liberals since the end of the Napoleonic Wars. Adding worker-oriented protections to a commercial arena that had always been surrounded by the interest of the state, they anticipated—even as they also contributed to—a welfarist "new liberalism" more commonly associated with the pre–World War I thought of L. T. Hobhouse and J. A. Hobson and the politics of David Lloyd George, 1906–14.[53] At a deeper level, the Plimsoll-era battle over maritime reform engaged arguments that would re-echo from the late nineteenth century through the early twentieth century (and indeed be rekindled in a latter-day era of "deregulation") over the proper role for state regulation in commercial life.

The maritime debates also indicated that a substantial reactionary fraction would both resist government oversight and blame the workers themselves for their particular afflictions. A restriction on advance notes (proposed and withdrawn in 1875, before being passed in 1880) thus represented for some a broader ideological provocation. For his part, Conservative MP for Haddingtonshire Lord Elcho, a founder of the London Scottish Golf Club, "deprecated any interference on the part of the State between two grown men in their contracts and dealings with each other. To say they should not pay a man his wages on Saturday because he might get drunk and be unable to go to church on the Sunday. It was a case of State-help *versus* self-help." When Liberal MP Edward Knatchbull-Hugessen for the town of Rochester protested that the clock had long since turned toward "factory" legislation, Lord Elcho corrected him, insisting that "the Liberalism of those days was in favour of the removal of restrictions on freedom of contract, except in the case of women and children, [whereas] the Liberalism of these days was in favour of restriction upon full-grown men."[54] Principled resistance to state regulation of the economy was also at the core of opposition from the "old liberal" *Westminster Review*, for whom the penchant for a legislative fix reflected a problem of modern-day culture: "The impatience for quick results is a notable feature in the high pressure life of the present day. It is the moral sequence to railways, penny postage, the telegraph, and the commercial practice of quick returns and small profits."[55]

Such more or less laissez-faire sentiments were paired with a counterattack on the supposed beneficiaries of the welfare state, the sailors themselves. A "much more fruitful cause of loss of life than unseaworthy ships," argued George Cavendish-Bentinck, Tory MP for Whitehaven, "was unseaworthy seamen." Shipmasters, he suggested, needed more control over intoxication and indiscipline.[56] Eugene Collins, moderate Liberal MP for Kinsale, quite agreed. Rather than "agitating the minds of sailors and impressing them with a belief that their interests were not provided for, whilst the capitalist classes got all the benefit of legislation affecting shipping," it would be far better, Collins insisted, to advocate temperance, education, and "other such measures as might rescue [them] from degrading habits, and render them more respectable than they were."[57] Defending criminal imprisonment in cases of sailor desertion, C. M. Norwood, shipowner and Liberal MP from Hull, pointed to the "exceptional character" of a "seafaring occupation." Special protections already surrounded the signing of the seaman's contract; moderation of long-standing legal remedies would do "extensive injury" to the shipowner, while civil penalties alone would prove inadequate for a class of workers who had "no local habitation nor property which his creditors could seize."[58]

For their part, the Liberal reform majority who pressed the measures of 1875, 1876, and 1880 alternated between moral principle and political pragmatism. On the moral front, reformers defined the status quo for the seaman not as a realm of economic freedom but as one of slavery. Sailors, they argued, turned to desertion as their only recourse from "servile dependence on crimps" and "an organized system of debauchery." "Far worse than the mere loss of money," explained Liberal peer Lord Sudeley in the debate of 1880, "was the loss of character, and the slavery [on board ship] thereby rendered necessary."[59] But the argument for reform also drew on precedent and a dispassionate appeal to the balance of interests within the body politic. It was thus that Chamberlain challenged those who insisted on the "pristine purity of their political economy . . . in face of the fact that freedom of contract had already been interfered with by the Legislature when the interest of any particular class seemed to demand it." If railroads could be subjected to liability laws and the truck system abolished in mining districts, then, he pleaded, could he not count on broad support for the government's "moderate little measure"?[60]

For reformers and opponents alike, however, the lines between government's necessary regulatory activity and individual responsibility sometimes blurred unpredictably. An example appeared in discussion of a proposed new scale of ship's provisions occasioned by an 1875 spike in the shipboard incidence of scurvy, a condition whose exact etiology remained unknown at the time, even as practical dietary antidotes (particularly lime juice—hence the North American slang reference to the British as "Limeys") to what would later be recognized as a vitamin deficiency were already legally mandated. Even as division reigned regarding the source of scurvy (for example, Plimsoll attributed it to pickled beef), one legislator quickly targeted "the large employment of Lascars and other foreign sailors, who were rather dirty in their habits," while another similarly blamed "black men" who ate "slush" (a concoction of cured beef and biscuits) for the problem.[61]

Ideologically, the median position regarding state action (and support for the government's bill) was reflected in the argument of William Rathbone VI, Liberal MP from Liverpool, that the measure met the test of "English principles of leaving the action and energy of our citizens free and unfettered by minute Government direction [in contradistinction to "the Continental plan of Government surveys and minute interference"], but holding them to a strict account for the use of that freedom, when they injured or attempted to injure others thereby."[62] Perhaps anticipating latter-day aversion to the "nanny state," supporters adamantly refuted description of the 1876 and 1880 merchant shipping bills as "grandmotherly legislation."[63]

Even those willing in principle to support further regulatory reform, moreover, hesitated when it came to the question of international market competition. Any measures that pushed the cost of operations up, opponents argued, would drive British ships from the sea. Reflecting the shipowner concerns of his district, "advanced Liberal" MP for Tynemouth T. E. Smith thus worried that "many ships would be transferred to foreign flags, and their owners would thus evade the provisions of the Act."[64] It was a point that the bill's advocates could not easily refute, unless they were to make the even more expansive move of regulating foreign as well as domestic shipping. Plimsoll himself acknowledged "that the House had a perfect right to legislate for foreign ships in British waters" but counseled that as of 1876, the timing was not yet right. Better, he suggested, "to pull the beam out of our own eye before attempting to pull the mote out of our brother's eye."[65] Without much fanfare, and drawing on a precedent applied to passenger steamers only since 1854, provisions for detention of improperly or overloaded ships and penalties for timber stored on deck (though not load line or other safety inspection provisions) were applied to foreign vessels in British ports in the 1876 legislation.[66] A principle of regulation only dimly perceived in 1876 would, indeed, take center stage thirty years later, on both sides of the Atlantic.

Finally, and of more immediate impact on New Liberal thinking, the maritime legislative debate dropped hints of a future political economy in which workingmen—whether landed or sea-based—might have more of a say themselves. Though ultimately held back from the 1876 Merchant Shipping Act, discussion had begun on the legal iniquities faced by sailors, particularly their (unique) liability to criminal conviction—with likely imprisonment at hard labor—should they break a contract by deserting in port. Interestingly, the legislator who ventured farthest down this path in the mid-1870s was Tory Democrat John Eldon Gorst, a Disraeli confidant from Chatham.[67] No element of public welfare, Gorst argued in 1876 in relation to the criminal penalties still imposed on deserting seamen, justified treating them "like children, and not like other people."[68] In the course of his own advocacy for legal reform, Gorst pointed to the seamen's political weakness. "They would never have been treated in this manner," he suggested, "if they had had the same electoral influence as other working men" or as the shipowners did.[69] In the same spirit, Liberal Newcastle manufacturer and publisher Joseph Cowen proposed, rather idealistically, the election of seamen to local marine boards and thus "by recognizing seamen as fellow-citizens, to induce more friendly feeling between shipowners and their men."[70] Though utterly unsympathetic to the proffered maritime regulations, the *Westminster Review* equally invoked the principle of sailor self-representation. Rather than seek legislative relief, it counseled, sailors ought to "follow the example of other workers and . . . form a Sailors' Trades Union." With such an agency of collective self-help, argued the editors, "there would be no call for legislation to protect seamen, coerce owners, or harry and worry a most important element of our national greatness."[71]

From Liberalism to Social Democracy

Sailor trade unionism would indeed become a potent force in the succeeding years. Unfortunately for the apostles of self-help, however, its presence, combined with a general thickening of organized labor's political presence, would only stimulate and reinforce the regulatory regime imposed upon the shipping industry. Rather than an alternative to "plimsollism," trade unionism proved its most effective ally.

The connection, as it happened, began with Plimsoll himself. To this end, he could count on George Howell—a loyal acolyte since the 1870s Plimsoll defense committee, elected to a Bethnal Green constituency as a Lib-Lab, 1885–95—to serve as chief spokesman for the seamen's cause.[72] More important for the long run, however, was the emergence of a national British seamen's union in 1887 (subject of chapter 5), headed by retired sailor from Sunderland Joseph Havelock Wilson, who would himself be elected to Parliament as an "Independent Labour" (1892–95, 1906–10) and Coalition Liberal (1918–22) candidate.[73] At age sixteen in 1874, Wilson had returned home from a voyage in the midst of Plimsoll's parliamentary agitation. "He was my hero," Wilson would remember. When Wilson blended several local organizations into the National Amalgamated Sailors' and Firemen's Union of Great Britain and Ireland in 1887, Samuel Plimsoll presided (as he would for the next five years) as ceremonial president.[74] It was Plimsoll who induced Wilson to stand for Parliament and likewise Plimsoll who greeted Wilson in a carriage upon the latter's release from prison following a disruptive strike in Cardiff in 1891.[75] In his memoir of 1925, Wilson recalled his early days under Plimsoll's tutelage in lobbying MPs from seaport towns on maritime legislation. At Plimsoll's order, Wilson would be dispatched to hold "indignation meetings" to pressure a recalcitrant member: "If the meeting was a large and successful one, the old gentleman [Plimsoll] would almost do an Irish jig in the outer lobby of the House of Commons; then he would send for the unfortunate Member, read him a lecture, and show him the photograph [of the attending crowd]. I was like a Red Indian bringing in scalps."[76]

Arriving in Parliament a dozen years after Plimsoll had left it, Wilson engaged in a legislative activism—like George Howell before him—that represented at once a continuity and a break from the model of his early mentor. Most obvious was the difference made by a direct representative from an interest group. Rather than a humanitarian-by-sympathy like Plimsoll, Wilson might better be categorized as a kind of "parliamentary shop steward" for the merchant seamen. Incapable of the charisma of the grandiloquent gentleman-reformer, Wilson worked the trenches. His most common interventions on the House floor involved demands for Board of Trade inquiries: into the death and mistreatment of an individual seaman by a tyrannical captain, into the loss of a specific ship alleged to be undermanned, and, increasingly by 1899, into the alleged excess of non-English speakers (that is, foreigners) and mistreatment of lascars on board British ships.[77] These last matters (which had not concerned Plimsoll at all) suggested the particular job-protection strategies of an English trade unionist dealing with an ever more international labor market. Identified with no legislative achievement of his own and defeated in his attempt in the 1890s to incorporate seamen in the terms of the Employers' Liability Act (1880) or Workmen's Compensation Act (1897), Wilson nevertheless contributed to both incremental and larger changes in the regulatory regime affecting the shipping world. In particular, his testimony and steady advocacy before the 1894 Royal Commission on Labour contributed to several pro-labor recommendations—including an eight-hour day, better accommodations, an official food scale, and worker representation on local marine boards—that would eventually be incorporated in later legislation.[78]

Lacking the galvanizing force of a Plimsoll, Wilson's style and very presence nevertheless indicated something of a widening of British democracy, in part the direct effect of near-universal male suffrage achieved by 1884. As Wilson argued in 1899 in relation to the omission of sailors from a prior act, "Unfortunately, Sir, at that time the seafaring man was not directly represented in this House, and consequently it was possible for the shipowner Members of the House of Commons to persuade the House that it would be an unjust thing to include seamen in the Employers' Liability Act."[79]

The distinction was recognized, at least implicitly, by all around him. Even in opposing Wilson, for example, Conservative home secretary Sir Matthew White Ridley saluted the "assiduity and energy" that Wilson delivered on behalf of the "class he represents in this house."[80] Another Tory, Thomas Gibson Bowles, was more openly hostile: "[Wilson] has been in the habit of making all kinds of statements, putting them down on the paper as Questions and of not being here in his place to ask his Questions. These Questions are full of the most infamous insinuations, and he has always failed to prove them. . . . It is rather hard for the honourable Gentleman to carry on his business in this House in that manner. If he carries on his business outside this House on the same principles as he carries it on in the House, I do not think I can predict for him any great success in his calling in life."[81] In the face of such Conservative criticism, Wilson enjoyed voluble support from Liberal allies, including Herbert Asquith, MP, who would serve subsequently as chancellor of the exchequer (1906–8) and prime minister (1908–16).[82]

In short, the very impertinence that Wilson represented to some on the House floor reflected a significant shift from indirect to direct representation of working-class citizens in political life. Moreover, for his favored constituency—the sailors—Wilson was every bit as narrowly "interest"-minded as any MP with a vested connection to his own economic group. Some workers, at least, now had at least modest access to the levers of power. Such a view would be in keeping with a recently revived appreciation of the role of previously scorned trade union leaders working within the late-nineteenth-century liberal tradition.[83]

Looking Out for One's Own

As regulatory controls on the British merchant marine ranged ever more ambitiously in topic and breadth, they inevitably broached a question not prominently featured in the debates surrounding the Plimsoll era's original agitation. This was the issue of international versus merely national norms: how, in short, to "reform" national safety and welfare standards without upsetting national economic competitiveness in a global market? The issue came most forcefully and self-consciously into play on the British side in the 1906 Merchant Shipping Act, even as it would receive an even more prominent encore performance ten years later in the United States in the form of the La Follette Act of 1915 (see chapter 4).

Substantively, the 1906 act—piloted through Parliament by new Board of Trade president (and future prime minister) David Lloyd George, in the immediate aftermath of a sweeping Liberal victory over Joseph Chamberlain and a Conservative-Unionist campaign for a return to tariff duties and "imperial preference"—offered a consensual resolution of long-standing problems in the industry.[84] Its incremental strengthening of the apparatus of safety and welfare measures stretched back in inspiration to the legislative aftermath (1850, 1854) of the Navigation Acts repeal as well as to Plimsoll's instigations of the 1870s and early 1880s that had ended in a truly massive consolidation act of 1894 (at 747 sections across 300 pages of text, the longest British statute of the century).[85] New in the 1906 law were extensions of crew space, a much-elaborated food scale together with a requirement for certified cooks and inspections of provisions, the option of Board of Trade advisory boards (with an invitation to seamen as well as shipowner representatives), and a provision that all seamen hired on British ships in the United Kingdom or in European ports understand orders in the English language. It was the last clause, moreover—alongside kindred clauses that extended previous load line and grain cargo restrictions to foreign as well as British ships—that revealed the cutting edge of the 1906 initiative. More than simply raising the bar for British seamen and shipowners, legislators were attempting to shield both classes of constituents from international market pressures.

The degree to which such state intervention—approved in principle by both Conservative Opposition and Labour MPs (in loose affiliation with the government)—heralded a larger break from liberal "free trade" norms dominated contemporary debate. Preferring to cast the 1906 act as a regulatory corrective to a preferred course of commercial noninterference, Lloyd George offered a very positive summary of the development of the nation's shipping industry. Whereas in 1870, British ships manned by 200,000 British seamen and 18,000 foreigners (as well as a negligible number of lascars) carried 5,500,000 tons of shipping, by 1904, 176,000 British seamen supplemented by 39,000 foreigners and 42,000 lascars were carrying nearly twice the 1870 load. Indeed, by the latter date, British ships carried not only two-thirds of their own nation's trade but 54 percent of the entire world's commercial cargo. As the government minister fairly gushed, "There had not been anything like it in history." Specific abuses, Lloyd George suggested, should be addressed, but there was no cause for alarm about the nation's maritime preeminence.[86]

Even as they repeated the mantra of free trade, therefore, the Liberal government's officials ingeniously stole the thunder of protectionists by regulating foreign shipping instead of foreign trade. The results, they promised—fair competition, improved safety, and better lives for seafarers—would be the same. As "one of the most valuable of measures [offered] to one of the most neglected classes," insisted Liberal MP Munro Ferguson, the 1906 law occasioned "never any suspicion of . . . any protectionist character." The English language requirement was thereby introduced "on the ground of safety"; similarly, the broader application of the load line was "needed in the interests of the safety and welfare of the sea-faring population." Liberal MP J. C. Guest from Cardiff likewise steadfastly denied "any protective instincts or protective ideas in the Bill," even while forced to acknowledge its "slightly protective effect."[87]

Conservatives, who had already adopted the logic of retaliation against cutthroat international competitors, were largely reduced to sputterings that the government's measure did not go far enough. The "Tory Romantic" from Dover, George Wyndham, for example—fresh from failure in setting Irish policy under the previous government—burnished his literary credentials in mock congratulation of Lloyd George's defense of the bill. Calling it "a stage on the road which leads away from the high and dry theory of free trade," Wyndham noted the "anxious care" that the government had taken "to assure us that all this interference on the part of the State was solely in the interest of human life and the safety of human limb. Did it occur to him whilst framing this interesting piece of legislation that the result might have a protective value?" If so, Wyndham continued his baiting, where might such revisionist logic stop? "Is he going to look after the meals of the seamen on foreign ships which compete with British ships?"[88]

Relieved of the responsibility of governance, Tory critics rhetorically erased all limits on British jurisdiction over foreign ships. Making his maiden appearance on the House floor, Lord Inverclyde, heir and director of the Cunard Line, proposed load line restrictions on foreign ships "bound to as well as actually within any port of the United Kingdom." He dismissed the claim of pursuing violations only against ships already docked in British waters (which government officials insisted was the limit of their legal powers) as "more of less of a bogey." "Foreign vessels, when they left a foreign port, might have their bunkers full [of coal], and possibly overloaded, but they arrived in this country in proper loading trim, because they had burned the coal."[89] In a similar vein, future Conservative Party leader Andrew Bonar Law questioned the conventionally delimited construction of national legal sovereignty. Speaking speculatively, and perhaps mischievously, he pointed to American law, which had been setting various safety and welfare restrictions on *embarking* emigrant passenger ships since the early nineteenth century![90] Confounded by the government's insistence that "absolute equality with the foreigner" was a "very difficult thing to do," a few Conservatives pushed abstractly for future "international agreements" on load lines and other issues that would assure common standards. Otherwise, as Inverclyde insisted, British shipping could never enjoy "fair competition."[91]

As the official voice of the seamen's union on maritime reform, Wilson knew that once the government's ministers had put their heads together on the matter in 1906, he could command little more than a hearing for any further changes. Still, his interventions in debate revealed the degree to which his trade union constituents now worried especially about their job security in an international labor market. Insisting that shipowners "had the best of the bargain" in the new legislation, he accused them of inserting "protection" from foreign ships while "screaming out against anything that would interfere with the employment of the lowest kind of foreigners who competed with British sailors."[92] He was referring, in particular, to the growing numbers of lascar (and, to a lesser degree, Chinese) seamen—once largely confined to tropical latitudes where they were hired at much lower "Asian article" rates—on transoceanic voyages.[93] Rather than an outright ban on lascars, Wilson sought in vain both to re-restrict their geographical presence and to undermine their hiring advantage by demanding equal allotments of space and food for lascars, so that they would not "be brought into competition with the Britisher in this country, thus depriving British seamen of the chance of employment."[94] It is noteworthy, however, that the legislator who ventured the furthest toward labor "protection" was not Wilson but Tory MP Sir Howard Vincent, who had beaten Plimsoll at Central Sheffield on a tariff reform platform in 1885. Perhaps hoping to consolidate the supporters of his old rival, Vincent proposed in 1906 "that the wages paid on foreign ships coming into British ports [be] on the same scale as the wages paid to British seamen on British vessels."[95] Such talk, responded Board of Trade president Lloyd George, touched "dangerous ground," a "quagmire [that] I would rather avoid . . . at the present moment."[96]

Even as the shift of advocacy from Samuel Plimsoll to Joseph Havelock Wilson reflected larger transformations in the nature of the liberal reform-

FIGURE 3.3. *A Tribute to Samuel Plimsoll.* Befitting his renown as the "sailor's friend," the *London Graphic*, an illustrated weekly newspaper, offered this heroic portrayal of Samuel Plimsoll in August 1875. *London Graphic*, Aug. 28, 1875.

ism, the former's influence on maritime policy continued for years after he had departed the public scene. Both advocates and critics of subsequent maritime legislation, like the extension of the liability act, readily identified themselves with Plimsoll's crusade against "unseaworthy ships."[97] Though Wilson's own ascension in public life generally coincided with Plimsoll's effective retirement—a consequence both of diabetes and the responsibilities of a second marriage, including three young children—the connection between the reformer and his sailor union friends remained an intimate one. Within hours of Plimsoll's death at Folkestone on June 3, 1898, "all the ships in Folkestone harbour had their flags at half mast," and on June 7, "a contingent of sailors drew his hearse to St. Martin's Church, Cheriton, Kent, for his funeral and burial."[98] In its back-handed eulogy to a "sincere, if not well-regulated, mind," the *Times* puzzled over a man who "really knew in his own person very little of the subject to which his public life was devoted, and in which, in spite of the difficulties thrown in his way by want of experience, he did a great deal of valuable service." In a letter to the editor, seamen's union activist and former sailors' chaplain Edward W. Matthews tried to explain. Plimsoll, Matthews reported, had told him years before that "he heard a voice from the sea, and believed God had called him to this service."[99]

However he came to the sea, the mark Plimsoll left on it went beyond his namesake load line. By coupling safety not only to the welfare but ultimately to the self-government of seamen themselves, Plimsoll set off a wave of reform thought, agitation, and organization that continued long after his death. Beginning, to be sure, with a British accent, the very reach of the empire, the logic of the industry, and the "motley" composition of the seagoing labor force also ensured that the efforts of the Sailor's Friend would ultimately carry broad international consequences.[100]

4

The Nationalist Solution

THE LA FOLLETTE ACT OF 1915 AND THE JANUS FACE OF PROGRESSIVE REFORM

Nineteenth-century American seamen and their advocates had long called for "emancipation" from coercive regulations. By the end of the century, workers in this most "unfree" of occupations were still subjected to various forms of physical punishment from superiors and denied the "right to quit" work without facing potential criminal prosecution. Famously, the seamen finally won their freedom in one of the hallmarks of Progressive Era legislation, the U.S. Seamen's Act, signed by President Woodrow Wilson on March 4, 1915, a date that Senator Robert M. La Follette, the bill's chief author, called the seamen's "emancipation day."[1] Upon reexamination, the La Follette Act (as it was commonly known) was both more and less than it appeared. Though initially presented as a catch-up measure for matters of freedom, rights, and safety at sea, both the legislation and the contemporary debate that enveloped it tilted at larger, more forward-looking issues. The problem was no less than the inability of U.S. seamen as well as U.S. ships to compete in the world market. Indeed, within a comprehensive and complex piece of legislation (requiring twenty-one pages of dense, single-space type to enumerate its twenty sections), the act might well be considered the first serious and systematic policy response to the pressures of the world market on the American workplace. As a kind of dress rehearsal for latter-day themes of labor and globalization, both the mechanism and ideology of regulation take on a heightened interest here. So too do the tensions, which would prove recurring ones, between internationalism, nationalism, and racial prejudice in the formation of national regulatory policy.

Crafting a Legislative Juggernaut

An extended body of protective and regulatory labor legislation, the Seamen's Act surely was. A moral compass fixed on the measure's contents would likely first point to its "free labor" provisions. Centered on the decriminalization of desertion (now reduced to a forfeiture of wages earned), the act effectively gave sailors the same employment rights available to all other non-incarcerated Americans since the passage of the Thirteenth Amendment. The free labor imperative also mandated the formal abolition of flogging and other forms of corporal punishment (replaced by a graduated code of punishment for disorderly conduct), an anti-crimping ban on advance wages or the allotment of wages to any but the sailor's immediate family, and a "half-wage clause" allowing the sailor to depart at any port during a voyage with half his earnings to date. A second objective spelled out in several clauses legislated improvement of seamen's working conditions. Dividing sailors into two watches at sea and limiting all seamen to nine-hour days (and Sundays off) in port, these work-related measures also specified minimal requirements for shipboard diet, sleeping space, and adequate toilet facilities.[2] Third, explicit concern for passenger as well as crew safety mandated lifeboat design, access, and certified emergency training by the crew. Fourth, the act added sections that clearly sought to enhance trade union power in hiring and job protection: within five years of the passage of the act, for example, 65 percent of the deck crew were to be rated as "able seaman," defined by three years' service at sea or on the Great Lakes. In addition, in a move justified as a safety measure, an English-language requirement (technically, crew members had to understand orders from the captain) aimed to shift crews toward higher homegrown quotients. Finally, in perhaps its boldest but least advertised move, the authors of the act specified its application not only to all U.S.-flagged ships but also, and within a year, to "foreign vessels"; any treaties to the contrary, moreover, were to be abrogated in short order.[3]

The political history of the Seamen's Act is reasonably well documented. It has long been recognized that behind the eponymous author of the act, Robert La Follette, was the real father of the maritime labor reforms, International Seamen's Union of America (ISU) leader Andrew Furuseth. A crusty, Oslo-born sailor and fisherman who jumped ship in 1880 to make his home in San Francisco, Furuseth was a self-taught exponent of sailor union federation, craft unionism, and ultimately political regulation of the waterfront. Though American sailors organized, staged protests, and several times struck as early as the colonial and early national eras, more stable unionization awaited the 1880s.[4] Begun as an outgrowth of the radical International Workingmen's Association, the Coast Seamen's Union, which Furuseth joined shortly after its founding in 1885, soon took on the conventional, job-control objectives of a craft union, initially as the Sailors' Union of the Pacific following a merger in 1889 and then, after a further regional federation, as the ISU in 1893.[5]

Together with San Francisco Democratic congressman James G. Maguire, Furuseth had begun crafting seamen's reform bills as early as 1894. After 1900, he practically turned his leadership of the Coast Seamen's Union into a full-time lobbying position in Washington, D.C.[6] Across twenty years of advocacy, Furuseth (as Hyman Weintraub demonstrates in his excellent 1959 political biography) became the iconic, even legendary representative of the American seafarer. The power and pathos of his argument together with his sheer persistence of effort won this ascetic, lifelong bachelor (with a face that some compared to the "prow of a Viking ship") a growing circle of influential allies.[7] Though ultimately mired in myriad political conflicts with erstwhile friends (particularly the syndicalists, communists, and industrial unionists to his left), upon his death in 1938 he was widely mourned as "father and mother and priest to his men."[8]

By far, Furuseth's and maritime reform's most important connection was to Republican senator Robert La Follette. The union leader had originally gained the progressive senator's respect when, breaking with most of his San Francisco labor colleagues, he sided with the graft prosecution of the Union Labor Party's "boss" Abe Ruef in 1907–8. Soon, the two men, who were of the same age, became fast friends. Beginning in 1910, La Follette introduced the Seamen's Bill in every Congress until it passed.[9] In the wake of the *Titanic* disaster of April 1912, the force behind maritime labor and safety reform gained inexorable logic. By the end of the year, both major party conventions had adopted resolutions sympathetic to the sailors' cause.[10] A watered-down version of the Furuseth-backed measures, in fact, passed Congress in 1912–13 but died by pocket veto in the final hours of President William Howard Taft's term.[11] Labor reform forces gained the edge they needed only when the Democrats retook the White House and both houses of Congress in November 1912 and William B. Wilson, the bill's former cosponsor, became secretary of labor.[12]

Tellingly, La Follette's successful proposal in 1915 was officially labeled

COAST SEAMEN'S JOURNAL

FOR THE SEAFARING PEOPLE OF THE WORLD.
Official Paper of the International Seamen's Union of America.

"SAFETY FIRST" EDITION

VOL. XXVII, No. 45. SAN FRANCISCO, WEDNESDAY, JULY 22, 1914. Whole No. [illegible]

UNSKILLED SEAMEN AT WORK

WHILE THE "SAFETY FIRST" SLOGAN HAS BEEN GENERALLY ACCEPTED ASHORE, THERE ARE POWERFUL FORCES AT WORK TO PREVENT ITS ADOPTION AT SEA. SAFETY AT SEA DEPENDS LARGELY UPON EFFICIENT AND SUFFICIENT CREWS. THE LA FOLLETTE SEAMEN'S BILL (S. 136), WHICH PASSED THE SENATE LAST OCTOBER, PROVIDES FOR BOTH. FOR PURELY SELFISH REASONS, SHIPOWNING INTERESTS HAVE PERSISTENTLY OPPOSED THIS BILL AND HAVE SUCCEEDED IN PREVENTING ACTION UPON IT IN THE HOUSE OF REPRESENTATIVES. IF THE TRAVELING PUBLIC WILL USE THEIR INFLUENCE WITH MEMBERS OF CONGRESS THE BILL WILL PASS AT THIS SESSION. WILL YOU WRITE YOUR CONGRESSMAN TO-DAY?

FIGURE 4.1. "Unskilled Seamen at Work." In pushing the La Follette Act, Andrew Furuseth's International Seamen's Union, as represented here through its *Coast Seamen's Journal*, stressed the need for skilled workers with proper equipment in event of emergencies. This angle was particularly highlighted following the 1912 *Titanic* disaster. *Coast Seamen's Journal*, July 22, 1914.

an "act to promote the welfare of American seamen . . . abolish arrest and imprisonment as a penalty for desertion . . . and to promote safety at sea."[13] In its own agitation for the bill, the Seamen's Union neatly packaged post-*Titanic* apprehensions with the horror of New York City's 1911 Triangle Fire: "No one will claim it is safe to crowd people into a theater or a shirtwaist factory and then to lock the doors. Is it not even more dangerous to jam a steamer full of passengers and then to send it out of harbor without having on board the means whereby they may be taken off quickly and safely in case of need?"[14] In the hands of a skillful orator like Senator La Follette, the prosaic mass of regulatory detail contained in the Seamen's Bill was instantly turned into a drama of life and death, the crucial difference for those caught in some future oceanic emergency, utterly dependent on workingmen who today would be called "first responders." "Take a vessel manned by men who know the sea," he lyricized, ". . . and when the hour comes that in all its fury the raging storm breaks, their boat is prepared for it."[15]

Alongside "safety," the "freedom" argument was a relatively easy sell for maritime reform advocates. Reformers could draw on a long history—and extended literary tradition—likening life in a forecastle to imprisonment. As folklorist Archie Green has noted, wordplay comparing service in the British "fleet" to London's Fleet prison goes back to the seventeenth century, while in the eighteenth century Samuel Johnson reportedly likened the sailor's lot as "being in a jail with the chance of being drowned."[16] The issue of actual sailor imprisonment had, of course, reared its head in the 1895–98 *Arago* case (*Robertson v. Baldwin*; see chapter 2) that critics quickly labeled the "Second Dred Scott Decision." Furuseth and his supporters positively reveled in the high ground of this issue. Though the White Act (1898) further extended immunity from imprisonment—irrespective of the nature of the voyage—to all domestic and nearby foreign ports and recommended a month-limit on any imprisonment for desertion, the noxious principle remained.[17] Furuseth's own famous (but perhaps apocryphal) words on the subject of sailor incarceration have been oft-repeated: "You can put me in jail, but you cannot give me narrower quarters than as a seaman I have always had. You cannot give me coarser food than I have always eaten. You cannot make me lonelier than I have always been."[18] In December 1909, a parade of 1,800 seamen in New York City culminated in a mass meeting at Cooper Union to promote the sailor's freedom; in attendance were not only British seamen's leader Joseph Havelock Wilson and American Federation of Labor (AFL) chief Samuel Gompers (who arrived straight from Supreme Court arguments in the *Buck's Stove* case) but also the son of William Lloyd Garrison, who "sent a message for the men who were not freed by the Emancipation Proclamation."[19]

In the run-up to the bill's passage, the issue was in high gear. The still-sitting congressman William B. Wilson in 1912 had defined the issue starkly: "It is needless in this age to argue for the right of men to be free. . . . Labor power is a part of man; it is generated within him and can only be exercised and utilized through his brain power and will. To compel him to use it against his will is to make him to all intents and purposes a slave."[20] Raising the ante even higher, Mississippi senator James K. Vardaman, a champion of hill country poor whites (but as a virulent racist no friend of real ex-slaves), declared, "If the Sermon on the Mount were delivered to this body today for the first time . . . some Senator in this Chamber would rise in his place and object to the application to governmental questions of the eternal principles enunciated in that sacred message, lest the order of things might be disturbed. . . . Mr. President, I am afraid the rule of gold has taken the place of the golden rule in matters of legislation."[21]

Not surprisingly, few legislators chose to stand up against the Golden Rule. A lonely defense of the desertion law (this from a steamship executive) likened a sailor's contract to a marriage contract: "I can not go back to my wife, if I want to break my marriage contract, and say to her, 'You can keep my old socks and loose change I have around the house, and we are quits.' That is exactly what this bill provides for the seaman. The State [under current law] steps in and says: 'We have an interest in that. You must perform specifically. You must either support your wife and family or go to jail.'" Furuseth quickly rejected the marital metaphor. "When we talk about a ship," he explained, "we always say: 'Thank God, I am not married to her.' I have seen men go ashore and commit misdemeanors to get clear of a vessel. I have seen men eat soap to get clear of a vessel. I have seen men go and put their feet through plate-glass windows to get clear of a vessel. . . . I have run from a vessel and left £50 due me and was glad I had a chance to run away."[22] Ohio Republican senator Theodore Burton, a moderate progressive, predicted that if only the bill were limited in application to abolishing desertion arrests of *American* seamen, "every Member of the Senate will approve."[23] A sign of the emotional wedge of the desertion issue came at a key moment in the bill's deliberations in 1915 when Furuseth "personally begged" President Woodrow Wilson "to make me a free man." It moved the president, according to Senator La Follette, as "[I] had never seen him moved on any other occasion."[24]

Rather than attack its signature plank, opponents of the seamen's legislation preferred to cast it as special-interest legislation, a boondoggle for a pampered occupation, and an unfair limitation of employers' authority over their property. A steamship representative summed up the industry view of the bill as "union labor tyranny" and "one of the worst bills in restraint of trade . . . ever."[25] Provision for better food, as included in the bill, was dismissed on grounds that "the poor, downtrodden sailors" have "more meals and more to eat than any class of men in the country."[26] Senators who worried about excessive heat and inadequate ventilation on board steamships were told they had read too many "Jack London stories."[27] As the attorney for the American Steamship Association, the shipowners' group, testified, "The seamen may not be seeking as much the protection of human life as to give themselves a dominating position over the vessel owners."[28]

Indeed, unable and unwilling to defend the draconian statutes on de-

FIGURE 4.2. U.S. Progressive reformers, ca. 1915. This rare photo captures Senator Robert M. La Follette flanked by seamen's leader Andrew Furuseth (left) and writer-reformer Lincoln Steffens (right). Courtesy of the Wisconsin Historical Society, Image # WHi-73349.

sertion, most opponents of the La Follette Act preferred not to directly contest but rather to belittle its likely humanitarian impact. For whatever their position on the legislation, all parties acknowledged that relatively few American seamen would be immediately affected by its enactment. This was because the new legislation merely extended to foreign ports the immunity from desertion prosecution already accorded domestic-related trade and because relatively few U.S.-flagged ships still traveled the high seas.[29] "They tell you," declared Republican representative Willliam E. Humphrey of Washington, "that the emergency for the passage of this bill is to keep the American seamen from being imprisoned. . . . We have no American sailors to free. We have not today 500 American sailors upon the Pacific Ocean. We have very few anywhere."[30] According to Representative Humphrey's data, 93 percent of U.S. foreign trade was carried by foreign ships with foreign crews, and, of the remaining 7 percent, "not 10 per cent of their crews are American citizens."[31] For Representative Joseph Moore, a Pennsylvania Republican with personal ties to the banking and international merchant circles, the bill's moral fervor was thus much ado about nothing: "The gentleman from Texas [Hardy] makes a most brilliant and eloquent speech about the gyves [bands] that are upon the wrists and the shackles that are upon the legs of American seamen. If there are no American seamen, it is useless to talk of shackles upon American seamen."[32]

There was clearly some substance to the debunkers' point. The combination of mid-nineteenth-century "navigation laws" that required U.S.-built ships for U.S.-flagged vessels, together with comparatively high U.S. wages and shipbuilding (especially for steam-powered vessels) costs, had taken a drastic toll on the American presence in the transoceanic carrying trades. A story circulated of a British captain in the South Pacific who, feigning great surprise at a ship bearing the American flag, exclaimed: "Why bless my heart, that must be a Yankee ship. I remember seeing that flag when I was a boy. The poor fellow must have drifted off the coast and got lost."[33] According to congressional testimony, whereas in 1840, some 80 percent of the U.S. carrying trade was in U.S. vessels, by 1883 that proportion was down to 15 percent.[34] In one belated response, Congress in 1912 lifted the restriction on American registry of foreign-built cargo ships.[35] Given such conditions, Representative Moore could scoff in 1915 that the La Follette bill "proposes inasmuch as we have no American sailors we shall give the American sailors' rights to foreign sailors, that inasmuch as we have no American ships we shall confer every American right upon foreign ships."[36] If they had been pressed, even its chief proponents would have had to admit that relatively few American seamen would immediately benefit from its protection.

In the eyes of its advocates, however, it was precisely the extension of coverage to workers on foreign ships that provided a crucial measure not merely of its expansive idealism but of its ultimate likely benefit to American seamen. Within the folds of its legislative logic, the La Follette Act presumed nothing less than a nationalist solution to the problem of discouragingly cheap, international maritime labor. The reformers' case began with an appreciation for the seaman's weak bargaining position within segmented national labor markets across the world's seas. Draconian national penalties against desertion (commonly augmented internationally by bilateral treaties for the return of captured seamen) prevented the operation of a "free market" in labor, segmenting sailors according to national wage norms and preventing lesser-paid sailors from taking advantage of opportunities at higher-wage ports of call. The system, ran the reformers' logic, both locked in cheaper rates abroad and made American labor and shipping prices utterly uncompetitive on the high seas. As a remedy, the act posited a single world market for seagoing labor in the foreign trade. If "sea labor," like any other commodity, advocates reasoned, were allowed to float at market price, then all would-be employers would have to pay that price. In a 1914 appeal to President Wilson, the ISU elaborated on this basic logic. By using the police power to capture and return seamen who attempted to quit the service of their ships, the U.S. government effectively helped foreign shipowners maintain a wage rate lower than that prevailing at American ports. Such intervention, argued the union, "marks the one advantage which foreign ships now hold over the American ships in the foreign trade, and which prevents the proper growth of our merchant marine. . . . If conditions can be brought about whereby the wage cost of operation will be equalized, the development of our merchant marine and our sea power will be unhampered. . . . The remedy is to set free the economic laws governing wages."[37]

Given a competitive market in shipping (that is, the option for shippers to choose the least expensive flag carrier), a right to quit and a "half-wage" guarantee on U.S. ships alone would hardly solve the larger problem. With average U.S. sailor wages nearly forty dollars per month compared to British rates at twenty to twenty-five dollars per month, Swedish rates at seventeen dollars per month, and Chinese rates at seven to nine dollars per month, restricted U.S.-only regulations would likely further drive U.S. ships from the sea.[38] Or, as Senator La Follette explained, "It will do us no good . . . so to equip, so to man, and so to regulate our merchant marine if all the craft that we meet on the watery way shall be undermanned, controlled by ignorance, and sailed by the very lowest element in all humanity." Rather—and here lay the audacity of the reform—"all foreign vessels which operate to our ports must also meet the requirements imposed by the bill. As well might you enact nothing as to leave that out."[39] As legal precedent for the extension of sovereignty, La Follette cited an otherwise obscure and uncontroversial passage in the 1898 White Act that had applied a ban on advances and allotments in seamen's wages to foreign as well as U.S. vessels.[40]

No doubt, the La Follette Act carried large expectations. Apply the new standards to foreign ships (what Texas Democratic representative Rufus Hardy called a "free seas" principle), its proponents promised, and you would see a gradual convergence of *all* sea wages at a higher rate.[41] Once the world's merchant marine (or at least any part of it that passed through a U.S. port) could demand, via the right to quit, comparable pay and conditions, foreign captains would have to hire new crews, or rehire their old crews, at the wages then prevalent in a given port. Moreover, to secure their crews, they had best make such adjustment well in advance of arrival in U.S. waters, thus at least theoretically creating what, in modern-day parlance, might be termed an economic "race to the top." "Just as sure as the United States passes this law," Furuseth thus told a congressional committee, "European nations will have to follow you, because you will take from them the cream of their seamen until you can develop your own. . . . The result will be, as a whole, the rebuilding of the [American] merchant marine."[42] In addition to its immediately felicitous impact on "150,000 American seamen," Furuseth modestly predicted that the legislation would also benefit the rest of an estimated 2 million other seafarers "throughout the world."[43] As eminent maritime authority Elmo Paul Hohman later summarized, the Seamen's Act rested on "a theory of wage adjustment which aimed at nothing less than a worldwide equalisation of wage rates."[44]

Nor was the logic behind Furuseth's vision merely abstract. For decades, world seafarers had been aware of the upward pull of wages on trips to North American ports. As historian Eric Sager documents for voyages from Liverpool in the 1870s, the average monthly wage for an able-bodied seaman headed for the United States was £3-17-0, while the average for "any other part of the world" was £3-3-0, a difference of more than 20 percent. As Sager infers, the only meaningful logic behind the difference (given no shortage of willing volunteers for such transatlantic voyages) was "to reduce the wage disparity upon arrival" and thereby avert massive defections via desertion common in North American ports. Yet, since the wage differential itself apparently proved insufficient in this regard, masters had resorted to other measures, most commonly denial of shore leave and/or denial of advance wages. By denying both of these employer restrictions and effectively placing U.S. law behind any sailor's right to quit, La Follette Act advocates squared public policy with their own extended experience of a "floating" international labor market.[45]

Not surprisingly, the projected international reach of the act equally excited its opponents. As early as 1912, a minority report blasted the La Follette bill as "the most extreme and revolutionary in all probability that has ever been favorably reported to this House."[46] On economic grounds, Georgia senator Hoke Smith worried that the legislation would scare off the foreign tramp steamers that carried his region's cotton to market.[47] On security grounds, the Senate Republican doyens of American foreign relations—Henry Cabot Lodge of Massachusetts and Elihu Root of New York—both expressed alarm at the idea of abridging treaty provisions, especially at a time of gathering diplomatic apprehension.[48] Fine to put an end to the "old system" of arrest for desertion, argued Lodge, but "I cannot conceive that any country in the world . . . would patiently submit to having its citizens and subjects who are the masters or officers of vessels arrested in a foreign port . . . for an act which is entirely lawful in their own country and under their own flag."[49] Root protested such "arrogant indifference to the interests and even the prejudices of other nations," lecturing his colleagues that while there may have been "a time when we, an agricultural country with all of our life confined within our own borders, could get down and ignore the fact that other people in the world had their own ideas and were entitled to entertain them . . . a country whose production and industries have been so organized that its life and prosperity are dependent upon the continuance of a commerce of thousands of millions of dollars . . . can not live upon any such method of legislation."[50] Even Senator William Stone, Democrat of Missouri, who acknowledged "the struggle between employees and employers" and conceded the legal grounds for the bill, nevertheless opposed the reach of the proposed remedy. "If [only] it had been confined in its operations to American seamen and American ships," Stone complained, "but when we go beyond that and undertake a sort of Utopian scheme of caring for foreign seamen and regulating foreign ships and imposing our standards of policy upon the Governments of the world, I am compelled to halt."[51] Despite such forebodings, Senator La Follette steered his legislative craft to victory in February 1915, setting aside a final move to reconsider the bill by a Senate vote of 39 to 33.

The Nation-State as a Vehicle for Global Standards

The appeal for an economic readjustment on behalf of American sailors wrapped itself tightly in nationalist bunting. Furuseth, for example, invoking the classic text of Admiral Alfred Mahan, labeled his analysis of the legislative saga "American Sea Power and the Seamen's Act."[52] Like other commentators, he connected the reform effort not just to workers' rights and welfare but also to the revival of an American merchant fleet. The simultaneous invocation of a "reform spirit" with assertion of national prosperity and power was, of course, a common denominator of Progressive Era thought. The notion of a "fair marketplace"—competitive but accessible to all participants—ran from Populist granaries and railroad regulation to Gompers's anti-injunction campaigns through Theodore Roosevelt's New Nationalism, Wilson's New Freedom, Herbert Croly's *Promise of American Life* (1909), Walter Weyl's *The New Democracy* (1912), and Walter Lippmann's *Drift and Mastery* (1914).[53] Like their larger Progressive cohort, therefore, the maritime reformers managed to champion state action while still embracing a competitive marketplace economy. As Croly would put it, there were "two indispensable economic conditions" to the higher development of democratic civilization: "the preservation of the institution of private property in some form, and the . . . radical transformation of its existing nature and influence."[54]

To be sure, the worker-centered rights and welfare priorities embodied in Progressive measures like the La Follette Act tempted its friends to go further toward out-and-out socialization, or public ownership, at least on a selective basis. Just such an economic-nationalist direction appealed to Washington's Progressive-Republican representative James Wesley Bryan. In Bryan's view, the shipowners—both by long-established navigation and restricted liability laws—had already purchased a kind of special-interest protection that would be called "the rankest socialism" if it came from "an ordinary public man": "We go to work and chart the seas, and build lighthouses, and make every arrangement to protect them in case of wreck, and then we organize our Navy to protect them against the enemy in all of the ports of the world at public expense."[55] Notwithstanding such support from their government, the patriotism of shipowners, warned Bryan, extended only "until it comes to the proposition of profit." "When it is found that an American ship can make a little bit more by going under the Japanese flag or the Russian flag or the Belgian flag they at once forget their patriotism, . . . [the shipowner] forgets the land of his birth . . . dries up about Old Glory and 'my flag and your flag,' and runs up a foreign flag because he can make more pennies by hiring men who do not have the privileges of American liberty and the American Constitution."[56] Opposing all subsidies to the industry, Bryan went so far as to advocate a nationalized maritime fleet, a federal monopoly on coastwise and hemispheric trade routes that would transport "our goods to South America at cost."[57] Though Bryan was a vocal member of the Seamen's Act majority coalition, his proposals were quickly shelved.

One of the trickier aspects of the Seamen's Act agitation was the simultaneous reliance on and avoidance of "international" norms in promulgating U.S. legislative standards. On the one hand, inspiration and justification for a number of features of the Seamen's Bill came from abroad. Fending off criticism that the reach of the reforms represented a grave violation of national sovereignties, Furuseth's Great Lakes lieutenant, Victor Olander, pointed to the British Merchant Shipping Act of 1906 as a key precedent: "The laws dealing with deck load, the laws dealing with freeboard [that is, the Plimsoll line], the laws dealing with everything that has to do with safety of life among passengers and among the employees [already] apply to foreign seamen in foreign vessels while in English ports."[58] In addition, when it came to the number of watches at sea, required sleeping space in the forecastle, food rations, and sanitary facilities, union advocates made regular, sometimes quite systematic reference to "modern European conditions." In a typical congressional committee exchange, Furuseth referred to a provision for washtubs as follows: "As a matter of fact, this provision was taken out of the German law, which is middle way between the French and the Scandinavian."[59] In short, U.S. reformers were eager to "bargain up" protective norms by reference to specific, model practices abroad.[60]

Yet, on economic, political, and moral grounds, the Furuseth–La Follette forces were loathe to bequeath actual regulatory authority to any international body. As early as 1908, Furuseth's attendance at an International Transport Workers' Federation convention in Vienna had left him bitterly disappointed at what seemed to him the Europeans' greater interest in seamen's welfare than freedom. Indeed, it was after the Vienna meeting that Furuseth determined to push for unilateral, American enforcement of the right to quit.[61] Similarly suspicious from the start of shipowner influence at the post-*Titanic* London Conference on Safety of Life at Sea in November 1913, Furuseth only reluctantly endorsed what he considered its tepid recommendations that went on to receive the endorsement of the U.S. Senate as an international treaty convention.[62] American wariness toward international reform efforts was spelled out in the 1914 debate on the seamen's bill by Kansas Democratic representative Guy T. Helvering, who challenged those "who would have us delay in the enactment of this legislation until such time as we can confer with the nations of the earth and formulate satisfactory rules": "Nothing is to be gained by such delay. The nations most interested have a selfish interest in the prevention of any legislation not satisfactory to the shipowners. They have coddled, nursed, and subsidized them in an endeavor to secure a large percentage of the trade of the world, and they will not aid in restrictions which will be opposed by such owners."[63] This same reluctance to countenance international authority (given its potential to dilute national labor standards) would ultimately propel Andrew Furuseth to adamant opposition to the very formation of the International Labor Organization in 1919, a position that alienated the seamen's leader even from the pragmatic nationalist president of the AFL, Samuel Gompers.[64]

The Underside of Progressive Reform

While the adherents of far-reaching labor standards regularly wrapped national group interest in appeals to universal freedoms, they sometimes tapped more openly racist and xenophobic impulses.[65] That was certainly the case with the Seaman's Act agitation. Although it has generally escaped the attention of those transfixed by a Whiggish view of the Progressive synthesis, a more ambivalent take on the Seamen's Act was sounded by earlier scholarship.[66] As early as 1961, Jerold S. Auerbach exposed both the protectionist and racial trappings of the maritime reforms. Identifying anti-Asian sentiment as a "cardinal" motivation behind the bill, Auerbach explained, "Furuseth's cry for seamen's rights would become indistinguishable from Nordic racism."[67] A mirror for both the good and bad of the Progressive reform era, the Seamen's Act, from this angle, reflected the "Progressive juxtaposition of idealism and imperialism, of regeneration and Anglo-Saxon superiority, or reform and nativism."[68]

For Furuseth and his supporters, global labor competition and a nostalgic view of changes in the trade merged into a single sense of grievance. The skill as well as romance and glamour attached to the age of "wooden ships and iron men" had disappeared into the drudgery of the era of steam. As a result, according to Furuseth, the sea was becoming more and more "the domain of those who fought life's battles and accepted defeat, of the sewage of the Caucasian race and of such of the races of Asia as felt that their condition could be improved by becoming seamen."[69] While the ISU supported the 1882 Chinese Exclusion Act and its increasingly restrictive follow-up amendments (as did most of the West Coast labor movement), the union remained frustrated by the courts' decision that such acts did not apply to the hiring of Chinese on American vessels. The Pacific Mail Steamship Company, for example, used Chinese "almost exclusively," while other U.S. companies hired them as stewards for one-fourth the wages of American seamen.[70] Characteristically, the union's *Seamen's Journal* played upon popular stereotypes in 1901 by suggesting that the "real struggle of to-day lies between the civilization that draws its breath from beef and barley and that which rests upon rice and dried fish."[71]

Thus, even as maritime reform advocates invoked the language of "standards" to attract American boys to the sea, they specifically derogated the growing numbers of Chinese, Japanese, and "lascars" plying international waters. "Our own countrymen began quitting the sea more than 50 years ago," explained California Democrat John Edward Raker to his

House colleagues in late August 1914. For decades, that left European nations to supply "not only our sailors and firemen, but also officers to man our merchant vessels." But now, he worried, the "same underlying cause" was equally eroding European seamanship. The "white man" was quitting the sea altogether, increasingly replaced by "men from India, China, and the Malay Islands." Especially at a time of escalating war, no nation, Raker warned, could depend on "alien races and alien nationalities" for its maritime security.[72] A similarly racialized appeal was sounded by La Follette in advocating for the language provisions of the Seamen's Bill:

> Suppose a vessel is at sea, in a storm, in a collision; it has encountered an iceberg, as the *Titanic* did; it has met some foreign boat, manned by Chinese stupefied by opium. They have not obeyed the rule of the road on the sea. There is a collision. The vessel is loaded with passengers. . . . It may have a crew representing many nationalities . . . some from the Mediterranean, some from India, some from South Africa, some from Germany, some from the Netherlands, some from China, and some from Japan. They know no word of English. One group can not communicate or converse with or have intercourse intelligently with the other.[73]

Argument for the Seamen's Act, in short, combined free market and protectionist principles. On the one hand, reformers sought to allow sailors, by withdrawing punishment for "desertion," to seek the highest price for their labor in the global marketplace. On the other hand, both the English language and skill provisions legislated limitations on open hiring. But what if the two principles collided?

Just that eventuality beckoned in 1912 with the proposal by Massachusetts Republican representative Augustus Peabody Gardner of an "alien seamen's bill," an extension of immigrant-restriction legislation spurred by the Dillingham Commission, 1907–11. Under Gardner's proposed bill, in order to avoid fines for discharging any unlawful alien or person of Chinese descent at an American port of call, shipowners were given discretion to hold their men on board. Furuseth and other union champions, however, preferred an automatic inspection by immigration officers, to see who might be admitted as an immigrant, followed by respect for the right of *any* sailor to "go over and buy a plug of tobacco; go on shore and look at the country [and then hire out to the highest bidder] . . . as if he came through Castle Garden."[74] Furuseth's seeming indulgence of the possibilities for desertion was not lost on the restrictive bill's sponsor. "You want to have people come in here and pass by our immigration laws," charged Representative Gardner, "because you think it will help those men you represent to have the foreign seaman come in, and thereby, when he goes out again, gets higher pay. Now, I say one wants immigration for one reason, and another wants to help people to come in here for another reason. I do not want to help them for any reason." Even a more sympathetic Democratic committee chairman, John Burnett of Alabama, a former member of the Dillingham Commission, agreed with Gardner: "I see great danger in the suggestion that is made to allow those fifteen or thirty or forty thousand to come in, as [Furuseth] suggests, and become part of the masses, but I think there is justice in his suggestion that there should be an examination [such as] at Ellis Island, and to see that they do not desert."[75] The xenophobia justifying the union's maritime labor law reforms, it seemed, was a retractable yardstick, extended (or not) depending on the issue—in this case, one that soon disappeared into the legislative miasma—at hand.[76]

If Furuseth had no problem endorsing the America-first tenor of the La Follette Act, his left-wing critics in the Industrial Workers of the World (IWW) also faced the challenge of reconciling support for employment security with their commitments to more universalist principles of worker rights. The Wobblies, as the members of the IWW were popularly known, had stepped in over the wreck of rival and mismanaged maritime unionism on the East Coast to build up their own Marine Transport Workers Union in the years 1911–14. With a temporary base among both Spanish-speaking firemen (who had quit the ISU) and port workers in New Orleans, Wobbly advocates were in no mood to grant Furuseth's larger legislative initiative a free pass.[77] In the first place, their syndicalist principles upheld workplace militancy over legislative strategies. Doubting as late as December 1914 that the Seamen's Bill would pass, the "meditating rebel" of the IWW's *Solidarity* newspaper scoffed, "Why bother with Congress at all, if you have [solid] organization?" Furuseth, he suggested, "very likely has a child-like faith in 'the state,' far exceeding his confidence in the workers whom he is supposed to represent."[78] More pointedly, the Wobblies took aim at the ISU's attempts to prioritize hiring of skilled, English-speaking seamen; instead, the IWW equally welcomed less-skilled firemen, cooks, stewards, longshoremen, bargemen, "or anyone who works in the industry."[79] Moreover, unlike most trade unionists, the Wobblies were not merely internationalists but practically race-blind in their inclusiveness; their first convention laid out the principle that "you could not and should not by any process of exclusion exalt yourselves above the working class of the most medieval province in China."[80] Curiously, however, when it came to challenging the protectionism of the ISU regarding the hiring of foreign, non-English-speaking workers, Wobbly critics relied less on egalitarian principle than on a practical, business-centered argument. Citing employer testimony from the congressional hearings, *Solidarity* editorialized that the La Follette bill's restrictive standards would drive American flag shipping from the seas. Bar the Chinese from employment for the U.S.-owned Pacific Mail Steamship Company, they suggested, and one of the firm's foreign rivals, not American mariners, would inherit the trade.[81] Opposing both protectionist labor legislation and long-established navigation laws denying foreign investment in U.S. shipbuilding, the syndicalist Wobblies ironically went further than their business unionist contemporaries in embracing the logic of the free market.

A Foul Occupation

While selectively playing the race card, the reform forces behind Furuseth had to defend their own ranks from public perceptions that the seafarers themselves were a class of already degraded lowlifes. Thus, in opposing projected legislative requirements for better sleeping and sanitary quarters, both shipbuilders and shipping merchants pinned the blame for substandard conditions on the sailors' own conduct. Objecting to making employers responsible for providing "clean" facilities, Charles Skentelbery, marine superintendent for the New England Coal Company, argued, "We have an excellent washing place for our firemen and sailors, and they will not keep it clean now, but say that the stewards and waiters should do so, which is not the case. We can not employ stewards as valets for the crew. . . . We have some very shocking, dirty conditions in those places due to the men themselves."[82] Insinuating that many sailors did not clean up their own washbasins or even flush their own toilets, a steamship manufacturer pleaded that "we can not carry a man to follow a sailor into the water-closet and wash and clean up after him."[83] One shipping company representative further contrasted the discipline of old sailing crews with the laxity of the current day's steamship crews: "A few years ago I fitted a vessel out on the Pacific coast with bathtubs, all up to date washing accommodations, and in about three months afterwards, I was going through the inspection and I found the bathtubs full of human excrement. No man will ever take a bath after he sees anything of that kind in the tub. . . . I took the bathtub[s] out." Reflecting another common image of the sailor, Superintendent Skentelbery pointed to the source of many of the sanitation problems: "The trouble is that in leaving port our firemen and sailors are mostly drunk, and they do create a nuisance in the places . . . not always in the washbowl."[84]

Against such collective denigration of his seafaring contemporaries, Furuseth's response reflected an ambivalence that made him at once a dogged and imperious champion of his trade. On the one hand, the seamen's leader blamed sanitary breakdowns on inadequate facilities, inadequate staffing of mess boys and stewards, and lack of planning by ship captains to have the deck watch attend to maintenance tasks.[85] Echoing this practical defense, the ISU's Victor Olander insisted, "The dirt referred to . . . comes not from the actions of the sailors . . . but from the fact that the water to the toilets is very often shut off in port, and there is no way of keeping it clean except to spend a lot of time getting a bucket, going up on deck, hoisting the water up over the side, carrying it down below, and washing it out. . . . If some of our friends among the vessel owners who are very anxious to get the men to keep clean should make some arrangement to furnish water on those occasions, they would not have that kind of trouble."[86]

On the other hand, Furuseth himself did not let his own members off the hook so easily. A gruff patriarch who regularly admonished his rank and file even while championing their cause, Furuseth regularly saw more to admire in the maritime past than in the present. The Seamen's Act, he pointed out to skeptical observers, did not remove the imperative for sailor discipline—"whether it is cleaning a washing place, or tarring the rigging, or steering, or keeping lookout. . . . [Once] a vessel is in motion . . . it is absolute obedience or imprisonment. That is what the law calls for, and this [legislation] does not change that at all."[87] Moreover, while insisting that seamen were "as cleanly as the average crowd of men as long as they had any chance to be," the union leader also allowed that "there is a constant deterioration going on . . . there is a lower personnel. The better class of men, the higher type of men, refuse to accept sea life under existing conditions."[88] Radical legislative relief, the seamen's leader counseled, would not only hold the line against incompetent, unsafe, and un-American crews but attract a proud, new class of skilled and fully civilized practitioners to the art of seafaring.

Enforcing the La Follette Act

It was one thing to pass innovative legislation but quite another to enforce it. One challenge raised against the Seamen's Act—and this by world merchant and shipbuilding interests—concerned its very legality. Conventionally—that is, according to the customs of admiralty or maritime law—a ship's flag determined the law that should apply to a given craft, no matter in which waters it was found.[89] Even where a legal proceeding was brought in the port state, the courts would normally apply the law of the ship's (foreign) flag state. The "rule of the flag" in admiralty, however, was hardly absolute; it depended on the specific consent of the nation whose port a ship entered. Otherwise, once in port (or within the recognized three-mile limit of "national waters"), every ship was subject to the jurisdiction and laws of that port's country. When, for example, a murder was alleged by a foreigner against another foreigner on a foreign ship in a New Jersey port, the matter would assuredly be handled by New Jersey's courts and according to New Jersey's laws. Yet, when it came to disputes over wages, injuries, or other matters germane to the normal "discipline" of a vessel, precedent, legal scholars suggest, was decidedly mixed. Even if it possessed the underlying right to do so, Congress would thus need to be clear and explicit whenever it counterposed its authority to the "rule of the flag" in order to pass muster in U.S. courts.[90]

So, the question arose: Did Congress have the power to apply the full range of the La Follette Act's provisions not only to American ships but to foreign ships as well, superimposing its own will on other nationals in disregard of their own laws and customs? The answer, initially elaborated in two outwardly conflicting decisions of the U.S. Supreme Court, was a cautious "yes." Justice Louis Brandeis, a close political friend of Senator La Follette as well as visionary reformer in his own right, figured in both—a fact that further tied the legislation to both the political and the legal sensibility of American Progressivism.

International application of the La Follette Act was initially tested in *Sandberg v. McDonald* (1918), wherein the litigant Sandberg, one among a group of petitioning international sailors, had signed up on a British freighter in Liverpool and, in keeping with British custom, had received an advance payment of wages. When their ship docked in Mobile, Alabama, the sailors demanded one half of wages earned under the La Follette Act. The ship captain promptly paid them but first deducted the amount advanced in Liverpool. Pointing to the La Follette Act's provision that advance payments (a classic lure for crimps) were unlawful, the men then quit the ship and brought suit. A narrow 5–4 majority of the Supreme Court ruled against the seamen. Looking to the "language of the act itself" rather than examining the legislators' likely intent, Justice William R. Day emphasized that the relevant section of the legislation was to apply to foreign vessels "while in waters of the United States," and therefore prior advances *paid abroad* were not affected. Parsing the decision some thirty-five years later, distinguished legal scholar Alexander M. Bickel suggested that in addition to relying on linguistic literalism—which was in any case vigorously contested by the Court's minority, including Brandeis—the Court hesitated to challenge long-standing deference to the "rule of the flag."[91]

It was Brandeis, according to Bickel, in a case very much like *Sandberg*, who soon moved the Court to a different conclusion. In *Strathearn S.S. Co. v. Dillon* (1920), John Dillon, another British sailor, applied for half-wages in a U.S. port but was rebuffed on grounds that his own prior contract and British law differed from the mandate of the La Follette Act. In an unpublished opinion circulated among his Supreme Court brethren, Brandeis took pains to demonstrate that Congress had both ample precedent and the clear intent to impose the full logic of the La Follette Act over foreign vessels. Brandeis concisely summarized 125 years of maritime regulation and emphasized that the 1915 legislation emerged determinedly out of a national protectionist economic argument: "The committees of Congress concluded that if seamen on foreign vessels were freed from liability to arrest in our courts for desertion and this exemption from arrest were coupled with a provision enabling the seaman to obtain here payment of a substantial part of all wages theretofore earned and remaining unpaid, foreign vessels engaged in the American trade would be compelled to raise wages and working conditions to practically the standard prevailing in our coastwise trade."[92]

The power of the Brandeis memorandum was enough to win the Court, utterly divided in *Sandberg*, to a unanimous decision sustaining the ambitious reach of the Seamen's Act, in *Strathearn*. Again speaking for the Court (but now with a new inflection), Justice Day pointedly borrowed from the Brandeis analysis of legislative intent: "Apart from the text, which we think plain, it is by no means clear that, if the act were given a construction to limit its application to American seamen only, the purposes of Congress would be subserved, for such limited construction would have a tendency to prevent the employment of American seamen, and to promote the engagement of those who were not entitled to sue for one-half wages."[93]

Alas, for reasons that will only briefly detain us here, the global reach of the Seamen's Act—sustained in principle by *Strathearn*—was severely limited in practice in the years to come. Suggesting a division within the Wilson administration, the Department of Commerce regularly favored the shipowners in its interpretation of the law. Safety inspections, for example, were dropped for foreign vessels whose national laws roughly met American standards. The language provision was similarly weakened by accepting pidgin English and even hand gestures as adequate communication between officers and crew. Forecastle provisions were deemed applicable only to ships built after 1915. Allowing fewer men for the evening "dog watch" undermined an intended incentive for new hiring.[94] Meanwhile, other nations determined to hold men on their ships. French law, for example, effectively discouraged desertions by defining the merchant marine as a naval reserve service.[95] Even if Americans declared desertion legal, foreign nations were under no such compunction should the offender ever return to his native soil. Out of both nationalist loyalties and economic calculation (the same attributes that had helped pass the act), even many foreign seamen's union officials "were opposed to the Act, and did not encourage their members to avail themselves of its opportunities."[96] The Great War, of course, utterly upset normal sea commerce for several years running. While the war initially drove up wages (and union membership), a disastrous strike in 1921 brought the ISU back to a low ebb, just as Republican administrations, utterly disinclined to push the regulatory envelope, took over, only to be followed by a long slump in world shipping, and then the Great Depression. In the circumstances, evidence for the wage "equalization" anticipated by the act was spotty, at best.[97]

By the time of the post–World War II revival of world trade, utopian hopes for the impact of the Seamen's Act were long gone. Just how much the act's intended reach had been foreshortened was evident in extended legal skirmishing—though less about the original act than a narrower corollary, passed in 1920 as part of the wide-ranging Merchant Marine (aka Jones) Act, to extend to seamen the rights enjoyed by railroad workers to sue for damages in case of accident or injury.[98] Among its revisions of prior legislation, the Merchant Marine Act reiterated the half-pay provisions, including for "seamen on foreign vessels, while in the United States," and then guaranteed the right to trial by jury to any seaman injured in the course of his employment.[99] Following on the "equalization" arguments elaborated in Seamen's Act debate, New Mexico Democratic senator Andrieus Jones openly asserted that the purpose of his legislative initiative was "to bring the foreign seamen up to a level with our own seamen by giving them the remedy here in our own ports that our seamen have."[100]

In the post–World War II era, however, application of the statute fell to an American judiciary increasingly reluctant to intervene in international commercial matters. The extraterritorial reach of the earlier maritime statutes was now met with incredulity as well as a most narrow literal construction by the courts. Thus, in denying access to the Jones Act to a British seaman injured on a British ship while on the high seas, Second Circuit judge Learned Hand allowed in 1947 that while the U.S. Congress might have the power to so extend its jurisdiction, it would be "as extreme an exercise of power as one can imagine; a bit of absolution beyond all ordinary conventions."[101]

An even more telling decision was that of the Supreme Court in *Lauritzen v. Larsen* in 1953. Following Hand's logic, U.S. Supreme Court justice Howell E. Jackson ridiculed the legislative draftsmanship as well as outsized ambition of the La Follette Act and its stepchild, the Jones Act: "Three sections [of the former act] were made specifically applicable to foreign vessels, and these provoked considerable doubt and debate. Others were phrased in terms which on their face might apply to the world or to anything less."[102] Despite the apparent openness of its language, Jackson inferred, Congress surely did not mean its statutory remedy to apply to a Danish seaman hired onto a Danish ship in the New York harbor and injured in Havana, Cuba.[103] In the absence of what it termed "more definite directions" than were contained in the statutes, the Court declared, jurisdiction would be decided by "the usual doctrine and practices of maritime law."[104] Suggesting both the tenor and contemporary illogic of the laborist appeals, Justice Jackson added the following parenthetical note to his decision: "In apparent recognition of the weakness of the legal argument, a candid and brash appeal is made by respondent and by *amicus* briefs to extend the law to this situation as a means of benefiting seamen and enhancing the costs of foreign ship operation for the competitive advantage of our own. . . . The argument is misaddressed. It would be within the proprieties if addressed to Congress. Counsel familiar with the traditional attitude of this Court in maritime matters could not have intended it for us."[105]

The open ignorance of the Supreme Court of arguments that had produced the maritime acts some three decades before testified not only to a change in the manner of legal reasoning but to a revised world order.[106] With international commerce a key to revived prosperity in an era of newly forming multilateral economic and regulatory agencies, the unilateralist approach to labor equalization that animated the La Follette Act appeared arcane, unworkable, even absurd. So much for what had once appeared a panacea for sailor and indeed world labor problems. In June 1953, approaching their 100th anniversary celebration of Furuseth's birth, the Friends of

Andrew Furuseth Legislative Association rhapsodized, "If [only] the Seamen's Act had been enforced from 1917 on, it might not have been necessary to have spent 19 billion dollars under the Marshall Plan, because the standard of living of European countries would have advanced more nearly to a parity with our own."[107] Unfortunately, outside its commemorative partisans, such arguments by the 1950s surely fell on deaf ears. What was once the dominant, underlying logic of the Seamen's Act was now a dead letter.

IN RETROSPECT, BOTH THE PASSAGE and subsequent emasculation of the Seamen's Act invite a few observations about the early pursuit of "global" regulatory labor reform. First, the latter-day witness cannot help but marvel at the ambition of the act in both substance and its reach across national borders. When not otherwise disabled by the "commerce" or "due process" clauses of the Constitution, the Progressive Era Congress demonstrated a penchant for robust regulatory relief on behalf of working people. Second, the act surely reminds us that ours is not the first age to confront the debilitating aspects of a competitive global marketplace, nor the first to try to do something about it. Moreover, more than mere trade protectionism, the act sought to enlist both regulatory and marketplace dynamics in the pursuit of social justice. While much can be said on the positive side to commemorate the Seamen's Act, however, its uglier underside must, of course, also be weighed in the balance. Very well and good, we might suppose, to raise wages as well as safety levels for crewmen around the world, but what of its scarcely veiled attempt to drive a lower class of laborers (defined in terms utterly conflating race and economic standing) from the sea? Unfortunately, a unilateral presumption of virtue masking both racism and a narrow economic nationalism was utterly on display in the agitation for the Seamen's Act. To be sure, most latter-day globalization critics prefer to imagine a supranationalist approach to the problems of the "global sweatshop." Yet, even in more legitimately internationalist garb, the challenge of reconciling the needs and interests of the world's most miserable and exploited workers with those of their higher-skilled and better-remunerated counterparts remains a daunting one.

5

Workers of the Sea, Unite?

THE INTERNATIONALIST LEGACY OF THE PRE–WORLD WAR I YEARS

In August 2005, the *American Prospect*'s savvy editor-at-large, Harold Meyerson, noted with approval that within the umbrella of the recently formed Union Network International, a new alliance of service sector unions had determined to coordinate organizing campaigns of janitors and security guards across India, Poland, Holland, Germany, South Africa, and the United States. "As recently as two years ago," exulted Meyerson, "it was unlikely that any labor-force futurologist would have predicted that the first de facto global union would consist of the people who guard and clean office buildings and factories." Focusing on U.S. participation in the new alliance, Meyerson credited a changeover at the AFL-CIO (American Federation of Labor and Congress of Industrial Organizations) in 1995 when a newly elected president John Sweeney "shifted the focus of the federation's international department from fighting the Cold War . . . to winning global support for unions involved in strike actions here, and attempting to create a global trade order that didn't function solely for the benefit of corporations and investors." A key recruit to the new strategy was Service Employees International Union president Andy Stern, who (despite a subsequent organizational split from Sweeney) likewise reckoned that union strategy would have to change when, in the midst of a school-bus driver campaign in Minnesota, he discovered that the company was owned by a British employer immune from local politics and grassroots pressure. "We have to recognize," Stern declared, "that in real, 21st-century terms, 'Workers of the world, unite,' can't be just a slogan. It's the way of succeeding in a global economy." Meyerson seized on the labor leader's literary quotation. "And why is it that it took the world's workers a century and a half to get around to that charge given them by Karl Marx and Friedrich Engels in *The Communist Manifesto*? Because it took the capitalists a century a half to build the world that Marx described."[1]

Meyerson, like most other contemporary commentators, exaggerates the newness of today's conditions while also missing the longer history of "global unionism." The fact is, Union Network International was not the first global union—not by a century. That claim belongs to the International Federation of Ship, Dock and River Workers, established in 1896 and still a force today as the International Transport Workers' Federation. International market competition has always loomed as a potential obstacle to national labor standards. Indeed, early-nineteenth-century advocates for restrictions on hours and child labor like Robert Owen, Jerome Blanqui, and Daniel Legrand recognized the limits of national legislation alone. As Blanqui wrote as early as 1838, "There is only one way of accomplishing [the reform] while avoiding its disastrous consequences: this would be to get it adopted simultaneously by all industrial nations which compete in the foreign market."[2] Workers' own activity to attain such ends began soon after. Apart from the more political formations begun in Marx's and Engels's own lifetimes—particularly the "First" and "Second" Internationals of the socialist movement—the most sustained cooperation of workers across national borders occurred among waterfront workers centered in Europe, with a political base in London, in the 1890s.[3] Just as a "global economy" long preceded the contemporary focus on "globalization," so, too, did the workers' movement attempt to grapple with the challenge of a labor market—and employer power—that transcended national boundaries.

To be sure, no amount of awareness, even advanced thinking, about the global economy could serve as an "open sesame" to effective trade union action along those lines. No figure, for example, was more central to this earlier internationalist initiative than British sailor union leader Joseph Havelock Wilson (henceforth Havelock Wilson). That Wilson's general historical reputation should be linked, however, not to militant labor internationalism but rather to its polar opposite—that is, national chauvinism, racist protectionism, and even open collusion with employers versus worker unrest—is a testament not only to the changes affecting one man over time but also to the turbulence and tragedy encountered in one of labor history's most daringly cooperative endeavors.

Formed originally from a few local unions centered on England's northeast coast in 1887, the National Amalgamated Sailors' and Firemen's Union of Great Britain and Ireland (NASFU)—which after two reorganizations and three name changes emerged in 1926 as the National Union of Seamen (NUS)—was internationalist in spirit and action almost from the beginning. This was, in part, a matter of necessity, as a large section of the seagoing labor force were themselves neither British-born nor British citizens.[4] Since the repeal of the generally protectionist Navigation Acts of 1849, shipowners and merchant shippers were freed from previous domestic quotas requiring 75 percent native workers. A British ship, putting in at a foreign port, could henceforth hire at will. Eager to slash costs, shipowners took ready aim at higher-than-Continental British wage rates. For sailor-unionists, such structural features opened the door either to a strategy of international organizing or of nationalist protectionism. When they chose the former, they regularly relied on what would become the ITF. Through such international affiliation, British along with fellow European and North American sailor and dockworker unions attempted to coordinate workplace actions against an employer front, the Shipping Federation, that was equally and often more efficiently outfitted for international combat.

Havelock Wilson was heading only a local seamen's union in Sunderland when he first declaimed on international unionism. Protesting the fact that Britain's Employers' Liability Act of 1880 (which first extended compensation to workers in case of injury or loss of life due to employer negligence) exempted sailors from its coverage, Wilson promised a mass meeting that "the day would come when seamen would have, not only a national union, but an international union extending throughout the world. It might sound to many like a dream, but [I am] confident that, at some day or other, it [will] be accomplished."[5] Engagement with the larger world came logically, and almost inevitably, to a seaman like Wilson. Born in the coastal town of Sunderland, he had gone to sea at age twelve and joined the Australian Seamen's Union before returning home, marrying, and setting up a temperance hotel from which, with help from his wife, he could also direct local union affairs.[6] His own early analysis of obstacles facing sailor welfare balanced the problem of shipowner control of local marine offices—whereby "seamen had lost one set of crimps, but they had obtained in exchange Government-paid crimps"—with the problem of foreign competition driving down wages. British ships, he observed, were increasingly swamped by "the sewer rates of Europe," as British shipowners engaged entire crews at Continental ports like Hamburg, Antwerp, Rotterdam, and Bremen. Regarding the frequent complaint by owners that British seamen were unruly and unreliable, Wilson was sympathetic to a point: "The class of Britishers going to sea had degenerated to a marked degree," he allowed, as many native-born seamen had readily deserted to American ships with better rates of pay.[7]

Wilson's moves to strengthen sailor organization were connected to a period of expansive organizing and militant tactics within the larger British labor movement. This so-called New Unionism is most commonly associated with the middle-class rediscovery of poverty, socialist agitation among the poor as in the 1888 match-girl strike, and, most famously, London's "Great Dock Strike" of 1889, which would give rise to a new generation of socialist labor leaders including Ben Tillett, Tom Mann, John Burns, and Will Thorne.[8] To be sure, the entity that became the NUS was distinct from other "new unions" in certain respects. Like the higher-dues "new model" craft unions of the mid-nineteenth century, the Seamen emphasized accident and funeral benefits from the start; while including unskilled workers, they were "industrial" (or single-industry) rather than "general-unionist" in structure; and, while militant in action, they generally avoided political and ideological claims.[9] The timing of seafarer unionism may have been linked as well to changing technology and demographics. Three-quarters of oceangoing commerce was carried by steam by the turn of the century, making voyages speedier and family absences shorter. As a result, the figure of footloose "Jack Tar" had given way to the married man, who in turn adopted the skilled worker's "provider ideal" toward his immediate dependents.[10] Whatever its distinctive dynamic, the Seamen's takeoff as both a national and an international phenomenon was also intimately linked to interaction with the other leading figures and organizations of the times, especially Tillett's and Mann's dockworkers. From early on, the organizations of workmen who regularly met at the quayside realized their practical dependence upon one another.[11]

The Seamen were, in many ways, at the very center of the first wave of New Unionism, 1889–96. Their initial success in gaining both union recognition and wage increases at once preceded and succeeded the famous battle for the "dockers' tanner" (or wages at sixpence an hour) in August–September 1889. By 1890, what had begun as a mere local fragment claimed 60,000 members in control of all but the southern ports. Exemplifying the new militancy, unionized sailors and firemen at Liverpool reportedly "stormed the Sailors' Home, where the masters were enlisting rats [that is, strikebreakers] and drove them from their holes."[12] Yet, even as they helped precipitate action by other low-paid and previously unorganized workers, the Seamen's initiative also unleashed a powerful employer counterattack. When Wilson extended his support not only to the organization of the forecastle but to a newly rebellious association of ships' officers, even threatening to strike against the employment of non-union officers, shipowners in September 1890 formed the Shipping Federation to "[maintain] liberty of contract and [resist] the new union methods of coercion."[13]

Within a year, the Shipping Federation—demanding a "Federation ticket" by which Seamen's members had to accept employment alongside non-unionists—had set both the sailors' and dockers' unions back on their heels.[14] The fiercest struggles occurred at Hull and Bristol in 1892–93. Pushing back against the employer counteroffensive before a massed crowd of 5,000 at Bristol, Ben Tillett veered toward revolutionary license in suggesting that the struggle "must not finish until the workers of all grades and degrees commanded absolutely the whole machinery of the state, the whole machinery of government, of production, control and distribution."[15] Though never embracing Tillett's socialist vision—instead sticking to a demand for conciliation and collective bargaining—Wilson also spread the strike fever in these years and reportedly even pushed for a general strike until overruled by Tillett and the other leaders.[16] Wilson's centrality to this whole upheaval period cannot be denied. "The Seamen," summarizes a scholarly account of the New Union moment, "were embroiled in a dispute which affected almost every port in the kingdom, and caught up both the major dockers' unions in battles for which they were ill-prepared yet could not avoid."[17] Amid the turmoil of industrial conflict, Wilson himself was imprisoned for six weeks for threatening the peace at Cardiff in 1891, the popular reverberation from which would help secure him a parliamentary seat at Middlesbrough a year later. Overall, the employer counterattack (with the military protecting strikebreakers at Hull in 1893) and a slipping economy sent an increasingly bleak message to the new unions. Using ships as "mobile dormitories" to insert blackleg workers (the favored British term for strikebreakers) into various local disputes, employers increasingly checked strike action at every turn.[18] Extending themselves too far, too fast and regularly being vanquished by the Shipping Federation's more ample resources, the organized dockers' ranks in 1896 were a fifth of what they had been in 1890; meanwhile, the NASFU dissolved in financial ruin in 1894.[19]

In addition to catalyzing the period of labor-management conflict, the sailors took the lead in drawing the British trade union movement toward serious international connections. As early as 1889, for example, the sailors' union had supported striking Danish seamen, effectively urging its dock-worker allies in Newcastle to boycott ships arriving with blackleg crews. By 1890, to discourage the dumping of British crews abroad and to adjust to a labor force growing to 40 percent foreign-born by 1900, NASFU also briefly opened branches in Hamburg, Antwerp, Rotterdam, and Copenhagen.[20]

Battle-scarred but undaunted, the New Unionist generals determined by the mid-1890s to take the workers' fight to a wider plain. What would soon become formally institutionalized, however, began, as political projects often do, as an offshoot of prior ad hoc activity. In 1896, even as Havelock Wilson and Tom Mann were discussing a more effective coordination of shipping and carrying unions against interlocking shipping interests, Wilson learned that a British sailing crew from Liverpool had been discharged after refusing to permit the loading of their ship by strikebreaking longshoremen in Rotterdam. After a call went out to "black" (or boycott) the ship throughout the British Isles, a coordinating meeting of British and a few international representatives followed in July 1896. The result was the formation of the International Federation of Ship, Dock and River Workers, a dockworker-sailor alliance, and then, with the affiliation of railroad and streetcar workers, the International Transport Workers' Federation in 1898. With Mann as president and Wilson and Tillett as key associates, the new, still-British-centered movement (the Swedish seamen's and dockers' federation, led by Wilson's old Sunderland sailing partner Charles Lindley, was the first foreign affiliate) prepared to take on the world.[21] "Every year," declared Mann in 1897, "shows more clearly to the ordinary observer how thoroughly International the capitalists are as regards the use of the capital they control. . . . What we do now stand in urgent need of is an international working alliance among the workers of the whole world."[22] Mann envisioned a "maximum working day" and "uniform rates of pay, rations, and conditions of work wherever practical" in all ports of the world.[23]

A string of campaigns testified to the welling interest in international worker cooperation, even though results were mixed. Tom Mann, for example, a hero of the London dock strike of 1889, campaigned among Hamburg dockers in 1896. Though their organizing strike ultimately proved unsuccessful, the proto-ITF effectively did its part by stopping blackleg traffic to Hamburg. Within a couple years, moreover, tangible support was offered to striking Stockholm dockworkers, while Mann, Wilson, and Tillett—the latter arrested while hoping to sneak into the country in a cycling outfit—intervened on behalf of port workers attempting to form a Seamen's branch in Antwerp, Belgium.[24] With high expectations, Liverpool dockworkers' leader Edward McHugh even ventured to New York City in 1896, where he quickly aided the creation of the American Longshoremen's Union.[25]

International solidarity sentiment, it seemed, was popping up all over. Thomas J. Elderkin, Great Lakes representative and secretary of the American International Seamen's Union, reached out through the ITF corridor to Charles Lindley in Sweden: "We have made our National Organization an International one. And if it were possible I would like to see your organization attached to it. The cost is three cents per month per member in good standing. . . . We in America feel that Seaman should be recognized the World over when carrying a Union Card."[26]

No one, initially, was happier with the internationalist turn than Wilson and his Seamen's Union, who effectively drove the action. Indeed, the semiofficial historian of the ITF suggests that in its first few years, the ITF and the Seamen's Union were nearly identical, "since it was in fact the same organization in everything but name and its officers."[27] No wonder that the British sailors' unofficial organ would happily report that the "Sailors' and Firemen's Union is peculiarly well adapted for the extension and consolidation of an international federation. . . . [The] members are continually visiting other countries and fraternizing with foreign people and we hope to live to see the day when London shall be headquarters of a great extensive and powerful international union of all sailors and firemen of whatever colour and race. Why should it not be so?"[28]

The very formation of an international body in 1896 also touched off dreams of a transoceanic general strike to raise standards in all the port industries. Flush with a sense of power and possibility, the British dockside labor leaders reached out with considerable diplomacy to potential long-distance allies. Looking to time an international action, they thus sought the Swede Lindley's advice on avoiding "bad weather" in the Scandinavian ports. Learning that the Swedes were contemplating May actions, Wilson implored Lindley to wait until July, for "otherwise you will upset the arrangements of the men in America, France, the Continent and United Kingdom."[29] While the big event did not come off in 1897, coordination remained the name of the game. Amid a strike on the Tyne in 1899, Wilson, for example, bent over backward to draw on Lindley's sympathies. His own men, he told Lindley, had decided to demand the British union rate for Swedish and Norwegian vessels docked in Newcastle. "With regard to your countrymen, I must give them every credit for the noble manner in which they have stood their guns. The only blacklegs we have at present time are Britishers. Very few foreign ones indeed. And the hardest part of the fighting has been done by Swedes and Norwegians."[30]

The spirit of cross-border militancy, perhaps not surprisingly, proved at once intoxicating and frustrating to the affected labor leadership. On the one hand, Tom Mann, a kind of one-man troubadour of discontent, found an expanded market for his early proto-syndicalist dreams. In a leaflet, presumed to be written by Mann, ITF affiliates were encouraged to consider the strategy of "ca'canny," or worker slowdowns: "It is a simple and handy phrase which is used to describe a new instrument or policy which may be used by the workers in place of a strike. If two Scotchmen are walking together, and one walks too quickly for the other, he says to him, 'ca'canny mon, Ca'canny!' which means 'Go easy, man, go easy.'"[31] On the other hand, while all ITF signatories might endorse an international strike in principle, the mechanics of mobilization could prove difficult and irksome. Mann summarized the problems of coordination with his own Anglocentric inflection in 1897: "Germany declared strongly in favour of complete organisation, but was by no means enthusiastic in favour of striking. The French were very pronounced in favour of a general strike as soon as the organisation were sufficiently perfect in the respective countries. The Belgian and Dutch declared themselves ready for action immediately the signal should be given."[32]

Even as ITF membership increasingly shifted toward railway and other land-based transportation affiliates that diluted its original British-based maritime base—with the international headquarters moving to Hamburg in 1904—sailor unionism continued to provoke the biggest international upheavals.[33] Undoubtedly, the largest prewar action—and one that still must rank highly in the annals of multilateral labor militancy—was the seamen's and dockworkers' strike of 1911. The product of a full two decades of skirmishing with the Shipping Federation, which itself had officially gone international in 1909, the actions begun by Wilson's Seamen were carefully calculated. Having previously demanded that the Shipping Federation accept creation of a National Conciliation Board to hear issues of wages, manning, port payments, and unimpeded union representation, Wilson, by mid-1910, was beating the drums for international strike action.[34] With plans ratified in August by the ITF International Congress meeting in Copenhagen, Wilson counseled ITF general secretary Herman

Jochade, "We should hold propaganda meetings and preach the doctrine of 'Get Ready for the fight' at any moment."[35]

When the fight began, a bit ahead of the secretly circulated June 14, 1911, starting date, it proceeded with great verve. With coincident seamen's actions in the Netherlands, Belgium, the U.S. Atlantic coast, as well as England, and with immediate sympathy actions—followed up by collective bargaining demands of their own—by dockworkers in the affected countries, shipowners felt an immediate sting.[36] A big break for the strikers came when Liverpool ocean liner companies, the biggest group of shipowners outside the Shipping Federation, allowed each of their affiliated companies to make its own settlement. As a result, concessions by one firm set a pattern for the next. For its part, the Shipping Federation, practiced at assembling blacklegs to break strikes at a single port, had no solution to replacing an estimated 120,000 workers across multiple port sites.[37] Equally fortuitously, the British Liberal government, led by Herbert Asquith and David Lloyd George, allowed Local Government Board minister John Burns, a hero of the 1889 dock strike, to press employers for a conciliatory settlement.[38]

Ten days into the conflict, Wilson reported to ITF headquarters like a dutiful, and triumphant, field commander: "We have badly defeated the Shipping Fed. at London, Glasgow, Liverpool, Shields, Newcastle, Sunderland, Blyth, Middlboro, Bristol, Swansea, Newport, Barry including substantial advances in wages and wiped the Shipping Fed. clean out at these places, compelled shipowners to give absolute recognition to the Union.... Such a victory is unknown in England for Seamen. . . . Dear Comrades, many owners surrendering the [Shipping] Federation blood ticket, now our policy is to wage war on the non Unionist, drive him into the Union at the point of a bayonet."[39] And indeed, by December, with the breadth of U.K. ports under its control, the Seamen had reportedly added 70,000 members, making it a major trade union power for the first time in twenty years.[40] In the process, the seamen's strike in Britain had spread to dockworkers, railway workers, and, beyond the transport nexus, flour milling workers at Hull, cottonseed meal workers in Liverpool, and, in London, "15,000 women and girls employed in biscuit, jam and other factories."[41]

Some have even pointed to the influence of a "syndicalist" or direct-action socialist streak in the unfolding events, as symbolized by the presence of Tom Mann, who associated himself with small but vociferous organizations backing revolutionary industrial unionism by the time of

FIGURE 5.1. "In Mid-Ocean during the Seamen's Strike." The highpoint of prewar ITF effectiveness (as well as Havelock Wilson's last hurrah as a committed trade union internationalist), the great maritime strike of June 1911 idled some 120,000 seamen and dockworkers across the Atlantic world and won sweeping contract advances for the affected national unions. In this cheeky cartoon equally unsympathetic to both the striking workers and the rich clientele of passenger liners, the *New York Times* imagines the role reversals hypothetically enforced by the strike. *New York Times*, June 18, 1911.

his return to England from Australasia in May 1910.[42] Less dependent on theory than on the short-term coincidence of trade union militancy and employer recalcitrance, what might be called the "syndicalist mood" of the day drew primarily on pent-up hatred for the strikebreaking practices of the Shipping Federation among industrial workers themselves. Thus, when a boat of blacklegs appeared at Liverpool in June 1911, Mann drew cheers from a crowd of strikers with this visceral denunciation: "If that boat were sunk before she had time to moor correctly, [I] would for [my] part rejoice. If [I] were able to sink the ship [myself, I] would do it. . . . As for the scabs on board, the sooner they went to heaven or hell—according to which they were most fitted—the better for the world."[43]

For both seamen and dockworkers, the 1911 strike was a smashing success. What had begun as a demand for negotiations with a seemingly all-powerful Shipping Federation had ended, port by port, in major concessions from Shipping Federation–affiliated employers. Though out-and-out union recognition proved the exception to the rule, the hold of the employers' "Federation tickets" had been broken.[44] In Liverpool, for example, cooperating seamen and ships' stewards had won a ten shilling per week pay increase, abolition of the employer-run medical examination, no victimization of strikers, and union recognition, including the right to wear the union badge and permission for union officials to enter the companies' ships.[45] Similarly, New York strikers on coastal steamers extracted significant concessions from management on matters of food, quarters, and wages after a mere two-day walkout.[46] Dockworkers, at most of the striking ports, had done just as well, generally gaining 20 percent in wages along with a slight reduction in hours. At the strike's settlement in August 1911, Ben Tillett virtually taunted his capitalist antagonists: "A hard world, my masters, but we demagogues manage to live in it; and to live virilly [*sic*], pugnaciously, agitating, and winning; to the disgusted amazement of hireling slanderers and refined futilities. But the fight's the thing: the strike."[47] Even the moderate *New York Times* found something to commend about strikers who "gained as much as this and have done it so quickly, with few breaches of the peace and those not serious." With sympathetic condescension, the *Times* allowed that perhaps its middle-class readers should "[revise] accepted opinions as to the intelligence and character of the men who form the crews of the modern steamer." No longer the rough sailor type of yore but rather a mixture of hotel stewards and engineers, the steamship worker had proved "a good deal of a man, after all."[48] Even as the international reach of what was originally envisioned as a "world-wide walkout" proved limited, the significant achievements won by the strikers seemed to augur well for the larger project.[49]

Organizing a Multinational, Multiracial Workforce

To be sure, the translation of solidarity from rhetorical commitment to international union practice had, from the beginning, proved an uneven process. Union leaders themselves clearly recognized the grip that national and even more localistic loyalties carried among rank-and-file workers. When push came to shove in labor-management disputes, the appeal to "nation" (or ethnic peoplehood) often took precedence over "class." The Seamen's campaign against Shipping Federation tickets in Glasgow in 1898 was typical. Engaging its hard-core base, even as it hatched an international strategy via the ITF, the union appealed to "the men on the Clyde [who] are standing true and staunch and loyal—as Scotsmen are expected to do. Scotsmen—the real natives—would sooner starve than act as blacklegs."[50]

Such appeals to blood ties among union men worked fine unless or until one "blood" came up against another in the workforce. Then, union leaders had to decide whether to try to muffle or placate national and ethnic divisions. Maritime unions etched a zigzag pattern here. Joining the internationalist mobilization as secretary of the incipient ITF in 1896, British dockworkers' chief Ben Tillett grandly declared, "The interests of Labour the world over are identical, and fully recognizing this fact are prepared to help on International action. Capitalists and the [upper] classes generally cunningly contrive to keep the workers in their respective countries fighting each other with Industrial instruments, or military weapons, creating racial and national hatred, and it is our desire to bury such hatred to ensure the International Solidarity of Labour." Addressing his Swedish counterpart, Charles Lindley, Tillett openly apologized for and repudiated the action of any British countrymen who had scabbed on Swedish dockers or seamen in a recent strike at the port of Stockholm.[51] Yet, this was the same Tillett who, as champion of London dockers in 1889, had assailed government policy that permitted the "dregs and scum of the Continent to make foetid, putrid and congested our already crowded slums."[52]

In retrospect, the ideologically more conservative Havelock Wilson seems to have taken a more consistently pragmatic and calculating view toward cooperation across borders. By 1890, some 40,000 out of a claimed total membership of 90,000 sailor union members were non-British nationals. Before the 1889 strike wave, Wilson sought incrementally to reduce the presence of foreign nationals; those with four years' or more experience on British ships (estimated at 40–50 percent of the total) would be accepted on the same terms as "Britishers," but other non-nationals would have to pay special union entrance fees of up to a prohibitive twenty pounds.[53] Later, Wilson allowed that his policy caused friction with the very international sailor forces he was trying to coordinate in industrial action, but he saw no direct contradiction. "My view was that as long as foreign seamen accepted wages lower than ours it would always be a menace to our trade, and our policy should be directed towards encouraging the foreign seamen to organize in their own countries, so as to remove unfair competition. Foreigners of all kinds were plentiful, and I found them good Trade Unionists."[54]

Not surprisingly, the early ITF found the search for agreement across national lines a difficult matter at both a practical and political level. British unions regularly complained that their international union counterparts were in arrears in assessments to the federation treasury. Moreover, there were seemingly infinite points of view on political subjects. At the Amsterdam Congress in 1904, French delegates set up several barriers to international strike action; the Dutch and Swedes quarreled over the proper control of new machinery; and the French, Italians, and Germans divided over the propriety of an antimilitarism resolution at a trade-union conference. Indeed, reverberations from the still-fresh Boer War and resentment by many delegations of what appeared a British-Swedish leadership alliance helped spur the move of ITF headquarters to Germany that same year.[55] As the two largest bodies of organized workers, British and German labor federations regularly sparred during the early ITF years. The Hamburg-based Secretariat, for example, complained of an "ostrich policy," adopted by British unions to the problem of British-based strikebreakers. British labor leaders responded that they regularly confronted blacklegs, but, given the huge unemployment problem in British ports, it was unrealistic to expect full compliance with trade union norms. British representatives further explained that the Germans were "too young in the movement and too excitable" while claiming that their own countrymen, "with their longer experience, took things more coolly." Paul Muller, the German ITF and transport workers' leader, responded that the Germans had objectively reported the facts and that the Brits should "hardly expect to be given a diploma for the mass export of blacklegs."[56]

Among all the major maritime union delegations, the least inclined toward strong international organization were undoubtedly the Americans, as represented by Andrew Furuseth, head of the International Seamen's Union. Perpetually fearing that relatively high U.S. wage rates would be diluted by any move toward international standards, Furuseth's interest in collaborative engagements was always tepid at best. In 1896, for example, just as the federation that would become the ITF was being formed, the Norwegian-born Furuseth cautioned fellow Scandinavian Charles Lindley against "raising hopes to have them dashed to the ground" and "talk for talk [*sic*] sake." Noting that the U.S. merchant marine was "about 50% Scandinavian," Furuseth declared himself "in favor of international organization amongst seamen especially but think it must be based upon national Unions."[57] By 1913, following a generally dyspeptic U.S. response to the 1911 uprising, bitter divisions had grown within U.S. seamen's ranks, with both the Atlantic coast and Great Lakes constituents of the U.S.-based ISU in open rebellion against Furuseth's leadership.[58] One of the leaders of the opposition, New York attorney and former sailor George Bodine, appealed to Jochade, the ITF, and the "European system of organization" as a lifeline for those caught in Furuseth's "'one-man' out-fit": "[Furuseth] believes in keeping each craft separate with no central affiliation of any kind if he can help it. He is opposed to any kind of Waterfront Federation of Waterfront Trades or in fact to any kind of Transportation Department and the International Seamen's Union of America is only part of the [ITF] because the Seamen forced the American International into it against Mr. Furuseth's opposition."[59]

The challenge of mutual understanding was likely exacerbated by basic language barriers as well as political-cultural divides. Judging from ITF publications, even the most basic communication sometimes broke down. The *Korrespondenzblatt* ("Correspondence Sheet"), published out of Hamburg in five languages, thus tripped over its appeal to English-language readers: "The first number of this official paper . . . was received very kindly by all the organizations. The necessity of this was confessed on every side because one cannot think of a Central-organization without such intellectual joining-link. The pulsation of the vital-power of our ITF shall be expressed in our *Korrespondenzblatt*. . . . The comrades of all countries ought to take it as their duty to make the *Korrespondenzblatt* a crystal-bowl, into which all our intellectual interests flow together."[60] Similarly, it is likely that the passion behind General Secretary Jochade's invocation—"The right of self-preservation of all the organizations commands imperiously the connexion with similar beings, which carry on the same battle with the same interests"—lost something in translation.[61]

However halting was the international partnership between European, North American, and Australasian trade unionists, the presence of Africans and Asians in international waters posed yet more contentious issues for the Atlantic-based movement. On repeated occasions, for example, ITF leaders made mention of the need to extend Western-based trade union standards to the poorer regions of the world; for example, the first resolution of the British NUS at the Vienna conference in 1908 called for greater organizational and propaganda activity among "foreign-tongued and coloured seamen."[62] Even as a matter of abstract principle (let alone practical priority), however, the idea triggered dissent. Furuseth, leader of the American delegation, opposed the motion. Though defending the long-established inclusion of Negro sailors in the merchant marine, he insisted—in anticipation of the English-language clauses in the La Follette Act of 1915—that it "would be impossible to tolerate the yellow race on American ships—that would mean handing over all our jobs to them."[63] Indeed, two years previously, Furuseth and other ISU representatives vigorously defended their formal ban on permitting Japanese sailors on U.S. vessels. Fending off criticism from the German ITF newspaper editor, a Furuseth confidant, Walter Macarthur, struck back that "when our friends, who seem to have not even the faintest idea of the subject matter, advise us to organize the little brown men, we begin to lose patience. . . . If the Oriental hordes ever commence to invade Germany then we will carefully consider the arguments of the German [correspondent] Paul Muller."[64] Lindley backed the American position: "I am firmly against Socialism being used as a dogma to justify overpopulation by the yellow race. . . . They have been living in their own way for a large number of years and it is not possible to persuade them to reach a higher level of culture." Lindley himself, it should be noted, was quickly chastised by a Norwegian representative for discriminatory attitudes that had, in the past, extended to opposing the employment of Galicians (Poles) in the Swedish merchant marine.[65]

Yet, out-and-out racism or overt stigmatization of entire culture groups was notably a minority position within the ITF prior to World War I. The dominant position within the multilateral body was more idealistic, a cautious yet willing embrace of "the other" within the confines of trade union standards of conduct. German sailors' union leader Paul Muller represented the majority view at the Vienna Congress in attempting to soft-pedal ethnic divisions within the world's sea traffic, without actually denying the problem of ethnic difference. Unions, he argued, could not control hiring in any case; that was in the employers' hands. If others were willing to work under the same conditions as European or American seamen, then there should be no objection. Yet in his exchange with the Americans over Japanese exclusion, Muller himself lapsed into ethnic stereotyping. While insisting that the "Japanese are [an] industrial nation, a culture-nation of [the] first class," whose workers, once organized, could be counted on "to battle against . . . the brutality of the sea-capitalists," Muller allowed that the Chinese were another story. Because they appeared to forswear the material needs of other workers, the Chinese admittedly represented "under certain circumstances really a danger for the maritime workers of all the culture countries."[66] The slur against the Chinese notwithstanding, the British-German alliance that defined ITF policy was formally color-blind. The principle of transferability—that is, that unionized seamen could transfer freely from one national ship to another—was already written into the ITF constitution. To be sure, a "utopian" British proposal for uniform membership dues worldwide never came to pass. Yet, the broad principle of free exchange of members as well as the idea of paying one's union dues at any authorized port (from which they would be re-sent to one's home country) remained bedrock policies.[67]

No doubt, sea labor functioned through the decades (and indeed centuries) not only as a forum for interethnic and interracial contact but also as a conveyor belt for political radicalism. Not for nothing did socialist and syndicalist factions abound in maritime unions the world over. Likely, part of the controls that national governments tried to attach to maritime occupations stemmed from fears of alien and subversive thoughts as well as the "disreputable" lifestyles associated with sailor-town culture. Just as historians Peter Linebaugh and Marcus Rediker tracked the "hidden history of the Revolutionary Atlantic" for an earlier era, one could certainly extend their narrative (though that is not the task here) of "motley"-based, oceanic rebellion into the early twentieth century. To take but one example, future Vietnamese Communist leader Ho Chi Minh first enlarged his worldview while serving as a kitchen helper on a French steamship liner in 1911. A stay in Marseilles first connected him to books and newspapers, even as further maritime employment facilitated travel to the United States, where he reportedly heard Marcus Garvey speak in Harlem and encountered Korean nationalists who left a lasting imprint on his political outlook.[68] In and of themselves, in short, seafaring occupations offered some degree of political and personal openings whatever the formal policies of employer, nation, or even trade union dictated.

Questions of the "foreign-born" and the "colored" sailor took on special meaning within the demography of the British empire itself. As early as the 1820s, the East India Company had hired native Indian seafarers on special work contracts, including wages at one-fifth to one-third of those prevailing for European sailors. Subsequent British legislation codified such "Asiatic articles" for "lascar" (South Asian) or "Chinese" (East Asian) hires, limiting them to round-trip voyages beginning and ending in Asia or restricting their geographical reach altogether.[69] Contemporary concerns were enhanced by the falloff of homegrown recruits. "Steam and the screw propeller," lamented one 1895 observer, "have almost killed that spirit of adventure which has helped to make the British flag evident and respected on every sea. . . . Prudent parents more often prevail upon their boys to seek safer and more lucrative employment on dry land."[70] According to parliamentary testimony in 1906, an estimated 176,000 British seamen had been supplemented by 39,000 "foreigners" and 42,000 lascars; deep-sea voyages, moreover, were often nearly half-manned by recruits from abroad.[71]

At least until World War I, Havelock Wilson, as both trade union and parliamentary representative (1892–95, 1906–10, 1918–22) of the seamen's cause, trod a position that might be characterized as one of indirect protectionism.[72] His collaboration in the passage of the Merchant Shipping Act of 1906, which tried implicitly by means of accommodation directives, safety standards, and language tests to limit the numbers of both foreign and colonial seamen in British ports (see chapter 3), is illustrative. While shipowner advocates played the "difference" card, suggesting that lascars really did not like so much air and that overly drafty quarters would not suit people of a tropical "temperament," Wilson insisted that he had "no objection to any man on the ground of his nationality or his colour, . . . but it is not right in principle that foreign seamen should be used for the purpose of lowering the conditions of employment of our own men in our own country." Denying any racial aversion to lascar (or Chinese) hires, Wilson stuck to the trade union principle that the regulations regarding sailor welfare on board British ships should be universal and uniform. In particular, he challenged the separate standard of forty to fifty cubic feet of sleeping space for lascars versus the standard seventy-two cubic feet for white men. Indeed, he cited a medical argument that lascars needed a larger, healthier space, precisely because they were, on balance, "physically weaker."[73] To be sure, Indian seamen themselves were hardly mollified by what one Bombay protest petition called the "fatal philanthropy" of those who would willingly sacrifice Indian seafarers' very livelihood for the principle of better shipboard lodgings.[74]

FIGURE 5.2. An exoticized view of Indian seamen (1929). This staged portrait of Indian seamen on board the SS *Viceroy of India* (1929) offers, as historian Ravi Ahuja has documented, a good example of official ship photography meant to exoticize lascars, who ordinarily wore Western clothing unless specifically "outfitted" in native garb for their role as stewards on passenger lines. See Ravi Ahuja, "Mobility and Containment: The Voyages of South Asian Seamen, c. 1900–1960," *International Review of Social History*, 51 (2006): 122. Photograph courtesy of the National Maritime Museum, Greenwich, United Kingdom.

Wilson and the union advocates failed, in any case, in overcoming the imperial division of maritime labor standards, when British subjects on "Asiatic articles" were pointedly exempted from the rules governing accommodation and language competency in the 1906 act.[75] The issue of Chinese labor, with rising complaints of the substitution of Chinese for white crews in the oceangoing trade, increasingly rankled in the prewar years. In words that would echo on both sides of the Atlantic, a British union leader railed in 1914 that "white seamen are doomed. They cannot compete with a handful of rice and 8d per day. . . . The man who talks equality in this respect is not a Socialist; he is simply crazy and beyond hope."[76] By 1913, Wilson, who had remained restrained on this point (perhaps due to his own early friendship with Chinese fishermen in the Pacific Islands), was himself calling for the complete exclusion of Chinese labor from British ships.[77]

So long as they remained indirect rather than openly discriminatory in their methods of employment protection, Wilson's attitude and the Seamen's position on foreign and even "colored" labor jockeyed restlessly in these years with the ambitious call of the ITF for international solidarity. The latter was eloquently represented by one Eugene Gildermeisen, who, identifying himself as a "foreigner" who had sailed the previous twenty years on British ships and joined the sailors' union as a union pioneer in 1887, appealed in 1905 "to my comrades (Britishers and foreigners) to cease caviling amongst themselves as regards the place of their birth":

> I have heard Britishers often argue that they could not see their way to join a Union which admitted foreigners to membership. Now, to my mind, this is foolnishness [*sic*] of the worst kind. If the Britisher were to study his interest his one effort would be to get as many foreigners as possible to join the organization. . . . When first I commenced to sail in British vessels a decided preference was given to Scandinavians. When it became evident that these were just as keen on the question of wages and rights as the Britishers, shipowners turned their attention to the Germans, who, they said, were more obedient and reliable and not so likely to give the trouble which Britishers and Scandinavians did. After a year or two more it was discovered that the Germans also had their ideas about decent wages, good food, reasonable hours, etc. Then came the Italians, then the Greeks, then the Turks, and in the last resource, the Lascars and Chinamen are hailed as the salvation of the shipowning community. The fact is that the owners saw that these various nationalities, on acquiring experience of British ships, insisted upon having the same conditions as Britishers had.[78]

If Gildermeisen's logic seemed more than confirmed by his own experience, the events of his era too often scrambled the cooperative logic he held so dear.

Impact of World War

The springtime of international maritime solidarity decidedly ended in World War I. The toll, as it turned out, was taken both by the war itself and by a less-predictable turn in labor-management relations (especially in Great Britain) triggered by wartime circumstances.

The conflict that pitted German and English armed forces directly against each other by August 1914 tore at the political foundation of the ITF, not to mention any larger project of Euro-American working-class unity. Immediately sensing the costs involved, key parties at the time initially tried to keep communicative and cooperative channels open across enflamed borders. Thus, as thousands of merchant mariners docked in "enemy" ports were arrested and interned by both the Central Powers and the Allies, labor leaders on both sides initially tried to ease their burden while hoping for a quick end to the war. The American Andrew Furuseth, for example, generally friendly to the Germans and even a confessed admirer of the emperor, sought reassurance from German ITF leader Herman Jochade that British detainees not be "ill-treated in any way—that would not be German."[79] In England, Havelock Wilson went further. For the 5,000 German seamen initially taken ashore at the beginning of the war, the Seamen stepped in, with permission from the British government, and purchased Eastcote, a remote estate near Northampton. There, without barriers or guards, and equipped with a hospital and rations of beer and tobacco, the men were housed and fed on a mere pledge of honor not to escape.[80]

Of all the maritime leaders, the most politically conservative and generally least interested in measures of international cooperation, Furuseth, was also the most sanguine about the war's likely impact. Writing Jochade in April 1915, he could not stem his admiration for German seamanship and technology: "If war had been delayed another fifteen years, Germany would have driven the English from the Ocean. Seapower is in the Seamen, and your submarines are surely proving this up to the hilt." War between nations, in Furuseth's view, was inevitable, and the sooner such natural forces resolved themselves, the better. "I believe that [the war] came out of the ground—the human mind—and could not be prevented while it might have been delayed. . . . About the cry of peace of our socialist friends I never took that to mean anything but lack of serious thought. I was perfectly sure that when the struggle should come the socialists would lay aside their theories and become real Germans, Englishmen, Frenchmen and so forth. The feeling of RACE is too strong to be overcome by half-baked theories. When the war is over there will be struggles between men about the best means to promote human welfare and that is proper."[81]

Perhaps it was also inevitable that once war came, fellow feeling across belligerent national lines would vanish. In the seamen's case, the fatal blow to solidarity fell with U-boat attacks on Allied shipping, punctuated by the May 7, 1915, attack on the *Lusitania*. Inflamed not only by the latter atrocity but by the seeming indifference, even exultation, of the German detainees in England to the loss of British civilian life, Wilson dramatically changed his tune. "I always thought we were at war with the Pan-Prussian Military

Party," he reportedly told a friend. "Now I know we are at war with the German People."[82] The Seamen's Union soon turned Eastcote over to the military, and the German seamen were relocated behind barbed wire and bayonets. Wilson's own outrage against the Germans now knew no bounds. By August 1917, an international conference he organized in London blamed German seamen (many of whom had been conscripted into naval service) as much as their leaders for the "inhuman conduct of submarine warfare" and demanded both reparations and a boycott of German seamen themselves when the war was over.[83]

Attempting in vain to ride out the storm, the ITF's newspaper was itself a fair barometer of the period's rising tensions. In December 1914, British ITF secretary Robert Williams sparred respectfully with General Secretary Herman Jochade over the causes of the war. In laying blame, Williams tried to separate the "Prussian War Lords" and "German militarism" from the mass of German workers. "Let us who can," he counseled, "be calm during the next few weeks. Let us rigorously suppress the blood lust in ourselves, and among those whom we can influence. . . . When we succumb to the 'news' fever, fostered and inflamed by a reactionary Press, and purchase their loathsome gloatings, may we remember that this army repulsed, or that army slaughtered, was composed of the flower of the European manhood. Conscripts today and potential trade unionists tomorrow." Then Williams made direct appeal to recent labor history of pan-European, white working-class cooperation: "[The] German fleet may easily contain reservists from the German working class who contributed £5000 to the London Transport workers when they were fighting the Patriotic London Employers. . . . Let it never be forgotten that the Patriotic shipowners of this Country have displaced 60,000 seamen and firemen in our mercantile marine by 60,000 Chinese and other Asiatics." Jochade, himself a young reservist soon to be called to active duty, politely chided his British comrade for hanging the war on "German militarism." "What about British militarism?" he countered. "It seizes all sea-routes and oppresses the seafaring trade of all nations in the most reckless manner possible." Hatred of the British, he argued, explained "why every German stands behind his government, ready to sacrifice everything . . . for the downfall of German commerce and industry would also cause a disruption of our political and trade union movement."[84]

Soon, the tone of fraternal exchange worsened, appreciably. By June 1915, dockers' union leader Ben Tillett, previously a self-styled "internationalist," identified a struggle between England fighting for the "liberty of the world" and "the terrible power of the Prussian brute [which must be] destroyed forever."[85] After December 1916, all communication from the Berlin Secretariat of the ITF came to an end.[86]

Nor did some tempers heal even after German military defeat. In 1917, British Trades Union Congress delegates, attempting to attend a Stockholm conference regarding postwar aims among a revived international labor movement, were stopped by a Seamen's Union blockade of ships. In a tear-filled explanation of his union's action, Wilson denounced those who would attend for being willing to "take the bloodstained hands of murderers within your own."[87] Under the left-wing Dutch socialist Edo Fimmen, the ITF generally sought to reconstitute the forces of international unionism via a new Amsterdam-based Secretariat beginning in 1919. Indeed, as early as 1924, Fimmen was envisioning a world where national union federations took a backseat to what today are called "global unions." As Fimmen analogized, "When capitalism changed in the direction of national organization, the conduct of the industrial struggle passed from the control of local trade unions to that of national trade unions. So now, in the period of struggle which has begun with the world war . . . , the leadership must pass from the national organizations to the International Trade Secretariats."[88] Wilson would have none of it. Demanding a formal apology from German trade union officialdom for U-boat attacks and a two-year blacklist of all German merchant seamen, the Seamen disdained reaffiliation with the ITF. Instead, with backing from the isolationist Furuseth, Wilson led seamen's unions from thirteen Allied and neutral countries into the breakaway International Seafarers' Federation, which would constitute the official voice of the seamen at the founding conferences and early convention-setting sessions of the International Labor Organization (see chapter 6). The International Seafarers' Federation ultimately expired in 1925, and its affiliates returned to the ITF.[89]

But Wilson's differences with the postwar trade union movement rested on more than war-induced emotions. The fact was that the maritime labor relations, in his eyes at least, had arrived at a happy state of mutual interests that left no further room for strategies of class-wide mobilization or even trade union militancy. Wilson's longtime aim had been to achieve negotiated agreements between shipowners and the union—effectively, a seat at the table. Now he had what he wanted. The new departure began at the war's outbreak with a flat increase of one pound per month (raised another pound per month by the end of the year) above the official union rate for all seamen in merchant vessels requisitioned by the admiralty. Pledging cooperation—including a no-strike, no-slowdown pledge—while resisting out-and-out conscription, the union facilitated the transfer of some 8,000 seamen to His Majesty's Service during the first two days of war. The real breakthrough for British seamen, however, came from outside pressure. American entry into the war in April 1917 occasioned an "Atlantic Agreement" among U.S. shipowners, Furuseth's ISU, and the U.S. Shipping Board that raised wages for able-bodied seamen and firemen to a level nearly twice that prevailing in the British trade. This combination of high wages and a newly expanded U.S. fleet, together with the "right to quit" already enshrined in the new La Follette Act, effective as of March 1916, set off alarm bells in the British government. By mid-1917, recent British recruits composed a full third of the U.S. merchant marine, and British prosecutions for desertion multiplied. Never had the seamen on either side of the Atlantic possessed greater economic and political leverage. The result was the formation of the British National Maritime Board (NMB) in November 1917, at once stipulating a new, national wage at nearly double prewar rates and centralized, collective bargaining. Henceforth, an industry-wide union shop would prevail across Britain, in a kind of cartelized arrangement between the sailors' union, the Shipping Federation, and the NMB, presided over by shipowner Sir Walter Runciman. The arrangement was further consolidated in 1922 by institution of the "PC5 system," a work ticket dispatched only to Wilson's own loyal union members.[90]

In the end, however, creation of the NMB also "precipitated a critical shift to collaboration."[91] Wilson's insider status with industry leaders led him to readily accede to shipowner demands in light of falling postwar freight rates. In an attempt to maintain employment levels, pay cuts of £4.50 were accepted in stages from 1921 to 1923. After acceding to another 10 percent wage cut in August 1925, Wilson, the former international strike leader, helped squash international sailor resistance centered in South Africa and Australasia.[92] More famously, Wilson's refusal to permit the seamen to join other transport workers in support of the miners as part of the General Strike of 1926 permanently "blackened" his reputation in labor circles and contributed to the temporary disaffiliation of the NUS from the TUC in 1928.[93]

Moreover, not only did the union abandon militant or solidaristic action; but as the postwar labor market shrank, it also presided over an intricate wage hierarchy defined by racial and citizenship status and fully codified in NMB regulations. Despite patriotic talk of "British men for British ships," growing numbers of colonial seamen were hired well below NMB rates as contract laborers. But rather than contest the multiple standards for non-white workers as he once had done, Wilson now consented to a hardening of official racial inequalities. A Yellow Peril campaign, already indulged before the war, attracted even greater support and political success amid nationalistic wartime passions: in 1919, the NMB at once gave preference to British subjects over non-British Chinese and "Alien Colored" seamen while also generally excluding the targeted minorities from standard (white) pay rates.[94] The discriminatory initiatives culminated in the Home Office's Coloured Alien Seamen's Order of 1925, which, by singling out black seamen to produce British passports or register as aliens (at a time when few seamen, white or black, carried passports), sought to exclude black seamen from Britain altogether.[95] The result, an ever more divided sea-laboring force rather than an all-white one, ultimately weakened the union and played into shipowners' hands in the form of wage cuts and other concessions. The constant threat by employers to hire cheaper labor outside standard, national rates, however, also allowed union officials to control their own rank and file. For the union, there was a certain material payoff as well. While openly condemning foreign hires, the union quietly benefited from the lesser contracts of lascars and others who, though ineligible to collect from union pension funds, nevertheless paid into them in weekly installments.[96]

Although consistently hardheaded and resolutely result-oriented in his moves, Havelock Wilson unquestionably underwent something of a "sea change" as a union leader in World War I. From being one of the most aggressive of the prewar "new unionists," he emerged, post-NMB, as perhaps the foremost union spokesmen for labor-management cooperation, a position that helped win him awards as a Commander of the British Empire in 1917 and as Companion of Honour in 1922. Such newfound respectability was clearly a source of pride for a former ship's cook. Among the highlights of his life, his truncated 1925 autobiography (meant to encompass two volumes but never getting beyond the 1890s of volume 1) recalls an early encounter with the Prince of Wales (the future King Edward), who, unlike the condescending Board of Trade negotiators, treated the then-controversial labor leader with respect. "I found him," wrote Wilson, "a real English Gentleman, and I can say, without qualification, that there is nothing finer in the world than an English Gentleman."[97] In addition to the pull of social acceptance, the combination of mistrust bordering on hatred for those who had joined the Central Powers and a racial disdain for "backward" peoples now pushed Wilson away from internationalist organizing strategies. Perhaps not surprisingly, therefore, by the time he penned his memoir, he was openly disparaging the "solidarity mania" of his younger days.[98]

PART III

A World Fit for Seafarers?

6

A Sea of Difference

THE INTERNATIONAL LABOR ORGANIZATION AND THE SEARCH FOR COMMON STANDARDS, 1919–1946

If the age of sail regularly rendered seafaring a romantic, if also forbidding, occupation in the eyes of landlubbers, the realities of the age of steam presented a rather different picture. Though sailing vessels continued to carry a substantial portion of the world's trade up to World War I (even if these often applied steam engines as auxiliary means of propulsion), the twentieth-century configuration would be one of iron (and later steel) hulls and steam (and later diesel) engines. The transformation also inevitably complicated an older comradeship below deck. Employers increased the percentage of unskilled workers: not only was the crew now divided between deckhands, firemen (or engine-room coal stokers), and stewards (where there were passengers), but the distinctions in pay and status between officers and engineers on the upper end and "ratings" on the lower grew ever starker. Just as the scales had measurably tipped in Britain from sail to steam, gentleman-sailor-politician Thomas Brassey, reportedly the first to circumnavigate the world in a private yacht, pointedly declared, "The rise of steam caused the separation of seamen into classes more distinctly than was previously the case."[1] By 1913, the president of the American Steamship Association utterly dismissed union attempts to maintain a three-year service requirement for "able-bodied" quotas and status: "The work performed by the deck hands aboard a modern steamer, with short masts, little rigging, and almost no sails, is of the most ordinary kind of unskilled labor that can be imagined, consisting for the most part of washing decks, scrubbing paint, and polishing brasswork, the center of gravity, so to speak, having shifted from the deck to the engine department, where the really technical part of a steamer's work is now performed. . . . To insist that it requires three years' experience to acquire adequate facility is 'absurd'—three months at most would be amply sufficient."[2]

Industrial Seamen in Popular Culture

However exaggerated some claims to the diminution of required seafaring skill might prove, the apparent transformation of maritime work certainly left an outsized mark on both the writers and the lawmakers who represented the seamen before a larger public. If early-nineteenth-century Anglo-American writers, for example, famously presented the seaman as something of a symbol of human freedom under threat from various antagonists, their early-twentieth-century descendants reconstructed the mariner's image for more modern but less heroic times. As a jumble of unskilled and none-too-bright laborers recruited from across the world for an arduous but predictable work-life, the image of the seaman had lost its exotic luster. The dean of the new, realist "sea writers" was Joseph Conrad, who, as a young Polish émigré, had worked on eighteen (mostly British) ships during eleven years of employment.[3] In what would become a common trope, Conrad juxtaposed an idyllic, manly, pre-industrial age of sail to the conflictual, degraded, and utterly regimented routine of the steamship. Highlighted by his depiction of the disgraceful abandonment by quarreling officers and crew of beleaguered passengers on the wrecked tramp steamer *Patna* in his 1900 novel *Lord Jim*, Conrad effectively disparaged the "industrialization" of the merchant marine.[4]

The theme equally resonated with Eugene O'Neill, who, first inspired by a Conrad novel, shipped out at age twenty-one on one of the disappearing square-riggers and then included the sea in nineteen of his forty-four plays as "an integral part of the action."[5] Driscoll, the hard-living protagonist of O'Neill's early *S.S. Glencairn* series, disparages his steamship workmates who have asked him for a song: "Ye've heard the names av chanties but divil a note av the tune or a loine av the words do ye know. There's hardly a rale deep-water sailor lift on the seas, more's the pity."[6] In starker terms still, Irish stoker Paddy speaking to his American buddy Yank in *The Hairy Ape* (1921) contrasts the days of "clippers wid tall masts touching the sky—fine strong men in them" with that of "bloody engines pounding and throbbing and shaking . . . choking our lungs wid coal dust . . . caged in by steel from a sight of the sky like bloody apes in the Zoo!" Marginalized both on

FIGURE 6.1. Yank in *The Hairy Ape*. Reflecting an increasingly pessimistic, early-twentieth-century view of merchant seamen as an exploited and even brutalized industrial working class, Yank, the fireman on a cruise ship in Eugene O'Neill's *The Hairy Ape* (1921), is a man bereft of family, country, and education "dat don't belong." From the Irish Repertory Theatre production of *The Hairy Ape*, New York City, Nov. 21, 2006, © Carol Rosegg.

ship and off by respectable society, Yank's combustible anger lands him in prison, from where he can identify vicariously with working-class political rebels. Listening from his cell to a denunciation by a U.S. senator of the Industrial Workers of the World as "the Industrial Wreckers of the World," Yank erupts, "Wreckers, dat's de right dope! Dat belongs! Me for dem!"[7]

Another gripping illustration of the downward passage of sailors from exotics to drudges occurs in *The Death Ship* (1926 German edition, 1934 first English edition), a novel by the biographically mysterious writer B. Traven, best known for *The Treasure of the Sierra Madre* (1935). Likely (but not transparently) a German-born national who then moved to the United States and Mexico, the pseudonymous Traven evokes a maritime world of bureaucratic coercion and lifeless toil as witnessed by protagonist Gerald

Gales, an American merchant sailor stranded in Europe without proper papers. With sardonic humor, Traven sketches the struggles of the lower depths of a floating international proletariat amid rising nationalist barriers. Continually deported and effectively locked out of "civilized" society for want of demonstrable citizenship, Gales thus finds a berth only on the "death ship" *Yorikke*, filled with other workers in the same situation: "There have never been so many [death ships] as since the war for liberty and democracy that gave the world passports and immigration restrictions, and that manufactured men without nationalities and without papers by the ten thousand."[8] Literally cast adrift, Gales's shipmates evolve a communicative strategy apparently common to a British-dominated shipping world: "Every sailor of any nationality knows some thirty English words, which he pronounces in such a way that after half an hour you may get a rough idea of what he wishes to say."[9]

Jamaican-born Claude McKay experienced the ethnic diversity of the sea firsthand. Bound for a meeting of the Communist Congress in Moscow in 1922, McKay first worked his way over from New York to London as a stoker on a merchant ship.[10] Both of his two early novels, *Home to Harlem* (1928) and *Banjo* (1929), make reference to the friction of race and work from the author's experience at sea and portside in New York, London, and Marseilles. In the first novel, the main character's freighter "stank between sea and sky: The white sailors who washed the ship would not wash the stokers' water-closet, because they despised the Arabs. And the Arabs themselves made no effort to keep the place clean, although it adjoined their sleeping berth."[11] In the second novel, the southern black vagabond Banjo, hanging out with Afro-Caribbeans in Marseilles, in the end rejects a life at sea, given the hostility that "colored seamen" find there. In particular, he becomes aware of British policy (abetted by the national seamen's union) to drive colored seamen out of England: "Colored seamen who had lived their lives in the great careless tradition, and had lost their papers in low-down places to touts, hold-up men, and passport fabricators, and were unable or too ignorant to show exact proof of their birthplace, were furnished with the new 'Nationality Doubtful' papers. West Africans, East Africans, South Africans, West Indians, Arabs, and Indians—there were all mixed up together. . . . They were agreed that the British authorities were using every device to get all the colored seamen out of Britain and keep them out, so that white men should have their jobs."[12] As McKay, like Traven, recognized, state policy in the post–World War I world had come down hard on wayward, and especially racially marked, seaman.

Industrialized work routines, miserable pay and conditions, the tensions of a polyglot labor force, and the threat of radical upheaval—these were main themes of maritime fiction across the early twentieth century. They were also the themes that International Labor Organization reformers, seeking to bring order and stability to the world's shipping lanes, confronted during the organization's first decades of work. Conceived amid postwar expectations (apocalyptic or millennial, depending upon the observer) of worldwide mass strikes and armed worker uprisings, the ILO might best be considered a "reformers' redoubt" from revolution. The social democrats who led this postwar labor body sought to find capitalist partners willing to make a "deal" in the interests of long-term social stability as well as social justice.[13] That the air was already coming out of the revolutionary Bolshevik balloon as early as 1920 when the ILO got down to business immediately weakened the odds that it could pull off the grand social compromise it sought. Moreover, the ensuing years of rising nationalist tensions dwarfed the very "class conflict" that international labor standards were meant to allay. As a result, momentum slowed and resources dwindled for projects of international cooperation on almost every front, and at the political level one might fairly label the interwar ILO, like its mother-ship the League of Nations, "an almost total failure."[14] That said, the discussions within the organization on policy prescriptions that latter-day commentators would call the "global economy" have a remarkably present-day feel. The ILO thus stands out as *the* pioneer attempt to deal with the effects of globalization on working people.

The United States played a fitful role in the ILO's development. Just as President Woodrow Wilson laid the foundations for the League of Nations, then watched helplessly as his country failed to join, so American Federation of Labor president Samuel Gompers served as a moving spirit for the ILO, only to face the same rebuff from the U.S. Congress. During the Paris Peace Conference, Gompers presided over the Commission on International Labour Legislation that drafted the constitution for the ILO. Within his federation's own ranks, Gompers first prevailed over the vituperative objections to the international body by Andrew Furuseth of the International Seamen's Union. Having won La Follette Act standards, Furuseth was loath to subject his members to what he feared would be a British attempt to undo them. Though Gompers strongly argued for a La Follette–like sailors' right-to-quit-in-any-port article into the commission's charter, once it was rejected by the delegates, he stood firmly, and permanently, as an ILO advocate.[15] Yet, it surely pained the AFL leader, along with other eager American labor internationalists, to be forced to the sidelines during the inaugural International Labor Conference held in October 1919 in Washington, D.C.[16]

Like the League of Nations, the ILO soldiered on in the absence of the world's newest superpower, although, in the case of the ILO, sustained interest from key labor, business, and civic groups led to a reversal of policy and belated U.S. entry in the organization in 1934.[17] Buttressed from the beginning by enthusiastic support from Europe's leading trade union federations, the ILO officially justified its support for labor organization as a contribution to world "peace and harmony": "injustice, hardship and privation," read its charter, stoked "unrest" (that is, Communist revolution) and a downward economic spiral likely only to spur further world war.[18]

Though organically tied to the organizational structure of the League of Nations (and subsequently the United Nations), the ILO took on a distinct representational and juridical process.[19] Adopting the British War Cabinet's formula for incorporating both business and trade union representatives in its counsels, the ILO embraced "tripartism," with each national delegation composed of government (2 votes), employer (1 vote), and worker (1 vote) members.[20] From its inception, the ILO sought to establish "international labor standards" that would, in turn, be accepted and incorporated into the national laws of affiliated governments. Such standards took the form either of conventions (international treaties to be ratified by member states and considered legally binding upon the signatories once adopted by at least two member states) or recommendations (nonbinding guidelines), either of which required a two-thirds majority of voting delegates to be adopted.[21]

The first ILO director, Albert Thomas, a French socialist politician and wartime minister of munitions, approached the organization (which he affectionately called "la maison") with great expectations. As his English-language deputy recalled, "He sensed the stirring of new forms, a recasting of ideas, a greater response and responsibility of the masses. Like Columbus, he saw a world beyond the horizon of his fellows, and he laid his plans and settled his methods on other assumptions than theirs."[22]

Fashioning the ILO's Maritime Conventions

Nowhere, moreover, were the aims and principles of the ILO more quickly on display than within the maritime field. The wartime collaborative efforts

FIGURE 6.2. Albert Thomas and shipowners, 1920. Albert Thomas *(fourth from left)*, French socialist and first International Labour Organization director, 1920–32, meets with shipowners at the Second International Labour Conference in Genoa in June 1920. Courtesy of the ILO Department of Communication.

of Havelock Wilson's National Union of Seamen and the Shipping Federation spilled over into larger efforts of standard-setting within the umbrella of the ILO and its effective sponsorship of a series of seamen's conferences. Beginning in Genoa, Italy, in June 1920, these conferences initially joined representatives of the International Transport Workers' Federation (ITF) and the International Seafarers' Federation (the British-American maritime spinoff from the ITF) with their counterparts from the employers' International Shipping Federation, which had in turn sprouted from its British parent. Despite considerably smaller numbers than other occupational groups like railway workers or dockers, seamen drew more immediate international attention. As historian Bob Reinalda documented, "The ILO adopted more international regulations for the seafarers than for any other group: in the inter-war period a total of 13 conventions and six recommendations [with another 16 added in the immediate post-WW2 (1946–1949) period]."[23]

Those seeking to draft what they called an "International Seamen's Code" at the 1920 Genoa conference—the first targeted industrial conference in the life of the infant ILO—justified their work with reference to both seamen and shipping interests. First, unlike most other workers, seamen were a polyglot, multilingual lot, regularly working "in several countries" as well as "on the world's highway, far removed from the usual reach of public authorities." As such, as an "international community," conference organizers asserted they would be best served by a "uniform law." Second, anticipating the postwar return of cutthroat commercial competition between merchant fleets, the would-be legislators pointed to the difficulties in adopting "any new [national] legislation because of its possible reaction to the advantage of the merchant fleet of a competing country. If, for instance, one State attempts by legislation to secure the improvement of seamen's living accommodations, it may find itself at a disadvantage vis a vis another State which fails or refuses to make a similar change in its laws."[24]

However compelling the larger logic, when it came to international standards, the devil was in the details. In the maritime field, a cardinal illustration of the difficulties of agreement lay in the basic principle of a limitation of working hours. Though "eight hours" had been adopted as a principle as early as the Versailles Treaty, attempts to apply it to maritime work had been tabled at the initial 1919 Washington Labor Conference and left to the 1920 Genoa conference to adjudicate. The thirty countries assembled there, however, quickly confronted a fact that would frustrate the search for common standards for the next century: there was not one encompassing maritime labor market but several. The question thus arose: Could the world body collapse the labor markets into one, or, failing that, could it effectively legislate sliding standards for discrete geographical or ethnic labor forces?

Reporting from a special subcommittee meeting, governmental delegate Charles Hipwood, from the British Board of Trade, first voiced the problem to the assembled delegates in Genoa. Though all British parties agreed that "the present hours of Lascars should be reduced," he averred, "further than that we found it very difficult to go." On top of a draft convention, Article 1 that would adopt the universalistic "principles of the 8 hr day and 48 hr week applied to every seamen employed on board a vessel of whatever nature, public or private" and "without distinction of nationality or race," Hipwood therefore proposed a special "lascar article" allowing for a lower standard, to be subsequently negotiated among government, shipping, and Indian seamen representatives.[25]

As reports from the proceedings made clear, openly imperial powers like Belgium and France as well as the shipping colossus Great Britain, which clothed its South Asian empire in quasi-autonomous legal forms, could not square their interests with a simple, global "eight-hour" labor standard. Rather, they sought to allow for racially and/or geographically derived corollaries to the main trunk of an international principle. As Belgian government spokesman and director of the Royal Observatory Georges Lecointe explained of the African seamen employed by French boats on the Red Sea and black Belgian boatmen in the Congo, "They have not the same ability to work as the white men of course, and so, if a uniform régime were applied to them, the Belgian shipowners could no longer engage these people, and so instead of helping them, they would be deprived of their work." "Certainly," added Lecointe, such "exceptions" would "not last forever. We shall try to suppress them as soon as we can." To encompass all the members of the population targeted for special treatment, he broadened Hipwood's language into a generic-sounding regulatory exception: "Identical principles shall regulate the conditions of employment of all members of the crew working on board a ship in a distinct group, and under the control of a special supervisor."[26]

Among international labor legislators, however, it was not just "imperialist" nation-states or employers who invoked the race card. Several Western ILO worker delegations also feared—and openly sought to curtail—economic competition from a cheaper, "colored" labor force. Australian government delegate Robert Storrie Guthrie, a former seaman and trade union leader whose subsequent legislative advocacy would earn him the title of the "Australian Plimsoll," was perhaps most explicit in rejecting a separate lascar provision within the regulation of hours. Proud of his own country's "white" labor policies ("in Australia [we have] no black labour carrying one pound of cargo or one passenger along the 12,000 miles of our coastline"), he warned that Indian crews must be "confined to the Indian trade" or else "this Conference will have failed." By accepting a reduced standard for Indians, warned Guthrie, the ILO would inadvertently sanction the dreaded "Kalashi watch"—"it means men, with supervisors over them who use a whip, yes, a whip for the purpose of getting them awake when something has got to be done." In short, argued Guthrie, there could be but one seamen's code: "The war has been won, and in the conditions of the settlement of that war was this, that there should be a standardization throughout the world. Whether they were black or white did not matter to ourselves."[27]

Guthrie's logic was echoed by other delegates. Giuseppe Giulietti, Italian seamen's leader, urged Indian seamen to trust the power of the international workers' movement rather than national employer or governmental interests to lift them up: "The seamen of every nation belong to the same class, and we are fighting and working in order to unite all the seamen of the world.... Do not forget the great war! Do not forget that at the present time, in Paris and other great cities, representatives of African people and of Indian people are organising big societies in order to get complete freedom for the people they represent."[28] Ken Okasaki, a Japanese workers' delegate and a captain in his nation's merchant marine, similarly sided with Australian, Italian, Canadian, and Argentinian labor representatives in demanding a single eight-hour standard for all classes of workers—deckhands and stewards as well as engine room stokers—of whatever nationality.[29]

The Indians, for their part, insisted that the hoary hand of protectionism lay behind nearly every claim for universal standards. Government spokesman D. F. Vines, a captain in the Royal Indian Marine, pleaded for respect for the Indians' place in international waters within a calibrated ILO standard of hours regulations to make up for their own lack of strong unions. Responding to the arguments of the union delegates, Vines reminded them that during the war, Indian seamen had carried food and merchandise to Britain, France, and Italy: "You did not want to push them out then. Are you now going to try and push them aside?" A. M. Mazarello, president of the fledgling Asiatic Seamen's Union in Bombay, endorsed Vines's support for a "Lascar" article that "will permit India to follow the international movement without going too quickly, and will provide at the same time a protection for Indian sailors."[30] With each side sticking to its own "principled" position, maritime shorter-hours legislation failed by a single vote in 1920. A breakthrough on this issue would wait another seventeen years.[31]

Even as substantive reform lagged, the tone of international discussion noticeably changed during the interwar years in one important respect. The protective, if condescending, discourse on the part of European governments toward the workers in their imperial possessions diminished and was replaced by the beginnings of self-representation from the developing world itself. In particular, new voices of anger and frustration were registering from the representatives of Asian seamen, who experienced conditions far worse than those of their Western brethren and who no longer put any faith in separate "Asian articles." In 1929, Indian ILO workers' delegate Muhammed Daud, a Calcutta lawyer who gave up his practice during the non-cooperation movement to become president of the Indian Seamen's Union, described a desperate situation where 250,000 seamen were competing for 50,000 jobs and expressed "disappointment regarding the benefits for which we had hoped from this Organization." Despite repeated calls since the Versailles Treaty for "better wages, better regulation of hours of work, better treatment from the shipowners, and better treatment when in port," he saw little evidence of progress. "If the different Governments continue to act in this way," Daud warned in 1929, "there is the danger workers in the East will begin to turn their attention to the programme of Moscow."[32]

Joining Daud in demanding a special study of Asian sea labor, Chau Chit Wu, adviser to the Chinese Workers' Delegation, claimed that 160,000 of his countrymen were employed by foreign shipowners in highly unfavorable conditions. Typically, he reported, they received two to three pounds per month compared to the non-Asiatic rate of nine or ten pounds per month; similarly, hours restrictions (along with overtime pay) and workplace accident compensation were regularly relaxed for Chinese seamen. Indeed, they twice conducted prolonged strikes during the 1920s against the "general contempt" and "inequality of treatment" shown them. Together, Wu and Daud urged support for state employment bureaus as well as protection for the "freedom of association" in the conduct of trade unionism. In addition to securing an "Asiatic enquiry" in 1929, the rising new nationalist voices militated against separate "Asian articles" to any agreement. As late as the preparatory meeting for the 1936 International Labour Conference, British-based shippers were reportedly still proposing the old policy. But the Indian worker delegation (led by the Bengali coal trimmer Aftab Ali) now joined by shipowner representatives of Indian-owned firms prevailed on the Indian high commissioner, Faroz Khan Noon, politically sensitive heir to a wealthy Punjabi landowning family and future prime minister of Pakistan, to refrain from reviving what they viewed as an outdated and insulting formula.[33]

After years of deadlocked conferences and dashed hopes, ILO maritime reform was again propelled by the twin storm clouds of worldwide depression and Communist insurgency. The opening for global standards on hours and manning provisions came at a special maritime conference in Geneva in 1936.[34] The government delegate from France and chairman of the conference preparatory committee, André Haarbleicher, director of the

French Merchant Marine and officer of the Legion of Honor who would later die at Auschwitz, opened discussion with a warning that "there is considerable risk of social disturbance if this Convention is rejected."[35] British trade union leader and Labour Party stalwart Ernest Bevin, who served as adviser to the worker delegation from the British empire, pressed the point. Bevin condemned rising trade barriers and increasing restrictions on emigration that he likened to medieval Britain's Five-Mile Vagabond Act, which limited peasants from leaving their villages. "World organization," he suggested, "must take the place even of empires if we are going to solve modern economic and other difficult problems." Start with the "regulation of hours of labour on terms of equality," he counseled the trading powers of the globe, then proceed to further "narrow the field of competition" by eliminating selective government subsidies, quotas, and varying currency standards. Ensuring the seamen's welfare, believed Bevin, was thus "but a step towards something bigger and better": "Anyone who votes against this Convention today is voting for the continuation of the miserable world chaos which we find around us, whereas a vote in favour of the Convention will be one contribution, however small, to the removal of that chaos."[36]

Even as the Depression's heightening impact hardened resistance to higher standards among many employers—the British, Dutch, and Norwegians, for example, persisted with the twelve-hour day—two new factors had come into play on behalf of international standards. First, in many countries, as two contemporary researchers discovered, "the wider extension of subsidies gave seamen an opportunity to appeal to their governments to grant subsidies only where reasonable labor standards were in force."[37] Perhaps more significant still was the inaugural (and instantly very active) presence of a U.S. delegation within the ILO itself. With a suspension of the rules and a special joint resolution that Massachusetts Republican congressman George H. Tinkham labeled "one of the most contemptible intrigues ever attempted in the parliamentary history of this country," President Franklin D. Roosevelt had secured U.S. participation in the ILO in June 1934.[38] In keeping with the regulatory spirit of the early New Deal, the bill's supporters, like Democratic representative Samuel Davis McReynolds of Tennessee directly linked the move to the domestic standards-setting machinery of the National Industrial Recovery Act (NIRA) and Agricultural Adjustment Act (AAA). "We can proceed faster and farther in this direction of standards," advised McReynolds, "if standards are also being raised in most of the other countries of the world."[39] Democratic representative Charles J. Colden of California went so far as to call the ILO the "foundation stone upon which enlightened souls of every nation are attempting to build a new deal."[40]

Indeed, for some of its U.S. enthusiasts, the ILO beckoned not only for its potential international benefits but also, at least briefly, as a savior of sorts of the New Deal's domestic reform agenda. After the Supreme Court's *Schechter* decision of May 1935 striking down both the NIRA and the AAA—thus leaving the president's industrial and agricultural recovery plans in shambles—the ILO convention process (like the more famous "court-packing" plan) offered a theoretical way around a constitutional bottleneck.[41] Picking up a thread from Columbia University political scientist Joseph Perkins Chamberlain, U.S. commissioner of labor statistics Isador Lubin and U.S. ILO delegation chief John Winant conceived an ILO route for labor and social welfare policy.[42] Suggesting an alternative to the normal legislative process susceptible to court review, Lubin wrote Secretary of Labor Frances Perkins in May 1936, "We should establish the precedent of submitting [ILO] conventions to the Senate so that in the event we wish to test out the treaty-making power as a vehicle for securing social legislation a definite precedent will have been established."[43] The stratagem appeared to take immediate effect, as indicated by a presidential message to Congress in June 1936 urging consideration of five ILO draft conventions, including "reduction of hours of work to 40 a week"—this a full year and a half before the president's domestic Fair Labor Standards Act, embodying the same principle (now facilitated by a more obliging Supreme Court) that was enacted by Congress.[44]

However grandiose their expectations for the world body in general, the Americans clearly arrived at the ILO's 1936 maritime conference with enthusiasm. The U.S. delegation was led, across 1935–36, by government delegate Robert W. Bruere, erstwhile editor of the Progressive reform journal *Survey* and National Recovery Administration administrator. He was accompanied by an employer representative from the U.S. flag carrier Moore & McCormack Co. and a labor delegate from the near-moribund ISU (first the ailing eighty-three-year-old Andrew Furuseth, then chief union legislative counsel Paul Scharrenberg, both eager, despite earlier misgivings about the international organization, to extend principles originally codified in the 1915 La Follette Act), creating one of the few tripartite delegations united by strong reform and regulatory predilections. The rationale for unanimity was not far-fetched. Like France and Russia, the United States already enforced the eight-hour day and three-watch system—as opposed to the traditional two-watch system of four hours on and four hours off that added up, for most of the world's sailors, to a twelve-hour day. As Harvard economist Carl J. Ratzlaff had argued in 1932, "American employers and laborers [will be] directly [and positively] affected by the 'leveling' up work of an international economic organization such as the ILO."[45] Again second only to Great Britain as a maritime power, the U.S. presence decidedly advanced the chances for maritime reforms inside that world body.[46]

Pressure for regulatory economic action was generally intense by mid-1936. To fend off plunging price and production schedules, labor and governmental delegates at the Twentieth Session of the International Labour Conference in Geneva pushed for hours limits in multiple industries. Yet, despite an energetic push for standards, particularly the forty-hour week, the textiles convention, the symbolic center for international industrial agreement, failed to reach the needed two-thirds threshold for passage, as did similar measures for construction, iron, and coal industries.[47] Indeed, of all the "landed" industries, only the peculiar arenas of the glass bottle industry (a classic repository of child labor) and public works (which, by definition, lacked private sector opponents) secured conventions limiting hours of work.[48]

Finally, in the fourth such attempt since 1920 and amid what American delegate Bruere called "miserable world chaos," the Hours of Work and Manning Convention sailed through the 1936 conference. Though applying only to "international" voyages, exempting catering and clerical employees, and allowing exceptions according to "national regulations" or "collective [bargaining] agreements," the three-watch, eight-hour day-at-sea and six-day week-in-port system was thus enshrined as an international norm and slated to "come into force" as soon as it had been ratified by at least five of the big (that is, 1 million tons–plus of cargo volume) maritime countries.[49] Still, U.S. labor commissioner (and Columbia University economic historian) Carter Goodrich marveled that "in this most international of industries," the advocates of regulation had "won a signal and unexpectedly complete victory."[50] Indeed, ratification had even overcome the combined opposition of the British shipping and seamen's representatives, who continued to collaborate in a two-track system subordinating Indian and Chinese labor.[51]

Yet, even the passage of a convention exposed a degree of cynicism as well as the practical limits associated with ILO diplomacy. The assenting majority, for example, included many votes from countries effectively unaffected by the outcome. Even as the Mexican government happily subscribed to the "fundamental principles of social doctrine," it allowed that the subject had "no immediate repercussions" upon the national economy. China similarly offered eager support for the eight-hour day, even though "we have no such [internationally trading] ships in our country." The Soviet Union, while giving lip service to the measure, preferred to score its own propaganda point: "In our country, the abolition of private ownership of the means of production, the nationalisation of shipping, the liquidation of the capitalist class and the absence of private shipowners have put an end to the exploitation of seamen. Soviet seamen are working for themselves, for their own society, and consequently they work shorter hours than those of any other country in the world."[52]

Opponents of regulation, to be sure, did not find the convention terribly constricting. The government delegate for India, for example, though not casting a negative vote, made clear that the draft convention, representing too much of a departure from the contemporary practices, would never be adopted by his country. Likewise, the Dutch, who claimed to have lost nearly 20 percent of their shipping due to industry subsidies and protectionist trade policy of others, would not countenance further intrusions on their marketplace maneuverability by paying overtime rates. "I am not in the easy position," rued C. J. P. Zaalberg, director of the Dutch National Society for the Protection of Shipping Interests, "of those . . . who say to themselves 'We have no merchant marine, but we want everybody in the world to have a happy life, and so we shall vote for this convention.'"[53] After all the argument and all the waiting, the 1936 Hours of Work and Manning Convention never came into force: ten years after its passage, only three nations (Australia, the United States, and Belgium) had ratified its terms.[54]

Protectionism, or the "National" Approach to Regulation

Even as a model debating forum for competing visions of industrial regulation, the ILO proved a source of unrequited love for even its most active suitors. The British had long been cautious regarding the ILO's reach. The Americans, as well, who had belatedly but all the more eagerly turned to the ILO to raise worldwide standards to a level in at least some minimal correspondence with its own, soon adopted other strategies. Indeed, witnessing the timing of events developing across congressional, parliamentary, and ILO clocks, it appears that government officials and their labor allies, even as they "played the international field," had simultaneously been hatching plans to "marry the girl next door" in the form of national shipping subsidies and seamen's protective legislation.

Protection, indeed, was the name of the international game by the mid-1930s. With their economies spiraling downward, the shipping nations sought to hold onto their share of the world market by various forms of subsidy. Great Britain had notably abandoned its signature free trade posture—adopting heavy duties then later devaluing the pound and jettisoning the gold standard—in the years after the Great War. By 1935, Britain had also followed Japan, Italy, Germany, Holland, and France in establishing operating subsidies for its tramp steamers in the British Shipping (Assistance) Act.[55] The United States, having built itself overnight, or at least between 1917 and 1922, into the world's second-largest merchant fleet, was equally determined not to fall behind. By the 1930s, with most of the government-built vessels again either in mothballs or private hands, many worried that the country was once again drifting into maritime impotence.[56] The coincidence of disasters aboard the *Morro Castle* (September 1934) and *Mohawk* (January 1935)—the first by fire, the second by seeming crew incompetence—further raised public anxieties.[57]

The result was the U.S. Merchant Marine Act of 1936. Modeled on regulatory rates and hours legislation adopted for the railroad and trucking industries in the Emergency Railroad Transportation Act (1933) and Motor Carrier Act (1935) and extending and amending preferences previously offered in a series of ocean-mail subsidy acts in the 1920s, the Merchant Marine Act simultaneously curried favor with the marine unions and the U.S. shipping and shipbuilding industries.[58] By justification, it hearkened back to Adam Smith's original exemption of a national shipping industry from free-trade principles on grounds of national defense and economic security. One of the bill's key proponents, Representative S. O. Bland, pointed to a litany of historical embarrassments due to the nation's chronically inadequate seagoing capacity. In addition to the scare of 1914 when the United States found itself suddenly "cut off from the markets of Great Britain, France, Italy, Germany, and other nations of Europe with few exceptions," Bland invoked "the spirit of the martyred war President, William McKinley, who knew the humiliation which we suffered in the Spanish-American War, when we had not American ships or seamen sufficient for the war, when we had to search the ports of Europe for transports and colliers . . . when we had to enlist landsmen and foreign seamen to man our fighting vessels, and when returns show that fully one third of our naval crews were foreigners." President Franklin Roosevelt echoed Bland's logic in his 1935 legislative message to Congress, urging new legislation to "square this traditional ideal [of an American merchant marine] with effective performance."[59]

Faced with a competitively adverse sea, American policy-makers, in 1936, acted decisively (however impractically) to establish a U.S.-owned and U.S.-manned oceanic fleet. Invoking the La Follette Act of 1915 as "one of the most humanitarian ever enacted by the Congress," New Dealer senator Royal Copeland of New York determined to realize its ambitions for American seamen in a new form. "If there is one place," declaimed Copeland, "if there is one institution under the American flag which should be under the domination and control of loyal, patriotic Americans, it is a vessel upon the high seas." In words that likely warmed the heart of the "grand old man of labor" Furuseth (who often frequented the public gallery during congressional debates), Copeland dipped into a rhetorical bag of nationalism, gender, and the basic mystique of the sea:

> There may be labor disputes in a factory; there may be disturbances somewhere on land; but by reason of the activities of the police force or the peace officers, or perhaps moral suasion coming from the homes and wives of the employees there is always a way to make certain that no great harm shall take place in one of our institutions on the land. However, when it comes to a vessel upon the high seas every passenger, every person upon that vessel is at the mercy of the sailors, of the officers, of those in command of the ship. Because of this it is essential, if we are to operate ships, to have them operated by a satisfied, contented, well-fed, well-housed, and well-cared for crew.[60]

Appealing across class, regional, and partisan boundaries, legislators sweetened a massive subsidy program for U.S. shipbuilders and shipowners (a newly created U.S. Maritime Commission would essentially fund the difference between the prevailing construction and operating price abroad and that at home) with an employment and welfare program for U.S. seamen.[61] The latter measures (divided between the act itself and amendments to the La Follette Act of 1915) authorized the new commission to prescribe minimum manning and wage scales for all U.S. oceangoing ships and required that within two years, 90 percent of crews on subsidized ships—and 75 percent on all U.S.-flagged ships—"be citizens of the United States, native-born, or completely naturalized." These stipulations were to be advanced by establishment of a government-sponsored Merchant Marine Academy for training seamen and officers and to be relaxed only under an emergency finding by the secretary of commerce.[62]

Unfortunately, any move to protect a single nation's seamen was likely to contain a nastier side as well. As in Britain's early lascar restrictions or in the English-language provisions of the U.S. La Follette Act, a racist, anti-immigrant, and specifically anti-Asian animus again infected Anglo-American maritime labor reform in the Depression era. The British mold was first set in the Coloured Alien Seamen's Order of 1925 (as discussed in chapter 5).[63]

Just as the 1925 measure made things difficult for non-white maritime workers on land, so the labor clauses of the 1935 tramp shipping subsidy bill discriminated against them at sea. In accepting industry subsidies, Labour MPs had insisted on a full reversal of open-hiring practices and demanded a British-only employment policy on British ships. As with the earlier order, however, precisely defining "British nationals" within an extensive and complex imperial order proved a difficult and contentious process. Initially, many veteran Indian seamen lost their jobs as employers scurried to comply with the new rules. Quickly, a labor shortage and internal conflicts within the seamen's union led to an agreement to treat British "protected persons" (from the war-acquired territories of southern Arabia and East Africa) and "all classes of British subjects" alike. Still, some, like the Goan seamen used to traveling on "Lascar" articles but technically Portuguese subjects, were left out. Moreover, when the subsidy scheme was renewed in 1939, shipowners risked losing the subsidy if they employed Indian seamen outside "customary" routes; in addition, Indian-crewed ships received a lower subsidy since wage increases affecting British seamen since 1935 had not applied to them.[64]

The U.S. move to subsidized shipping carried a similarly racialized taint when it came to manpower definitions. Within a general clampdown on 1930s immigration (including the "voluntary" return to their homeland of nearly 1 million Mexicans), immigration restrictionists reintroduced legislation that had been routinely backed for years by the AFL under the rubric of the Alien Seamen's Bill of 1933.[65] The rationale for the proposal lay in a perceived "loophole"—in fact, a component of the "right to quit"—of the 1915 La Follette Act itself, under which all sailors had enjoyed the right to depart their ships in any American port for up to sixty days before signing on to another voyage under the best terms they could find. On the grounds that an appreciable number of seamen (and "bogus seamen")—estimates of total "deserter seamen" from all countries varied wildly from 50,000 to 500,000—otherwise excluded by law from entering the country were manipulating this sea passage to join the U.S. labor force, the bill proposed severe new restrictions. Every arriving alien seaman would be "examined in quarantine" to determine his eligibility to disembark the ship. No vessel that included crew members racially excluded from applying for citizenship in the United States would be granted entry into a port. Finally, no vessel could depart a U.S. port with a smaller crew than it had entered with. Identifying Asiatic aliens as people whose "willingness to work for low wages and under any conditions make it impossible for the American workmen to compete with them," Texas congressman Martin Dies (better known for his later service as the first chairman of the House Un-American Activities Committee) believed restriction would "not only help labor but promote law enforcement." "Many of these aliens," he explained, "become racketeers and criminals."[66] Likely due to the intense diplomatic pressure from U.S. allies, Senate leadership failed to match the ardor of the House, allowing the alien seamen initiative to lapse once again in 1933.[67]

Of course, the citizen-only clause that accompanied the 1936 shipping subsidy legislation offered another path toward restriction. Indeed, in addition to its strong native preference, by limiting even the potential 10 percent of noncitizens within a crew to those making a "valid declaration of interest to become a citizen," the bill neatly disqualified from service all Asians, since they were already barred from citizenship.[68] The degree to which cultural prejudice trumped even the most naked economic self-interest in such matters was nowhere more blatant than in one curious turn amid the 1936 congressional debates. Just as the final "t" was being crossed in the Senate version of the "personnel" section of the new legislation, concern was expressed about the total ban on Asians in the stewards' department on passenger liners. Speaking up for several West Coast shipping lines, Republican senator Frederick Steiwer of Oregon urged a special exemption of up to 20 percent "only in the stewards' department" for "aliens ineligible for citizenship." Such a measure, Steiwer urged his colleagues, was necessary to accommodate passenger liners on the trans-Pacific run that regularly employed "some Asiatics": "The reason for the necessity of doing so is that many of the passengers on some of the runs are themselves Asiatics, and the ship operators find that it is impossible to employ a good class of American citizen to serve the Asiatic passengers."[69] For fear of losing rich passengers' accounts, the restrictionists were thus asked to give way slightly and allow a minimal presence of an accursed "coolie" class on American-flag ships. Despite an initial show of support, the Senate ultimately buried the proposal.[70]

Even the most poignant absurdity within the citizenship clause of the 1936 act could not deflect the law's restrictionist impulse. As it happened, an estimated 3,000 Filipino seamen had entered the U.S. merchant marine—especially as stewards—following the Spanish-American War and since established permanent residency with their wives and families. Now, as Resident Commissioner Quintin Paredes appealed to Congress, they were in a "serious predicament." Subject as "resident nationals" to a call to arms in defense of the American flag, which still had complete sovereignty over their country, they nevertheless fit neither the "native born" nor "completely naturalized" categories of those eligible for employment under the 1936 Merchant Marine Act. Nor, except in special circumstances, could they apply for American citizenship. If further restricted to the quota for "aliens" under the new legislation, the ranks of Filipino seamen would drop from 3,000 to at most 750. Again, the appeal fell on deaf ears.[71]

Labor's Post–World War II Surge

Word War II opened a new chapter of maritime labor internationalism, wanted or not. Wartime demand, itself, raised the size and profile of Allied merchant marine fleets and accorded them an unprecedented domestic political influence—one that would afterward ripple out into international waters. In the United States, war nearly quadrupled the numbers of merchant mariners from 55,000 to 215,000. Of these, a casualty total of one in twenty-six represented a higher percentage of war-related deaths than any U.S. armed service. In a crisis atmosphere in which cooperative labor-management relations were facilitated by the government's War Shipping Administration, unions on both coasts dramatically expanded in membership, the Congress of Industrial Organizations' National Maritime Union (NMU) nearly doubling to a peak of 100,000 members and the AFL's Seafarers' International Union–Sailors' Union of the Pacific (SUP) multiplying from 15,000 to 62,000. Significant adjustments in pay, insurance benefits, and war risk bonuses (converted to a forty-five dollars per month wage increase at the end of hostilities) substantially advanced the able seaman's economic position. The unions' still-strong public standing was perhaps best demonstrated when SUP chief Harry Lundeberg personally prevailed on Senator Robert Taft of Ohio to exempt the industry from the general prohibition imposed by the 1947 Taft-Hartley Act on union hiring halls.[72]

FIGURE 6.3. American Merchant Marine Memorial. The American Merchant Marine Memorial, inspired by a photograph of survivors of a German U-boat attack, was dedicated in Battery Park, New York City, on October 8, 1991. Designed by the Parisian-born artist known as Marisol, the project was conceived by the American Merchant Mariners' Memorial Inc., as chaired by the president of the AFL-CIO, Lane Kirkland, to commemorate the thousands of merchant ships and crews pressed into military service since the Revolutionary War. Photograph by Daniel E. Beards.

For their part, the British NUS also exercised a renewed influence based on their crucial contribution to the war effort. A national mobilization summoned every man, aged eighteen to sixty, with merchant ship experience since 1936, of whom more than a quarter (twice the figure for World War I) composed a devastating 32,000 war-related deaths. The turning points of the war—from Dunkirk to North Africa to Murmansk—depended on their sacrifice. Like their American counterparts, British seamen were rewarded with an advance in pay, war risk bonuses, and "continuity of pay" while shipwrecked or waiting for employment in the Merchant Navy Reserve Pool.[73] By war's end, though losing 60 percent of its homegrown fleet, enemy prize tonnage and wartime acquisitions from the United States and other Allies left the United Kingdom with a still robust merchant navy only 21 percent reduced from its prewar levels—and this at a time when former commercial rivals like Greece and France (not to mention Italy, Germany, and Japan) had virtually to start up again from scratch.[74] In such circumstances, it was perhaps not so surprising that the NUS, under the leadership of Charles Jarman, would be at least temporarily restored as the world's leading voice in maritime labor affairs. Jarman's initiatives, in association with the ITF, included the convening of two wartime London conferences of allied and neutral countries that produced an International Seamen's Charter of worker protections. Anticipating the return to peace, the signatories insisted that "seafarers would not be pawns in any effort made by owners to cut one another's throats. We intend to demand [of the ILO] that there shall be international observance of conditions of employment and these shall be in direct conformity with the sacrifices made by the seafarers in the successful waging of this war."[75] At the ILO's ensuing fifth Special Maritime Conference in Seattle in 1946, Jarman reminded the assembled delegates, "More than 30,000 British merchant seamen had lost their lives in the war. If any of the contributions to victory needed no emphasis, it was theirs. The seafarers were entitled to expect that the Governments would show their appreciation of the sacrifice made in fulfilling the pledges given them during the war."[76]

On paper, the pledges were indeed fulfilled. Major breakthroughs in 1946 came with revised "hours and manning" articles that extended the previous eight-hour pledge to all ratings. Even more dramatically, they established the first global minimum wage for any occupation, setting the "basic pay for a calendar month of service" at "not less than sixteen pounds" or "sixty-four dollars." In a separate convention, the required supermajority of delegates added an extra three days to the minimum vacation package. In reaching for a universal standard, the problem of "third-world" (that is, Chinese, Indian, and African) seamen on "first-world" ships was finessed in an elegant, if temporary, manner. The preparatory committee reportedly was thus "unanimous in its view that there ought not to be any discriminatory treatment of these seamen by reason merely of their race. . . . The majority were agreed, however, on the necessity for taking account of the fact that it is at present the practice to employ these seamen in larger numbers than would be the case if the crew were composed of nationals of the country of the ship's flag." Thus, without specific mention of any racial or national-origin group, article 6 of the 1946 convention singled out "the case of ships in which are employed such groups of ratings [non-officers] as necessitate the employment of larger groups of ratings than would otherwise be employed." For these "groups" who once would have fit under the rubric of "Asian articles," an "adjusted equivalent" of the minimum scale would thus be created—a rate to be negotiated between shipowners and seafarer unions or, failing agreement, between the governments of origin of both employer and employee.[77] With delegates united in principle on a "leveling-up" strategy for seafaring labor, shipowners did receive consideration in their concern to ensure "fair competition." The labor delegates agreed that the convention would not become operational until at least nine of the major shipping powers had ratified its terms.

Before the vote, some employer delegates still openly worried. A Norwegian shipowner had predicted in the preparatory sessions, "If this Convention were ratified it would mean a revolution, and they were not prepared to assist in bringing about the obsequies of their industry."[78]

Those who feared ILO lawmaking might have saved their angst for another forum. As had occurred with its 1936 forebear, the far-reaching 1946 convention never came into operation. Indeed, it did not get close. Until yet another special conference revised and updated maritime measures in 1958, only Australia had ratified the "revolution" of 1946.

To be sure, the internationalism imposed by wartime exigency took forms beyond legislation. In 1947, *New Yorker* writer Richard O. Boyer offered a colorful reminiscence of his wartime experience on a troop transport ship and the heroic struggles of the left-wing NMU.[79] A central theme of Boyer's story was the shipboard realization of the classic in-unity-there-is-strength view of working-class identity: "Union leaders were proud of the fact, moreover, that there was little racial discrimination aboard the *Marquette*—although they said they had to fight to keep this so, since new officers and new crewmen appeared on each trip. They said that some of the best men in the crew were Negroes and that on the ship's muster roll were Egyptians, Chinese, Swedes, Persians, Englishmen, Liberians, Welshmen, Hondurans, Frenchmen, Italians, Russians, Irishmen, Serbs, Mexicans, Croats, Ecuadorians, Puerto Ricans, South Africans, Spaniards, Icelanders and Filipinos, all of them naturalized Americans."[80]

Solidarity and Its Limits

Tales of interracial and interethnic solidarity are a mainstay of the survival narratives of the trade union movement around the world, including its British and American component parts. And there was likely no occupational group with more experience of international and cross-cultural contacts than merchant seamen. Indeed, it was that very experience that had set Anglo-American seamen's organizations as early as the turn of the twentieth century on a path to define a set of common, livable standards for all the world's seamen. That quest continued through a vigorous pursuit of ILO seamen's conventions. Yet, even those of a most democratic disposition in the West faced a difficult dilemma. Should they engage a worldwide market of people and products and try to impose humane standards there, just as they had done across a century of struggle in their home countries? Or should they withdraw behind selective national standards to cushion the competitive market pressures?

For seamen's representatives of the two greatest shipping powers of the early twentieth century, the "global sea" of competitive shipping and motley maritime crews proved a tough, uninviting environment. As the initial decades of ILO experience suggested, there existed no obvious instrument by which minimal worldwide codes of skill, safety, and conditions of labor could be imposed. Both Great Britain and the United States, in a period of social-democratic currents stirred by strong labor movements, thus initially opted to insulate their maritime labor forces as well as their shipping industries from outside competition. The economic impact of such measures, discussed in the following chapter, only accelerated the long-run decline of both shipping powers on the world stage. The social consequences were more immediate. As a result of the protectionist legislation, the "world" found aboard both British- and U.S.-flagged ships increasingly mirrored that found at home. The kicker in Boyer's paean to NMU pluralism was the final, almost invisible phrase—"all of them naturalized Americans." "Diversity" in the post–World War I Atlantic world would determinedly be limited to "naturalized" citizens. No matter the slogans or projected ideals, as B. Traven had recognized early on, this was not the stuff of which international solidarity could easily be fashioned. One is reminded of veteran sailor-author William McFee's comment on the disparity between the "internationalism" of maritime law and commerce and the attitudes of those involved in the trade. "It may be doubted," he offered in 1950, "whether the seaman is not even more nationalist in his ideas than his contemporaries ashore."[81]

For all its travails, internationalism on the high seas did not—perhaps could not—go away. Try as the Atlantic superpowers might to turn away from the rest of the maritime laboring world, that world did not stand still. In particular, both the Chinese and the Indian seafaring populations—the accursed objects of much Western restrictive activity—already by World War II had gained important new leverage. In both cases, wartime service in the Allied cause together with rising nationalist sentiment at home, the latter accentuated by resentment of imperial and/or racist disdain from

Western "superiors," triggered a rising assertiveness. Amid the collective fight against Japan, mass desertions by Chinese seamen in U.S. ports effectively forced an attenuation of long-functioning exclusion laws. In the case of the Indians, a succession of wartime strikes together with pressing labor shortages produced a dramatic jump in wages and benefits. Yet, as Gopalan Balachandran has argued, it was "only . . . in the context of the self-consciously modern project of the new nation-state—that Indian seamen finally shed their badge as 'coolies' to emerge as workers."[82] An important step on that path was the 1948 complaint to the ILO by A. K. Serang, son of founding Indian seamen's leader Mohamed Serang, about the corrupt hiring practices associated with the shipping company–recruitment broker monopoly control of the labor market. The First Asian Maritime Conference, held in 1953 in Ceylon, proved a turning point. Shortly thereafter, government-run seamen's employment offices were established in Bombay and Calcutta, as well as in Pakistan, Singapore, and Hong Kong.[83] The story, to be sure, carries a broader point. If Western trade unionists often found international organizations like the ILO to be toothless tigers, their counterparts in developing nations often looked to them as both political and economic lifelines.[84] Moreover, in the post–World War II era, particularly with mounting concerns about conditions on ships attached to "flags of convenience," both ILO standards like the global minimum wage and the mobilization of developing-country seafarers would assume a new public prominence.

7

Cooperation and Cash

LABOR'S OPPORTUNITY IN A POST-DEREGULATORY ERA

I recently visited a ship in New Orleans that had a sign proclaiming "We Speak English Only." The ship was Chinese built, German-owned, and registered under a Marshall Islands flag, and for the benefit of its twenty-member crew derived from eight different nationalities, the sign was translated into half a dozen foreign languages.
—*Peter Schauer, President, Orion Marine Corporation, May 10, 2009*

Old Man: "To end man's inhumanity to man we need limitless limitless limitless cash."
—*Eugene Ionesco, "The Chairs"*

The presence of strong trade unions in the maritime industry, as in many other industries in the United States and Britain, was all but taken for granted in the mid-1960s. Neither the unions nor their employer counterparts likely imagined that their worlds would be shaken to the core within just two decades. Yet, if the loss of union influence became a common theme of contemporary political history across Europe as well as North America, the sustained "renewal" of maritime unionism at the end of the twentieth century stood out as a dramatic exception. The players involved in this transformation, encompassing both national and international organizations spread across the globe, offered a testament to the power of transnational civil society. Moreover, that such a renewal should come at the very hands of the world economy that was otherwise shredding traditional worker protections made the latest chapter of maritime labor regulation perhaps the most surprising of all.

Fall of the Postwar Order

In 1965, former U.S. senator Joseph H. Ball, Republican of Minnesota, launched a full-scale tirade against union power in the U.S. shipping industry that, in retrospect, offers a valuable perspective on the sweeping changes affecting maritime labor worldwide in the post–World War II era. Ball was a partisan, but on this subject, he was no yahoo. As chair of the Labor Subcommittee of the Senate Committee on Labor and Public Welfare in the 80th Congress, he had been a principal architect of the Taft-Hartley Act aimed at limiting union power in 1947. Defeated for reelection in 1948 by Democratic-Farmer-Labor candidate Hubert Humphrey, Ball wrote his own "labor letter" for several years before entering the shipping business himself and ultimately heading up labor relations for the largest unsubsidized U.S. carrier, States Marine Lines.[1]

Granting that maritime labor, both offshore and on the docks, had long suffered mistreatment and thereby justified the workers' initial organizing efforts, Ball charged in a book-length study that since the mid-1930s, the balance of power in the industry had shifted drastically toward an economically noncompetitive "union monopoly." As Ball documented, of the twenty-three times that the president had invoked the "national emergency," strike-delaying provision of the Taft-Hartley Act, nine were occasioned by strikes or threatened strikes in the maritime industry. The owners' fears and projected financial weakness in the event of a long strike were such as to compel the largest employer association (in vain) to support compulsory arbitration, an almost-unheard-of position from the business community. The source of union power, Ball explained, was a combination of fierce worker loyalty ingrained over decades of conflict combined with the union hiring hall, established for both port and seafaring workers since the late 1930s. Almost alone, the maritime unions had resisted Taft-Hartley's attack on the closed shop (under which all workers hired must be members of the union) with "union preference" or "seniority" alternatives that accomplished the same ends. Indeed, after 1948, even officials of the Pacific Maritime Association, an employer group that included some of the most virulently anti-union executives in the industry, gave up their challenge to the hiring halls. The result, as Ball ruefully summarized, was that "in this industry the unions, and not the employers, control the jobs." Certainly, seafarers' rising wages and benefits reflected a strong union influence. From a low point in the 1920s and early 1930s of a comparative annual income less than half that of average shore-based manufacturing, seamen's income closed the gap during World War II and maintained a steady rise through the mid-1960s. Indeed, with whipsawing constantly bidding up wages among rival unions (the Sailors' Union of the Pacific and the International Longshoremen's and Warehousemen's Union [ILWU] competed on the West Coast, as did the National Maritime Union and the International Longshoremen's Association [ILA] on the East Coast), contract reopeners and even multiple wage increases within a single year were regular occurrences during the 1950s. By 1965, dockworkers ranked with steelworkers among the highest-paid wage earners in the country. Seafarers also made tremendous gains, generally winning a forty-hour workweek at sea by 1951–52 and the right not to cross other unions' picket lines, while also bettering the earnings of most jobs ashore, even as their fringe benefits added another 40 percent to employers' total labor costs.[2]

Always more organizationally unified than their American counterparts, unionized British seamen were no less assertive in the early postwar decades. Indeed, having recently braved torpedoes, shipwrecks, collisions, and prisoner of war camps, British merchant seamen, like other parts of the unruly postwar working class, determined to grab their share of decision-making as well as prosperity once peacetime returned. The result was an upheaval within the National Union of Seamen itself. As if collectively throwing off the mantle of accommodation and tripartism carefully constructed by Havelock Wilson, the Shipping Federation, and the National Maritime Board, the early postwar years witnessed a version of the shore-side "shop stewards movement" in a rash of maritime strikes and demands for greater rank-and-file control within the union. Challenging the Established Service Scheme (a very centralized labor-management system dependent on salaried union officials), a sailors' Reform Movement had captured the union leadership by 1974. The revolt climaxed in the tumultuous 1966 shorter hours strike. Demanding the forty-hour week and rejecting their own leadership's acceptance of a forty-four-hour week, rank-and-file militants (with strong Communist Party support) hung on for seven weeks, even as Labour prime minister Harold Wilson declared a national state of emergency and accused them of striking "against the state." An economic disaster for all concerned (and costing the nation one-fifth of its gold and currency reserves), British sailors had chosen an expensive way to banish a reputation as "second-rate" or "Uncle Tom" trade unionists that had dogged them since Wilson's refusal to join the General Strike of 1926.[3] The changed postwar situation of U.S. and British seafarers echoed across the membership of the International Transport Workers' Federation. When Swedish seamen's leader (and old-time Furuseth friend) Charles Lindley retired from the ITF executive board in 1946, General Secretary J. H. Oldenbroek offered a tribute: "If he were to be asked for what in life he felt most grateful, I feel sure his reply would be—for the chance I have had of helping to bring a sense of culture into the lives of those who fifty or sixty years ago were stamped the scum of the earth."[4]

To be sure, the seafaring life continued to carry its share of burdens and complaints. Yet, even the complaints registered by Western seafarers in the postwar boom years (as in the British upheavals) suggested a standard of measurement far removed from the occupation's rough-hewn and marginalized past. Now thoroughly integrated into the consumer marketplace, sailor wants—income security, more leisure time, a safe and dependable workplace, even *fulfilling* work—more closely mirrored desires ashore. In the wake of the seamen's strike, a Tavistock Institute study conducted in the late 1960s for the National Marine Board found that one-third of recruits to the British merchant marine quit by the end of their first year. In an increasingly youth-centered labor force, "marriage/low pay/boredom" were listed as the chief inducements toward early leaving or job "wastage." Even for those who stayed longer, the inevitable separation—mental as well as physical—between home and sea lives reportedly could give rise to "almost unbearable tensions when the two 'halves' begin to approach one another: the irritability of a seafarer approaching port is known as 'the channels.'"[5] Similarly, a survey of Swedish seafarers in 1974 identified stress caused by a reduction in crew size (and consequent forced overtime) and injurious noise levels as the biggest workplace hazards. Beyond these specific grievances, however, floated more intangible, lifestyle-centered concerns. Given the reduction in turnaround time in port, maritime labor offered less chance than anticipated to "see the world." At the same time, an unwelcome holdover of tradition lingered in the age-old system of seaboard "class distinctions." Even with the eclipse of the cat-o'-nine-tails and other forms of direct abuse, the desire for "comradeship" and "community" was still checked by the differences between the officers' and ratings' mess and recreation rooms and the fact that "a twenty-five year old navigating officer [might] enjoy a cabin twice the size of that assigned to a fifty year old able seaman."[6] Rank-and-file discontents associated with a more general, youthful rebellion against "alienating" work combined with a worldwide shortage of skilled officer candidates gradually brought changes in both the recruitment and treatment of the maritime labor force.[7] In Britain, for example, the Tavistock inquiry focused on ways of relieving the "tedium" at sea, while other programs across the following decade experimented with enhanced worker autonomy and participatory decision-making. And, in measures that finally broke down barriers between seafarers and other workers, new U.K. Merchant Shipping Acts in 1970 and 1974 removed all criminal penalties for "desertion" while also eliminating the sometimes-intimidating public signing of articles-of-agreement, or the seafarer's contract of employment.[8]

Of course, one way around the "unnatural environment" and "tedious" routine of seafaring was to open the portals to women. With the exception of the Soviet Union, however, even wartime exigency had drawn few women into the world's merchant service. In the postwar period, a slow trickle of female entrants began, with Sweden leading the way in hiring stewardesses as well as female cooks and radio officers. Then, the 1960s witnessed the first women officers within the European merchant marine, while by the 1970s both U.S. and European fleets were slowly bending to the growing demands for employment equity from the international women's movement. However, nothing in the West matched China's launch of the first all-women-officered cargo ship, the *Fengtao*, amid the Cultural Revolution.[9] By the 1980s, a more general economic shift in the industry, as discussed below, set back seaborne feminism, even as female recruitment spiked again—but mainly in traditionally gendered service jobs—with the rise of the middle-class cruise industry in the late 1990s. By 2009, women still represented only 2 percent of the worldwide maritime labor force.[10]

As it happened, the early 1970s embrace of quality-of-work and gender revolution issues proved a high-water mark for Western seafarers and their unions. For the next two decades, conditions deteriorated, the native workforce turned sharply away from the sea, and union membership shrank. Adversity derived from three related sources: new labor-saving technologies and ship design, a decline in the fortune of "older" sea powers, and the rise of open registries or "flags of convenience" (FOCs) that, in turn, tapped cheaper, global labor pools.

Technological innovations transformed the workplace in several important ways. The 1960s rise of commercial airline service dramatically set back the ocean liner trade (and hence steward employment), even as huge new tankers and container ships—known now as "megaships"—carried more cargo and, with the aid of computerization, at a fraction of the previous man-hour requirements.[11] In the oil trade alone, supertankers that in the late 1950s topped out at 28,000 DWT (deadweight tonnage) gave way to the 250,000 DWT very large crude carriers of the 1970s and soon after to their half-million-ton replacements. For the general cargo sector, a single container vessel regularly handled the load of seven conventional break bulk carriers. Cost-cutting pressures grew after the October 1973 Yom Kippur War, disruption of the Suez Canal, and resulting "oil shock" of the OPEC (Organization of Petroleum Exporting Countries) boycott. A boom in shipbuilding fueled by easy credit was suddenly cut short by general cutbacks in production and trade; as freight rates fell, "owners now had to meet inescapable interest and capital payments above all else."[12] Labor costs proved an immediate—and long-term—arena for savings. Over the coming years, diesel fuel largely replaced steam (and requisite steamfitters) on cargo ships, even as computerization eliminated radio officers and self-docking mechanisms reduced the need for tugboats. Indeed, according to one account, the Japanese "actually researched the possibility of fully automated megaships carrying no crew at all on the open sea."[13]

If U.S. and British shipping fortunes declined in a roughly parallel, post–World War II two-step, the immediate causes were somewhat distinct. Even as enormous government shipbuilding subsidies (dating from the interwar period and beefed up again in the late 1950s and 1960s) upheld the prominence of the British Red Ensign upon the seas, British shipping supremacy was afterward fading fast. Already fallen behind a rebuilding Japan and FOC newcomer Liberia in the early 1970s, by the late 1980s the United Kingdom had dropped out of the world's top ten carriers. With less-privileged commercial relations to the member-states of its former empire and with cheaper commercial rates beckoning from other quarters, the United Kingdom was conducting less than a third of even its own trade in British-flagged vessels. Employing some 150,000 seafarers as late as 1951 (with these divided two-to-one between U.K. nationals and Indian and other Commonwealth residents), the merchant navy dropped to 30,000 by 1990, with a third working the coastal trade, while many of the rest seldom ventured beyond the English Channel and the North Sea.[14] Looking back from the end of the century, Conservative MP David Gilroy Bevan had cause to contrast a long history when "Britain rules the waves" to an era in which "Britain rues the waves."[15]

U.S. shipping (and accompanying employment) fortunes faced the same bottom-line economic and technological challenges but with a few added twists. First, as had happened after World War I, a prevailing free-enterprise ideology dictated the sale and dispersion of a government-built fleet of 6,000 new ships, which by the end of the war was ferrying two-thirds of the world's oceangoing commerce. Priced out of competitive shipping markets for most of the previous century—and about to collapse altogether before the ascendancy of the FOCs—U.S. shipbuilder and seamen interests alike clung to one fail-safe argument to keep American flags in the water: national security. Outside the armaments and defense industries, it is safe to say that no economic and employment sector had a bigger direct stake in the Cold War (or its national-security-conscious aftermath) than the U.S. merchant marine. Based directly on the "security" argument, Congress, for example, in 1954 amended the Merchant Marine Act of 1936 (which itself had used the same justification for elaborate ship subsidies) to mandate that at least 50 percent of government cargoes, such as food aid, must be transported in U.S.-flagged (that is, U.S.-built and U.S.-manned) ships. Similarly, the National Defense Reserve Fleet, initially comprising a variety of vessels specifically from the postwar sell-off of 1946, was repeatedly summoned at moments of crisis, including the Korean War, Suez and Lebanon, the Cuban blockade, and the Vietnam War. Close alignment of the shipping industry's future with Cold War foreign policy, moreover, carried direct implications for the maritime unions themselves. The fortunes of Joseph Curran's NMU–Congress of Industrial Organizations may thus have been temporarily stabilized by his forceful break with the union's left-wing minority in 1947–48.[16] Perhaps most notoriously, the rival Seafarers' International Union (SIU), with the complicity of both the Canadian and U.S. governments, muscled in on the Communist-led Canadian Seamen's Union (CSU), precipitating a tumultuous worldwide sit-down strike in 1949 that crushed the CSU and eventuated in a several-year "reign of terror" by Canadian District SIU leader Hal Banks.[17]

Yet, for all their carefully cultivated ties to the federal government and linkage of the national merchant marine to strategic foreign policy designs, unions like the NMU and the SIU (into which a much-shrunken NMU ultimately merged in 2001) could exact only a token return from the alliance. Following a deregulatory agenda in the early 1980s, the Reagan administration effectively de-funded the differential subsidies of the 1936 Merchant Marine Act. As Gunnar Lundeberg, president of the SUP lamented, "there was blood all over the walls" as one domestic steamship company after another closed up shop, and the total number of U.S. seafaring jobs dropped from 71,000 in 1952 to 7,500 by 1996.[18] With union hiring halls operating as a job trust in an ever-shrinking market, the demographics were telling. When writer John McPhee spent a year aboard a U.S.-flagged freighter in 1988, the average age of the crew was fifty-one. "This is now an old man's business," the captain told him.[19]

The Rise of Flags of Convenience

By 1990, many social commentators testified to the phenomenon that would most commonly be christened "globalization." A dramatic upsurge in international economic activity—at once facilitated by the transportation revolution touched on above, a communications revolution identified with the Internet, and political deregulation identified as a trend toward "neo-liberalism"—suggested a qualitative change in the world socioeconomic order. For good or ill, national legislatures had less and less control over the tide of economic life, and workers in any one country suddenly found themselves in direct competition, and sometimes face to face, with those from other parts of the world. The tiny transport section of the Communist-led World Federation of Trade Unions (WFTU) thus ideologically hailed what it called the "internationalization of economic life" for "[bringing] workers closer together, forcing whole nations to pool their efforts for the sake of common goals," even as it took note of "new forms of exploitation" produced by "augmenting the competition amongst the wage laborers."[20]

In global shipping, the competition chiefly took the form of FOCs, a social fact that in turn produced one of the most original, far-reaching, and sustained campaigns in all world labor history. Amid a general rise in international investments, growth of transnational corporations, and even the "off-shoring" of production by industrial (and subsequently service) enterprises, FOCs, at least for workers, were a stunningly unique economic phenomenon. In one sweep of a pen—for the re-registration of shipping tonnage was quickly facilitated in a liquid (in more ways than one) marketplace—an entire ship's labor force could be transferred overnight to the jurisdiction and sovereignty of a new national "master." In the process, a raft of job rights, expectations, and leverage built up over decades could be dismissed in an instant. As a former international trade union official described "the sheer audacity and enormity of the FOC device" to his academic interlocutor: "[Imagine] the prospect of turning up at the office next Monday to be handed a new contract enforceable under the laws of the Republic of Liberia."[21] Multiple complaints of wage theft, abandonment, and arbitrary dismissals—as compiled by an academic study of FOC voyages in 1999—lent credence to the forebodings attached to the untying of flags from their effective owner states.[22]

In retrospect, the rise to dominance of FOCs in the contemporary era appears a little like the spread of kudzu vines across the U.S. Southeast (as well as Australian Northeast) countryside, in that they were introduced for one purpose but then prospered for other reasons. FOCs ultimately spread across the shipping landscape based on their economic advantage. Yet, like kudzu, the original rationale for FOC use was different. Nearly two centuries ago, some U.S. vessels took refuge behind the Portuguese ensign in the War of 1812 and transferred registers to avoid the British slave-trading fleet. Again, in the late nineteenth century, some American shippers registered in Great Britain to avoid construction costs. The continuous history of the modern-day system, however, began with U.S. use of the Panamanian registry following World War I. Transportation magnate (and future diplomat/politician) W. Averell Harriman initiated the Panama connection to evade Prohibition Era restrictions on his "gambling ships" in 1922.[23] With its "special relationship" to the United States—a government "stabilized" by Washington diplomats, currency pegged to the dollar, and English-language fluency—Panama soon beckoned to other shippers as a way of evading La Follette Act eight-hour workdays as well as collective-bargaining contracts. The beginnings of World War II also witnessed a flight from the U.S. flag to Panama as a neutral refuge, though the ruse did not fool the Germans, who sank some 150 Panamanian-flagged ships during the course of the war.[24] After the war, on the so-called trade out and hold principle, the U.S. Shipping Board openly encouraged further transfers to the Panamanian flag as a way of getting rid of debt-ridden craft that could theoretically be requisitioned back in case of emergency. Soon, the re-registered ships sought out multinational crews at a scaled-down "Japanese" wage.[25] And quickly, following Panama's lead, Honduras (building off its United Fruit Company base) and Liberia (making a special bid to oil tankers) entered the trade through the open-registry door.

The FOC exception ultimately became the rule in world shipping. By 1990, for example, only a quarter of British shipowners opted for their own Red Ensign.[26] As a U.N.-related agency reported in 2006, "It is not unusual to find that the owners, operators, shippers, charterers, insurers, and the classification society, not to mention the officers and crew, are all of different nationalities and that none of these is from the country whose flag flies at the ship's stern." Indeed, according to the most recent statistics from the International Maritime Organization (IMO), 45 percent of the world fleet came from the major open registries—a list topped by Panama, Liberia, Bahamas, Marshall Islands, Malta, and Cyprus—representing 47 percent of oceanic world trade, compared to 27 percent carried by traditional maritime powers, a list including, in rank order, Greece, Norway, Japan, the United Kingdom, Italy, and the United States.[27]

Not surprisingly, the ready resort to FOCs, and particularly the rapid postwar turnover of U.S.-owned ships (including considerable obsolete tonnage) to third-world flags, set shipowners on a collision course with the main international body of seafaring and dockworker unions, the ITF. As early as its 1948 Oslo Congress, the ITF called for an international boycott of Panamanian- and Honduran-flagged ships, since "it is only through such drastic action that the menace can be eliminated." Though the initial FOC fleet included old tonnage that opened their owners to the charge of flagrant disregard of shipping standards, the dominant ITF argument from early on identified the chief threat as the one "to the very jobs of their members."[28] Taken aback by the boycott threats, the Panamanian government itself requested time to consult with the International Labor Organization in order to establish the rudiments of maritime labor administration. Although several Panamanian-flag shippers moved quickly to sign ITF agreements at prevailing "British" seafarer rates, some traditional strong-union stalwarts within the ITF Boycott Committee openly grumbled at a delay in collective action. Norwegian seamen's leader Ingvald Haugen questioned whether mere adoption of some ITF decree "would guarantee satisfactory safety standards, working conditions, social security, etc. on Panamanian ships? Where was the Panamanian seafarers' movement which would have to guarantee the implementation of such instruments? In Norway they knew full well that, even with a Labour Government, a sound trade union movement was indispensable to ensure the enforcement of the laws' regulations and collective agreements." But a British delegate sounded the majority call for caution: "Were they competent," he asked, "to decide who was not competent to be a maritime nation?" The ITF must be wary of "anything savoring of flag discrimination."[29]

Still, the "PanLibHon" dragon (named after the three top FOC flags) only grew over the next decade, assuming top strategic priority for the ITF's powerful International Fair Practices Committee. In preliminary political skirmishing, the union forces succeeded in incorporating a "genuine link" principle (requiring effective administrative control, not a mere paper trail, between a state and ships registered under its flag) as a matter of United Nations–sanctioned international law in 1958.[30] Within months, this moral victory was followed up by ITF direct action in a four-day international boycott led by Scandinavian unions as well as the reconciliation of long-feuding NMU and SIU U.S. affiliates. Only months later, the Fair Practices Committee further cracked down on FOCs by refusing to accept wage levels at the prevailing rate of the home country of the majority of the crew. To prevent the gaming of the maritime labor marketplace, ITF agreements were "henceforth to be concluded through the affiliated unions of the country in which actual control of the shipping operation is vested."[31] Since most FOCs were subsidiaries of American-owned companies, the ruling made the world-leading standards of U.S. unions the measure of the FOC campaign. In cases where no strong national union could logically assume jurisdiction, the crew was to be affiliated directly to the Special Seafarers Section of the ITF itself.

Though constituting a strong warning shot, the ITF's direct action initiative also revealed cracks in the international labor armor. Cold War politics, which split the ITF from its WFTU counterparts, deprived the boycott of the participation of the industry's left-leaning unions in France and Italy, while the abstention of powerful West German unions was explained by a standard clause in collective bargaining agreements forbidding "secondary" industrial action. What was more, the near-unanimous hostility registered by world shipowner forces dashed earlier hopes of a labor/management entente of the "traditional" maritime states against the upstart FOCs.[32]

The anti-FOC boycott campaign soon stalled for another reason. The biggest prop to the seamen's boycott campaign, solidarity actions among U.S. seafarers and dockworkers, ran into a roadblock in the form of the U.S. Supreme Court. The key issue lay in the reach of lawful trade union activity—as defined by the National Labor Relations Act (NLRA, 1935, 1947) and the Norris-LaGuardia Act of 1932—in cases of a non-U.S. flag or non-U.S. crew. At bottom, the issue revisited the limits of national labor law that, a half century earlier in a slightly different guise, had equally bedeviled proponents of the La Follette Act.

Initially, the U.S. unions might have been excused their ignorance of what they were up against, given a series of seemingly contradictory court decisions. An early jolt to international solidarity activity, for example, was delivered by the case of *Benz v. Compania Naviera Hidalgo* (1957). The case dated to actions aboard the SS *Riviera*, a U.S.-built but Panamanian-flagged ship crewed principally by German and British sailors when it docked in Portland, Oregon, in September 1952. Though the crew had signed articles of agreement in Bremen, specifying a two-year commitment at then-prevailing British wages, they went on strike upon arrival in Portland, demanding higher wages and back pay and designating the SUP as their collective bargaining representative. Union pickets (involving the SUP, the Masters, Mates, and Pilots, and the SIU) were set up, effectively preventing ship repairs or cargo-loading for the next three months until a district court enjoined the picketing and awarded damages against the unions. With only Justice William O. Douglas dissenting, the Supreme Court sustained the action of the district court on grounds that the NLRA "is concerned solely with the labor relations of American workers between American concerns and their employees in the United States."[33] In the immediate aftermath of the *Riviera* episode, North Dakota senator William Langer, a Republican isolationist, tried and failed to extend the Jones Act and NLRA to more clearly cover "runaway" ships.[34]

The same court in 1960 (again by an overwhelming eight-to-one decision) supported the West Coast's Marine Cooks and Stewards union, American Federation of Labor, which was blocking another Panamanian steamship with foreign crew from unloading a cargo "to protest against the loss of livelihood of union seamen to [foreign seamen] with substandard wages and working conditions." In this case, the Supreme Court dismissed an injunction issued by a Washington State district court and upheld by the court of appeals that the picketing amounted to unlawful interference with foreign commerce. The distinction, the high court held, was that this time the American seamen were picketing "on their own behalf" and "concerning terms or conditions of employment" (unlike the *Benz* case, where American unions picketed a foreign ship in sympathy with a strike of foreign seamen)—thus immunizing their actions from court injunction as specified under Norris-LaGuardia. "The fact that a foreign ship enters a U.S. court as a plaintiff," concluded the justices, "cannot enlarge the jurisdiction of that court."[35]

In 1963, following a variety of National Labor Relations Board (NLRB) decisions that had generally validated the ITF's FOC boycott campaign, a court and presidential administration that would be popularly remembered for its "liberal" leanings now applied a tourniquet. In two major FOC-related cases, *Incres Steamship Co., Ltd. v. International Maritime Workers Union* and *McCulloch v. Sociedad Nacional de Marineros de Honduras*—both decided on the same day in February 1963—the Court, siding with amicus briefs filed by President John F. Kennedy's solicitor-general Archibald Cox, denied U.S. unions any legitimate collective bargaining action against foreign-flag ships. In both cases, U.S. unions had engaged in workplace sanctions to affect labor relations among the crew of FOC ships. Italian workers on the *Incres*, an Italian-owned cruise ship flying a Liberian flag, struck for higher wages while their ship was docked in New York, and U.S. unions spiritedly supported this workplace action. In the *McCulloch* case, the maritime unions sought the right to petition for representation of Honduran-flagged *Empresa* line vessels, which were chartered by the U.S.-owned United Fruit Company and engaged in a regular course of trade between foreign ports and the United States. Though even the government acknowledged that the degree of U.S. ownership and control should be relevant factors in the Court's deliberations, the justices—citing the lack of any explicit citation in the NLRA permitting the extension of activity to foreign flags—ruled the unions' activity in both cases entirely out of bounds.[36] If it were to parse the ownership question in its decision, explained the Court, it would have to "inquire into the internal discipline and order of all foreign vessels calling at American ports. Such activity would raise considerable disturbance not only in the field of *maritime* law but in our international relations as well." Justice Douglas, though bowing to the judgment of his colleagues since his own views on the same matter had been rejected in the *Benz* case, nevertheless worried that the "practical effect of our decision is to shift from all the taxpayers to seamen alone the main burden of . . . assuring the availability of an adequate American-owned merchant fleet for federal use during national emergencies."[37]

The weight of the Warren Court in limiting American labor activity to the "water's edge" of national citizenship and nationally owned property grew even heavier in the successive Burger era. In 1974, pounding the last nail into the coffin of collective international waterfront activity, the Supreme Court decided (with future chief justice William Rehnquist writing the majority opinion) in *Windward Shipping v. American Radio Assn.* that the very picketing of a low-wage foreign flag—in this case a Liberian freighter in the port of Houston—would provoke consequences unforeseen (and thus unsanctioned) by the labor act. Justice William Brennan (whose dissent was joined by Justices Douglas and Thurgood Marshall) penned a fitting epitaph: "Ninety-five percent of our export trade has already fled American-flag vessels for cheaper, foreign-registered shipping. In holding that the respondents' picketing against foreign flag vessels does not give rise to a dispute 'affecting commerce' within the National Labor Relations Board's jurisdiction, the Court effectively deprives American seamen, among all American employees in commerce, of any federally protected weapon with which to try to save their jobs."[38] The net result of this "hammer blow" of the U.S. court decisions was to limit the effectiveness of the international anti-FOC campaign for much of the next two decades.[39]

During the 1970s, the ITF, with the U.S. affiliates now decidedly removed from the center of the action, tried various other angles to contain the ever-growing traffic of FOCs. In 1972, the ITF tightened its administrative apparatus, among other things issuing a standardized "blue certificate" for FOC carriers meeting the designated ITF rate and paying into the organization's Seafarers' International Assistance, Welfare, and Protection Fund (aka Welfare Fund). What became known as the ITF's "standard agreement" was targeted to the able-bodied seaman rank, from which other ranks' rates, up or down, were traditionally calculated, and set at a kind of Western European mean—that is, less than the Swedes but more than the Greeks.[40] Designating official ITF "inspectors" at ten specific ports, the measures generally suggested a new level of seriousness for the international campaign. That same year, recruitment of the left-wing Australian dockworkers into the ITF provided a powerful new ally alongside Scandinavian, British (at least until adverse "Thatcherite" labor law reforms), and other European union federations in enforcing boycotts against or inducing strikes aboard noncompliant FOC vessels. At least in intent, therefore, the campaign thus remained true to its original goal of depriving the upstart carriers of a labor market advantage and thus driving registration back to the country of ownership where the strong unions were based.[41]

Yet, it was not mainly anti-union employers or restrictive courts that stood in the way of the ITF's international campaign. Rather, especially after the "oil shock" and slump in world trade placed enormous pressure on the shipping industry to cut costs, the cheap labor markets of the developing world proved an irresistible and growing factor in maritime recruitment. This was facilitated by newly opened labor recruiting agencies operating across national borders. Inevitably, this issue re-opened a split between "Western" and "third-world" workers (including affiliates of the ITF) just as it had in a previous generation of standard-setting within the precincts of the ILO. Even as the FOCs doubled in market share to nearly 30 percent of world trade in the early 1980s, constituting a majority of gross tonnage by the turn of the century, so too did global seafaring crews take on an increasingly third-world character.[42] Postwar FOC crews initially drew heavily from northern Europe, but, given the sustained economic boom, interest in seafaring careers had generally dwindled in the West. Beginning in the 1970s, new global labor contracting agencies turned eastward, first to India, Hong Kong, and South Korea and then, with further leaps in economic development, to other sources, including, most prominently, the Philippines.[43] Indeed, whereas Asians had composed 15 percent of the world's seamen in

1960, their share reportedly rose to 67 percent by 1987.[44] Within an ever more competitive shipping market, moreover, these new "labor-supplying" countries resisted restrictions from "the West" that might limit their market access. In point of fact, of course, Indians and other Asians were by no means "new" to seafaring, for they had long labored under the effective control of a largely British imperial apparatus that had segmented and sequestered them into distinct employment spaces. Now, however, they were recruited both by their own aspiring new national fleets and by the polyglot FOCs. In both cases, the proffered wages and conditions ignored established Western trade union norms. Moreover, in response to the heightened price competition, traditional maritime powers like Norway, France, and Denmark unveiled "second registry" fleets, tapping the lower, global wage levels for ratings even as they generally preserved at least the top officer positions for their own nationals. In another accommodation to changing crew structures, the British NUS in the 1970s successfully extracted a lucrative "Asian levy" on every non-domiciled seaman employed on British-flagged ships; without in the least interrupting the employment shift, the measure nevertheless provided a key prop to the union's home finances.[45]

That state policy itself could play an important role in the acceleration of globalization is neatly demonstrated in the case of the Philippines. To be sure, Filipino seafaring stretched back at least to the Acapulco-to-Manila runs of Spanish galleons of the sixteenth century and continued during both the American and Japanese occupations of the early through mid-twentieth century. Filipinos also had a built-in advantage in the world labor market in speaking English and in receiving formal certification from training schools directly modeled on the U.S. merchant marine.[46] Yet, beginning in 1974 with the creation of the National Seamen's Board (subsequently redefined as the Philippines Overseas Employment Administration, or POEA), the Philippine government—two years after the declaration of martial law and beginning of extended dictatorship by President Ferdinand Marcos—also seized on seafaring as a prime component of a larger development strategy. The government henceforth actively recruited and trained an exportable labor force, focused on male seafarers and female domestic workers and nurses. Stressing the national type abroad as reliable, friendly, and hard-working, the POEA hailed them at home as *Bagong Bayani*, or "new heroes" of the nation. Responsible for establishing minimal contract terms for its hired-out laborers, the POEA was also careful to set its seafarers' rate just shy of the ILO minimum, not to mention well below the ITF's standards.[47] Throughout its moves, the government enjoyed the support of the Associated Marine Officers' and Seamen's Union of the Philippines (AMOSUP). In 1960, taking a lead from his older brother Roberto, who had earlier organized the Manila stevedores and chartered the Transport General Workers Organization, Captain Gregorio S. Oca, a graduate of the nation's merchant marine academy, formed the union that became AMOSUP with 500 members serving on national flag ships in 1960. Stressing the American education, English facility, and Christian affiliation of Filipino mariners, Oca also quickly aligned himself with the pro-American, anti-Communist policies of the Marcos government and was rewarded by appointment to the board of the powerful POEA, among other official positions.[48] As a result of joint government-union efforts, Filipino employment skyrocketed from 25,000 seafarers in 1974 to 250,000 in 1990. Oca recalled, in the late 1970s, "We [AMOSUP] were signing agreements practically every day."[49] Growth continued at a dramatic rate through the 1990s until reaching a peak market share of 28 percent in 2002, a year in which remission payments from seafarers (80 percent of contracted salary income) were estimated as a nearly $2 billion boost to the Philippine economy.[50]

The ITF and the Challenge of Organized Asian Seafarers

Still weighted numerically toward the traditional maritime powers, the London-based ITF struggled to harmonize its commitment to universal standards with the interests of members from newer labor markets. Push first came to shove in the 1970s. As early as 1973, when several Asian governments and their affiliated unions (worried about market share) openly rejected a newly constituted ILO minimum wage of forty-eight pounds per month (well above then-common thirty-two pounds per month national rates), the parties found temporary agreement in an arrangement that offered a lower-wage dividend to national shipowners in developing countries. As even the aspiring national flags, however, fell far behind the growing FOC behemoth, the employment dilemma for third-world seafarers grew. Indeed, even ITF affiliates began to cut corners in signing contracts with FOC owners. Still attempting to maintain a single "European" rate for FOC shipowners (many of whom were now hiring the same Asian seamen indigenous to the Asian national fleets), the ITF called a historic boycott in 1978 against an Indian-crewed Liberian freighter docked in Glasgow. The crew, on orders from the National Union of Seafarers of India (NUSI) trade union leadership, not only refused the "solidarity" action but collaborated in an employer-initiated injunction against the ITF boycotters.

Outraged, the ITF suspended its 24,000-member NUSI affiliate. Equally irate, NUSI general secretary Leo Barnes attacked the ITF for hypocrisy in allowing the FOCs to supplant the national flags in the first place: the ITF's "blue certificates," he suggested, were no more than a "license for prostitution"![51] With NUSI rallying other Asian unions to its defense, the international body sought to mend fences with its Asian affiliates who represented nearly a fifth of its global membership. Still, even with NUSI back in the fold by 1980, ITF general secretary Harold Lewis was still criticizing Asian seagoing unions for collaborating with anti-labor governments as well as with FOC operators.[52]

For an extended moment, the FOCs threatened to undo the ITF's entire seafarer campaign. Given the pervasive presence of both FOCs and third-world crews, by the late 1970s, the ITF was clearly struggling to find an acceptable, international floor of wages and conditions applicable across its sprawling, global constituency. The result was an initially lower "Asian rate" for seafarers working exclusively in the Asian region and then, in 1986, the worldwide "TCC" or "total crew cost" agreement, hammered out between NUSI's Leo Barnes, AMOSUP's Gregorio Oca, and the London-based Secretariat.[53] Essentially, the labor body abandoned the effort to expel FOCs from the seas and gave up on high-wage standard agreements for all global carriers as well. Instead of a precise list of wages and benefits for each job level, ITF national affiliates and FOC shipowners could negotiate a more flexible contract so long as it met an ITF-determined labor cost bottom line, initially at approximately 60 percent of the standard contract for able-bodied seamen.[54]

But by no means did the TCC concession mean that the ITF was giving up on standards altogether. By accepting a more pragmatic accommodation to prevailing labor market levels, the ITF had actually discovered an effective way for organized labor to insert itself as never before as a factor in global shipping. Though forced to back off "Western" rates, ITF activists had nevertheless found a way to reunite a global occupational community around a common cause. Indeed, a remarkably robust world labor inspection regime emerged by the 1990s. Building up from the lower rates negotiated by national affiliates in the 1980s, the London-based ITF office gained broad support in 1994 for a TCC minimal able-bodied seaman rate contract of $1,100 per month, or more than twice the contemporary ILO standard. Though nowhere near the contemporary European rate ($1,804 per month), the contrast to shoreside wages in the chief labor supply countries was telling: the able-bodied seaman's monthly wage was more than seven times that of the average industrial wage in the Ukraine or the Philippines and some twenty-one times that of his shoreside counterpart in India.[55] Pressed on more and more global shippers, the TCC rates gathered collective force through the decade. With key support from both Indian and Filipino unions, the ITF contracts encompassed some 85,000 seamen, a quarter of the worldwide FOC trade, in 2001.[56] In addition, in 1999–2000, a group of large European-American-based shipowners—originally gathered in the International Maritime Employers' Committee (IMEC) to fend off ITF influence but now worried more about their own low-cost competitors—agreed to bargain directly with the union federation in talks that came to be known as the International Bargaining Forum (IBF). Adding Japanese and Korean counterparts, the employers' Joint Negotiating Group encompassed some eighty international shipping firms by 2003, and by 2007, the resulting "green certificate" awarded to signatories to its pattern agreements with the ITF—far more encompassing in its terms than the TCC minimums—covered some 70,000 seafarers of all nationalities serving on 3,500 ships.[57] All told, by the end of December 2008, the ITF counted 201 affiliated unions representing 720,000 seafarers (out of an estimated world total of 1.2 million), including 207,000 FOC workers covered by one form or another—standard agreements, TCC, or IBF—of ITF agreement.[58] Exercising an authority unknown to any other global labor secretariat, the ITF had achieved what industrial sociologist Nathan Lillie called "a *de facto* global trade union for seafarers," embodying "a form of global unionism different from traditional national unionism."[59]

The revival of seafarer unionism relied on its own version of the cash nexus in the form of the ITF's Welfare Fund. In exchange for a blue certificate, FOC operators (in addition to meeting ITF contract terms) effectively paid a per-seafarer tax ($230 a year in the 1980s–90s and since raised to $250) that sustained the campaign's worldwide network of inspectors and overall administrative costs while extending a variety of benefits to unemployed and retired seamen ashore. The entire edifice of the fund survived a crucial legal test in the House of Lords in 1982. In *Universe Tankships v. ITF*, the U.S. owners of a Liberian-flagged oil tanker that had been blacklisted by ITF affiliates in July 1978 until it had signed a wage agreement and "contributed" $6,480 to the Welfare Fund hired leading commercial law firm Holman, Fenwick and Willan (HFW) to challenge the legitimacy of the union action. After first being rebuffed on their claims relating to the boycott action itself (still judged legitimate under the labor legislation of the 1970s), HFW pursued claims against the Welfare Fund payment on grounds that the fund was a "trust," and thus legally limited to apply to the welfare of the individual crew members covered by the agreement, as opposed to the larger ends of the FOC campaign. (Such a reading of the law would likely have delivered a mortal blow to the entire campaign.) Following conflicting lower court rulings, the Judicial Committee of the Lords (what in October 2009 would become the Supreme Court of the United Kingdom) crucially ruled against the trust argument, 5-0—technically declaring that "the welfare fund was set up by way of contract . . . rather than by way of trust" and thus saving the campaign's London nerve center. In one telling courtroom exchange, the HFW barrister reportedly opined that "the Welfare Fund, my Lords, is nothing more than a war-chest." "Nothing wrong with that, is there?" responded the venerable liberal lord Leslie Scarman.[60]

With Welfare Fund payments far exceeding income from affiliate union dues, the ITF—alone among international union trade secretariats—soon swelled in size and influence.[61] Flush with new FOC revenue, by 1994 the Welfare Fund reportedly "had accumulated assets exceeding the equivalent of $100 million with negligible debt." By the end of the decade, the revenues from the fund (along with its charitable stepsister the Seamen's Trust) would bankroll a staff of one hundred inspectors in seaports around the world, including Poland, Russia, South Korea, and India.[62] As NUSI's Abdulgani Serang explained the system, hard bargaining and "loud arguments" regularly took place "within the ITF family" in determining acceptable TCC rates. "Western" and "Asian" delegates, as he recalled, came to the meetings with "different perspectives," and even within the regional blocs, "each union had its own vested interest." Yet, in a crucial move originated in 1983 and toughened in 1994, the ITF insisted that the relevant unions of the shipowner's country—that is, in most cases Euro-America or Japan—have priority on the representation of FOC fleets, with Welfare Fund payments and membership dues to be apportioned between them and the unions of the crew's home countries. Thus, even as the British (and likewise, U.S., Swedish, and others') seafarers' unions were drained of members at home by FOC competition, they nevertheless gained substantial new revenues from FOC collective bargaining agreements. In the 1990s, for example, Japanese and German transport unions willingly collaborated with the Filipino AMOSUP: AMOSUP members gained higher wages and benefits, including access to a union-run hospital, while in return their first-world union counterparts received a dues "tariff" of thirty to forty dollars per month directly from the seafarers' wages.[63] In similar agreements with "non-domiciled" members on Norway's "second register" cruise ships, the

Norwegian Seamen's Union notably reapportioned some dues monies "to compensate for shortfalls in paying benefits to Norwegian members who have lost work through being replaced by foreign seafarers."[64] Thus, in an important sense, the Welfare Fund "bought" peace between otherwise irreconcilable parties among seafaring labor's global ranks.

The consensus, always tenuous and fragile, among seafarer unions required constant cultivation. Again, the case of the Philippines provides a clear example. AMOSUP, the largest of the nation's three major maritime unions, enjoyed a fitful relationship to the ITF's FOC campaign until finally agreeing to authorize inspectors in Filipino ports in 2002. A likely reason for cooperation was a fear of the influx of still-cheaper labor from Myanmar and China into the world market. As Captain Oca himself wryly commented, "There will always be conflicts of interest [among labor suppliers]."[65] Indeed, even among the unions of a single country like the Philippines, different agendas played out on the international stage. Less than half the size of AMOSUP, the United Filipino Seafarers (UFS) has distinguished itself since its founding in 1994 in at least two respects. First, with publication of a bimonthly, English-language newspaper, *Tinig ng Marino* (Voice of the Seafarers), the upstart union uniquely touched base with hundreds of thousands of seafarers in some 400 ports worldwide.[66] More important, the UFS notably disdained ITF membership and openly touted its collective bargaining contracts at sub-TCC rates.[67] Such invidious intramural distinctions only exacerbated the problem of blacklisting for those Filipino sailors who willingly participated in ITF boycott actions.[68]

The Dockworker-Seafarer Alliance

Just as important as the ties among international seafarers, the FOC campaign depended on support from organized longshoremen. Indeed, when it came to brandishing a "stick" in both the securing and enforcing of seafarer contracts, the dockworker unions regularly supplied the heavy lifting. To be sure, the tactics of enforcement varied by country, and especially by legal restrictions. In Scandinavian ports, for example, where secondary boycotts generally remained legal, nonunion ships were simply "blacked" by boycotting port unions. In both the United States and the United Kingdom (post-Thatcher), however, the same forces resorted to more ingenious measures in the era of TCC and IBF contracts. By contract right, an ITF port inspector could board any ship with a union agreement. Once alerted to a problem (usually by a phone call from the ship but also by a ship's record of past violations), the inspector normally first requested a meeting with the crew, then spoke to the captain to attempt redress of any safety, wage, or welfare-related issue. (Long-distance communication was reportedly facilitated by the existence of English as the "official" language of the maritime world: "Someone always speaks English on almost any crew.") If the captain himself could not resolve the grievance, the inspector (or ITF higher-ups) sought direct contact with the shipowner or charter company. With each hour in port precious to the captain and his employers, extended delay could prove disastrous to the shipowner's bottom line. This situation was largely similar in the case of a nonunion ship that refused an inspector's request to board, for in both cases, the ship required "release" (usually including unloading and reloading) by dockworkers. As one inspector observed, "Any employer knows that longshoremen . . . unhappy with the working conditions or mistreatment of workers [who] are working side by side with them might lead to a labor disruption. Just the possibility of things getting sticky, many times things can get resolved. . . . There are laws that say that you can't do things but there are a lot of things you can do without breaking the law."[69] Invocation of "work-to-rule" tactics—including uncommonly deliberate work habits and safety inspections that predictably turned up further time-consuming violations—formed a regular part of the dockworkers' "solidarity" repertoire.[70]

No one disputed the centrality of the dockers' representatives within the FOC campaign, and, indeed, they were granted equal representation within the Fair Practices Committee. But why did dockworkers take on the enforcement work of a seafarers' campaign in the first place? The experience of the ILWU, the powerful West Coast dockworkers' union, in the FOC campaign offers one answer to a question otherwise puzzling in an age of disenchantment if not downright disillusionment with grand gestures of interunion, let alone international, labor cooperation. Formed after the militant West Coast Longshore Strike of 1934 and led for four decades by Australian-born former Wobbly and Communist sympathizer Harry Bridges, the ILWU had been expelled along with ten other "red-led" unions from the CIO in 1950 and remained adrift from both the AFL-CIO and ITF until a decade after Bridges's 1977 retirement. Though formal ITF reconnection came in 1988, it was not until 1993 that the ILWU took an active role in the FOC campaign. The move mixed idealism with hardheaded incentives. At the most immediate and practical level, the ILWU commitment came with a "quid pro quo" in the naming of ILWU appointees to several inspector positions on the West Coast.[71] But there were clearly larger considerations

FIGURE 7.1. ITF inspection. An International Transport Workers' Federation inspector and volunteers board a flag of convenience in 2000 in Tilbury port, England, during one of the ITF's international weeks of action. Courtesy of the International Transport Workers' Federation.

at work as well. Substandard conditions on ships, explained Ray Familathe, ILWU Director of International Affairs and one of the union's original inspectors, were likely to "roll onto the docks, [so] it's important that we help those [seafarers] organize and sustain [union] contracts." The ITF's "Dockers Clause"—a prominent part of every FOC seafarers' contract—thus specifically prohibited the performance of any "cargo-handling" work.[72] "Solidarity," summarized Familathe, "works both ways." Moreover, in recent years, amid attacks on unionized ports and dockworker protections (what the ITF has labeled a move toward "ports of convenience"), dockworkers have received as well as given international aid. In 2002, for example, during a lockout imposed by the Pacific Maritime Association during a contract impasse, the ILWU's ultimate triumph in the form of a favorable long-term contract was secured with significant support from ITF affiliates abroad.[73]

Apart from its strategic dimensions, cooperation between first-world FOC inspectors and third-world seafarers often proved an intense, personal experience for those involved. In 1996, Familathe, then in his second year with the ITF, called inspecting "the most gratifying job I have ever had—[defending] the rights of people who don't have the power to defend themselves." Looking back a dozen years later, his passions for the task had barely cooled. "Nobody would believe some of the deplorable conditions on some of these ships," he reflected. As an example, he cited a ship to which he had once been summoned in Long Beach, California, where seafarers were sleeping on plywood without mattresses and every toilet was backed up with feces all over the floor. With supplies run down, the men were "fishing off the fantail" for their food, and with water supply contaminated, they were sick to their stomachs. The Greek captain and the officers had already finished off the supply of bottled water. For Familathe, such experiences vividly reconnected union organizing to the immediate needs of seafarers. "We get kind of lost in this political world these days," he mused, "but when you see a worker who reaches his hand out, [while] the captain is holding his passport, and he can't just take off, and when you've got it in your ability to help . . . and all he says is, 'Hey man, can you help me?'—doing something like that is pretty good work. We're like social workers, union organizers, and chaplains [combined]—that's why we go up gangways."[74]

In sum, the ITF's FOC campaign may well stand as a classic political application of the adage "If you are given lemons, make lemonade." Faced with the likelihood of the permanent undoing of nearly a century of trade-union inspired protections for seafarers, the ITF coalition of developed- and developing-world constituencies pressed a compromise upon the shipping giants of the world. If the ITF's "blue" and "green" standard-of-living contracts remained, at least by 2009, a unique feature within the landscape of industrial relations, they shared in a global standard-setting process already more developed in the case of environmental and safety regulations as well as certain resource-scarce enterprises like deep-sea fishing rights. As political scientist Elizabeth R. DeSombre has convincingly argued, such political regulation of the global marketplace constitutes a welcome step away from a much-feared "race to the bottom" associated with cutthroat competition in favor of a "race to the middle"—bounded by business interests on one side and the restraining hand of government (as influenced by union or other popular lobbies) on the other. As in the case of fishing nations that banded together to keep rogue operators from despoiling maritime spawning grounds, DeSombre characterized the Joint Negotiating Group–ITF agreements as examples of the "power of clubs" wherein not only unions but shipowners agreed to contribute in order to obtain membership in a club that enforces behavioral standards on miscreant outliers. In this instance, even some developing nations like India, Singapore, and the Philippines—which were otherwise wary of "Western" hegemony—turned to the club to limit competition from newer, less-scrupulous players.[75] Excluding fishing and cruise ships, the ITF, according to a 2006 study, had signed an impressive one-third or more of FOC ships "under contract."[76] In forcing collective agreements on the industry, the ITF had, in turn, discovered a way to keep its own, otherwise unruly, house in order. Union contracts together with the Welfare Fund provided a formula for social justice of which the Old Man in Ionesco's "The Chairs" could only dream: "To end man's inhumanity to man we need limitless limitless limitless cash."[77]

Possibilities of Port State Control

We have seen how the effects of globalization have been cushioned, in the form of the ITF, by an organ of what might be called "transnational civil society." Yet, states themselves continue to play important roles in the maritime regulatory regime, as evidenced, most specifically, in the expanding agency of "port state control." The concept—emphasizing the right of port states to exercise some defined degree of jurisdiction over foreign vessels entering their harbors—first took on meaning in the International Convention for the Safety of Life at Sea (SOLAS) in 1914 on the heels of the *Titanic* disaster. More recent updates of the SOLAS convention—establishing standards for operational safety, ship design, and environmental protection—occurred under the auspices of the IMO, a specialized U.N. agency with headquarters in London, first convened in 1959.[78] The big push in enforcement, however, came only after the terror of oil spills hit the industrialized world following the 1967 *Torrey Canyon* and the 1978 *Amoco Cadiz* disasters, huge spills off the coasts of Cornwall and Brittany, respectively.[79] Notably, during the same period that U.S. courts were reaffirming the priority of flag state control on labor matters, international norms were undermining this same norm on the environmental front. Fulfilling a principle previously sustained by ILO and IMO conventions, the Hague Memorandum of Understanding (MOU) among several North Sea states in 1978 first authorized portside inspections of equipment and safety standards for merchant vessels irrespective of national flag.[80] This first initiative was followed by a stronger Paris MOU in 1982 and quickly imitated by other regional port state control networks. By 2002, the administration of the Paris MOU stretched to twenty-seven states encompassing all of Europe and Canada and mandating inspections of a minimum 25 percent of foreign flagged ships visiting affected ports.[81]

In the early stages of implementation, port state control regimes steered clear of labor-related issues. The one exception was represented in enforcement of standards of training and certification of crew members. Beginning in 1978 and then substantially strengthened in 1995 (STCW [Standards of Training, Certification and Watchkeeping for Seafarers] 95), a comprehensive IMO convention incorporated enforcement of this issue under the port state control safety inspection system. Though still only inadequately making up for the skill standards once enforced by the merchant marine academies and union hiring halls in the traditional maritime states, STCW 95 received support from both the ITF and shipowner associations as a way to stem both a skilled labor shortage and invidious low-standard competition on the high seas. Despite the continuing challenge of enforcement (for example, a report in 2002 branded the Philippines the "fake certificate capital of the world"), the training-and-certification model, enforceable at ports around the world, beckoned to reformers at both the ITF and ILO as a potential solution to much bigger problems.[82]

In negotiation since 2001 and concretized in the consolidated Maritime Labour Convention (MLC) of 2006, the ILO for the first time placed its historic set of some seventy seafarer conventions under the enforcement mechanism of port state as well as flag state inspection. A five-year action plan, including adoption of guidelines for inspections and the required ratification of the convention by at least thirty ILO member states responsible for at least one-third of the gross tonnage of world shipping, would bring the MLC into play in 2011. With the February 2009 ratification by Panama (the largest flag state in the world) added to the prior signatures of Liberia, Marshall Islands, the Bahamas, and Norway and together representing 45 percent of world tonnage, the treaty had not only met but far exceeded one of its two stipulated conditions for activation. Surprisingly, the post-2008 economic downturn that caused plunging freight rates, stalled and parked ships, and significant job loss did not notably slow the regulatory initiative. "Even in these difficult times," explained Cleopatra Doumbia-Henry, director of the ILO's International Labour Standards Department, "it is important and heartening to see that countries are moving forward on their international obligation to achieve secure decent work in a major international industry that is essential to the world trading system."[83] In addition to advancing the MLC, Panama's action appeared to confirm the "power of clubs" in the global marketplace. Branded as late as 2000 by the ITF as the "most deficient flag state" when it came to meeting world labor norms, Panama's early self-enlistment in the MLC ratification campaign suggested that "reputation"—together with regular arrests and disrupted voyages by ITF inspectors—mattered to any would-be shipping giant.[84]

Hailed by its supporters as an "international bill of rights" for the world's estimated 1.2 million seafarers, the MLC could fairly be seen as the humane culmination of two centuries of maritime labor regulations.[85] Encompassed within its vast protective umbrella, the MLC set minimal requirements for training, conditions of recruitment and employment, hours of work and rest, wages, leave, repatriation, accommodation and nutrition, recreational facilities, occupational safety and health protection, medical care, and welfare and social security matters. Both in its substantive reach and its enforcement via port control authorities among its signatory states, the measure—at least at first glance—inevitably summons up the image of a kind of "global La Follette Act." Might this, one wonders, be the realization of the updated dreams of devoted sailor-unionist Andrew Furuseth—no longer an ethnocentric bigot but now converted into a tolerant, universalistic world legislator?

Alas, there are at least two reservations that must be considered before joining in a "Hallelujah" chorus for the likely activation of the MLC in 2011. First, the guidelines mandated in 2009 for port state control officers carrying out MLC inspections called for wage rates—including the ILO's global minimum wage—to be left to the unions themselves to try to force upon the shippers. Whereas underage employment, inadequate food or drinking water, and repeated violation of work hours or nonpayment of wages were singled out in the guidelines as potential justification for the detention in port of an offending ship, the document drew no such specific attention to rates of pay and/or benefits.[86] Unlike environmental or safety standards that drew on governmental authority, workers and their unions were still left to do the heavy lifting—presumably via their own ITF enforcement mechanisms—in matters of economic justice. Thus, even as prospects for the MLC held out hope for a minimal, protective flooring for the welfare of the third-world seafarer, its power to affect living standards was likely to be severely limited. Most assuredly, it could do nothing by itself to harmonize the wage levels of the older seafaring supplier nations with those of more recent years. Despite a residual Western union yearning for some wage protection, there was no reason to think that European or North American sailors would return to the deep seas. Rather, the MLC was best seen as a resource, and potentially a powerful and important one, for a new era of seafarer organization centered on developing-world workers.[87]

Second, the MLC notably stopped short of empowering the seafarers *on their own behalf*. To be sure, this was a bigger problem than the MLC—or even the ILO—itself. Even the union-run ITF FOC campaign, operating as it did through the thickly woven tapestry of first- and third-world country unions, has largely neglected the political agency of the seafarers themselves. In collaborating on a "regime" of standards, the ITF balanced the interests of first- and third-world unions and seafarer and dockworker constituencies, while the ILO parsed the complex, conflicting interests of governments, unions, and employer groups. It is not to diminish the hard-won protections of the weak from exploitation in such efforts to ask a simple question—how might actual seafarers play a role in these standard-setting deliberations?

The fact was that neither the ITF's FOC campaign nor the ILO had much to say about workplace democracy. The latter, since 1999, had set as its "primary goal" "securing decent work for women and men everywhere." In short, in an era of "economic liberalization," with ever-greater disparities of wealth and privilege spread across the globe, priority for the world organization was perhaps necessarily focused on "employment promotion" and "improving the conditions of labour."[88]

The ITF, meanwhile, both by its federated constitutional structure and the organizational compromises necessary to maintain its political unity, appeared unable to impose even minimal standards of union democracy on its far-flung affiliates. Unfortunately, the result has been that of the hundreds of thousands of seafarers positively affected by the ITF boycott and inspection policies, very few of them enjoyed a tangible connection, let alone a decision-making role, within any specific union body. As Susan Cueva, a longtime Filipina activist and an early organizer of the first ITF office in Manila, noted of the international seafarer campaign, "[The unions] do not really organize the seafarers. . . . They do not train workers to become activists or shop stewards. Rather, they sign agreements with shipowners. It doesn't really matter who the crew are: the vessel will have the agreement, not the workers."[89] Pressed on this matter of rank-and-file activism in the campaigns carried out in their names, two union leaders of today's largest national seafarer constituencies offered only partial refutations of the charge. NUSI general secretary Abdulgani Serang, for example, first pointed to the regularity of grievance calls his office receives from shipboard Internet or mobile phone sources. He willingly allowed, however, that unions on most FOC ships are "not that strong" but attributed the lack of shipping crew self-government to economics. Compared to the exploitation of other third-world workers, seafaring "is not so bad." As a result, many will "not complain" but rather "bide their time until they get into a strong union port, then rely on the dockers" to ameliorate their grievance. A strong union, he suggested, "does not go well on an empty stomach"; as Serang reported, even a vessel's boatswain, normally designated by the union to witness any grievance hearing, often hesitates to step forward out of fear for his job.[90]

In the Philippines, AMOSUP president Captain Gregorio Oca pointed proudly to several union-provided hospitals, a seafarers' retirement home, and a major merchant marine academy. But a shop steward system like those that were once common on U.S., British, and other European ships probably would not work, he suggested, among today's crews. Emphasizing the diverse mixture of nationalities and religions on board a single ship, Captain Oca elaborated that the workers "have very different concepts" of political and social life; beyond "learning to work together," it is really "very hard." Given the workers' own "materialistic" priorities, Oca suggests, it makes sense for the union to focus on "wages and benefits."[91] Yet, a survey of nearly 400 Filipino seafarers conducted in 2002–03 found that while "most" had "positive views about their unions," they also had "very limited or zero awareness" of their rights of association, grievance procedures, or the collective bargaining process. Moreover, "no seafarer interviewed recalled participation in any union election, and many complained about not receiving any report, which explained or accounted for their union contributions."[92] Dissent was most unlikely, given the power relations within the unions. As the ITF's secretary for the Asia-Pacific Region put it, Oca was a "larger than life figure" to the Filipino seafarers: "He's god for those people."[93] The situation, according to Cueva, was still worse for the women employed on cruise ships: "Being women 'captured' in vessels, there is no place to run" from the daily barrage of sexism and threats of sexual assault.[94]

A focus on union education and rank-and-file participation (not to mention the extra burdens facing women workers) was hard to find within the ranks of the ITF campaign. One exception was the small Philippines nonprofit, the International Seafarers' Action Center (ISAC). Formed out of the original ITF office in Manila that Cueva and labor attorney Edwin Dela Cruz chartered in 1998, ISAC continued to espouse worker empowerment

FIGURE 7.2. Filipino sailors on Greek freighter, 1991. Thanks to competitive wage rates, close collaboration in recruitment and training between their government and a powerful union body, and their English-language abilities, Filipinos emerged in the 1990s as the ratings of first resort among both flags of convenience and traditional Western carriers. © International Labour Organization. Courtesy of the ILO Department of Communication.

in ways that sometimes bumped up against the established unions as well as manning agencies and government policies. Openly critical of the lack of regular elections within AMOSUP as well as a membership policy that denied union seniority and long-term health benefits, ISAC in cooperation with the Danish Seafarers' Union in early 2009 helped birth a new union, FILDAN, for Filipino seafarers on Danish second-registry ships. Organizers of this so-far tiny group (which as of June 2009 still lacked an official collective bargaining contract) committed themselves to the principle of "democratic unionism," including shipboard coordinators (shop stewards), lifetime membership, regular elections, and an annual general membership assembly.[95] Yet Susan Cueva herself, back in Britain while working with a Filipino/a public-sector union, voiced some skepticism: "To set up a separate union of seafarers in the Philippines, you need to invest quite a lot of resources and people willing to risk their lives to do it; not just the manning agencies, shipowners, and the government [will be] against it but unfortunately the existing seafarers' unions [as well]."[96]

ALWAYS SENSITIVE TO THE logic of the world order of their own times, seafarers have experienced a wide variety of conditions at work and treatment from their shipowner employers. Yet, at least a few things have long remained more or less the same in the shipping world. Whoever and wherever they are, both the ships and the people (overwhelmingly men) who work them have remained a major concern of national governments, which regard them as a key prop to national economic welfare and, in some cases, to national security as well. As such, regulation of the maritime laboring class likely offers the oldest, most seamless, and most complex body of labor law and legislation in the Western world. The same facts explain why this work realm has also emerged in the forefront of international regulatory law and administration in the twentieth and twenty-first centuries. Yet, if governments have always "cared" about seafarers, their ministrations have rarely extended to considering any realm for the active "citizenship" of those regularly working the world's sea crossings. Just as the majority of seamen were once considered "wards of the admiralty," they seem to have returned in more recent times to dependency on a new—if better intentioned—set of guardians. And even if the lash, imprisonment for desertion, and the death ship fortunately no longer menace the waves, the seafarer still floats on a world barely of his own making. Even the most "progressive" institutional innovations in defending seafarer interests have yet to bring their charges fully to life.

Despite these important limitations, the combination of the ITF's FOC campaign and the ILO's MLC presents an example of an occupational regulatory framework operating at a scale without parallel in the world today.[97] Might the maritime paradigm then have legs to carry some of its lessons to other industries and cover other groups of workers? On the doubtful side is the very weight of regulatory tradition in the shipping industry—a tradition that has always tied the health of the industry (and in more recent times the welfare of the seafarers themselves) to vital national interests. In turn, as national interests merged and/or collided with transnational economic forces, policy makers in government, in industry, and among organized workers themselves shifted to multilateral regulatory arrangements. Even more peculiarly—and serendipitously for seafarer rights and welfare—the union forces in this case discovered a hardheaded, practical mechanism for compelling agreements across divergent world labor markets as well as national borders. The ITF campaign notably did not succeed in dismantling the FOC system; however, it has to a great degree harnessed that system to a regime of labor standards, a regime that pays for itself. In an important sense, the ITF activists have emerged as the new Progressive reformers—rightful heirs to Richard Henry Dana Jr., Samuel Plimsoll, and Robert M. La Follette—for seaborne workers. Whether third-world workers themselves can take the baton from their Western and professional-class advocates and patrons, however, remains to be seen.

Despite their particularism, the maritime configurations may prove a harbinger of larger things to come. Certainly, there is a thirst for institutional innovation in the field of labor relations. As a distinguished U.S. labor historian has recently argued, "Just as durable industrial unions could not have been achieved independent of the political economy of the New Deal state, so the mass organization of post-industrial workers is not likely to happen without a new national and transnational regulatory regime."[98] The early and continuing experience of economic competition among workers, employers, and nations engaged in the shipping industry has made it a vanguard in efforts at international labor governance.

Certainly the exceptionality of the shipping industry as an arena "adrift" from national moorings (most evident in the FOC era) lessens with each passing year. As Nathan Lillie most convincingly argues, "The declining fortunes of labor in recent decades are related to a withdrawal of the state as guarantor of labor rights [and] the change in the role of the state is even more dramatic than that." Various forms of "off-shore" production and services, Lillie suggests—from telecom call centers to transnational subcontracting in the construction trades—have led to a situation of "variegated" or non-territorial sovereignty, effectively limiting the capacity of the nation-state to set and enforce regulatory standards.[99] At the opposite extreme from the world order of mercantilism and superseding the successor regime of free-trade and/or protectionist nationalism, a neoliberalist globalism currently threatens national social sovereignty in the name of worldwide market forces. As state protections for workers and citizens are increasingly weakened or rendered meaningless, what can take their place? The example of the shipping industry suggests that at least something other than a deregulated "race to the bottom" can emerge from the globalized shakeup. In that sphere, as we have seen, a transnational regulatory regime emerged, combining the powers of government and international agencies, labor unions, and employer associations.

Moreover, as one indicator of what might be done to harmonize the interests of first and third worlds as well as owners and workers, the example of the shipping industry suggests a hopeful, however imperfect, model of governance. To be sure, the days of "union monopoly" over a major industry, such as Senator Ball complained of, are unlikely to return in the foreseeable future. Yet, if the world stays "flat"—in the sense of an ever more competitive commercial playing field—a wave of regulation may just roll over it to try to make it "fair" as well.

Notes

Introduction

1. K. Wilson, *Island Race*, 173.

Chapter 1

1. Smith, *Wealth of Nations*, 1:34.

2. Ibid., 1:463.

3. See, e.g., ibid., 2:595–614. Cf. Samuel Fleischacker, who goes further to suggest, contra most conventional readings (and my own), that Smith is entirely ironic even in this limited defense of the Navigation Acts. *On Adam Smith's* Wealth of Nations, 10–11.

4. Smith, *Wealth of Nations*, 1:464–65. Outside of the protection of national shipping/navy interests, Smith allowed for one other case "in which it will be generally advantageous to lay some burden upon foreign for the encouragement of domestic industry" (1:465)—this being the use of a retaliatory (and carefully proportionate) tariff against a specific tax imposed on one's own goods.

5. "Laws Concerning Seamen," *Niles Register* 37 (Sept. 26, 1829), 74.

6. Hope, *New History of British Shipping*, 297. According to the first comparative statistical measurement of merchant shipping, in 1870, the United Kingdom possessed 2.6 million net tons of shipping, compared to its closest seagoing competitor, the United States, at 0.6 million net tons. Ibid., 308.

7. Though other projects, particularly the conquest of Canada and Indian removal, clearly surfaced as war fever developed, even the young "War Hawks," led by Westerners like Henry Clay, initially centered their resentments on British maritime policy, which, they feared, would suffocate American commerce. Horsman, *Causes of the War of 1812*, 167–69; Hickey, *Don't Give Up the Ship*, 87–91, 111–12.

8. Lemisch, "Jack Tar in the Streets"; Nash, *Urban Crucible*.

9. Lemisch, "Jack Tar in the Streets," 402–3.

10. Gilje, *Liberty on the Waterfront*, 24–25. In 1830, the U.S. population numbered nearly 13 million compared to Great Britain's 14 million; by 1850, the United States at 23 million had overtaken Britain's 21 million.

11. Linebaugh and Rediker, *Many-Headed Hydra*, 245–46, 334–38; Gilje, *Liberty on the Waterfront*, 25–26, 179; Horsman, "Paradox of Dartmoor Prison"; Bolster, *Black*

Jacks, 1, 31, 113–30. On African American service in the U.S. Navy, generally, see Langley, *Social Reform*, 92–96.

12. Lambert, *Barbary Wars*, 118–22; Allison, *Crescent Obscured*, 110; Gilje, *Liberty on the Waterfront*, 151–55.

13. Lambert, *Barbary Wars*, 120–21. For Franklin's own early years of "unfreedom" and the deep, complex mark they left on his relation to the slavery question, see Waldstreicher, *Runaway America*.

14. Gilje, *Liberty on the Waterfront*, 151. For a more extended account of the effect of stories of faraway captivity on emerging national and imperial identities, see Colley, *Captives*.

15. Hickey, *War of 1812*, 11; U.S. Congress, *Annals*, 12th Cong., 2d sess., 1813, 1033–34; Zimmerman, *Impressment of American Seamen*, 255–57; cf. Gilje, *Liberty on the Waterfront*, 157; cf. Latimer, *1812*, 32; Brunsman, "Subjects and Citizens." For a more thorough assessment of the subject, see Brunsman, "Evil Necessity."

16. Quoted in Lambert, *Barbary Wars*, 187.

17. Linebaugh and Rediker, *Many-Headed Hydra*, 145–49; Brunsman, "Evil Necessity," 353–55.

18. Linebaugh and Rediker, *Many-Headed Hydra*, 151.

19. Nicholas Rogers, "Impressment and the Law in Eighteenth Century Britain," in Landau, *Law, Crime and English Society*, 72–73, Walpole quotation, 74.

20. Brunsman, "Knowles Atlantic Impressment Riots."

21. Hutchinson, *Press-Gang Afloat and Ashore*, 79.

22. Rogers, "Impressment and the Law in Eighteenth Century Britain," 92.

23. M. Lewis, *Social History of the Navy*, 127–33, 137.

24. Horsman, *Causes of the War of 1812*, 27. The Treaty of Amiens (1802) interrupted but for a single year active hostilities between the French and the British that otherwise stretched uninterrupted from 1793 to 1815.

25. Indeed, according to an official survey of New York City's naval yard in 1808, half of naval enlisted men were "foreign nationals" and overwhelmingly of British origin. McKee, "Foreign Seamen."

26. Gilje, *Liberty on the Waterfront*, 97.

27. Ibid., 167. U.S. officials estimated in 1806 that half the seamen involved in the nation's foreign trade were British-born. Cray, "Remembering the USS *Chesapeake*," 463.

28. Hickey, *War of 1812*, 11, 17–19; "The Acts, Orders in Council, etc. of Great Britain, 1793–1812," ⟨http://www.napoleon-series.org/research/government/british/decrees/c_britdecrees1.html⟩. Stephen, *War in Disguise*, offers a substantive British contemporary take on the U.S. commercial threat of these years.

29. [A British Subject], "True Picture of the United States," 76, microcard. The British themselves played the citizenship card from both sides: whereas American law required five years' residency for naturalization, England made special provision for the naturalization of foreign seamen in two years. A Cosmopolite, "Further Important Documents Respecting the American Question," *Pamphleteer*, 2 (Sept. 1813), 259–60. Even if the British Admiralty likely exaggerated in claiming that 20,000 officially "British" subjects were serving in the U.S. Merchant Marine, U.S. treasury secretary Albert Gallatin admitted to a figure of 9,000 such seamen. Latimer, *1812: War with America*, 32.

30. Lloyd, *British Seaman*, 215.

31. Tucker and Reuter, *Injured Honor*; Morison, *Oxford History of the American People*, 372–73; Altoff, *Amongst My Best Men*.

32. Morison, *Oxford History of the American People*, 371.

33. Aside from impressments, the British Orders in Council (1807), authorizing the arrest of any ship suspected of trade with France or its colonies—and a direct response to Napoleon's Continental System or European embargo on trade with the British empire—especially drew the Americans' ire. To be sure, there is a considerable literature that suggests that below the surface, the eyes of the prowar forces were at least equally trained on vanquishing Canada and the Indian territories. On causes of the War of 1812, cf. Goodman, "The Origins of the War of 1812"; Horsman, *Causes of the War of 1812*; Egan, "Origins of the War of 1812"; Stagg, *Mr. Madison's War*; and Hickey, *War of 1812*.

34. James Madison, Second Inaugural Address, Mar. 14, 1813, ⟨http://www.bartleby.com/124/pres19.html⟩; Gilje, *Liberty on the Waterfront*, 170.

35. Gilje, *Liberty on the Waterfront*, 170. Commanded by James Lawrence, the refitted *Chesapeake* engaged the HMS *Shannon* on June 1, 1813. Lawrence was mortally wounded, and even his famous last command, "Don't give up the ship!," did not save the *Chesapeake* from capture. "Chesapeake, (U.S. ship)," ⟨http://www.britannica.com/EBchecked/topic/937759/Chesapeake⟩. The slogan remained a catchphrase for years to come. As late as 1834, for example, James S. Wright's plat of Chicago projected four parallel east-west streets named sequentially "Free," "Trade," "Sailors," and "Right"—though the names would never be officially assigned. Chicago map drawn by J. S. Wright according to survey (New York: P. A. Mesier's Lithograph, 1834), reference courtesy of Gerald Danzer.

36. Gilje, *Liberty on the Waterfront*, 162.

37. Foreign Office, "Papers Relating to America," 13, 15, 55.

38. Pope quoted in Schoen, "Calculating the Price of Union," 190.

39. William J. Novak, "The Legal Transformation of Citizenship in Nineteenth Century America," in Jacobs, Novak, and Zelizer, *American Experiment*, 85–120.

40. For elaboration on the distinctions among republican citizens and birthright subjects, see Eisanach, "Liberal Citizenship," esp. 200–201.

41. Zolberg, *Nation by Design*, 78–87.

42. Madison, "Extract of a Letter from the Secretary of State [Madison] to Mr. Monroe [U.S. Ambassador to England] Relative to Impressments."

43. Cray, "Remembering the USS *Chesapeake*," 453, 464, 467.

44. Historians J. C. A. Stagg (*Mr. Madison's War*, 295) and Donald R. Hickey (*War of 1812*, 110) themselves adopt the two different names for the bill.

45. As Stagg documents, "The British government had already rejected three times between July and November 1812 the American suggestion that the essence of the Seamen's Bill serve as a basis for discussions on impressment." *Mr. Madison's War*, 295.

46. U.S. Congress, *Annals*, 12th Cong., 2d sess., 1813, 937–38; cf. Hickey, *Don't Give Up the Ship*, 110.

47. U.S. Congress, *Annals*, 12th Cong., 2d sess., 1055; Zimmerman, *Impressment of American Seamen*, 199. Two significant amendments failed in the House: one, introduced by Robert Wright (Democratic-Republican, Md.), that if any naturalized sea-

men were impressed after passage of the bill, the president was authorized to hold a like number of the offending country's seamen on U.S. ships; the other by Timothy Pitkin (Federalist, Conn.) that after the war, three-fourths (following the same figure as in the British Navigation Acts) of all U.S. seamen must be American citizens. U.S. Congress, *Annals*, 12th Cong., 2d sess., 1010, 1017–22; Stagg, *Mr. Madison's War*, 297.

48. Stagg, *Mr. Madison's War*, 296.

49. U.S. Congress, *Annals*, 12th Cong., 2d sess., 961.

50. Ibid., 1003.

51. Hickey, *War of 1812*, 29–51. The War Hawks, one of several contentious factions within the Republican Party, were a collection of a dozen young, mostly southern and western legislators, grouped around their factional leader, Speaker of the House Henry Clay of Kentucky.

52. U.S. Congress, *Annals*, 12th Cong., 2d sess., 1813, 1000.

53. Ibid., 971, 975.

54. Ibid., 974, 976.

55. Ibid., 1000.

56. Ibid., 1042.

57. Ibid., 1043.

58. Ibid., 1033–34, 1037.

59. Ibid., 1051–52.

60. Such hesitation about the quality of new immigrant arrivals, seamen or others, would take further tangible form in the 1819 Passenger Act. Once viewed as a purely protective measure on behalf of immigrant welfare, more recent analysis detects a fearful rejection of unrestricted immigration here, just as its earlier British 1803 counterpart sought to limit emigration. Zolberg, *Nation by Design*, 104–13.

61. For the best description of these trends, see Vickers, *Young Men and the Sea*.

62. U.S. Congress, *Report from the Secretary of the Navy to the Senate*, May 26, 1828.

63. U.S. Congress, House Committee on Commerce, *Protections to American Seamen*; U.S. Congress, *Letter from the Secretary of State*; U.S. Congress, Senate Committee on the Judiciary, *Report*.

64. *U.S. Statutes at Large*, 13 (1864): 201.

65. Hickey, *War of 1812*, 282–85, 288–89.

66. Hutchinson, *Press-Gang Afloat and Ashore*, 311.

67. Lloyd, *British Seaman*, 267, 275–79, 282–83; J. S. Bromley, "In the Shadow of Impressment: Friends of a Naval Militia, 1844–74," in Foot, *War and Society*, 183–97.

68. Lloyd, *British Seaman*, 267.

69. Griffiths, *Impressment Fully Considered*, 2–3.

70. Ibid., 9–10.

71. Ibid., 50.

72. Ibid., 239. Griffiths's contemporary, naval lieutenant R. Standish Haly, offered a similar argument: a new era of enlightenment, he suggested, would bring an end to impressment just as it had earlier led to Catholic emancipation and the abolition of the slave trade. Haly, *Impressment*, 40. Another form of coercion, convict assignment to Australia, would be suspended in 1838. Eltis, *Coerced and Free Migration*, 19.

73. Steinfeld, *Invention of Free Labor*, 138–46, 163–72. The nineteenth-century rise of

"free labor," to be sure, involved numerous limits. Perhaps most relevant following the banishing of impressment was the legitimacy accorded military conscription *by one's own government*—a practice with roots as old as Hammurabi's Babylonian empire and first imposed by the U.S. government in the "war against slavery" in 1863. Ibid., 15–54. See also Orth, *Combination and Conspiracy*, 107–12; "Involuntary Servitude," *American Jurisprudence 2d*, s 9.

74. Gaskell, *Sylvia's Lovers*, 1:9.

75. D. Davis, *Slavery and Human Progress*, 170–72.

76. C. Lane, "African Squadron: The U.S. Navy and the Slave Trade, 1820–1862."

77. Ibid.

78. Ibid. Formal and effective collaboration between British and American slave trade patrols did not arrive until the Webster-Ashburton Treaty of 1843.

79. Hutchinson, *Press-Gang Afloat and Ashore*, 323–34.

80. Burn, *Age of Equipoise*, 149.

81. Frank Trentmann, "The 'British' Sources of Social Power: Reflections on History, Sociology, and Intellectual Biography," in Hall and Schroeder, *Anatomy of Power*, 296–97.

82. Senior quoted in Irwin, *Against the Tide*, 98.

83. T. P. Thompson, "Impressment and Flogging," 489, 493–94. It requires noting here that "liberalism," left to itself (or at least in the hands of middle-class employers and property owners), could still sanction considerable coercion—in the name of "free labor contracts" against workers. Only the persistent demands and resistant behavior of workers, as Robert Steinfeld has convincingly demonstrated in two major studies, would restrict the penalties available in enforcement of free labor contracts—in the United States by the 1830s and in Britain by the 1870s. *Invention of Free Labor*, 147–72; *Coercion, Contract, and Free Labor*, 189–91, 234–42.

84. I am using William Appleman Williams's broad definition of mercantilism as "the basic outlook of those who labored to build a dynamic balanced economy of agriculture and business organized on a capitalistic basis within a nationalistic framework." *History as a Way of Learning*, 247.

85. McCoy, *The Elusive Republic*, 9 (quotation).

86. Ibid., 174, 176–77. By coming to power, McCoy suggests, the Jeffersonians allowed themselves a subtle shift in their maritime stance: they were not corrupt (so that problem disappeared) and the free seas they coveted (for re-export as well as direct trade) required active support—and ultimately a declaration of war—to secure merchant shipping. Ibid., 186–87, 216, 233–35.

87. Lambert, *Barbary Wars*, 179–202; Colley, *Captives*, 43–72.

88. Lambert, *Barbary Wars*, 202.

89. Palmer, *Politics, Shipping and the Repeal of the Navigation Laws*, 40–42; Fisher, "Working across the Seas." See also Ewald, "Crossers of the Sea." With various forms of bilateral reciprocity negotiated since the 1820s, by 1845, "half of British trade was governed by exceptions to the Navigation Acts." Hope, *New History of British Shipping*, 282.

90. Conservative prime minister Sir Robert Peel defied his party's protectionist orthodoxy by repealing the Corn Laws in 1846, an act that led to the ouster of his

government. His dedicated followers, known as Peelites, soon made alliances with the Whigs and ultimately entered the Liberal Party under a former Peelite, William Gladstone. Hope, *New History of British Shipping*, 287–88; Palmer, *Politics, Shipping and the Repeal of the Navigation Laws*, 176–77.

91. United Kingdom, *Hansard Parliamentary Debates* (Commons), 3d ser., vol. 108 (1850): 110–13, 1445–46; Hope, *New History of British Shipping*, 287.

92. Fisher, "Working across the Seas," table 2, 36.

93. Heretofore a shifting mixture of factions in the aftermath of the Reform Act of 1832, the Liberal Party took initial shape in a formal alliance of Whigs, Radicals, and antiprotectionist Tory Peelites in 1859, a move that was consolidated by the party leader and prime minister William Gladstone beginning in 1868.

94. *Hansard* (Lords), 3d ser., vol. 106 (1849): 28. Labouchere further complained of "a great want of proper regulations and very imperfect discipline, in force amongst the crews of merchant vessels." Ibid., (Commons), vol. 107 (1849): 224.

95. Ibid., (Lords), vol. 106 (1849): 17.

96. Ibid., 30. On the larger internal debate among liberals over free-trade access versus slave-trade prosecution, see Searle, *Morality and the Market*, 48–76.

97. "Free Trade," *Quarterly Review* 86 (1850): 183.

98. *Hansard* (Lords), 3d ser., vol. 106 (1849): 21–22.

99. Anon., "The Navigation Laws," 1849, quoted in Palmer, *Politics, Shipping and the Repeal of the Navigation Laws*, ix.

100. Gilje, *Liberty on the Waterfront*, 139–41.

101. McCord, "Seamen's Strike of 1815."

102. Palmer, *Politics, Shipping and the Repeal of the Navigation Laws*, 119–20.

103. Hope, *New History of British Shipping*, 288; Course, *Merchant Navy*, 222–25; Flanagan, "Mid-Victorian Settlement?"

104. *Hansard* (Commons), 3d ser., vol. 130 (1854): 249.

105. Ibid. (Lords), vol. 128 (1853): 1229.

106. Ibid. (Lords), vol. 129 (1853): 1671.

107. Ibid. (Commons), vol. 128 (1853): 1223–25.

108. Ibid., 1230; vol. 129 (1853): 121.

109. Ibid., vol. 130 (1854): 228; vol. 129 (1853): 103.

110. Thornton, *British Shipping*, 65; Hope, *New History of British Shipping*, 309.

111. Thornton, *British Shipping*, 41–42.

112. Hope, *New History of British Shipping*, 298–303; Sager, *Seafaring Labour*, 13; Davis, Gallman, and Gleiter, *In Pursuit of Leviathan*, 261.

113. Hope, *New History of British Shipping*, 309.

114. Bullen, *Men of the Merchant Service*, 1.

115. McFee, *Law of the Sea*, 27.

116. *U.S. Statutes at Large*, 1 (1789): 55; 1(1792): 287–99; 1(1793): 308–18.

117. Ibid., 3 (1813): 351–52; U.S. Maritime Administration, "By the Capes." Interestingly, among those who had tried to soften U.S. cabotage policy in favor of more open trading access was historian and public official George Bancroft. A former secretary of the navy, as minister to Britain, 1846–49, Bancroft lobbied hard for repeal of the Navi-

gation Acts, though the quid pro quo he had envisioned—that the United States would, in turn, open its coastwise trade—did not materialize. Handlin, *George Bancroft*, 232–33, 242–43.

118. Hutchins, *American Maritime Industries*, 314.

119. Hope, *A New History of British Shipping*, 309.

120. Roland, Bolster, and Keyssar, *The Way of the Ship*, 211–24; Hope, *New History of British Shipping*, 309. Regarding shipping subsidy politics, see Bensel, *The Political Economy of American Industrialization*, 189–90; and Heinrich, *Ships for the Seven Seas*, 107–11, 125–26.

121. Tyrrell, *Transnational Nation*, 28, 38.

122. Whitehurst, *U.S. Merchant Marine*, 113–15. See also U.S. Shipping Act of 1984, sec. 1. (46 App. U.S.C. 1701 note, 2002).

123. Prados-Torreira, *Mambisas*, 112–13.

Chapter 2

1. Philbrick, "Cooper and the Literary Discovery of the Sea."

2. Cooper, *Pilot*, 73. Though still bathed in a romantic glow, *The Pilot*'s coxswain, Long Tom Coffin, also offers the first extended positive portrayal of a common sailor. Previous references to seagoing life, e.g. by Lord Byron and Sir Walter Scott, as well as the contemporaneous works of British captain Frederick Marryat, concentrated (as did Cooper's stories for the most part) on the adventures of the officer class, with ordinary sailors taking only subordinate, often comic, roles. Hugh Egan, "Cooper and His Contemporaries," in Springer, *America and the Sea*, 69; John Seelye, "Introduction," in Dana, *Two Years before the Mast*, xi.

3. Vickers, *Young Men and the Sea*, 163–213.

4. Dana, *Two Years before the Mast*, 12, 376.

5. Ibid., 376, 381.

6. Melville, *Redburn*, 162–63; Crews, rev. of *Melville: His World and Work*, 6–12.

7. Melville, *Redburn*, 160–61. On Melville's perceptions of ordinary seamen, see Valerie Burton, "'As I wuz a-rolling down the Highway one morn': Fictions of the 19th Century English Sailortown," in Klein, *Fictions of the Sea*, 142.

8. James, *Mariners, Renegades and Castaways*, 24–25. It is worth singling out *Moby Dick*'s chap. 54, "The Town-Ho's Story"—a fascinating tale of an ordinary whaler doling out final retribution to an Ahab-like first mate—as a striking exception both to James's thesis and the general thematic thrust of the novel. Melville himself sets it up as a kind of contrapuntal diversion from the narrative: indeed, it was a story so secret (and potentially subversive to the maritime social order) that "it never transpired abaft the Pequod's main-mast." ⟨http://www.princeton.edu/~batke/moby/moby_054.html⟩.

9. For an extended assessment of Melville's class and racial blinders, see Myra Jehlen, "Melville and Class," in Gunn, *Historical Guide*, 83–103.

10. Vickers, *Young Men and the Sea*, 178. Cf. Charles Dana's estimate of three-quarters foreign crew. Dana, *Two Years before the Mast*, 381.

11. Vickers, *Young Men and the Sea*, 196.

12. Hutchins, *American Maritime Industries*, 3–4; Macarthur, "American Seaman," 726. John G. B. Hutchins, the dean of shipping industry historians, notes that British ships, circa 1830–60, were "required to carry four men and a boy per 100 tons on sailing vessels" versus the U.S. custom of two to three men and a boy. A combination of hard driving and an increasing gap between "officers on quarterdeck and men in the forecastle" resulted in "the almost total disappearance of native-born seamen." *American Maritime Industries*, 306. David Alexander, "Literacy among Canadian and Foreign Seamen 1863–1899," in Ommer and Panting, *Working Men Who Got Wet*, 3–4.

13. Hohman, *History of American Merchant Seamen*, 7. Indeed, as late as the 1870s, an English steward on board an American sailing ship gave vent to the still-current opinion: "Boys, do you know this isn't a bad ship after all? I've always heard that an American ship one must steer clear of unless you want to be kicked about like a dog by the officers." Harlow, *Making of a Sailor*, 300.

14. Trent et al., *History of American Literature*, 3:349; Hale, *Man without a Country*, 8.

15. Ruskin quoted in Land, "Customs of the Sea," 170, though note that Land argues that the seaman's acceptance as worthy British subject developed only over time and in contradistinction to racial "others." John Peck, *Maritime Fiction*, identifies Great Britain among the "maritime nations" that "construct a national fiction in which the sea is seen as part of their being" (27).

16. J. Peck, *Maritime Fiction*, 31, 33, 50. On Austen's ultimately more nuanced view of the navy, see ibid., 36–41.

17. Booth, *English Melodrama*, 99–100. Reference courtesy of Laura Kasson.

18. Ackroyd, *Dickens*, 26. Even the harsher portrait of sailor violence contained in Captain Frederick Marryat's fiction (e.g., *Frank Mildmay* [1829], *Mr Midshipman Easy* [1836]) celebrates a kind of antimodernist, male heroism. J. Peck, *Maritime Fiction*, 50–69.

19. Trodd, "Collaborating in Open Boats," ⟨http://muse.jhu.edu/journals/victorian_studies/v042/42.2trodd.html⟩. See also Ackroyd, *Dickens*, 25–40.

20. The Phrase Finder, ⟨http://www.phrases.org.uk/meanings/ship-shape%20and%20Bristol%20fashion.html⟩. The phrase binds the seventeenth-century term "shipshape" with reference to the heyday of the trading port of Bristol. J. Peck, *Maritime Fiction*, 36.

21. Cf. Lee, "Return of the 'Unnative,'" 449–78. The loss of her sailor brother John at sea when she was eighteen years old helps explain Gaskell's personal preoccupation with the subject. As her biographer notes, "The figure of the sailor in peril moves through her fiction with the power of a recurring dream." Uglow, *Elizabeth Gaskell*, 53–54.

22. Disher, *Blood and Thunder*, 13, 141; Booth, *English Melodrama*, 108.

23. J. Peck, *Maritime Fiction*, 28.

24. Robinson, *British Tar*, 329.

25. Jerrold, *Mutiny at the Nore*, 12.

26. Trodd, "Collaborating in Open Boats."

27. Macarthur, *Seaman's Contract*, x–xi; Macarthur, "American Seaman," 718–31.

28. Macarthur, *Seaman's Contract*, xviii; *U.S. Statutes at Large*, 1 (1790): 131–35; 1 (1792): 229–32.

29. R. Morris, *Government and Labor*, 228.

30. Rao, "Visible Hands," 26.

31. Story quoted in Norris, "Seaman as Ward," 486 fn. 35.

32. Steinfeld, *Invention of Free Labor*, 138–46, 163–72. As Steinfeld neatly explains (290–314), removal of criminal sanctions led American employers to resort to other legal means of enforcing contracts. In particular, the common law doctrine of "entirety," wherein pay could be withheld until completion of the full contract period (unless otherwise authorized in the contract), remained a major source of worker grievance until state wage payment laws, beginning in the late 1870s, restricted such "entire" contracts.

33. *U.S. Statutes at Large*, 1 (1790): 131–35; Macarthur, "American Seamen," 724. I am indebted to private discussions with Robert Steinfeld for this comparative insight.

34. Steinfeld, *Invention of Free Labor*, 116–17, 153, 231 n. 78.

35. Randolph quoted in McFee, *Law of the Sea*, 173.

36. Langley, *Social Reform*, 24–25.

37. Leggett, "Brought to the Gangway," in *Naval Stories*, 153–79, quotation 160.

38. Macarthur, "American Seaman," 721, 727–28; Macarthur, *Seaman's Contract*, 148. Though flogging was outlawed in the United States by the 1850 act, other forms of physical punishment remained legal and, apparently, all too common until the La Follette Act of 1915. Macarthur, "American Seaman," 726–28; Rafferty, "Republic Afloat," 74.

39. Cobbett quoted in Spater, *William Cobbett*, 234.

40. E. Thompson, *English Working Class*, 604 n. 2.

41. Langley, *Social Reform*, 46–66, 91.

42. *Sailor's Magazine*, as cited in Glenn, *Campaign against Corporal Punishment*, 44.

43. Glenn, "Troubled Manhood."

44. Cooper, *Pilot*, 8; http://www.kirjasto.sci.fi/jcooper.htm.

45. I am still drawn to the influential argument of Mathews, *Slavery and Methodism*.

46. Glenn, *Campaign against Corporal Punishment*, 89.

47. Mayer, *All on Fire*, 20, 269–70.

48. Land, "Customs of the Sea," 177.

49. Ibid., 181; Visram, *Ayahs, Lascars and Princes*, 38–51.

50. Dinwiddy, "Campaign against Flogging," 309; Rasor, *Reform in the Royal Navy*, 10–11, quotation 147 fn. 29. Post-1860, "safe forbearance" was counseled in the use of physical punishment, with all physical punishment suspended in peacetime as of 1871 and extended to all contingencies in 1879. "Confinement" henceforth replaced physical force as the standard disciplinary tool in the Royal Navy (55–58).

51. *Congressional Globe*, 31st Cong., 1st sess., 1850, vol. 9, pt. 2: 2058–59; Sewell, *John P. Hale*, 137–39, 209–11. Perhaps to persuade more conservative legislators, Senator Hale's remarks pointedly overlooked the extended service of African Americans as well as "white citizens" in the U.S. Navy since its establishment in 1798. Bolster, *Black Jacks*, 68–69, 91, 103–4; encyclopedia.com, ⟨http://www.encyclopedia.com/doc/1O126-AfricanAmericansinthMltry.html⟩.

52. *Congressional Globe*, 31st Cong., 1st sess., 1850, vol. 9, pt. 2: 1907; N. Morris, *Oxford History of the Prison*.

53. *Congressional Globe*, 31st Cong., 1st sess., 1850, vol. 9, pt. 2: 1907.

54. Langley, *Social Reform*, 192–205. The House vote was more lopsided, 131 to 29 for abolition, with the opposition dominated by southerners and New York merchant interests. *Congressional Globe*, 31st Cong., 1st sess., 1850, vol. 9, pt. 2: 1850.

55. Rafferty, "Republic Afloat," 74.

56. *Senate Journal*, 31st Cong., 1st sess., Sept. 28, 1850, 691; *Statutes at Large*, 9, Naval Appropriation Act, 31st Cong., sess. 1, 1850, ch. 80: 515. The unintended (at least by its sponsor) extension of the measure foreshadows the famous case of the extension of anti-discrimination language of the Civil Rights Act of 1964 on the basis of "sex" as well as "race."

57. U.S. Congress, *Report from the Secretary of the Navy on the subject of the discipline of the Navy*.

58. "Flogging in the U.S. Navy," Naval Historical Center, Department of the Navy, ⟨http://www.history.navy.mil/library/online/flogging/htm⟩.

59. Elizabeth Schultz, "African-American Literature," in Springer, *America and the Sea*, 237–38; Equiano, *Life of Olaudah Equiano*; on controversy surrounding the interpretation of Equiano's text, see Carretta, *Equiano, the African*.

60. Douglass, *Narrative of the Life of Frederick Douglass*, 91; Douglass, *Life and Times* (1881), quoted in Schultz, "African-American Literature," 240.

61. Sokolow, *Charles Benson*, 45–47.

62. Bolster, *Black Jacks*, 190–214. In the 1850s, some states liberalized the Negro Seamen's Acts by requiring only that black seamen stay on board ship (as opposed to being placed in custody). Hamer, "British Consuls."

63. Hamer, "British Consuls," 144.

64. Hamer, "Great Britain."

65. U.S. Congress, House Committee on Commerce, *Free Colored Seamen*, 3, 6.

66. Hamer, "Great Britain," 22–23.

67. *Free Colored Seamen*, 40–42. On the state-delimited definitions of citizenship in this era, cf. William J. Novak, "The Legal Transformation of Citizenship in Nineteenth Century America," in Jacobs, Novak, and Zelizer, *American Experiment*, 85–120.

68. Opinions of Attorneys General, Message from the President of the United States, 31st Cong., 2d sess., 1851, "Rights of Free Virginia Negroes," 329–31.

69. *Free Colored Seamen*, 51, 55; on the contemporary invocation of state quarantines, see Bloom, *Mississippi Valley's Great Yellow Fever Epidemic*, 36–37, 45–46.

70. Wilson quoted in Hamer, "Great Britain," 11.

71. Taney quoted in Fehrenbacher, *Dred Scott Case*, 70.

72. Fehrenbacher, *Dred Scott Case*, 343.

73. Fitzhugh, *Sociology for the South*, 85.

74. D. Williams, "Mid-Victorian Attitudes to Seamen," 126.

75. *Congressional Globe*, 42d Cong., 2d sess., 1872, vol. 17 pt. 3: 2173.

76. Ibid., 2208.

77. Ibid., 122; Course, *Merchant Navy*, 217.

78. D. Williams, "Mid-Victorian Attitudes to Seamen," 114.

79. Walkowitz, *Prostitution and Victorian Society*, 72–73; D. Williams, "Mid-Victorian Attitudes to Seamen," 126.

80. *Hansard*, 3d ser., vol. 130 (1854), 574–75; Hope, *New History of British Shipping*, 282.

81. Subsequent restriction of government regulative powers in the United States, especially during the Progressive Era (as we will see in chapter 4), would derive more from the courts than from any anti-government or anti-regulatory impulse from the legislative branch.

82. *Congressional Globe*, 42d Cong., 2d sess., 1872, vol. 17, pt. 3: 1838.

83. Rafferty, "Republic Afloat," 42–43; Fingard, *Jack in Port*, 8–45. With her focus on British shipping to Canadian ports, Judith Fingard offers a subtle and sympathetic reading of the crimp's role in what she calls the "sailor labour market," including examples of crimp-sailor solidarity in pursuit of higher wages. Similarly, David Montgomery cites the 1867 case of a master stevedore's association bringing suit against waterfront tavern owners for effectively bargaining up the minimum wages of Boston seafarers. *Citizen Worker*, 48.

84. *Hansard*, 3d ser., vol. 130 (1854): 576, 582. Another form of the "advance" was the "allotment" system, wherein a designated portion of the seaman's wages could be allotted to his wife, mother, or the like or to an "original creditor," i.e. the crimp. See Macarthur, "American Seaman," 724–76.

85. *Statutes at Large*, vol. 17, 42d Cong., 2d sess., 1872, 266-sec. 17; vol. 23, 48th Cong., 1st sess., 1884, 55, 56-sec. 10; Roland, Bolster, and Keyssar, *Way of the Ship*, 235.

86. A statistical sample of U.S. seamen in 1796–1803 and 1812–15, for example, revealed a mean age of twenty-three years old. Dye, "Early American Merchant Seafarers," 334–35.

87. Norling, *Captain Ahab Had a Wife*, 214–61; Sokolow, *Charles Benson*, 70–77.

88. Valerie Burton, "The Myth of Bachelor Jack: Masculinity, Patriarchy and Seafaring Labour," in Howell and Twomey, *Jack Tar in History*, 179.

89. For a comprehensive treatment of the interaction of wage labor and domestic contracts, see Stanley, *From Bondage to Contract*.

90. Dixon, "Seamen and the Law," 101–5.

91. Great Britain, Public General Acts, Merchant Shippig Act, 17 & 18 Vict. (1854), cc. 104: 667–69.

92. Fingard, *Jack in Port*, 150.

93. Dixon, "Seamen and the Law," 297.

94. MacArthur, "American Seamen," 721; R. Morris, "Labor Controls in Maryland in the Nineteenth Century."

95. *Congressional Globe*, 42d Cong., 2d sess., 1872, pt. 3: 2206. Congressman and shipowner Fernando Wood of New York opposed the bill as a bureaucratic nightmare, modeled on a "failed" English law, unfit for "republican" government (2173–76).

96. Stanley, *From Bondage to Contract*, 35–40. For discussions of the extension of coercive practices within regimes of nominally free contract labor, see Gunther Peck, "Contracting Coercion"; Stanley, "Beggars Can't Be Choosers"; and Montgomery, *Citizen Worker*, 52–114.

97. *Congressional Globe*, 42d Cong., 2d sess., 1872, pt. 3: 2206.

98. Macarthur, "American Seaman," 721.

99. General Butler's formative experience with the administration of labor contracts

had come in 1862, when, administering the liberated sugar plantations of Louisiana, he devised policies to keep blacks—still technically slaves—at work according to a newly imposed wage system. Foner, *Reconstruction*, 55, 491.

100. *Congressional Globe*, 42d Cong., 2d sess., 1872, pt. 3: 2206.

101. In addition to the case of merchant seamen, Steinfeld has called attention to several other instances of late-nineteenth- and even early-twentieth-century enforcement of penal sanctions in labor contract enforcement, seemingly at odds with the spirit of both the Thirteenth Amendment and subsequent anti-peonage laws. *Coercion, Contract, and Free Labor*, 275–89.

102. Rafferty, "Republic Afloat," 56.

103. Fingard, *Jack in Port*, 242.

104. Lewis R. Fischer, "A Dereliction of Duty," in Ommer and Panting, *Working Men Who Got Wet*, 54–58; Sager, *Seafaring Labour*, 194–98. On the underreporting of desertions, see Fingard, *Jack in Port*, 142.

105. Sager, *Seafaring Labour*, 196.

106. Ibid., 303 fn. 59.

107. Rediker, *Between the Devil and the Deep Blue Sea*, 100–115.

108. Course, *Merchant Navy*, 221–22; Macarthur, "American Seaman," 229.

109. Weintraub, *Andrew Furuseth*, 31–34. A legal anomaly had, in fact, allowed prosecution of desertion in U.S. ports to lapse since an 1874 bill had eliminated the coastal trade from the bureaucracy of the far-reaching Shipping Commissioners' Act of 1872. As Furuseth, then with the Coast Seamen, discovered in 1887, the 1874 legislation unintentionally also withdrew the sailors from the sanctions of desertion in U.S. home ports, thus giving the union a powerful new strike tactic. Shipowners responded with remedial legislation in 1890, restoring "desertion" penalties for the coastal trade—and thus also setting up the agenda for the Maguire Act. Taylor, *Sailors' Union*, 76–79.

110. Schwartz, *History of the Sailor's Union*.

111. U.S. Supreme Court, *Robertson v. Baldwin*, 281, 283–86, 287–88.

112. Ibid., 292–93, 298–99.

113. Weintraub, *Andrew Furuseth*, 35; Macarthur, "American Seaman," 723.

114. Steinfeld, *Coercion, Contract, and Free Labor*, 266, 273, 277.

115. Macarthur, *Seaman's Contract*, 221–22; Weintraub, *Andrew Furuseth*, 42–43.

Chapter 3

1. Jones, *Plimsoll Sensation*, 12–13.

2. On early animal rights, see, e.g., Guither, *Animal Rights*, and Pearson, "'Rights of the Defenseless'"; on campaigns regarding "white slavery," see Walkowitz, *Prostitution and Victorian Society*, and *City of Dreadful Delight*.

3. See Stuart Hall, "The Rise of the Representative/Interventionist Sate, 1880s–1920s," in McLennan, Held, and Hall, *State and Society*, 7–49.

4. International Maritime Organization, "Historical Background Leading to the Adoption of the Load Lines Convention, International Maritime Organization."

5. nmm.ac.uk, "Ships, seafarers, & life at sea," http://www.nmm.ac.uk/explore/sea-and-ships/facts/ships-and-seafarers/load-lines; Fred Albert, "A Cheer for Plimsoll,"

Vocal Music (1876); John Guest, "A British Cheer for Plimsoll!" *Guest Vocal Music* (1875); vocal music in British Library, London. In its July 29, 1877, issue, the *New York Times* reprinted "The Meteorology of the Future," from the journal *Nature*, which, invoking the nightmare of shipwreck, included the following stanzas:

> I answered him: "But knowst thou not
> That Plimsoll's noble band
> Board every ship, and punch its ribs
> Before it leaves the land?"
> "No rotten beam but would be seen
> By such a skilled detecter.
> The dead man groaned—'*Alas! dear mate,*
> *They jobbed the ship's inspector.*'"

6. Course, *Merchant Navy*, 254.

7. *Coast Seamen's Journal*, 3 (Mar. 5, 1890) (San Francisco).

8. Peters, *Plimsoll Line*, v.

9. *New York Times*, Oct. 1, 1897.

10. *Seamen's Record*, Aug. 9, 1902, International Transport Workers' Federation (hereafter ITF) Papers, Seafaring; Jewell, *Among Our Sailors*.

11. Peters, *Plimsoll Line*, 5–24, 30–36; Masters, *Plimsoll Mark*, 76–83. On advanced manufacturers, see Jonathan Spain, "Trade Unionists, Gladstonian Liberals and the Labour Law Reforms of 1875," in Biagini and Reid, *Currents of Radicalism*, 116. Other Liberal manufacturer-politicians often sympathetic to workers' concerns, Spain notes, were Sheffield hosiery magnate A. J. Mundella, an advocate of industrial arbitration; Samuel Morley, a Nottingham textiles owner who supported Joseph Arch's agricultural laborers' union; and Derby brewer M. T. Bass, an advocate for the railway unions. Plimsoll would also find occasional common cause with newsagent W. H. Smith, worsted spinner Alfred Illingworth, and wire manufacturer Peter Rylands. Jones, *Plimsoll Sensation*, 126.

12. Indeed, between 1870 and 1873, 2,287 seamen were imprisoned from fourteen days to three months for reporting unseaworthy ships that went uncorroborated by subsequent Board of Trade surveys. Course, *Merchant Navy*, 231.

13. Peters, *Plimsoll Line*, 42, 51–53; Masters, *Plimsoll Mark*, 98–101, 124. While initially friendly, as Masters indicates, James Hall's relations with Plimsoll soured as the latter largely monopolized public attention on behalf of their shared cause.

14. Himmelfarb, *Idea of Poverty*, 155–56, 312–23, 354–55.

15. I am particularly indebted for explanation of this theme to Pearson, "'Rights of the Defenseless.'" Among key, complementary sources here is Fiering, "Irresistible Compassion." Another excellent, related treatment is Clark, "'Sacred Rights of the Weak.'" On the social inequality built into the "paradox of sentimentalism," see Silverman, "Sympathy and Its Vicissitudes." For a descriptive account of related movements, see also Glenn, *Campaign against Corporal Punishment*.

16. Quotation from Chichester Fortescue, *Hansard* (Commons), 3d ser., vol. 214, (1873): 1341.

17. Plimsoll, *Our Seamen*, 1.

18. Ibid. (illustrative insert from Annual Report of Board of Trade, opposite page), 2, 30.

19. Ibid., 55.

20. Ibid., 4–5.

21. Ibid., 11.

22. Ibid., 19–20.

23. Ibid., 88.

24. Ibid., 64.

25. Quoted in Peters, *Plimsoll Line*, 77.

26. Glover, "Plimsoll Sensation: A Reply," in Fortescue, *Hansard*, 1341–43.

27. Masters, *Plimsoll Mark*, 158, 176; Royal Commission on Unseaworthy Ships quoted in (unsigned) "Merchant Shipping Legislation," 474.

28. Farrer, "Merchant Shipping and Further Legislation."

29. "Merchant Shipping Legislation," 457.

30. As cited in Jones, *Plimsoll Sensation*, 101.

31. Peters, *Plimsoll Line*, 63–64.

32. Ibid., 105–8; Stenton and Lees, *Who's Who*, 2:25.

33. Masters, *Plimsoll Mark*, 214.

34. Vincent, *Derby Diaries*, 20, 22. Shaftesbury may well have likened Plimsoll's treatment to that of William Dodd, whose own exposé of child labor conditions, crucial to Shaftesbury's legislative proposals in the 1840s, had also been subjected to personal as well as political attacks in the House of Commons. Lord Ashley Earl of Shaftesbury, ⟨http://www.spartacus.schoolnet.co.uk/IRashley.htm⟩; Thomas Hughes, ⟨http://www.spartacus.schoolnet.co.uk/REhughes.htm⟩.

35. Leventhal, *Respectable Radical*, 140. Robert Knight, president of the skilled Boilermakers' Society (centrally concerned with steamship-building), was another early recruit to Plimsoll's side. Alastair J. Reid, "Old Unionism Reconsidered," in Biagini and Reid, *Currents of Radicalism*, 219.

36. "Unseaworthy Ships and Shipping Legislation," newspaper [name not discernible] report on public meeting in Liverpool, Apr. 7, 1875, George Howell Collection; Lamport, "Plimsoll Agitation," 117–37.

37. G. Howell, *Labour Legislation*, 269–70. Beginning in the mid-1870s and reaching its peak in 1885, the Lib-Lab formation expired when the unions threw their support to the incipient Labour Party after 1900.

38. P. Marsh, *Joseph Chamberlain*, 143; Peters, *Plimsoll Line*, 114.

39. Feuchtwanger, *Disraeli*, 177.

40. *New York Times*, July 24, 1875.

41. Great Britain, Public General Acts, Merchant Shipping Act, 39 & 40 Vict. (1876) c. 80.

42. Course, *Merchant Navy*, 236, 238.

43. Ibid., 246. In only four cases did shipowners appeal the Board of Trade survey's verdict; of those, only one case (against a verdict of unsafe construction) resulted in damages awarded to the shipowner for unnecessary delay of cargo. A short while later, the ship in question reportedly went missing "with all hands."

44. Masters, *Plimsoll Mark*, 224; *London Times* quoted in Peters, *Plimsoll Line*, 119.

45. Disraeli quoted in Masters, *Plimsoll Mark*, 224.

46. Vincent, *Derby Diaries*, 232–33, 20.

47. Plimsoll quoted in David M. Williams, "State Regulation of Merchant Shipping, 1839–1914: The Bulk Carrying Trades," in Palmer and Williams, *Charted and Uncharted Waters*, 66–67.

48. Plimsoll had again broken parliamentary decorum by campaigning against two opponents of maritime reform in their home districts, an offense that landed him a formal vote of censure in 1879. Masters, *Plimsoll Mark*, 246. Punch portrayed Harcourt as "A Man Overboard" rescued by "The Sailors' Friend" in Peters, *Plimsoll Line*, 144.

49. *Hansard* (Lords), 3d ser., vol. 254 (1880): 1460–62.

50. *Hansard* (Commons), 3d ser., vol. 290 (1884): 350.

51. P. Marsh, *Joseph Chamberlain*, 172–73.

52. Ibid., 171–73, 185.

53. Weiler, *New Liberalism*, 13–28.

54. *Hansard* (Commons), 3d ser., vol. 225 (1875): 168–70; Stenton and Lees, *Who's Who*, 2:204.

55. "Merchant Shipping Legislation," 456.

56. *Hansard* (Commons), 3d ser., vol. 227 (1876): 455; Stenton and Lees, *Who's Who*, 2:60–61.

57. *Hansard* (Commons), 3d ser., vol. 227 (1876): 464; Stenton and Lees, *Who's Who*, 1:86–87.

58. *Hansard* (Commons) 3d ser., vol. 251 (1880): 960–61.

59. *Hansard* (Lords), 3d ser., vol. 254 (1880): 1459–60; Stenton and Lees, *Who's Who*, 1:382.

60. *Hansard* (Commons), 3d ser., vol. 251 (1880): 964, 967.

61. Ibid., vol. 229 (1876): 74–77.

62. Ibid., vol. 227 (1876): 435.

63. Ibid., 440; 3d ser., vol. 251 (1880): 960. A linchpin of Margaret Thatcher's campaign for prime minister in 1979 was her attack on Britain's allegedly over-socialized "nanny state." The added-provisions clause that sparked the "scurvy debate" was subsequently withdrawn by its proponents before passage of the 1876 Merchant Shipping Act.

64. *Hansard* (Commons), 3d ser., vol. 227 (1876): 440.

65. Ibid., 228 (1876): 628–29.

66. Great Britain, Public General Acts, Merchant Shipping Act, 39 & 40 Vict. (1876) c. 80. Two considerations limited the practical effects of these initial measures: (1) without a load line provision, it was difficult to charge a vessel as overloaded, and (2) in the case of a detained foreign vessel, the consular agent of the foreign state could request an independent assessment with potential damages to be paid by the Board of Trade.

67. John Eldon Gorst, ⟨http://www.reference.com/browse/wiki/John_Eldon_Gorst⟩.

68. *Hansard* (Commons), 3d ser., vol. 228 (1876): col. 523.

69. Ibid., vol. 227 (1876): col. 436.

70. Ibid., vol. 229 (1876): col. 63; Stenton and Lees, *Who's Who*, 1:92.

71. "Merchant Shipping Legislation," 482–83.

72. Together, Chamberlain and Howell helped secure measures that gave the Board of Trade control over load lines (1890) and an additional inspection of provisions (1892). Leventhal, *Respectable Radical*, 207; Masters, *Plimsoll Mark*, 260.

73. Matthew and Harrison, *Oxford Dictionary of National Biography*, s.v. "Joseph Havelock Wilson," 59:612–13; Clegg, Fox, and Thompson, *History of British Trade Unions*, 1:55.

74. Course, *Merchant Navy*, 254.

75. Peters, *Plimsoll Line*, 155, 165; Masters, *Plimsoll Mark*, 258.

76. J. Wilson, *My Stormy Voyage*, 205.

77. *Hansard* (Commons), 4th ser., vol. 23 (1894): 21–22; vol. 24 (1899): 1001; vol. 66 (1899): 1292, 1451–52.

78. United Kingdom, "Further Recommendations of Report," *Fifth and Final Report of the Royal Commission on Labour*, 137.

79. *Hansard* (Commons), 4th ser., vol. 67 (1899): 69.

80. Ibid., 89.

81. Ibid., vol. 69 (1899): 666–67.

82. Ibid., vol. 67 (1899): 93–96.

83. See, in particular, Eugenio F. Biagini and Alastair J. Reid, "Currents of Radicalism, 1850–1914," in Biagini and Reid, *Currents of Radicalism*, 1–20.

84. Gilbert, *David Lloyd George*, 323–34.

85. Great Britain, Public General Acts, Merchant Shipping Act, 57 & 58 Vict. (1894) c. 60; Clegg, Fox, and Thompson, *A History of British Trade Unions*, 1:239 n. 1.

86. *Parliamentary Debates* (Commons), 4th ser., vol. 154 (1906): 244. Lloyd George also minimized concern about the diminution of numbers of native seamen. In part a function of a growing navy (64,000 in 1868 compared to 129,000 in 1905), in part due to the undesirable schedules of many British ships that sailed for months in distant waters, he pointed out that even Lord Nelson's glorious fleet reportedly contained 20 percent foreign crews, so there was surely "no danger" at the present moment. Col. 244.

87. Ibid., 279, 246, 1089–90.

88. Ibid., 255.

89. *Parl. Deb.* (Lords), 4th ser., vol. 165 (1906): 53–54.

90. *Parl. Deb.* (Commons), 4th ser., vol. 165 (1906): 1037; vol. 163 (1906): 70. Bonar Law's point was likely stronger as a debating point than a legal one. Though the U.S. Passenger Acts did mandate conditions on ships setting out for America, they effectively inspected and sanctioned them only for violations discovered once in U.S. ports—thus still applying "conventional" tests of sovereignty. See "Common Carrier Defined," ⟨http://www.lectlaw.com/def.c069.htm⟩.

91. *Parl. Deb.* (Lords), 4th ser., vol. 167 (1906): 55; *Parl. Deb.* (Commons), 4th ser., vol. 154 (1906): 1101; *Parl. Deb.* (Lords), 4th ser., vol. 165 (1906): 53.

92. *Parl. Deb.* (Commons), 4th ser., vol. 165 (1906): 1045; vol. 163 (1906): 73.

93. Hired in large numbers by the British since the late eighteenth century and serving on special two-year contracts first codified in 1834, Indian lascars "were paid one-third to one-fifth as much as white or Black seamen who operated in the nominally free European labor market." A virtual "captive pool of cheap labor," lascars were hired in the colonies for round-trip voyages only; they were required to be discharged and

re-engaged only in British India or else under the direct orders of the Lascar Transfer Office. Though "lascar" agreements were most commonly applied to Indian seamen, the British possessions of Singapore and Hong Kong also led to similar forms of "irregular" (versus "standard") Asiatic articles. Tabili, *"We Ask for British Justice,"* 42–47.

94. *Parl. Deb.* (Commons), 4th ser., vol. 165 (1906): 1047; vol. 154 (1906): 1114. A racial denigration of lascars—most obvious in Wilson's slippage in defining British Indian and British Chinese seamen as "foreigners"—infected even their defenders among policy makers. Extending a helping hand to an occupational group displaced by more advanced British ships, Lloyd George described the lascar as a "hereditary sailor . . . bound by rules of his caste to pursue the trade his ancestors have pursued from time immemorial." Discountenancing any need for further regulation on lascar conditions, J. D. Rees (Montgomery Boroughs) further claimed, "It was a well-known fact that if a native of India owned a palace, he would sleep in a corner. He disliked space and absolutely enjoyed crowding." *Parl. Deb.* (Commons), 4th ser., vol. 154 (1906): 245; *Parl. Deb.* (Lords), 4th ser., vol. 154 (1906): 1095–96.

95. *Parl. Deb.* (Commons), 4th ser., vol. 154 (1906): 290.

96. Ibid., 291.

97. See, e.g., the remarks of Conservative MP Admiral Field from Essex, *Hansard*, 4th ser., vol. 67 (1899): 81.

98. Matthew and Harrison, *Oxford Dictionary of National Biography*, s.v. "Samuel Plimsoll," 44:583.

99. *London Times*, June 4, June 6, 1898.

100. On the derivation of the "motley crew," see Linebaugh and Rediker, *Many-Headed Hydra*, 27–28, 213–14.

Chapter 4

1. For the best prior treatment of the act, see Auerbach, "Progressives At Sea." La Follette's quotation in Weintraub, *Andrew Furuseth*, 132.

2. The two-watch system (assuming a rotation of crew at four-hour intervals) was posed as a restriction on the Kalashi watch where all men served during the day but only a skeleton crew served at night—an arrangement that had drawn union criticism as a safety hazard. Weintraub, *Andrew Furuseth*, 111–12. In accord with the eight-hour day demand on land (not yet seen as practical for deck hands), the act specified a three-watch system for engine room employees.

3. *Statutes at Large*, 63d Cong., 3d sess. (1915), 38, pt. 1, 1164–85. Application of the act's provisions to foreign vessels was spelled out repeatedly in specific subsections: the half-wages provision (sec. 4) explicitly "provided further that this section shall apply to seamen on foreign vessels while in harbors of the United States, and the courts of the United States shall be open to such seamen for its enforcement"; similarly, not only did the manning (i.e., able-bodied quotient) and language provisions apply to "any vessel" under sec. 13, but the custom's agent, "upon the sworn information of any reputable citizen [read union representative] of the United States," was authorized to "muster the crew" and prevent a ship's departure until the ship complied with these provisions. Finally, secs. 16 and 18 not only extended the freedom-from-desertion-arrest to "seamen

on foreign vessels while in harbors of the United States" but, on an expedited procedural calendar, moved to annul all prior treaty agreements to the contrary.

4. Gilje, *Liberty on the Waterfront*, 249–58.

5. Schwartz, *History of the Sailors' Union*, commissioned by the union and available online. The pertinent section here is ch. 1, "The Lookout of the Labor Movement."

6. Weintraub, *Andrew Furuseth*, 2–3, 31–33, 51–56; Auerbach, "Progressives at Sea," 347. The International Seamen's Union of America (initially called the National Seamen's Union) was formed in 1892–99 as an amalgamation of Furuseth's old union, the Sailors' Union of the Pacific (an outgrowth of the older Coast Seamen's Union of the Pacific, est. 1885), with the Atlantic Coast Seamen's Union and Lake Seamen's Union on the Great Lakes. Taylor, *Sailors' Union*, 62; Hohman, *History of American Merchant Seamen*, 25–26; *Coast Seamen's Journal*, Mar. 9, 1910.

7. Taylor, *Sailors' Union of the Pacific*, 139. An anonymous clipping at the 1954 centenary celebration of his birth remembers him as "always dressed in a much-wrinkled baggy blue suit which flapped about his bony frame." ITF Papers, 159/5/3/1275 "Modern Documentation, USA," Modern Records Centre, University of Warwick. That Furuseth not only did not marry but never showed interest in women's company sparked quiet rumors of his homosexuality. While rhetorically often complaining that a sailor's life and wages made marriage difficult, he never publicly addressed his own solitary lifestyle. Weintraub, *Andrew Furuseth*, 92. As a matter of record, the homosocial environment at sea, not surprisingly, at once facilitated homosexual behavior and stigmatized it aboard ship. See, e.g., Burg, *Sodomy and the Pirate Tradition*.

8. *San Francisco Chronicle*, Jan. 25, 1938.

9. Weintraub, *Andrew Furuseth*, 87–88. Regularly joining the La Follettes for Sunday breakfasts in D.C., Furuseth "came as close to leading a family life . . . as he ever did in his entire life" (88). Thelen, *Robert M. La Follette*, 112.

10. Weintraub, *Andrew Furuseth*, 120–21.

11. The truncated version of the Furuseth reforms was introduced in the Senate by Senator Theodore Burton, a leading spokesman for shipping interests. *Cong. Rec.*, 63d Cong., 1st sess., Oct. 18, 1913, 50, 5696; Auerbach, "Progressives at Sea," 350.

12. Hohman, *History of American Merchant Seamen*, 30.

13. *Statutes at Large*, 63d Cong., 3d sess. (1915), vol. 38, pt. 1: 1164–85.

14. *Cong. Rec.*, House, 63d Cong., 2d sess. (1914), 51, pt. 14: 14359.

15. *Cong. Rec.*, Senate, 63d Cong., 1st sess. (1913), 50, pt. 6: 5718. A rather weak riposte by the reformers' opponents on the safety issue was sounded by steamship attorney Edwin H. Duff. Loosening long-standing strictures on the seamen's freedom would, he claimed, "absolutely destroy discipline." And, "without the discipline there can be no safety." Ibid., 5698.

16. Green, *Calf's Head and Union Tale*, 237.

17. Macarthur, *Seaman's Contract*, 221.

18. Furuseth quoted here in McFee, *Law of the Sea*, 181. On the still-mysterious genealogy of these words, which appear, among other places, under a bust of the sailor union leader at the National Portrait Gallery as well as at the Sailors' Union of the Pacific headquarters in San Francisco, see Green, "Furuseth's Credo," in *Calf's Head and Union Tale*, 229–46.

19. Weintraub, *Andrew Furuseth*, 116.

20. U.S. Congress, House Committee on Merchant Marine and Fisheries, *Report*, pt. 1: 6.

21. *Cong. Rec.*, Senate, 63d Cong., 3d sess. (1915), 52, pt. 5: 4808.

22. Senate Commerce Committee, *Hearing on HR 23673, Involuntary Servitude Imposed upon Seamen*, 39–41.

23. *Cong. Rec.*, Senate, 63d Cong., 3d sess. (1915), 52, pt. 5: 4803.

24. Auerbach, "Progressives at Sea," 359.

25. Senate Commerce Committee, *Hearing on HR 23673, Involuntary Servitude Imposed upon Seamen*, 75, 85.

26. Ibid., 74.

27. Ibid., 120.

28. *Cong. Rec.*, Senate, 63d Cong., 1st sess. (1913), 50, pt. 6: 5698.

29. Hohman, *History of American Merchant Seamen*, 31.

30. *Cong. Rec.*, House, 63d Cong., 3d sess. (1915), 52, pt. 5: 4643. In testimony to Congress, for example, one steamship company president identified only six U.S.-flag steamers left on the Pacific Ocean (with all six owned by railroad companies who operated them at a loss).

31. House Committee on Merchant Marine and Fisheries, *Report*, pt. 2: 1–2.

32. *Cong. Rec.*, House, 63d Cong., 3d sess., 1915, 52, pt. 5: 4647.

33. As quoted in Weintraub, *Andrew Furuseth*, 37.

34. Testimony of New York congressman Cox, *Cong. Rec.*, House, 48th Cong., 1st sess. (1884), 15, pt. 4: 3449.

35. Bickel, "Strathearn S.S. Co. v. Dillon," 1184.

36. *Cong. Rec.*, House, 63d Cong., 3d sess. (1915), 52, pt. 5: 4647.

37. Ibid., 2d sess. (1914), 51, pt. 14: 14359.

38. Auerbach, "Progressives at Sea," 353–54.

39. *Cong. Rec.*, Senate, 63d Cong., 1st sess. (1913), 50, pt. 6: 5718.

40. Ibid., 3d sess. (1915), 52, pt. 5: 4814.

41. *Cong. Rec.*, House, 63d Cong., 2d sess. (1914), 51, pt. 14: 14356; The Handbook of Texas Online ⟨http://www.tsha.utexas.edu/handbook/online/articles/view/HH/fha69.html⟩.

42. Senate Commerce Committee, *Hearing on HR 23673, Involuntary Servitude Imposed upon Seamen*, 57.

43. *Coast Seamen's Journal*, July 14, 1915.

44. Hohman, *History of American Merchant Seamen*, 34.

45. Sager, *Seafaring Labour*, 198.

46. Quotation from Weintraub, *Andrew Furuseth*, 120.

47. *Cong. Rec.*, Senate, 63d Cong., 3d sess. (1915), 52, pt. 5: 4813.

48. Two Balkan Wars as well as continuing German-British naval buildups raised international tensions across 1912–13.

49. *Cong. Rec.*, Senate, 63d Cong., 3d sess. (1915), 52, pt. 5: 4736.

50. Ibid., 4740.

51. *Cong. Rec.*, Senate, 63d Cong., 3d sess. (1915), 52, pt. 5: 4817.

52. Furuseth, "American Sea Power and the Seamen's Act."

53. For elaboration, see Fink, *Progressive Intellectuals*, 13–26. On the AFL's Progressive Era attempts to thread the needle between its avowed principle of "voluntarism" and strategic state intervention, see Fink, "Labor, Liberty, and the Law," in *In Search of the Working Class*, esp. 153–58. For a more extensive discussion of the same issue, see Greene, *Pure and Simple Politics*. For further exposition of these themes, see, e.g., Destler, *American Radicalism*, and Goodwyn, *Democratic Promise*. Croly, allowing that his own recipe for a more powerful, democratic state contained socialistic elements, insisted nonetheless that it "be characterized not so much socialistic, as unscrupulously and loyally nationalistic." *Promise of American Life*, 209.

54. Croly, *Promise of American Life*, 209.

55. *Cong. Rec.*, House, 63d Cong., 2d sess. (1914), 51, pt. 14: 14342–343. The *Titanic*, Congressman Bryan estimated, whose liability was roughly $3,000,000 under British laws, would have had to pay less than $100,000 to victims' families under American statutes. The Limitation of Shipowners' Liability Act of 1851 substantially limited responsibility for losses from negligence or unseaworthiness arising without the shipowner's participation and knowledge. Akpinar, "Defeating Limitation of Liability in Maritime Law."

56. *Cong. Rec.*, House, 63d Cong., 2d sess. (1914), 51, pt. 14: 14343. For the contemporary usage of the notion of an "American standard" in labor and economic debates, see Glickman, *Living Wage*.

57. *Cong. Rec.*, House, 63d Cong., 2d sess. (1914), 51, pt. 14: 14345.

58. Hearings of 1913 quoted in *Coast Seamen's Journal*, Feb. 5, 1913. Most novel about the U.S. legislation, of course, was the extension of standards, especially the desertion and half-wages clauses, to seafarers themselves.

59. Senate Commerce Committee, *Hearing on HR 23673 Involuntary Servitude Imposed upon Seamen*, 21.

60. The union published an elaborate synopsis of maritime labor laws in eleven countries, not counting its own frequent invocation of British precedents. *Coast Seamen's Journal*, Aug. 11, 1909.

61. Weintraub, *Andrew Furuseth*, 98–99, 115.

62. Ibid., 126–27.

63. *Cong. Rec.*, House, 63d Cong., 2d sess. (1914), 51, pt. 14: 14352.

64. Lorenz, *Defining Global Justice*, 73, 78.

65. For an extended development of this theme in a related context, see Frank, *Buy American*.

66. An exemplary modern textbook relates: "The product of stubborn agitation by the eloquent president of the Seamen's Union, the act strengthened safety requirements, reduced the power of captains, set minimum food standards and required regular wage payments. Seamen who jumped ship before their contracts expired, moreover, were relieved of the charge of desertion." Tindall and Shi, *America*, 1040.

67. Auerbach, "Progressives at Sea," 347. See also Weintraub, *Andrew Furuseth*, 112–13.

68. Auerbach, "Progressives at Sea," 360.

69. Quotation from Furuseth in *American Federationist*, 1915, as cited by Weintraub, *Andrew Furuseth*, 109.

70. Before branching out to a range of other themes, anti-Chinese complaints and pan-Asian exclusion demands provided the initial staple of content for the ISU's *Coast Seamen's Journal*, 1887–90, passim. Weintraub, *Andrew Furuseth*, 112. On seamen's union and exclusion politics, see Saxton, *Indispensable Enemy*, 252–57.

71. As quoted in Nelson, *Workers on the Waterfront*, 50.

72. *Cong. Rec.*, House, 63d Cong., 2d sess. (Aug. 27, 1914), 51, pt. 14: 14347.

73. *Cong. Rec.*, Senate, 63d Cong., 1st sess. (1913), 50, pt. 6: 5715.

74. U.S. Congress, House Committee on Immigration, "Alien Seamen and Stowaways." Gardner was the son-in-law of Henry Cabot Lodge.

75. Ibid., 20–21; *Biographical Directory of the American Congress 1774–1971*, s.v. "John Lawson Burnett," 674.

76. Without legislative resolution of the issue, the courts generally upheld the Chinese seaman's right to shore leave while gradually permitting the selective application of "bonding" (or the posting of bond as a hedge against desertion) to Chinese crew members, a practice uniformly applied to all ports by 1922. See the chapter "Sailors Should Go Ashore" in Ngai, *Lucky Ones*.

77. Cole, *Wobblies on the Waterfront*, 68.

78. *Solidarity*, Dec. 19, 1914.

79. Ibid., Nov. 14, 1914.

80. Industrial Workers of the World, *Proceedings of the First Convention of the Industrial Workers of the World*, 138 (reference courtesy of Gerald Ronning); G. Hall, *Harvest Wobblies*, 57–59.

81. *Solidarity*, Dec. 19, 1914.

82. Senate Commerce Committee, *Hearing on Involuntary Servitude Imposed upon Seamen*, 15.

83. Ibid., 18.

84. Ibid.

85. Ibid., 14–15.

86. Ibid., 16–17.

87. Ibid., 16.

88. Ibid., 19.

89. Legal Information Institute, Cornell University Law School, ⟨http://topics.law.cornell.edu/wex/admiralty⟩; Legal Database, ⟨http://www.legal-database.com/admiralty-law-overview.htm⟩. The 1957 Ealing Studies film, *Barnacle Bill* (released in the United States as *All at Sea*), had fun with the conventions of admiralty law. When a retired Royal Navy captain, William Horatio Ambrose (Alec Guinness), is met by local opposition in attempting to rehabilitate an old amusement pier, he registers the property as a "foreign" naval vessel under the flag of "Liberama" (a play on the then-budding flags-of-convenience Liberia and Panama)—which puts it beyond the reach of town authority—and proceeds to organize its stationary inaugural cruise. Harolds, "Some Legal Problems," 295; ⟨http://en.wikipedia.org/wiki/Barnacle_Bill_(1957_film)⟩. This convention, moreover, was in keeping with a general principle of American case law that congressional legislation applies only within U.S. territorial jurisdiction, unless a specific intent to the contrary is indicated. Plummer, "Choice of Law or Statutory Interpretation?," 182, 185.

90. Bickel, "Strathearn S.S. Co. v. Dillon," 1185.

91. Ibid., 1194–95. Known for his defense of judicial restraint, the "conservative" Bickel would later become a persistent critic of the Warren Court.

92. Brandeis quoted in ibid., 1183. Brandeis's opinion was aided by the work of his law clerk, the future secretary of state Dean Acheson. Bickel linked Brandeis's near-encyclopedic knowledge of—not to mention obvious sympathy with—seamen's legislation to his contemporary friendships with both La Follette and Furuseth (1201).

93. Day quoted in ibid., 1202–3.

94. Thelen, *Robert M. La Follette*, 112–13; Weintraub, *Andrew Furuseth*, 134–35.

95. Knauth, "Alien Seamen's Rights," 74–80. Knauth's article also documents how the exclusion of Chinese and Indian seamen was first softened, for political-diplomatic reasons, during World War II (77–78).

96. Hohman, *History of American Merchant Seamen*, 43.

97. *Seamen's Journal*, July 2, 1919; Hohman, *History of American Merchant Seamen*, 39–44.

98. The Jones Act actually added a remedy to two others already available to seamen. From ancient times, an incapacitated seamen had the right to "maintenance and cure" and to wages during the life of the voyage. In addition, if he incurred injury due to the unseaworthiness of the vessel, he could sue for indemnity. The Jones Act particularly extended protection in case of negligence by a fellow crewman. Stumberg, "Jones Act."

99. Merchant Marine Act, 66th Cong., 2d sess. (1920), ch. 250, 988–1008, quotation 1007.

100. Senator Jones quoted in Harolds, "Some Legal Problems," 307.

101. *O'Neill v. Cunard White Star* cited in "Recent Cases," *Rutgers Law Review* 13 (1959): 605.

102. U.S. Supreme Court, *Lauritzen v. Larsen*.

103. Disdaining the statutory language, Judge Jackson resorted to a formalistic seven-factor test (amended by a later case to eight factors) to determine the degree of U.S. interest when weighing maritime tort actions. As one commentator notes, the new test, though subsequently regularly invoked, "did little to relieve the ritualistic agony through which the courts struggled each time the question of applicability of the Jones Act was presented." W. Thompson, "Notes," quotation 351.

104. *Lauritzen* quoted in Plummer, "Choice of Law or Statutory Interpretation?," 187.

105. Justice Jackson decision in *Lauritzen* quoted in Bickel, "Strathearn S.S. Co. v. Dillon," 1204–05.

106. Harolds, "Some Legal Problems," 310.

107. *Orange County (Calif.) Post*, June 25, 1953, advertisement from Friends of Andrew Furuseth Legislative Association.

Chapter 5

1. Meyerson, "Globalism for the Rest of Us."

2. Blanqui quoted in Ernest Mahaim, "The Historical and Social Importance of International Labor Legislation," in Shotwell, *Origins of the International Labor Organization*, 1:4.

3. Marx himself took a lead in the formation of the International Workingmen's Association (or "First International," formed in London in 1864), while the more formidable Socialist International (or "Second International"), based on mass political parties like the German Social Democratic Party, began to coalesce in Chur, Belgium, in 1881 and held the first International Socialist Congress in Paris in 1889. The single trades of different countries also united in international trade secretariats, beginning with the International Federation of Miners in 1890, followed by the transport workers in 1896 and metal workers in 1900. Among these early secretariats, however, only the transport workers reportedly took on the task of directly coordinating industrial actions. Lowe, *International Protection of Labor*, xxii.

4. Marsh and Ryan, *Seamen*, 11–13.

5. J. Wilson, *My Stormy Voyage*, 93.

6. Ibid., 65–69; Matthew and Harrison, *Oxford Dictionary of National Biography*, s.v. "Joseph Havelock Wilson," 59:612–13.

7. J. Wilson, *My Stormy Voyage*, 79.

8. Means, *Bitter of Outcast London*, and C. Booth, *Life and Labour of the People in London* (originally published as two volumes in 1889 and extended to seventeen volumes by 1902), helped stir middle-class sympathies for the plight of the working classes. Clegg, Fox, and Thompson, *History of British Trade Unions*, 1:55–96; Pelling, *History of British Trade Unionism*, 97, 101.

9. Clegg, Fox, and Thompson, *History of British Trade Unions*, 1:87–96; J. Wilson, *My Stormy Voyage*, 199.

10. Valerie Burton, "The Myth of Bachelor Jack: Masculinity, Patriarchy and Seafaring Labor," in Howell and Twomey, *Jack Tar in History*, 188–90. By the 1890s, a reported two-fifths of sailors were either married or widowed.

11. "When sailors strike, dock workers are out of a job; and strike in the docks can make it impossible for ships to sail. . . . It is therefore hardly surprising that the dramatic advent of the Seamen led not only to widespread organization among the dockers, but also to contact between the leaders of both groups." Clegg, Fox, and Thompson, *History of British Trade Unions*, 1:56. It is likely that Tillett's own early experience as a mariner helped cement his lifelong friendship with Wilson. Schneer, *Ben Tillett*, 6–7.

12. *Commonweal*, June 1889, as quoted in Clegg, Fox, and Thompson, *History of British Trade Unions*, 1:56.

13. Clegg, Fox, and Thompson, *History of British Trade Unions*, 1:73–74.

14. Ibid., 73–77.

15. Schneer, *Ben Tillett*, 85.

16. Tsuzuki, *Tom Mann*, 85; Wilson, *My Stormy Voyage*, 99. Though undoubtedly the most conservative of new unionist leaders at an ideological level, Wilson's more fiery collaborators also varied over time in their social prescriptions. Tillett, e.g., influenced by the Australian model, for years backed state-based arbitration as a solution to industrial conflict before turning to syndicalism and then back to ardent nationalism during World War I; Wilson's anti-ideological pragmatism was evident in a disdainful comment in 1910 during an attempted strikebreaking by the German Employers' Association: "What makes me sick are the number of our socialist representatives from England [who] attend the International Socialist Congress, and they talk about the solidity [*sic*]

of labour but yet they do nothing to prevent British strike breakers being sent to Germany." Wilson to Herman Jochade, Sept. 21, 1910, ITF Papers, 159/3/B63/1/NSFU.

17. Clegg, Fox, and Thompson, *History of British Trade Unions*, 1:73.

18. Lane, *Union Makes Us Strong*, 106.

19. Marsh and Ryan, *Seamen*, 35–40; Pelling, *History of British Trade Unionism*, 110; Clegg, Fox, and Thompson, *History of British Trade Unions*, 1:81, 83.

20. Marsh and Ryan, *Seamen*, 51; Wilson, *My Stormy Voyage*, 194; Bob Reinalda, "The Early Years of the ITF (1896–1914)," in Reinalda, *International Transportworkers Federation*, 39.

21. Reinalda, "The Early Years of the ITF (1896–1914)," 40.

22. Tsuzuki, *Tom Mann*, 112.

23. Tom Mann to Edmund Cathery, IFSDRW, Jan. 21, 1897, ITF Papers, 159/3/a/2 NFDRW correspondence.

24. Tsuzuki, *Tom Mann*, 112–14.

25. K. A. Golding, "In the Forefront of Trade Union History," *ITF Journal* 31 (Summer 1971): 32; Barnes, *Longshoremen*, 110–23. The short-lived American Longshoremen's Union was but one of a series of discontinuous waterfront organizations in New York City before the establishment of Local 791 of the International Longshoremen's Association (ILA) in 1908.

26. Elderkin to Lindley, Dec. 23, 1895, ITF Papers, 159/3/A/1/1-14 Seafarers' Correspondence.

27. Ken Golding, "ITF History, Part 1, draft," ITF Papers, 159/3/0/254, p. 14. Golding was the ITF research officer from the 1950s to 1970.

28. Ibid.

29. Wilson to Lindley, Mar. 30, 1897, ITF Papers, 159/3/a/2 NFDRW correspondence.

30. Wilson to Lindley, Sept. 18, 1899, ITF Papers, 159/3/a/2 NFDRW correspondence.

31. Quoted in White, *Tom Mann*, 112–13.

32. Quoted in Tsuzuki, *Tom Mann*, 115.

33. By 1910, e.g., of nearly 500,000 ITF members, 57 percent were railroad workers, 18 percent dockworkers, and merely 6 percent seafarers. Reinalda, "The Early Years of the ITF," 42.

34. Taplin, *The Dockers' Union*, 82; *New York Times*, May 7, 1911.

35. Wilson to Jochade, Sept. 28, 1910, ITF Papers, 159/3/B/63/1/NSFU.

36. ITF Records, 159/B/63/1/NSFU, 1907–1911, re. 1911 strikes, International Seafarers' Movement minutes, May 1, 1911; *Weekly Report* of the ITF, July 3, 1911; White, *Tom Mann*, 174–79; cf. Clegg, Fox, and Thompson, *History of British Trade Unions*, 2:33.

37. Clegg, Fox, and Thompson, *History of British Trade Unions*, 2:34.

38. Ibid., 35.

39. Ibid. Wilson to Jochade, June 23, 1911, ITF Records, 159/3/B/63/1/NSFU 1907–1911, re. 1911 strikes.

40. Ibid., Wilson to Jochade, Dec. 29, 1911.

41. Holton, *British Syndicalism*, 91; *New York Times*, Aug. 19, 1911.

42. Holton, *British Syndicalism*, 52–69.

43. Taplin, *Dockers' Union*, 100; quotation reprinted in Holton, *British Syndicalism*, 94–95.

44. Clegg, Fox, and Thompson, *History of British Trade Unions*, 2:35.

45. Taplin, *Dockers' Union*, 86.

46. *New York Times*, June 20–21, 1911.

47. Tillett, from the *Clarion*, Aug. 18, 1911, quoted in Frow, Frow, and Katanka, *Strikes*, 137–41.

48. *New York Times*, June 22, 1911.

49. Ibid., Jan. 14, 24, 1911.

50. *Seafaring*, I, Nov. 19, 1898.

51. Tillett to Charles Lindley, May 20, 1896, ITF Papers, 159/3/a/2 NFDRW correspondence.

52. Tillett quoted in Schneer, *Ben Tillett*, 60.

53. Golding, "ITF History, Part 1, draft," 5.

54. Wilson, *My Stormy Voyage*, 127, quotation 98.

55. Tsuzuki, *Tom Mann*, 120.

56. Golding, "ITF History, Part 1, draft."

57. Furuseth to Lindley, Aug. 14, 1896, ITF Papers, 159/3/A/1/1-14 Seafarers' Correspondence.

58. Weintraub, *Andrew Furuseth*, 100–107. In 1911, only the Atlantic Coast Seamen's Union, an often discontented wing of the Furuseth-led ISU, had joined in the 1911 uprising.

59. Bodine to Jochade, Aug. 20, 1913, ITF Papers, 159/3/B/102 Correspondence with ISU of America.

60. *Korrespondenzblatt*, Jan. 20, 1905, ITF Papers, 159/4/1-3. The *K-blatt* was published in English, French, German, Italian, and Swedish.

61. Ibid., Apr. 1, 1905.

62. Golding, "ITF History, Part 1, draft," 116–18.

63. Ibid.

64. *Korresondenzblatt*, Apr. 1, 1905, ITF Papers, 159/4/1-3.

65. Golding, "ITF History, Part 1, draft," 116–18.

66. *Korresondenzblatt*, Apr. 1, 1905.

67. Golding, "ITF History, Part 1, draft," 118–19.

68. Linebaugh and Rediker, *Many-Headed Hydra*, 212–14; Duiker, *Ho Chi Minh*, 44–54.

69. Tabili, *"We Ask for British Justice,"* 185–86, 171. The demography of British imperial crafts was further complicated by other non-English "Britishers," also on lesser articles, including other Asians engaged at Singapore or Hong Kong and engine room "seedies" from Zanzibar. Ewald, "Crossers of the Sea," 87; Moving Here: Tracing Your Roots, ⟨http://www.movinghere.org.uk/galleries/roots/asian/ukrecords/lascars3.htm⟩.

70. "Supply of Seamen," *Chambers's Journal* 12 (May 4, 1895): 276.

71. *Hansard*, 4th ser., vol. 154 (1906): 244; "Supply of Seamen," 277.

72. Wilson served variously during 1892–95, 1906–10, and 1918–22; cf. Tabili's term of "pragmatic internationalism" (*"We Ask for British Justice"* 85).

73. Tabili, *"We Ask for British Justice,"* 36; parliamentary testimony as cited in *Korrespondenzblatt*, Aug. 1, 1906.

74. Balachandran, "Conflicts in the International Maritime Labour Market," 92.

75. Conrad Dixon, "Lascars: The Forgotten Seamen," in Ommer and Panting, *Working Men Who Got Wet*, 272. Dixon suggests that after the 1911 strike (in which lascars played a determinedly "neutral" role), the hostility of Wilson and others to the lascars abated.

76. Marsh and Ryan, *Seamen*, 70–71, quotation 71.

77. Wilson, *My Stormy Voyage*, 50; Marsh and Ryan, *Seamen*, 72.

78. *Seamen's Record*, Nov. 5, 1905, ITF Records, 159/5/3/479-81.

79. Furuseth to Jochade, May 27, 1915, ITF Papers, 159/3/B/102.

80. Marsh and Ryan, *Seamen*, 74–75.

81. Furuseth to Jochade, Apr. 15, 1915, ITF Papers, 159/3/B/102 Correspondence with the International Seamen's Union of America.

82. Seamen's union official Edward Tupper quoted in Marsh and Ryan, *Seamen*, 75.

83. Ibid., 75.

84. *Weekly Report of the ITF* (formerly *Korrespondenzblatt*), no. 137, Dec. 12, 1914, ITF Papers.

85. Schneer, *Ben Tillett*, 185.

86. Golding, "ITF History, Part 1, draft," 232.

87. Schneer, *Ben Tillett*, 193–94.

88. Bob Reinalda, "Interruption of Internationalism: The ITF during World War One and its New Start in 1919," in Reinalda, *International Transportworkers Federation*, 60.

89. Hartmut Rübner, "The International Seamen's Organizations after the First World War," in Reinalda, *International Transportworkers Federation*, 77–88.

90. Marsh and Ryan, *Seamen*, 76–83, quotation 81; Clegg, Fox, and Thompson, *History of British Trade Unions*, 2:141, 164.

91. Tabili, *"We Ask for British Justice,"* 93.

92. Clegg, Fox, and Thompson, *History of British Trade Unions*, 2:328–29; Hisson and Vivian, *Strike Across the Empire*.

93. Called by the General Council of the TUC in an unsuccessful attempt to force the government to act to prevent wage reduction and worsening conditions for coal miners, the General Strike of 1926 lasted ten days, May 3–12, 1926; Pelling, *History of British Trade Unionism*, 203; Clegg, Fox, and Thompson, *History of British Trade Unions*, 458.

94. Tabili, *"We Ask for British Justice,"* 93–94.

95. Ibid., 114.

96. Ibid., 110, 95.

97. Wilson, *My Stormy Voyage*, 206.

98. Ibid., 134.

Chapter 6

1. Sager, *Seafaring Labour*, 245–49. Sager notes that 1876 was the last year that total tonnage from sailing vessels exceeded that of steamships in U.K.-registered vessels but that as late as 1910, a majority of U.S. and Scandinavian tonnage was still powered by sail. Brassey, *British Seamen* (1877), quoted in Burton, "The Myth of Bachelor Jack: Masculinity, Patriarchy and Seafaring Labour," in Howell and Twomey, *Jack Tar in History*, 181.

2. H. H. Raymond testimony in *Cong. Rec.*, Senate, 63d Cong., 1st sess. (1913), 50, pt. 6: 5697. Despite apparent de-skilling, Sager insists that the able-bodied seaman of a steamship was "no mere scrubber of decks" but rather responsible for an "extensive" range of tasks including the tending of new machinery and proficiency with wire, rope, and cargo-handling equipment. *Seafaring Labour*, 261.

3. Jurgen Kramer, "Conrad's Crews Revisited," in Klein, *Fictions of the Sea*, 157.

4. Peck, *Maritime Fiction*, 170–73; Lillian Nayder, "Sailing Ships and Steamers, Angels and Whores: History and Gender in Conrad's Maritime Fiction," in Creighton and Norling, *Iron Men, Wooden Women*, 189–90. Likewise, Hester Blum perceives a more alienated work world in Conrad's fiction in contrast to earlier nineteenth-century sailoring characterized by a "desire to make labor and thought coextensive. . . . Nineteenth century sailors did not imagine their practical knowledge to be wholly divorced from figurative understanding." *View from the Masthead*, 112.

5. Gelb and Gelb, *O'Neill*, 157.

6. O'Neill, *Early Plays*, quotation from "The Moon of the Caribbees" (1917), 6.

7. O'Neill, *The Hairy Ape*, in *Three Great Plays*, 104, 129. O'Neill also provided one of the best testaments to how a young male writer might be drawn to the otherwise unsavory life of the merchant marine. As quoted in Gelb and Gelb, *O'Neill*, 168–69, his 1911 poem "Ballad of the Seamy Side" begins:

> Where is the lure of the life you sing?
> Let us consider the seamy side:
> The fo'c'stle bunks and the bed bugs' sting,
> The food that no stomach could abide,
> The crawling "salt horse" flung overside
> And the biscuits hard as a cannon ball;
> What fascination can such things hide?
> "They're part of the game and I loved it all."

8. Traven, *Death Ship*, 216. The "death" or "coffin" ships, said to be dispatched to be sunk for their insurance value by unscrupulous owners, were a prime target of the investigations of British reformer Samuel Plimsoll in the 1870s and 1880s.

9. Ibid., 237.

10. Cooper, *Claude McKay*, 171.

11. McKay, *Home to Harlem*, 1.

12. McKay, *Banjo*, 312; Elizabeth Schultz, "African-American Literature," in Springer, *America and the Sea*, 244. Fellow Harlem Renaissance author Langston Hughes recorded his own maritime work experience in *The Big Sea*.

13. As a British government delegate to the Paris Peace Conference later recalled, "the reasons" for convening the early labor conferences and for drafting an eight-hours plank as "one of the first acts" of the Paris Peace Conference were "the same":

> Labor everywhere was expecting and demanding reforms of a far-reaching character in the industrial world. It had claimed that these should form part of the Treaty of Peace. Though that was not possible, there was no unwillingness, on the part of the principle governments at any rate, to consider these claims; and

the fears of possible labor troubles and disturbances made them ready to treat the matter as one of urgency. That such fears were seriously felt was evident from the fact that M. Clemenceau considered it necessary to concentrate sixty thousand troops in the streets of Paris on the first of May to keep a labor demonstration from getting out of hand.

Sir Malcolm Delevingne, "The Organizing Committee," in Shotwell, *Origins of the International Labor Organization*, 1:286.

14. Hobsbawm, *Age of Extremes*, quotation 34, and see more generally his treatment of the "Bolshevik biennium" (1917–19) and its collapse, 54–84. Authors focused on ILO impact beyond the "Western" powers tend to offer a more positive assessment: see, e.g., Broeze, "The Muscles of Empire"; and Seekings, "ILO and Welfare Reform in South Africa, Latin America and the Caribbean, 1925–50" (copy courtesy of the author).

15. Edward J. Phelan, "The Commission on International Labour Legislation," in Shotwell, *Origins of the International Labor Organization*, 1:191–95. "Speeches," in Shotwell, *Origins of the International Labor Organization*, 2:421–40, includes exchanges between Furuseth, Gompers, Matthew Woll, and others. In deference to Gompers's pleadings and as a reassurance to the Americans that "American standards" would not run the risk of being undermined by lower ILO standards, a paragraph was added to the commission's final report, which appeared as an appendage to the Treaty of Versailles as follows: "In no case shall any of the High Contracting Parties be asked or required, as a result of the adoption of any Recommendation or draft Convention by the Conference, to diminish the protection afforded by its existing legislation to the workers concerned." Phelan, "Commission on International Labour Legislation," 163.

16. Harold B. Butler, "The Washington Conference," in Shotwell, *Origins of the International Labor Organization*, 1:305–30.

17. Lorenz, *Defining Global Justice*, 75–103. To woo U.S. policy makers, ILO advocates appealed directly to the similarities between the originating spirit of the international organization and the emergency measures of the Depression-era New Deal—particularly, the National Industrial Recovery Act of 1933—to construct a new "partnership between industry, labor, and government." Shotwell, *Origins of the International Labor Organization*, 1:357–67, quotation 359.

18. The constitution of the ILO formed Part 13, or the Labor Section, of the Treaty of Versailles. The Avalon Project, Yale Law School, ⟨http://avalon.law.yale.edu/imt/partxiii.asp⟩. Regarding the ILO as an anti-Communist buffer, see Ratzlaff, "International Labor Organization," 455.

19. Though league members automatically became chartered members of the ILO, an opening was left for non-league members to the join the ILO.

20. Edward J. Phelan, "British Preparations," in Shotwell, *Origins of the International Labor Organization*, 1:105–26.

21. International Labor Organization, *Rules of the Game*, 12–16.

22. Tribute by Francis Blancard, in International Labor Organization, *Albert Thomas*, 5; Phelan, *Yes and Albert Thomas*, 58.

23. Bob Reinalda, "Success and Failure: The ITF's Sectional Activities in the Context of the ILO," in Reinalda, *International Transport Workers Federation*, 138–40. By 2005,

the ILO had adopted 185 conventions and 195 recommendations, more than 60 of which pertained to seafaring. International Labor Organization, *Rules of the Game*, 17, 64.

24. International Seamen's Code proposal, International Seamen's Conference, Genoa, Italy, June 1920, as reprinted in *Coast Seamen's Journal*, Sept. 29, 1920.

25. "Hours of Labour and Their Effect on Manning and Accommodation," League of Nations, International Labour Office, Seamen's Conference, Genoa, July 9, 1920, 416.

26. Ibid., 417. Mandating a minimum presence on deck at night, the Kalashi watch required the fuller crew to be instantly aroused from sleep in the event of rough seas.

27. Australian Dictionary of Biography, online edition, ⟨http://ww.adb.online.anu.edu.au/biogs/A090139b.htm?hilite=Guthrie⟩; "Hours of Labour and their Effect on Manning and Accommodation," 421.

28. "Hours of Labour and their Effect on Manning and Accommodation," 421.

29. Ibid., appendix 2, July 8, 1920, 510–11.

30. Ibid., July 9, 1920, 423–24. Gopalan Balachandran suggests that Mazarello (and thus the decisive maritime hours vote) may have fallen victim to the influence of the giant P&O passenger line company or government interests who supplied his interpreter. "Conflicts in the International Maritime Labour Market," 94–95.

31. Less controversial than the hours and manning proposals but still something of a breakthrough was the "placement of seamen" convention—banning mercenary intermediaries, whether boardinghouse bosses in the West or licensed recruitment brokers (e.g., Indian *ghat serangs*) in the East. Otherwise, prior to 1936, the only maritime measures to reach the two-thirds threshold for creation of an ILO "convention" pertained to child labor (no one under fourteen) (1920), requirement of articles of agreement for all seagoing vessels (1926), and the repatriation of foreign seamen to their home country (1926). Broeze, "Muscles of Empire," 52–55; ILOLEX: Database of International Labour Standards, ⟨http:// www.ilo.org/ilolex/english/convdisp1.htm⟩.

32. Record of Proceedings, International Labor Conference, Geneva, 12th sitting, Oct. 24, 1929, 157. Allowing that it "was doubtful whether Moscow will be able to do anything," Daud nevertheless warned governments that it was "time for them to see that they ratify the Conventions that are passed with their consent in these International Labor Conferences."

33. Ibid., 171–74, 176; International Labor Organization, Report of the Director, 244; Record of Proceedings, International Labour Conference, 21st and 22nd sessions, 126–27; Broeze, "Muscles of Empire," 18, 61. It is noteworthy that the young Aftab Ali had taken advantage of La Follette Act provisions to jump ship in 1923 and spend three years in the United States before returning to India.

34. Reawakening fears of worldwide revolution and social breakdown, the stock market crash and economic depression of the 1930s paradoxically lifted the global profile of the ILO as a potential agent in dealing with the employment crisis. Moynihan, "United States and the International Labor Organization," 469.

35. Record of Proceedings, International Labour Conference, 21st and 22nd sessions, 117.

36. Ibid., 133.

37. Rice and Chalmers, "Improvement of Labor Conditions on Ships by International Action," quotation 1191.

38. Moynihan, "United States and the International Labor Organization," xi; *Cong. Rec.*, 74th Cong., 1st sess. (1935), 78, pt. 2: 1683.

39. *Cong. Rec.*, 73d Cong., 2d sess. (1934), 78, pt. 11: 12580.

40. Ibid., 74th Cong., 1st sess. (1935), 79, pt. 3: 2583.

41. New Deal advocates certainly had reason to fear for the future of national labor and welfare legislation. Not until March 1937 did the Supreme Court (in the famous "switch in time saves nine" case) reverse itself and uphold a state minimum wage law. Within weeks, it likewise upheld the National Labor Relations Act and the Social Security Act, thus both averting a constitutional crisis and rendering unnecessary such radically alternative paths as the ILO to domestic social legislation. McElvaine, *Great Depression*, 286; Lorenz, *Defining Global Justice*, 108.

42. Lorenz, *Defining Global Justice*, 96–110. Winant, a former New Hampshire Republican governor, would serve briefly as ILO director general, 1939–41, before assuming a wartime role as U.S. ambassador to Great Britain.

43. Lubin quoted in Lorenz, *Defining Global Justice*, 109.

44. *Cong. Rec.*, 74th Cong., 2d sess. (1936), 80, pt. 9: 9999.

45. Ratzlaff, "International Labor Organization," 450–51.

46. Rice and Chalmers, "Improvement of Labor Conditions," 1195.

47. On the 1936 world textile conference, see Lorenz, *Defining Global Justice*, 113–19.

48. Chalmers, "International Labor Organization," 323.

49. ILOLEX: Database of International Labour Standards, Hours of Work and Manning (Sea) Convention, 1936, ⟨http:// www.ilo.org/ilolex/english/convdisp1.htm⟩.

50. The same conference passed an additional convention establishing a minimum paid vacation of not less than nine days for all crew members. Goodrich, "International Labor Relations," 349, 354. A British collective bargaining agreement the previous summer adopting the rudiments of the three-watch system reportedly paved the way for the needed supermajority of delegate votes.

51. Balachandran, "Conflicts in the International Maritime Labour Market," 96–99.

52. Record of Proceedings, International Labor Conference, 21st and 22nd sessions, 120, 127, 129. The Soviet delegate, a Mr. Markus, pointedly did not mention the suppression of the Kronstadt sailors' uprising in March 1921.

53. Ibid., 129, 121–22.

54. International Labour Conference, 91st session, Report 3 (Part 2), "Lists of Ratifications by Convention and by Country," 91st Session, 2003.

55. Hope, *A New History of British Shipping*, 365–66.

56. Roland, Bolster, and Keyssar, *Way of the Ship*, 273, 325. The World War I–era oversupply of ships combined with the Depression-era trade slump drastically affected U.S. shipbuilding: "Between 1920 and 1928 not a single vessel for foreign trade was produced in American yards." Jeffrey J. Safford, "The U.S. Merchant Marine in Foreign Trade, 1800–1939," in Yui and Nakagawa, *Business History of Shipping*, 111.

57. Goldberg, *Maritime Story*, 182.

58. Hawley, *New Deal*, 233–34. The adoption of the 75 percent rule likely borrowed from the same number adopted for the coastwise trade in the 1920 Merchant Marine (Jones) Act, as well as perhaps going back much further to the same formula in the British Navigation Acts.

59. *Cong. Rec.*, 73d Cong., 2d sess. (1934), 78, pt. 1: 665; 74th Cong., 1st sess. (1935), 79, pt. 3: 2859.

60. Ibid., 74th Cong., 2d sess., 80. Furuseth's epithet and frequent presence at debates was invoked by Democratic representative William P. Connery (Mass.) on Mar. 5, 1934. *Cong. Rec.*, 73d Cong., 2d sess. (1934), 78, pt. 4: 3739.

61. The measures, tied together in debate, were passed as the ship-subsidy Merchant Marine Act of 1936 and as an amendment to the Seamen's Act of 1915. On the subsidy measures, see Dewey, "Merchant Marine Act"; and Roland, Bolster, and Keyssar, *Way of the Ship*, 294–99.

62. *Cong. Rec.*, 74th Cong., 1st sess. (1936), 79, pt. 9: 10194; 2d sess. (1936), 80, pt. 7: 7259; Joint Conf. Rept. 3041 (June 18, 1936), 1–8, quotation 6. Reference to the late-shifting of the "personnel" sections of the 1936 legislation is made within the House debates: *Cong. Rec.*, 74th Cong., 2d sess. (1936), 80, pt. 10: 10571–10572; Merchant Marine Act of 1936, Public Law No. 835, 74th Cong., 2d sess., 1936, sec. 301 (a) and (b). The "75 percent" Seamen's Act rule had been applied to the coastal trade since the Merchant Marine (aka Jones) Act of 1920, but the selected numerical quota enjoyed a much older pedigree—it dated to the British Navigation Acts of the mid-seventeenth century. In a clause removed from the issues discussed here, the shipping subsidy act also authorized the commission to issue continuous-discharge (registry) books to each seaman. Taking the place of the dreaded "fink" books long manipulated by employers, the new books, though accepted by the ISU, quickly became the target of a militant seafarers' strike in 1936–37. Goldberg, *Maritime Story*, 184–87.

63. Tabili, *"We Ask for British Justice,"* 113–34. For an account of the intimidating effect of such legislation, see McKay, *Banjo*, 312. On the political gamesmanship (and limited real effect) behind the order, see T. Lane, "Political Imperatives."

64. Balachandran, "Conflicts in the International Maritime Labour Market," 71–100, quotation 89.

65. Zolberg, *Nation by Design*, 267–70.

66. *Cong. Rec.*, 73d Cong., 2d sess. (1934), 78, pt. 4: 3735–3741, quotation 3738.

67. Ibid., 3737; on international pressures, see "Representations by Foreign Governments regarding Congressional Bills for the Deportation of Certain Alien Seamen," U.S. Dept. of State, Foreign Relations of the United States, diplomatic papers, 1932, General, Vol. 1 (1932), ⟨http://digicoll.library.wisc.edu/cgi-bin/FRUS/FRUS-idx?id=FRUS.FRUS⟩.

68. Merchant Marine Act of 1936, sec. 301 (c).

69. *Cong. Rec.*, 74th Cong., 2d sess. (1936), 80, pt.9: 9916.

70. Ibid., pt. 10: 10068–69.

71. House Committee on Merchant Marine and Fisheries, Hearings on HR 8532, 710–12. It is most likely (though warranting further research) that the Filipino mariner issue was buried in wartime mobilization. Special acts, for example, invited Filipinos into the U.S. Army, the Coast Guard, and Coast Guard Reserve in 1941 and 1942. Otherwise, the anomalous status of Filipinos in U.S. law vanished with independence in 1946. U.S. Congress, *Permitting Filipinos to Become Members of Coast Guard Auxiliary and Coast Guard Reserve*. For an excellent overview of American immigration law and restrictionism as applied to the Philippines, see Ngai, *Impossible Subjects*, 96–126.

72. U.S. Merchant Marine in World War II, ⟨http://www.usmm.org/ww2.html⟩; Goldberg, *Maritime Story*, 198–218, 225; National Maritime Union, *On a True Course*, 65. In addition, a move to incorporate merchant seamen under GI Bill benefits tried but failed due to the opposition of the armed services (Goldberg, *Maritime Story*, 212); Schwartz, *Brotherhood of the Sea*, 132.

73. Marsh and Ryan, *Seamen*, 149–50; Hope, *New History of British Shipping*, 382–89.

74. Hope, *New History of British Shipping*, 389.

75. Marsh and Ryan, *Seamen*, 153–54.

76. Preparatory Committee, Report 9, "Wages, Hours, Manning," International Labour Conference, 28th session, 1946, 47.

77. ILOLEX: Database of International Labour Standards, ⟨http://www.ilo.org/ilolex/cgi-lex/conved.pl?C076⟩. Record of Proceedings, International Labour Conference, 28th session, 1946, Seattle, Wash., 306.

78. Preparatory Committee, Report 9, "Wages, Hours, Manning," 47.

79. The NMU had arisen amid the failed 1936–37 strike as a revolt of rank-and-file militants versus a sclerotic and corrupt ISU leadership. On the complicated and often bitter maritime interunion battles of the 1930s, see Goldberg, *Maritime Story*, 130–62, and Nelson, *Workers on the Waterfront*, 223–49.

80. Boyer, *Dark Ship*, 23. On the U.S. waterfront, the NMU, with strong Communist ties until 1946, committed itself in principle, if not always in practice, to racial integration. Rubin, *Log of Rubin the Sailor*, 274–75. On the other hand, the Seafarers' International Union openly defended segregation in the assignment of crews, which led it into confrontation with the government's wartime Fair Employment Practices Committee. Goldberg, *Maritime Story*, 211–12.

81. McFee, *Law of the Sea*, 24.

82. Hyslop, "Steamship Empire," 63–64; Balachandran, "Producing Coolies."

83. Telephone interview with Abdulgani Serang (grandson of A. K. Serang and currently general secretary of the National Union of Seafarers of India), Mar. 3, 2009; "The ILO and Seafarers," *ITF Journal*, 59.

84. Broeze, "Muscles of Empire"; Seekings, "ILO and Welfare Reform."

Chapter 7

1. Ball, *Government-Subsidized Union Monopoly*, v–vi.

2. Ibid., 3, 5, 165, 167–69, quotations 5, 224, 241.

3. Marsh and Ryan, *Seamen*, 149, 160–64, 181, 184, 187. Union leaders had also accepted an "essential work" clause that could bring the workweek up to fifty-six hours. Hope, *New History of British Shipping*, 439.

4. "Charles Lindley Leaves the ITF," *ITF Journal* 7 (Sept. 1946), 10.

5. "The Seafaring Career," *ITF Journal* 34 (Summer 1974), 21. The Tavistock Institute of Human Relations was founded in London in 1946 as a center for education, research, and consultancy in the social sciences and applied psychology.

6. Leif Riso, "A Seaman's Life—Hard Work and Low Pay," *ITF Journal* 34 (summer 1974), 20–21.

7. The pattern of maritime discontent echoed a larger generational rebellion at the

workplace. In the United States, for example, an unruly three-week strike by young workers at the Lordstown, Ohio, GM plant in 1972 was quickly labeled an "industrial Woodstock." Georgakas and Surkin, *Detroit, I Do Mind Dying*, 105.

8. Marsh and Ryan, *Seamen*, 206–7, 214; Hope, *New History of British Shipping*, 440.

9. Belcher et al., *Women Seafarers*, 9–12.

10. Whitfield, "Waves of Resistance," *Transport International Online* (2003). ⟨www.itfglobal.org/transport-international/ti11resistance.cfm⟩.

11. Hope, *New History of British Shipping*, 392, 413, 426–27, 467. Until the 1960s, the largest cargo ships registered a carrying capacity of 10,000 DWT (deadweight tonnage) and the largest tankers registered 28,000 DWT; yet, by the 1980s, cargo ships at 200,000 DWT and tankers of 250,000 DWT were common. DeSombre, *Flagging Standards*, 79. Containerization, pioneered in 1956 by U.S. trucking company owner Malcolm McLean, so accelerated the transfer of goods from ships to rail (i.e., "intermodalism") that within twenty years, vessels longer than four contiguous football fields and too wide for the Panama Canal were dominating dry cargo oceanic runs. Bonacich and Wilson, *Getting the Goods*, 52–53.

12. Couper, *Voyages of Abuse*, 9–11, quotation 10.

13. Roland, Bolster, and Keyssar, *Way of the Ship*, 368–69.

14. Hope, *New History of British Shipping*, 392, 485.

15. Bevan quoted in Marsh and Ryan, *Seamen*, 200.

16. Goldberg, *Maritime Story*, 250–56. The NMU affiliated with the Seafarers' International Union in 1999 and completed a merger in 2001.

17. Kaplan, *Everything That Floats*, 189. After successfully negotiating contracts with much of the industry and forming a powerful bloc within the Trades and Labour Congress of Canada, Banks, as Kaplan documents, established a tyrannical authority within the Canadian District SIU that included blacklisting opponents, demanding bribes from would-be members, and even authorizing the brutal beating of a deck officer's union leader who refused the SIU's merger demands. Across an extended legal process, Banks was removed from office in Canada in 1963 under the newly legislated Trusteeship Act. When he evaded a conspiracy-to-assault charge by fleeing to a yacht in New York City and was subsequently offered a directorship at the SIU's training school, Canadian authorities sought extradition. Their quest was ultimately denied by U.S. secretary of state Dean Rusk in early 1968 in a further invocation of the national security argument. As AFL-CIO president George Meany strongly lobbied Rusk on Banks's behalf, the labor leader was said to be engaged in the vital role of "filling the manpower needs of the Merchant Marine necessitated by the present Viet Nam conflict." See esp. 49–50, 62–65, 73, 75, 82, 92, 145–51, 180, fn. quotation 181.

18. Gunnar Lundeberg interview, Feb. 24, 2009; Roland, Bolster, and Keyssar, *Way of the Ship*, 375–76, 370; Bonacich and Wilson, *Getting the Goods*, 86.

19. McPhee, *Looking for a Ship*, 85.

20. ITF Papers, Conference Documents (special issue, June 1990), ILWU Archives.

21. Harold Lewis, email to author, Aug. 5, 2009.

22. Couper, *Voyages of Abuse*, 41–55.

23. Johnsson, *Funny Flags*, 16.

24. Carlisle, *Sovereignty for Sale*, 2–4, 74–75, 101.

25. Ibid., 6–14; DeSombre, *Flagging Standards*, 76–78.

26. Sarah Palmer, "British Shipping from the Late Nineteenth Century to the Present," in Fischer and Lange, *International Merchant Shipping*, 138.

27. IMO, "International Shipping and World Trade: Facts and Figures" (2006 and 2008 updates), ⟨http://www.imo.org/includes/blastDataOnly.asp/data_id%3D13865/InternationalShippingandWorldTrade-factsandfigures.pdf⟩, 9–10; ⟨http://www.imo.org/includes/blastDataOnly.asp/data_id%3D220166/InternationalShipping2007.pdf⟩, cited in French; and Wintersteen, "Crafting an International Legal Regime." As French and Wintersteen note, a list of FOC states published by the ITF in 2008 included utterly landlocked Bolivia.

28. Northrup and Rowan, *International Transport Workers' Federation*, 43, 49.

29. ITF Boycott Committee Minutes, 159/1/5/b/1, Apr. 1949, ITF archives.

30. Northrup and Rowan, *International Transport Workers' Federation*, 45–46.

31. Ibid., 47–49, quotation 49. More than 150 vessels, a large share of the docked FOC fleet, were reportedly tied up by the boycott, mainly in U.S. ports.

32. Harold Lewis, email to author, Aug. 5, 2009.

33. U.S. Supreme Court, *Benz v. Compania Naviera Hidalgo*.

34. Schwartz, *Brotherhood of the Sea*, 137; "Modern Documentation, USA," 159/5/3/1275, ITF archives.

35. U.S. Supreme Court, *Marine Cooks & Stewards v. Panama SS Co.* The Norris-LaGuardia Act of 1932 effectively liberated organized labor from the crippling restraints of federal court injunctions.

36. U.S. Supreme Court, *Incres Steamship Co., Ltd. v. International Maritime Workers Union*. The IMWU was a short-lived joint venture of the SIU and NMU to create a single organizational entity for seafarers on "flagged out" but U.S.-owned ships. U.S. Supreme Court, *McCulloch v. Sociedad Nacional de Marineros de Honduras*. Cox, attempting to balance administration foreign policy with President Kennedy's campaign pledges to organized labor to stop "runaway ships," had argued for a slightly more nuanced and less-declarative ruling than was signaled in Justice Clark's written opinion. Carlisle, *Sovereignty for Sale*, 166–70.

37. Carlisle, *Sovereignty for Sale*, 166–70.

38. U.S. Supreme Court, *Windward Shipping v. American Radio Assn.*

39. "The Fight against Flags of Convenience," *ITF Journal* 33 (Spring 1973): 2. Former ITF general secretary Harold Lewis recalled the U.S. court decisions as "hammer blows." Harold Lewis, interview by author, June 22, 2005; Northrup and Rowan, *International Transport Workers' Federation*, 53–55; Lillie, "Union Networks," 97.

40. Harold Lewis, email to author, Aug. 26, 2009.

41. Johnsson, *Funny Flags*, 101–4; Northrup and Rowan, *International Transport Workers' Federation*, 21, 55–89; Lillie, *Global Union*, 42. The Thatcher-era reforms arrived in two giant leaps in the form of the Employment Acts of 1980 and 1982. The latter included a specific prohibition on "disputes on foreign matters unless the jobs of the workers striking in Great Britain are likely to be affected by the outcome of the dispute. Immunity is removed from secondary action when taken by workers of one company to pressurize another company where there is no dispute between their workers and employers." Wikipedia, ⟨http://en.wikipedia.org/wiki/Employment_Act_1982⟩.

42. Northrup and Rowan, *International Transport Workers' Federation*, 37–38. Lloyd's Register of World Fleet Statistics noted a jump in the FOC share of cargo to 43 percent by 1994; by 2000, five of the top ten flags in the world were FOCs, including the four largest flags. Northrup and Scrase, "International Transport Workers' Federation," 371; Lillie, *Global Union*, 32.

43. Lillie, "Global Collective Bargaining," 52–53; Lillie, "Union Networks," 93.

44. Steven C. McKay, "Filipino Sea Men: Identity and Masculinity in a Global Labor Niche," in Parrenas and Siu, *Asian Diasporas*, 66.

45. "Fight against Flags of Convenience"; Northrup and Rowan, *International Transport Workers' Federation*, 103–4. At a rate of thirty pounds per seaman, the levy, a kind of home-front tax on foreign hires, reportedly provided "over 50 percent of the NUS income" for a few years.

46. McKay, "Filipino Sea Men," 67.

47. Ibid., 71–72.

48. Captain Gregorio S. Oca, telephone interview, May 22, 2009; Associated Marine Officers' and Seamen's Union of the Philippines, ⟨http:// http://www.amosup.org/about-us/our-history⟩.

49. Oca interview.

50. Talampas, Roli. "Opportunities and Challenges in the Emerging Global State," *Tinig ng Marino* (Voice of the Seafarers), Mar.–Apr. 2004, ⟨http://www.ufs.ph/tinig/marapr04/03040414.html⟩; Amante, "Philippine Global Seafarers," 4–6.

51. Northrup and Rowan, *International Transport Workers' Federation*, 96–102; Report on Activities, Asian Seafarers' Conference, Singapore, May 1973; ITF Congress, Stockholm, Aug. 1974, 159/1/1/189, ITF archives; quotation from Arora, *Voyage*, 24.

52. Northrup and Rowan, *International Transport Workers' Federation*, 102; Arora, *Voyage*, 25–26; New York *Journal of Commerce*, July 24, 1980. One theoretically progressive solution to the interunion conflict surfaced in the 1979–80 United Nations Conference on Trade and Development. For an extended moment, the ITF found common ground in this Geneva forum with both third-world and Communist bloc countries in pushing for a policy of "cargo-sharing." The idea as originally formulated was that in exchange for the abolition of open registries for FOC shipping, both labor and capital-supply countries would agree to a formula whereby trade between any two nations would be divided on a 40–40–20 basis—with 40 percent going to ships of each trading partner and 20 percent to third-flag carriers. The formula would at once benefit the fledgling fleets and balance-of-payments of less-developed countries while still securing a maritime future for the big Western commercial powers. In the end, however, what looked good on paper could not fly politically or economically. Critics ranged from Western governments (who were not about to surrender their own control of bilateral trade relations) to unions from traditional third-flag carriers including the Scandinavians, the Dutch, and the British (who feared a bilateral squeeze against them) to a general business fear of economic meddling and predictions of overbuilding—assuming the developing countries could ever find the capital to sustain their side of the imaginary bargain. Except as a nebulous debating point, therefore, cargo-sharing went nowhere. Northrup and Rowan, *International Transport Workers' Federation*, 113–15; *Journal of Commerce*, July 23, 1980.

53. Lillie, *Global Union*, 52; Report on Activities, Fair Practices Committee, 1977–79, p. 122 (ITF document courtesy of Harold Lewis); Harold Lewis, emails to author, Aug. 26, Aug. 30, 2009; Serang interview; Oca interview.

54. Lillie, *Global Union*, 43; Northrup and Scrase, "International Transport Workers' Federation," 378–79.

55. Lillie, "Union Networks," 99; Lillie, "Global Collective Bargaining," 56; Lillie, *Global Union*, 41, 44; Northrup and Scrase, "International Transport Workers' Federation," 378, 384. Moreover, by 2001, the $1,200/mo. AB ITF rate contrasted to the typical $800/mo. nonunion rate. Lillie, *Global Union*, 40.

56. Lillie, *Global Union*, 41.

57. Ibid., 46–49; International Bargaining Forum Agrees Seafarers Pay, ⟨http://www.imec.org.uk/editoriles/File/PressRelease, Sept. 27, 2007⟩; Enrico Esopa interview, Feb. 13, 2009.

58. Statistics from ITF maritime coordinator Steve Cotton, as communicated through ITF public affairs agent Sam Dawson, email, July 7, 2009.

59. Lillie, *Global Union*, 146.

60. United Kingdom, House of Lords, *Universe Tankships Inc. of Monrovia v. International Transport Workers Federation*, 366–409. Trial conversation as recalled by eyewitness Harold Lewis, email to author, Aug. 28, 2009; cf. Northrup and Rowan, *International Transport Workers' Federation*, 86–88. Given the general political climate in the United Kingdom at the time, the ITF must have thanked its lucky stars at this ruling. By way of further elaboration, the original appeal of the owners against the blacking of the ship on grounds of "duress" was abandoned after an unfavorable House of Lords ruling in 1979 that the boycott action was exempted from tort action under the Trade Union and Labour Relations Act, 1974—thus leaving the Welfare Fund payment the one aspect of the case still open to question. Yet, by the time of the latter ruling on the "trust" issue in April 1982, the legal landscape had notably worsened for trade union action. Under the Employment Act of 1980 and then notably further tightened by the Employment Act of 1982—passed a few months after the ruling and self-consciously aimed at ITF's tactics, among other trade union tactics, by Prime Minister Thatcher's parliamentary stewards—secondary boycotts (or trade union action targeted beyond one's own immediate employer) were no longer granted their former immunity. Even in the *Universe Tankships* decision, though dismissing the employers' trust claim, a 3–2 judgment (from which Lord Scarman dissented) of the Lords forced the ITF to return the $6,000+ welfare contribution to Universe Tankships on the more technical grounds of "economic duress"—a concept that situationally limited immunity from tort. Collectively, post-1982, ITF boycott action was necessarily suspended in Britain even as the larger campaign (as conducted through boycotts elsewhere and Welfare Fund payments funneled back through the London Secretariat) picked up speed.

61. Northrup and Rowan, *International Transport Workers' Federation*, 17. In 2003, contractual payments into the ITF Welfare Fund by FOC employers "worked out to around $20 per crew member per month." "Flags of Peace."

62. Quotation Northrup and Scrase, "International Transport Workers' Federation," 389; Lillie, *Global Union*, 44.

63. Esopa interview.

64. Lillie, "Global Collective Bargaining," 58.

65. Oca interview; see also Bonacich and Wilson, *Getting the Goods*, 167–68. The one solace that both the ITF and other labor-supplying countries enjoyed regarding China was the fact that it had so far largely excluded its workers from the FOC system, employing most of its native labor force on its own nationally flagged ships. Lillie, *Global Union*, 151.

66. United Filipino Seafarers, ⟨www.ufs.ph/2009-10/ufs_story⟩.

67. "Fight for Better Salaries, Benefits Continues," *Tinig ng Marino* (Voice of the Seafarers), Nov.–Dec. 2000, ⟨http://www.ufs.ph/tinig/novdec00/11120001.html⟩.

68. Sampson, "Powerful Unions."

69. Ray Familathe interview, Mar. 11, 2009.

70. Interviews with former ITF inspectors Esopa and Familathe.

71. Brian McWilliams interview, Feb. 26, 2009.

72. Lillie, "Union Networks," 102–3.

73. Nathan Lillie and Miguel Martínez Lucio, "International Trade Union Revitalization: The Role of National Union Approaches," in Frege and Kelly, *Varieties of Unionism*, 168–69. In the 2002 dispute, ITF affiliates in Japan, New Zealand, Australia, Spain, and Denmark all "made specific threats that they would not handle cargo from the US loaded by scab labour" (169). Turnbull and Wass, "Defending Dock Workers," 582–612.

74. Familathe interview.

75. DeSombre, *Flagging Standards*, 3, 5, 53, 55–58, 65.

76. Lillie, *Global Union*, 175 fn. 7.

77. Eugène Ionesco, *The Bald Soprano, and Other Plays*, http://books.google.com/books?id=actou57plegC&printsec=frontcover&dq=Bald+Soprano+and+other+plays&hl=en&ei=F5dpTPCvKsP88AabqamzBA&sa=X&oi=book_result&ct=result&resnum=1&ved=0CCkQ6AEwAA#v=onepage&q&f=false.

78. International Maritime Organization, ⟨http://www.imo.org/About⟩.

79. Carlisle, *Sovereignty for Sale*, 186; DeSombre, *Flagging Standards*, 90.

80. Kasoulides, *Port State Control*, 142–45.

81. Politakis, "Updating," 345; Bloor, "Problems of Global Governance."

82. *Tinig ng Marino* (Voice of the Seafarers), Mar.–Apr. 2002, referencing a study by Bernardo Obando-Rojas, research fellow at the Seafarers International Research Centre, Cardiff University, ⟨www.ufs.ph/tinig/marapr02/03040202.html⟩; Lillie, *Global Union*, 89–104. Administration of port state control conventions varies by country; in the United States, for example, control is vested in the Coast Guard.

83. International Labor Organization, "Achieving the Seafarers' International Bill of Rights."

84. *Tinig ng Marino*, Mar.–Apr. 2000 ⟨www.ufs.ph/tinit/marapr00/03040002.html⟩.

85. "Achieving the Seafarers' International Bill of Rights."

86. My reading of the MLC draft and especially the "Guidelines for Port State Control Officers Carrying Out Inspections under the Maritime Labour Convention, 2006" is confirmed by Jon Whitlow, secretary of the ITF Seafarers' Department, via Sam Dawson, ITF public affairs officer, email, June 23, 2009; Maritime Labour Convention, 2006, ⟨http://www.ilo.org/ilolex/cgi-lex/convde.pl?C186⟩; Guidelines for port State control officers carrying out inspections under the Maritime Labour Conven-

tion, 2006 ⟨http://www.ilo.org/global/What_we_do/InternationalLabourStandards/MaritimeLabourConvention/lang—en/docName—WCMS_101787/index.htm⟩.

87. See also Lillie, *Global Union*, 149–50.

88. International Labor Organization, "Decent Work."

89. Susan Cueva, telephone interview, May 22, 2009.

90. Serang interview.

91. Oca interview.

92. Amante, "Philippine Global Seafarers."

93. Mahendra Sharma interview, March 23, 2010.

94. Susan Cueva, email, July 6, 2009. Cueva's own younger sister, she reports, "suffered terribly" as a cruise ship employee and "quit seafaring."

95. Edwin Dela Cruz, telephone interview, May 25, 2009. As Dela Cruz explains, Filipino union membership typically depends on "fixed contracts" that expire three months after leaving a ship, leaving the seafarer without medical coverage and legal services—and with no seniority to gain work on another vessel.

96. Cueva interview.

97. One recent study of applying labor standards via port state control thus concludes, "As any observer of the travails of the World Trade Organization could tell us, there are no successful models of global governance for the shipping industry to emulate." Bloor, "Problems of Global Governance," 21.

98. McCartin, "Democratizing the Demand."

99. Lillie, "Bringing the Offshore Ashore."

Works Cited

Primary Sources

Great Britain

Booth, Charles. *Life and Labour of the People in London*. London: MacMillan and Co., 1903 [1889].

[A British Subject]. "A True Picture of the United States of America . . . 1873 to the Present." London: Jordan and Maxwell, 1807. Englewood, Colo.: Microcard Editions.

Equiano, Olaudah. *The Interesting Narrative of the Life of Olaudah Equiano, Or Gustavus Vassa, The African Written By Himself*. Project Gutenberg, 2005 [1789]. ⟨http://www.gutenberg.org/files/15399/15399-h/15399-h.htm⟩.

Farrer, T. H. "Merchant Shipping and Further Legislation." *Quarterly Review* 141 (Jan. 1876): 250–84.

Foreign Office. "Papers Relating to America. Presented to the House of Commons, 1809." London: A. Straman, 1810.

Gaskell, Elizabeth. *Sylvia's Lovers*. Vol. 1. London: Smith, Elder and Co., 1863, 3 vols.

Glover, John. "The Plimsoll Sensation: A Reply." London: Effingham Wilson, Royal Exchange, 1873.

Great Britain. *The Public General Acts*. London: Printed by G.E. Eyre and W. Spottiswoode, 1870–1925.

Griffiths, Captain Anselm John, R.N. *Impressment Fully Considered with a View to Its Gradual Abolition*. London: J. W. Norie and Co., 1826.

Haly, Lt. R. Standish, R.N. *Impressment: An Attempt to Prove, Why It Should, and How It Could Be Abolished*. Poole: Moore and Sydenham, est. 1822.

Howell, George. *Labour Legislation, Labour Movements, Labour Leaders*. New York: E. P. Dutton, 1902.

George Howell Collection. Bishopsgate Institute, London.

Jerrold, Douglas. *The Mutiny at the Nore: A Nautical Drama in Three Acts* in *Cumberland's Minor Theatre*. London: Davidson, 1831(?).

Lamport, W. J. "The Plimsoll Agitation." *Theological Review* 11 (Jan. 1874).

Marryat, Frederick. *Frank Mildmay or, The Naval Officer*. Project Gutenberg, 2004 [1829]. ⟨http://www.gutenberg.org/etext/13010⟩.

———. *Mr. Midshipman Easy*. Project Gutenberg, 2004 [1836]. ⟨http://www.gutenberg.org/etext/6629⟩.
Means, Andrew. *The Bitter of Outcast London*. 1883.
"Merchant Shipping Legislation." *Westminster Review* 103 (Jan. 1875).
Plimsoll, Samuel. *Our Seamen: An Appeal*. London: Virtue & Co., 1873.
Smith, Adam. *An Inquiry into the Nature and Causes of the Wealth of Nations*. Edited by R. H. Campbell, A. S. Skinner, and W. B. Todd. Oxford: Oxford University Press, 1976 [1776].
Stephen, James. *War in Disguise, or, The Frauds of the Neutral Flags*. New York: I. Riley and Co., 1806.
Thompson, T. P. "Impressment and Flogging." *Westminster Review* 20 (Apr. 1834).
United Kingdom. *Fifth and Final Report of the Royal Commission on Labour*. Part 1. London, Eyre and Spottiswoode, 1994.
———. *Hansard Parliamentary Debates*. 3d series (1830–91).
———. House of Lords. *Universe Tankships Inc. of Monrovia v. International Transport Workers' Federation*. Transcripts of Judicial Proceedings (1983).
———. *Parliamentary Debates*. Commons, 4th Series (1892–1908).
———. *Parliamentary Debates*. Lords, 4th Series (1892–1908).
Wilson, J. Havelock. *My Stormy Voyage Through Life*. London: Cooperative Printing Society, 1925.

PERIODICALS

Chambers's Journal
Guest Vocal Music
London Times
Niles Register
Pamphleteer
Punch
Quarterly Review
Seafaring (later the *Seamen's Record* and *The Seaman*, publications of the National Union of Seamen and Firemen, which became the National Union of Seamen)
Vocal Music
Westminster Review

United States

Chicago. Map drawn by S. S. Wright according to survey. New York: P. A. Mesier's Lithograph, 1834.
Cooper, James Fenimore. *The Pilot: A Tale of the Sea*. Albany: State University of New York Press, 1986 [1823].
Croly, Herbert. *The Promise of American Life*. New York: Macmillan, 1963 [1909].
Douglass, Frederick. *Narrative of the Life of Frederick Douglass, An American Slave*. Boston: Bedford Books, 1993 [1845].

Fitzhugh, George. *Sociology for the South, or the Failure of Free Society*. Richmond: A. Morris, 1854.
Hale, Edward Everett. *The Man Without a Country*. New York: Macmillan, 1915 [1863].
Harlow, Frederick Pease. *The Making of a Sailor, or Sea Life Aboard a Yankee Square-Rigger*. Salem: Marine Research Society, 1928.
Hughes, Langston. *The Big Sea: An Autobiography*. New York: Hill and Wang, 1940.
Industrial Workers of the World. *Proceedings of the First Convention of the Industrial Workers of the World*. New York: New York Labor News Co., 1905.
Jewell, J. Grey. *Among Our Sailors*. New York: Harper and Brothers, 1874.
Leggett, William. *Naval Stories*. New York: G&C&H Carvill, 1834.
Macarthur, Walter. "The American Seaman under the Law." *Forum* 26 (Feb. 1899).
———, ed. *The Seaman's Contract, 1790–1918: A Complete Reprint of the Laws Relating to American Seamen, Enacted, Amended, and Repealed by the Congress of the United States*. San Francisco: James H. Barry Co., 1919.
Madison, James. "Extract of a Letter from the Secretary of State [Madison] to Mr. Monroe [U.S. Ambassador to England] Relative to Impressments." Washington, D.C.: A&G Watt, Feb. 5, 1806, microprint.
McKay, Claude. *Banjo*. New York: Harper and Brothers, 1929.
———. *Home to Harlem*. New York: Harper and Brothers, 1928.
Melville, Herman. *Moby Dick*. 1851. ⟨http://www.princeton.edu/~batke/moby/moby.html⟩.
———. *Redburn*. New York: Modern Library, 2002 [1849].
O'Neill, Eugene. *Early Plays*. New York: Penguin, 2001.
———. *Three Great Plays: Emperor Jones, Anna Christie, and The Hairy Ape*. Mineola, N.Y.: Dover Publications, 2005.
Traven, B. *The Death Ship: The Story of an American Sailor*. Brooklyn, N.Y.: Lawrence Hill Books, 1991 [1934].
United States. *The Statutes at Large*. Washington, D.C.: G.P.O., 1875–1936.
U.S. Circuit Court. *O'Neill v. Cunard White Star*, 160 F. 2d 446 (2d Cir. 1947).
U.S. Congress. *Annals of the Congress of the United States, 1789–1824*. 42 vols. Washington, D.C., 1834–56.
———. *Biographical Directory of the American Congress, 1774–1971*. Washington, D.C.: G.P.O., 1971.
———. *Congressional Globe*. 46 vols. Washington, D.C., 1834–73.
———. *Congressional Record*.
———. House Committee on Commerce. *Free Colored Seamen—Majority and Minority Reports*. 49–50, 27th Cong., 3d sess., 1843, Report no. 80.
———. House Committee on Commerce. *Protections to American Seamen*. 24th Cong., 2d sess., 1837, Report no. 1982.
———. House Committee on Immigration. "Alien Seamen and Stowaways." 62d Cong., 2d sess., 1912, pt. 6: 19–20.
———. House Committee on Merchant Marine and Fisheries. *Report*. 62d Cong., 2d sess., 1911–12, vol. 3, pts. 1 and 2.

———. House Committee on Merchant Marine and Fisheries. Hearings on HR 8532. 75th Cong., 2d and 3d sess., 1937–38.
———. *Letter from the Secretary of State . . . Certificates of Citizenship to American Seamen*. House. 27th Cong., 3d sess., 1843.
———. Opinions of Attorneys General. Message from the President of the United States. "Rights of Free Virginia Negroes." 31st Cong., 2d sess., 1851, Nov. 7, 1821. Ex. doc. no. 55: 329–31.
———. *Permitting Filipinos to Become Members of Coast Guard Auxiliary and Coast Guard Reserve*. S. Rep. 1636, 77th Cong., 2nd sess., 1942, Serial 10659.
———. *Report from the Secretary of the Navy on the Subject of the Discipline of the Navy*. 31st Cong., 2d sess., Jan. 10, 1851. Sen. ex. doc. no. 12: 5, 7.
———. *Report from the Secretary of the Navy to the Senate*. 20th Cong., 1st sess., May 26, 1828.
———. Senate Commerce Committee. *Hearing on HR 23673, Involuntary Servitude Imposed upon Seamen*. 62d Cong., 3d sess., 1913, pt. 1.
———. Senate Committee on the Judiciary. *Report*. 29th Cong., 2d sess., 1847.
———. *Senate Journal*.
U.S. Department of State. Foreign Relations of the United States diplomatic papers.
U.S. Maritime Administration. "By the Capes—A Primer on U.S. Coastwise Laws." ⟨http://www.marad.dot.gov/Publications/primer_laws.html⟩.
U.S. Supreme Court. *Benz v. Compania Naviera Hidalgo*, 353 U.S 138 (1957).
———. *Incres Steamship Co., Ltd. v. International Maritime Workers Union*, 372 U.S. 24 (1963).
———. *Lauritzen v. Larsen*, 345 U.S. 571 (1953).
———. *Marine Cooks & Stewards v. Panama SS Co.*, 362 U.S. 365 (1960).
———. *McCulloch v. Sociedad Nacional de Marineros de Honduras*, 372 U.S. 10 (1963).
———. *Robertson v. Baldwin*, 165 U.S. 275 (1897).
———. *Windward Shipping v. American Radio Assn.*, 415 U.S. 104 (1974).

PERIODICALS

American Federationist
American Jurisprudence
Coast Seamen's Journal
Forum
Journal of Commerce
New York Times
Pilot
Sailor's Magazine
San Francisco Chronicle
Seamen's Record
Solidarity

Transnational

International Labor Organization. "Achieving the Seafarers' International Bill of Rights: More than Half Way There!" Feb. 23, 2009. ⟨www.ilo.org/global/About⟩.
———. *Albert Thomas, 1878–1978*. Geneva: ILO Office, 1978.
———. "Decent Work." Report of the Director-General, ILO, 87th Session, Geneva,

June 1999. ⟨http://www.ilo.org/public/english/standards/relm/ilc/ilc87/rep-i.htm⟩ (accessed June 23, 2009).
———. ILOLEX: Database of International Labour Standards. ⟨http:// www.ilo.org/ilolex/english/index.htm⟩.
———. Record of Proceedings, International Labour Conference. 21st and 22nd sessions, Geneva, 1936.
———. Record of Proceedings, Seamen's Conference, Geneva, 1920.
———. Report from the Director. International Labour Conference. 14th Session, Geneva, 1930.
———. Report on Activities. Asian Seafarers' Conference. Singapore, May 1973.
———. *The Rules of the Game: A Brief Introduction to International Labor Standards.* Geneva: ILO, 2005.
International Maritime Organization. "Historical Background Leading to the Adoption of the Load Lines Convention." ⟨http://www.imo.org/Conventions⟩.
International Transport Workers' Federation (ITF) Papers. Modern Records Center, University of Warwick Library, U.K.
———. *ITF Journal.*
———. *Korrespondenzblatt.*
———. National Federation of Ship, Dock and River Workers Correspondence. Tom Mann to Edmund Cathery, International Federation of Ship, Dock, and River Workers, Jan. 21, 1897.
———. Transport International Online.
———. *Weekly Report.*
Tinig ng Marino (Voice of the Seafarers), publication of the United Filipino Seafarers.
World Federation of Trade Unions [Communist]. Conference Documents (special issue, June 1990), Tenth International Trade Conference of Transport, Port and Fishery Workers, Trade Unions International of Transport Workers, Apr. 23–27, 1990, Budapest, Hungary. Archives, International Longshore and Warehouse Union (ILWU), ILWU Library, San Francisco, Calif.

Secondary Sources

Books

Ackroyd, Peter. *Dickens.* New York: HarperCollins, 1990.
Allison, Robert J. *The Crescent Obscured: The United States and the Muslim World, 1776–1815.* New York: Oxford University Press, 1995.
Altoff, Gerald T. *Amongst My Best Men: African-Americans and the War of 1812.* Perry Group: Put-in-Bay, Ohio, 1996.
Arora, A. G. *Voyage: Chronicle of the Seafarers Movement in India.* Mumbai: NUSI, 1997.
Ball, Joseph H. *The Government-Subsidized Union Monopoly: A Study of Labor Practices in the Shipping Industry.* Washington, D.C.: Labor Policy Association, 1966.

Barnes, Charles B. *The Longshoremen*. New York: Arno, 1977 [1915].
Belcher, Phillip, et al. *Women Seafarers: Global Employment Policies and Practices*. Geneva: ILO Publications, 2003.
Bensel, Richard Franklin. *The Political Economy of American Industrialization, 1877–1900*. New York: Cambridge University Press, 2000.
Biagini, Eugenio F., and Alastair J. Reid, eds. *Currents of Radicalism: Popular Radicalism, Organised Labour and Party Politics in Britain, 1850–1914*. Cambridge: Cambridge University Press, 1991.
Bloom, Khaled J. *The Mississippi Valley's Great Yellow Fever Epidemic of 1878*. Baton Rouge: Louisiana State University Press, 1993.
Blum, Hester. *The View from the Masthead: Maritime Imagination and Antebellum American Sea Narratives*. Chapel Hill: University of North Carolina Press, 2008.
Bolster, W. Jeffrey. *Black Jacks: African American Seamen in the Age of Sail*. Cambridge, Mass.: Harvard University Press, 1997.
Bonacich, Edna, and Jake B. Wilson. *Getting the Goods: Ports, Labor, and the Logistics Revolution*. Ithaca: Cornell University Press, 2008.
Booth, Michael R. *English Melodrama*. London: Herbert Jenkins, 1965.
Boyer, Richard O. *The Dark Ship*. Boston: Little, Brown, 1947.
Bullen, Frank T. *The Men of the Merchant Marine, Being the Polity of the Merchant Marine for 'Longshore Readers*. London: Smith, Elder, 1900.
Burg, B. R. *Sodomy and the Pirate Tradition: English Sea Rovers in the Seventeenth-Century Caribbean*. New York: New York University Press, 1983.
Burn, W. L. *The Age of Equipoise: A Study of the Mid-Victorian Generation*. London: George Allen and Unwin, 1964.
Carlisle, Rodney. *Sovereignty for Sale: The Origins and Evolution of the Panamanian and Liberian Flags of Convenience*. Annapolis: Naval Institute Press, 1981.
Carretta, Vincent. *Equiano, the African: Biography of a Self-Made Man*. Athens: University of Georgia Press, 2005.
Clegg, H. A., Alan Fox, and A. F. Thompson. *A History of British Trade Unions since 1889*. 3 vols. London: Oxford University Press, 1964.
Cole, Peter. *Wobblies on the Waterfront: Interracial Unionism in Progressive-Era Philadelphia*. Urbana: University of Illinois Press, 2007.
Colley, Linda. *Captives*. New York: Pantheon, 2002.
Cooper, Wayne F. *Claude McKay: Rebel Sojourner in the Harlem Renaissance*. Baton Rouge: Louisiana State University Press, 1987.
Couper, A. D. *Voyages of Abuse: Seafarers, Human Rights and International Shipping*. London: Pluto Press, 1999.
Course, Captain A. G. *The Merchant Navy: A Social History*. London: Frederick Muller, 1963.
Creighton, Margaret S., and Lisa Norling. *Iron Men, Wooden Women: Gender and Seafaring in the Atlantic World, 1700–1920*. Baltimore: Johns Hopkins University Press, 1996.
Dana, Richard Henry, Jr. *Two Years before the Mast*. New York: New American Library, 2000 [1840].

Davis, David Brion. *Slavery and Human Progress*. New York: Oxford University Press, 1984.
Davis, Lance E., Robert E. Gallman, and Karen Gleiter. *In Pursuit of Leviathan: Technology, Institutions, Productivity, and Profits in American Whaling, 1816–1906*. Chicago: University of Chicago Press, 1997.
DeSombre, Elizabeth R. *Flagging Standards: Globalization and Environmental, Safety, and Labor Regulations at Sea*. Cambridge, Mass.: MIT Press, 2006.
Destler, Chester McArthur. *American Radicalism, 1865–1901*. Chicago: Quadrangle Books, 1966.
Disher, Maurice Wilson. *Blood and Thunder: Mid-Victorian Melodrama and Its Origins*. London: Frederick Muller, 1949.
Duiker, William J. *Ho Chi Minh: A Life*. New York: Hyperion, 2000.
Eltis, David, ed. *Coerced and Free Migration: Global Perspectives*. Stanford: Stanford University Press, 2002.
Fehrenbacher, Don E. *The Dred Scott Case: Its Significance in American Law and Politics*. New York: Oxford University Press, 1978.
Feuchtwanger, Edward. *Disraeli*. New York: Oxford University Press, 2000.
Fingard, Judith. *Jack in Port: Sailortowns of Eastern Canada*. Toronto: University of Toronto Press, 1982.
Fink, Leon. *In Search of the Working Class: Essays in American Labor History and Political Culture*. Urbana: University of Illinois Press, 1994.
———. *Progressive Intellectuals and the Dilemmas of Democratic Commitment*. Cambridge, Mass.: Harvard University Press, 1997.
Fischer, Lewis R., and Even Lange, eds. *International Merchant Shipping in the Nineteenth and Twentieth Centuries: The Comparative Dimension*. St. John's Newfoundland: International Maritime Economic History Association, Research in Maritime History, No. 37, 2008.
Fleischacker, Samuel. *On Adam Smith's* Wealth of Nations*: A Philosophical Companion*. Princeton: Princeton University Press, 2004.
Foner, Eric. *Reconstruction: America's Unfinished Revolution, 1863–1877*. New York: Harper and Row, 1988.
Foot, M. R. D. *War and Society: Historical Essays in Honour and Memory of J. R. Western 1928–1971*. New York: Barnes and Noble Books, 1973.
Frank, Dana. *Buy American: The Untold Story of American Nationalism*. Boston: Beacon Press, 1999.
Frege, Carola, and John Kelly, eds. *Varieties of Unionism: Strategies for Union Revitalization in a Globalizing Economy*. New York: Oxford University Press, 2004.
Frow, Ruth Edmund Frow, and Michael Katanka, eds. *Strikes: A Documentary History*. London: C. Knight, 1971.
Gelb, Arthur, and Barbara Gelb. *O'Neill*. New York: Harper and Brothers, 1962.
Georgakas, Dan, and Marvin Surkin. *Detroit, I Do Mind Dying: A Study in Urban Revolution*. Cambridge, Mass.: South End Press, 1998.
Gilbert, Bentley Brinkerhoff. *David Lloyd George: A Political Life; The Architect of Change, 1863–1912*. Columbus: Ohio State University Press, 1987.

Gilje, Paul A. *Liberty on the Waterfront: American Maritime Culture in the Age of Revolution*. Philadelphia: University of Pennsylvania Press, 2004.

Glenn, Myra C. *The Campaign against Corporal Punishment: Prisoners, Sailors, Women, and Children in Antebellum America*. Albany: State University of New York Press, 1984.

Glickman, Lawrence B. *A Living Wage: American Workers and the Making of Consumer Society*. Ithaca: Cornell University Press, 1997.

Goldberg, Joseph P. *The Maritime Story: A Study in Labor-Management Relations*. Cambridge, Mass.: Harvard University Press, 1958.

Goodwyn, Lawrence. *Democratic Promise: The Populist Moment in America*. New York: Oxford University Press, 1976.

Green, Archie. *Calf's Head and Union Tale: Labor Yarns at Work and Play*. Urbana: University of Illinois Press, 1996.

Greene, Julie. *Pure and Simple Politics: The American Federation of Labor and Political Activism, 1881–1917*. New York: Cambridge University Press, 1998.

Guither, Harold D. *Animal Rights: History and Scope of a Radical Social Movement*. Carbondale: Southern Illinois University Press, 1998.

Gunn, Giles. *A Historical Guide to Herman Melville*. New York: Oxford University Press, 2005.

Hall, Greg. *Harvest Wobblies: The Industrial Workers of the World and Agricultural Laborers in the American West, 1905–1930*. Corvallis: Oregon State University Press, 2001.

Hall, John A., and Ralph Schroeder, eds. *An Anatomy of Power: The Social Theory of Michael Mann*. Cambridge: Cambridge University Press, 2006.

Handlin, Lilian. *George Bancroft, the Intellectual as Democrat*. New York: Harper and Row, 1984.

Hawley, Ellis. *The New Deal and the Problem of Monopoly*. New York: Fordham University Press, 1995.

Heinrich, Thomas R. *Ships for the Seven Seas: Philadelphia Shipbuilding in the Age of Industrial Capitalism*. Baltimore: Johns Hopkins University Press, 1997.

Hickey, Donald R. *Don't Give Up the Ship: Myths of the War of 1812*. Urbana: University of Illinois Press, 2006.

———. *The War of 1812: A Forgotten Conflict*. Urbana: University of Illinois Press, 1989.

Himmelfarb, Gertrude. *The Idea of Poverty: England in the Early Industrial Age*. New York: Knopf, 1984.

Hisson, Baruch, and Lorraine Vivian. *Strike Across the Empire: The Seamen's Strike of 1925; In Britain, South Africa and Australasia*. London: Clio Publications, 1992.

Hobsbawm, Eric. *Age of Extremes: The Short Twentieth Century, 1914–1991*. London: Michael Joseph, 1994.

Hohman, Elmo Paul. *History of American Merchant Seamen*. Hamden, Conn.: Shoe String Press, 1956.

Holton, Bob. *British Syndicalism, 1900–1914: Myths and Realities*. London: Pluto Press, 1976.

Hope, Ronald. *A New History of British Shipping*. London: John Murray, 1990.

Horsman, Reginald. *The Causes of the War of 1812*. New York: A. S. Barnes, 1962.
Howell, Colin, and Richard J. Twomey, eds. *Jack Tar in History: Essays in the History of Maritime Life and Labour*. Fredericton, N.B.: Acadiensis Press, 1991.
Hutchins, John G. B. *The American Maritime Industries and Public Policy, 1789–1914: An Economic History*. New York: Russell and Russell, 1969 [1941].
Hutchinson, J. R. *The Press-Gang Afloat and Ashore*. London: E. P. Dutton, 1914.
Irwin, Douglas A. *Against the Tide: An Intellectual History of Free Trade*. Princeton: Princeton University Press, 1996.
Jacobs, Meg, William J. Novak, and Julian E. Zelizer, eds. *The American Experiment: New Directions in American Political History*. Princeton: Princeton University Press, 2003.
James, C. L. R. *Mariners, Renegades and Castaways: The Story of Herman Melville and the World We Live In*. London: Allison and Bushy, 1985 [1953].
Johnsson, Lennart. *Funny Flags: ITF's—Past, Present, Future*. Stockholm: Brevskolan, 1996.
Jones, Nicolette. *The Plimsoll Sensation: The Great Campaign to Save Lives at Sea*. London: Little, Brown, 2006.
Kaplan, William. *Everything That Floats: Pat Sullivan, Hal Banks, and the Seamen's Unions of Canada*. Toronto: University of Toronto Press, 1987.
Kasoulides, George C. *Port State Control and Jurisdiction: Evolution of the Port State Regime*. Boston: Martinus Nijhoff, 1993.
Klein, Bernhard, ed. *Fictions of the Sea: Critical Perspectives on the Ocean in British Literature and Culture*. Burlington, Vt.: Ashgate Publishing Company, 2002.
Lambert, Frank. *The Barbary Wars: American Independence in the Atlantic World*. New York: Hill and Wang, 2005.
Landau, Norma. *Law, Crime and English Society, 1660–1830*. New York: Cambridge University Press, 2002.
Lane, Tony. *The Union Makes Us Strong: The British Working Class, Its Trade Unionism and Politics*. London: Arrow Books, 1974.
Langley, Harold D. *Social Reform in the United States Navy, 1798–1862*. Urbana: University of Illinois Press, 1967.
Latimer, Jon. *1812: War with America*. Cambridge, Mass.: Belknap Press of Harvard University Press, 2007.
Leventhal, F. M. *Respectable Radical: George Howell and Victorian Working Class Politics*. London: Weidenfeld and Nicolson, 1971.
Lewis, Michael. *A Social History of the Navy, 1793–1815*. London: George Allen and Unwin, 1960.
Lillie, Nathan. *A Global Union for Global Workers: Collective Bargaining and Regulatory Politics in Maritime Shipping*. New York: Routledge, 2006.
Linebaugh, Peter, and Marcus Rediker. *The Many-Headed Hydra: Sailors, Slaves, Commoners, and the Hidden History of the Revolutionary Atlantic*. Boston: Beacon Press, 2000.
Lloyd, Christopher. *The British Seaman: 1200–1860*. London: Collins, 1968.
Lorenz, Edward C. *Defining Global Justice: The History of U.S. International Labor Standards Policy*. Notre Dame: University of Notre Dame Press, 2001.

Lowe, Boutelle Ellsworth. *The International Protection of Labor*. New York: Macmillan, 1921.
Marsh, Arthur, and Victoria Ryan. *The Seamen: A History of the National Union of Seamen*. Oxford: Malthouse Press, 1989.
Marsh, Peter T. *Joseph Chamberlain: Entrepreneur in Politics*. New Haven: Yale University Press, 1994.
Masters, David. *The Plimsoll Mark*. London: Cassell and Co., 1955.
Mathews, Donald G. *Slavery and Methodism: A Chapter in American Morality, 1780–1845*. Princeton: Princeton University Press, 1965.
Matthew, H. C. G., and Brian Harrison, eds. *Oxford Dictionary of National Biography*. 61 vols. Oxford: Oxford University Press, 2004.
Mayer, Henry. *All on Fire: William Lloyd Garrsion and the Abolition of Slavery*. New York: St. Martin's Press, 1998.
McCoy, Drew. *The Elusive Republic: Political Economy in Jeffersonian America*. Chapel Hill: University of North Carolina Press, 1980.
McElvaine, Robert. *The Great Depression: America, 1929–1941*. New York: Three Rivers Press, 1993.
McFee, William. *The Law of the Sea*. Philadelphia: J. B. Lippincott, 1950.
McLennan, Gregor, David Held, and Stuart Hall, eds. *State and Society in Contemporary Britain: A Critical Introduction*. Cambridge, U.K.: Polity Press, 1984.
McPhee, John. *Looking for a Ship*. New York: Noonday Press, 1991.
Montgomery, David. *Citizen Worker: The Experience of Workers in the United States with Democracy and the Free Market during the Nineteenth Century*. New York: Cambridge, 1993.
Morison, Samuel Eliot. *Oxford History of the American People*. New York: Oxford University Press, 1965.
Morris, Norval. *The Oxford History of the Prison: The Practice of Punishment in Western Society*. New York: Oxford University Press, 1997.
Morris, Richard B. *Government and Labor in Early America*. New York: Columbia University Press, 1946.
Nash, Gary B. *The Urban Crucible: Social Change, Political Consciousness, and the Origins of the American Revolution*. Cambridge, Mass.: Harvard University Press, 1979.
Nelson, Bruce. *Workers on the Waterfront: Seamen, Longshoremen, and Unionism in the 1930s*. Urbana: University of Illinois Press, 1988.
Ngai, Mai. *Impossible Subjects: Illegal Aliens and the Making of Modern America*. Princeton: Princeton University Press, 2004.
———. *The Lucky Ones: One Family and the Extraordinary Birth of Chinese America*. New York: Houghton Mifflin Harcourt, 2010.
Norling, Lisa. *Captain Ahab Had a Wife: New England Women and the Whalefishery, 1720–1870*. Chapel Hill: University of North Carolina Press, 2000.
Northrup, Herbert R., and Richard L. Rowan. *The International Transport Workers' Federation and Flag of Convenience Shipping*. Philadelphia: Wharton School Industrial Research Unit, University of Pennsylvania, 1983.
Ommer, Rosemary, and Gerald Panting, eds. *Working Men Who Got Wet: Proceedings*

of the Fourth Conference of the Atlantic Canada Shipping Project, July 24–July 26, 1980. St. Johns: Memorial University of Newfoundland, 1980.
Orth, John V. *Combination and Conspiracy: A Legal History of Trade Unionism, 1721–1906*. Oxford: Clarendon Press, 1991.
Palmer, Sarah. *Politics, Shipping and the Repeal of the Navigation Laws*. New York: Manchester University Press, 1990.
Palmer, Sarah, and Glyndwr Williams, eds. *Charted and Uncharted Waters: Proceedings of a Conference on the Study of British Maritime History*. London: National Maritime Museum, 1981.
Parreñas, Rhacel S., and Lok C. D. Siu. *Asian Diasporas: New Formations, New Conceptions*. Palo Alto: Stanford University Press, 2007.
Peck, John. *Maritime Fiction: Sailors and the Sea in British and American Novels, 1719–1917*. New York: Palgrave, 2001.
Pelling, Henry. *A History of British Trade Unionism*. Baltimore: Penguin, 1963.
Peters, George H. *The Plimsoll Line: The Story of Samuel Plimsoll, Member of Parliament for Derby from 1868 to 1880*. Chichester: Barry Rose Limited, 1975.
Phelan, E. J. *Yes and Albert Thomas*. New York: Columbia University Press, 1949 [1936].
Prados-Torreira, Teresa. *Mambisas: Rebel Women in Nineteenth-Century Cuba*. Gainesville: University Press of Florida, 2005.
Quinn-Judge, Sophie. *Ho Chi Minh: The Missing Years, 1919–1941*. Berkeley: University of California Press, 2002.
Rasor, Eugene L. *Reform in the Royal Navy: A Social History of the Lower Deck, 1850 to 1880*. Hamden, Conn.: Archon Books, 1976.
Rediker, Marcus. *Between the Devil and the Deep Blue Sea: Merchant Seamen, Pirates, and the Anglo-American Maritime World, 1700–1750*. New York: Cambridge University Press, 1987.
Reinalda, Bob, ed. *The International Transportworkers Federation, 1914–1945: The Edo Fimmen Era*. Amsterdam: Stichting beheer IISG, 1997.
Robinson, Charles Napier. *The British Tar in Fact and Fiction*. London: Harper and Brothers, 1911.
Roland, Alex, W. Jeffrey Bolster, and Alexander Keyssar. *The Way of the Ship: America's Maritime History Reenvisioned, 1600–2000*. Hoboken, N.J.: John Wiley, 2008.
Sager, Eric. *Seafaring Labour: The Merchant Marine of Atlantic Canada, 1820–1914*. Montreal: McGill-Queen's University Press, 1989.
Saxton, Alexander. *Indispensable Enemy: Labor and the Anti-Chinese Movement in California*. Berkeley: University of California Press, 1971.
Schneer, Jonathan. *Ben Tillett: Portrait of a Labour Leader*. Urbana: University of Illinois Press, 1982.
Schwartz, Stephen. *Brotherhood of the Sea: A History of the Sailors' Union of the Pacific, 1885–1995*. New Brunswick, N.J.: Transaction Books, 1986.
———. *History of the Sailors' Union of the Pacific*. Sailors' Union of the Pacific, 1985. ⟨http://www.sailors.org/pdf/history1-2.pdf⟩.
Searle, G. R. *Morality and the Market in Victorian Britain*. New York: Oxford University Press, 1980.

Sewell, Richard H. *John P. Hale and the Politics of Abolition*. Cambridge, Mass.: Harvard University Press, 1965.
Shotwell, James T., ed. *The Origins of the International Labor Organization*. 2 vols. New York: Columbia University Press, 1934.
Sokolow, Michael. *Charles Benson: Mariners of Color in the Age of Sail*. Amherst: University of Massachusetts Press, 2003.
Spater, George. *William Cobbett, The Poor Man's Friend*. Cambridge: Cambridge University Press, 1982.
Springer, Haskell, ed. *America and the Sea: A Literary History*. Athens: University of Georgia Press, 1995.
Stagg, J. C. A. *Mr. Madison's War: Politics, Diplomacy and Warfare in the Early American Republic, 1783–1830*. Boston: Little, Brown, 1983.
Stanley, Amy Dru. *From Bondage to Contract: Wage Labor, Marriage, and the Market in the Age of Slave Emancipation*. New York: Cambridge University Press, 1998.
Steinfeld, Robert J. *Coercion, Contract, and Free Labor in the Nineteenth Century*. New York: Cambridge University Press, 2001.
———. *The Invention of Free Labor: The Employment Relation in English and American Law and Culture, 1350–1870*. Chapel Hill: University of North Carolina Press, 1991.
Stenton, Michael, and Stephen Lees, eds. *Who's Who of British Members of Parliament*. 4 vols. Sussex: Harvester Press, 1978.
Tabili, Laura. *"We Ask for British Justice": Workers and Racial Difference in Late Imperial Britain*. Ithaca: Cornell University Press, 1994.
Taplin, Eric. *The Dockers' Union: A Study of the National Union of Dock Labourers, 1889–1922*. New York: St. Martin's Press, 1986.
Taylor, Paul S. *The Sailors' Union of the Pacific*. New York: Arno Press, 1971 [1923].
Thelen, David P. *Robert M. La Follette and the Insurgent Spirit*. Boston: Little, Brown, 1976.
Thompson, E. P. *The Making of the English Working Class*. New York: Pantheon, 1964.
Thornton, R. H. *British Shipping*. London: Cambridge University Press, 1959.
Tindall, George Brown, and David E. Shi. *America: A Narrative History*. New York: Norton, 1996.
Trent, William P., et al., eds. *A History of American Literature*. Vol. 3. New York: Cambridge University Press, 1921.
Tsuzuki, Chushichi. *Tom Mann, 1856–1941: The Challenges of Labour*. Oxford: Oxford University Press, 1991.
Tucker, Spencer C., and Frank T. Reuter. *Injured Honor: The Chesapeake-Leopard Affair, June 22, 1807*. Annapolis: Naval Institute Press, 1996.
Tyrrell, Ian. *Transnational Nation: United States History in Global Perspective since 1789*. Basingstoke: Palgrave Macmillan, 2007.
Uglow, Jenny. *Elizabeth Gaskell: A Habit of Stories*. New York: Farrar Straus, 1993.
Vickers, Daniel. *Young Men and the Sea: Yankee Seafarers in the Age of Sail*. New Haven: Yale University Press, 2005.
Vincent, John, ed. *Derby Diaries: A Selection from the Diaries of Edward Henry*

Stanley, 15th Earl of Derby, between September 1869 and March 1878. London: Royal Historical Society, 1994.
Visram, Roszina. *Ayahs, Lascars and Princes: Indians in Britain 1700–1947*. London: Pluto Press, 1986.
Waldstreicher, David. *Runaway America: Benjamin Franklin, Slavery, and the American Revolution*. New York: Hill and Wang, 2004.
Walkowitz, Judith R. *City of Dreadful Delight: Narratives of Sexual Danger in Late-Victorian London*. Chicago: University of Chicago Press, 1992.
———. *Prostitution and Victorian Society*. New York: Cambridge University Press, 1980.
Weiler, Peter. *The New Liberalism*. New York: Garland, 1982.
Weintraub, Hyman. *Andrew Furuseth: Emancipator of the Seamen*. Berkeley: University of California Press, 1959.
Whitehurst, Clinton H., Jr. *The U.S. Merchant Marine: In Search of an Enduring Maritime Policy*. Annapolis: Naval Institute Press, 1983.
Wilson, Kathleen. *The Island Race: Englishness, Empire and Gender in the Eighteenth Century*. New York: Routledge, 2003.
Williams, Appleman William. *History as a Way of Learning*. New York: New Viewpoints, 1973.
Yui, Tsunehiko, and Keiichiro Nakagawa, eds. *Business History of Shipping: Strategy and Structure*. Japan: University of Tokyo Press, 1985.
Zimmerman, James Fulton. *Impressment of American Seamen*. Port Washington, N.Y.: Kennikat, 1925.
Zolberg, Aristide R. *A Nation by Design: Immigration Policy in the Fashioning of America*. Cambridge, Mass.: Harvard University Press, 2006.

Articles

Ahuja, Ravi. “Mobility and Containment: The Voyages of South Asian Seamen, c. 1900–1960.” *International Review of Social History*, 51 (2006): 111–41.
Akpinar, Tim. “Defeating Limitation of Liability in Maritime Law.” *Trial* 40 (Feb. 2006): 44–45.
Auerbach, Jerold S. “Progressives at Sea: The La Follette Act of 1915.” *Labor History* 2 (Fall 1961): 344–60.
Balachandran, Gopalan. “Conflicts in the International Maritime Labour Market: British and Indian Seamen, Employers, and the State, 1890–1939.” *Indian Economic and Social History Review* 39.1 (2002): 71–100.
Bickel, Alexander M. “Strathearn S.S. Co. v. Dillon—An Unpublished Opinion by Mr. Justice Brandeis.” *Harvard Law Review* 69 (May 1956): 1177–1205.
Bloor, Michael. “Problems of Global Governance: Port-State Control and ILO Conventions.” SIRC Symposium 2003, Seamen’s International Research Centre, Cardiff, U.K. ⟨http://www.sirc.cf.ac.uk/⟩.
Broeze, F. J. A. “The Muscles of Empire: Indian Seamen and the Raj.” *Indian Economic and Social History Review* 18 (1981): 43–67.

Brunsman, Denver. "The Knowles Atlantic Impressment Riots of the 1840s." *Early American Studies* 5 (Fall 2007): 330–31.
Chalmers, W. Ellison. "International Labor Organization: Results of International Labor Conference, June 1936." *MLR* (1936): 316–28.
Clark, Elizabeth B. "'The Sacred Rights of the Weak': Pain, Sympathy, and the Culture of Individual Rights in Antebellum America." *Journal of American History* 82.2 (1995): 463–93.
Cray, Robert E., Jr. "Remembering the USS *Chesapeake*: The Politics of Maritime Death and Impressment." *Journal of the Early Republic* 25 (Fall 2005): 445–74.
Crews, Frederick. Rev. of *Melville: His World and Work*, by Andrew Delbanco. *New York Review of Books*, Dec. 1, 2005, 6–12.
Dewey, Ralph L. "The Merchant Marine Act of 1936." *American Economic Review* 27 (June 1937): 240–52.
Dinwiddy, J. R. "The Early Nineteenth-Century Campaign against Flogging in the Army." *English Historical Review* 97 (Apr. 1982): 308–31.
Dye, Ira. "Early American Merchant Seafarers." *Proceedings of the American Philosophical Society* 120 (Oct. 1976): 331–60.
Egan, Clifford L. "The Origins of the War of 1812: Three Decades of Historical Writing." *Military Affairs* 38 (Apr. 1974): 72–75.
Eisanach, Eldon. "Liberal Citizenship and American National Identity." *Studies in American Political Development* 13 (Spring 1999): 198–215.
Ewald, Janet J. "Crossers of the Sea: Slaves, Freedmen, and Other Migrants in the Northwestern Indian Ocean, c. 1750–1914." *American Historical Review* 105.1 (2000): 69–91.
Fiering, Norman S. "Irresistible Compassion: An Aspect of Eighteenth-Century Sympathy and Humanitarianism." *Journal of the History of Ideas* 37 (1976): 195–218.
Fisher, Michael H. "Working across the Seas: Indian Maritime Labourers in the India, Britain, and in Between, 1600–1857." *International Review of Social History* 51 (2006): Supplement, 21–45.
"Flags of Peace." *Economist*, Sept. 13, 2003, 59.
French, John D., and Kristin Wintersteen. "Crafting an International Legal Regime for Worker Rights." *International Labor and Working Class History* 75 (Spring 2009): 145–68.
Glenn, Myra C. "Troubled Manhood in the Early Republic: The Life and Autobiography of Sailor Horace Lane." *Journal of the Early Republic* 26 (Spring 2006): 59–93.
Goodman, Warren H. "The Origins of the War of 1812: A Survey of Changing Interpretations." *Mississippi Valley Historical Review* 28 (Sept. 1941): 171–86.
Goodrich, Carter. "International Labor Relations: Maritime Labor Treaties of 1936." *MLR* 44 (1937): 349–56.
Hamer, Philip M. "British Consuls and the Negro Seamen Acts, 1850–1860." *Journal of Southern History* 1 (May 1935): 138–68.
———. "Great Britain, the United States, and the Negro Seamen Acts, 1822–1848." *Journal of Southern History* 1 (Feb. 1935): 3–28.

Harolds, Louis R. "Some Legal Problems Arising Out of Foreign Flag Operations." *Fordham Law Review* 28 (Summer 1959): 295–315.

Horsman, Reginald. "The Paradox of Dartmoor Prison." *American Heritage Magazine* 26 (Feb. 1975): 12–17.

Hyslop, Jonathan. "Steamship Empire: Asian, African and British Sailors in the Merchant Marine, c. 1880–1945." *Journal of Asian and African Studies* 44.1 (Feb. 2009): 69–95.

Knauth, Arnold W. "Alien Seamen's Rights and the War." *American Journal of International Law* 37 (Jan. 1943): 74–80.

Land, Isaac. "Customs of the Sea: Flogging, Empire, and the 'True British Seaman,' 1770 to 1870." *Interventions* 3.2 (Aug. 2001): 169–85.

Lane, Calvin. "The African Squadron: The U.S. Navy and the Slave Trade, 1820–1862." *Log of Mystic Seaport* 50, 4 (1999): 86–98.

Lane, Tony. "The Political Imperatives of Bureaucracy and Empire: The Case of the Coloured Alien Seamen Order, 1925." *Immigrants and Minorities* 13 (1994): 104–29.

Lee, Julia Sun-Joo. "The Return of the 'Unnative': The Transnational Politics of Elizabeth Gaskell's *North and South*." *Nineteenth-Century Literature* 61 (Mar. 2007): 449–78.

Lemisch, Jesse. "Jack Tar in the Streets: Merchant Seamen in the Politics of Revolutionary America." *William and Mary Quarterly* 25 (July 1968): 371–407.

Lillie, Nathan. "Bringing the Offshore Ashore: Transnational Production, Industrial Relations and the Reconfiguration of Sovereignty." *International Studies Quarterly* (forthcoming).

———. "Global Collective Bargaining on Flag of Convenience Shipping." *British Journal of Industrial Relations* 42 (Mar. 2004): 153–79.

———. "Union Networks and Global Unionism in Maritime Shipping." *Relations Industrielles/Industrial Relations* 60.1 (2005): 88–111.

McCartin, Joseph A. "Democratizing the Demand for Workers' Rights." *Dissent* (Winter 2005): 61–66, 70–71.

McKay, Steven C. "Filipino Sea Men: Identity and Masculinity in a Global Labor Niche." In *Asian Diasporas: New Formations, New Conceptions*, edited by Rhacel S. Parreñas and Lok C. D. Siu. Stanford, Calif.: Stanford University Press, 2007.

McCord, Norman. "The Seamen's Strike of 1815 in North-East England." *Economic History Review* 21 (1968): 127–43.

McKee, Christopher. "Foreign Seamen in the United States Navy: A Census of 1808." *William and Mary Quarterly* 42 (July 1985): 383–93.

Meyerson, Harold. "Globalism for the Rest of Us." *American Prospect Online*, Aug. 30, 2005. ⟨http://www.prospect.org/cs/articles?article=globalism_for_the_rest_of_us⟩ (accessed Feb. 14, 2010).

Morris, Richard B. "Labor Controls in Maryland in the Nineteenth Century." *Journal of Southern History* 14 (Aug. 1945): 385–400.

Norris, Martin J. "The Seaman as Ward of the Admiralty." *Michigan Law Review* 52 (Feb. 1954): 479–504.

Northrup, Herbert R., and Peter B. Scrase. "The International Transport Workers'

Federation Flag of Convenience Shipping Campaign: 1983–1995." *Transportation Law Journal* 23 (1996): 369–423.
Peck, Gunther. "Contracting Coercion? Rethinking the Origins of Free Labor in Great Britain and the United States." *Buffalo Law Review* 51 (Winter 2003): 201–18.
Plummer, Mary Beth. "Choice of Law or Statutory Interpretation? The Fair Labor Standards Act Applied Overseas." *Indiana International and Comparative Law Review* 3 (Fall 1992): 177–97.
Politakis, George P. "Updating the International Seafarers' Code: Recent Developments." *International Journal of Marine and Coastal Law* 12.3 (1997): 341–63.
Ratzlaff, C. J. "The International Labor Organization of the League of Nations: Its Significance to the United States." *American Economic Review* 22 (Sept. 1932): 447–61.
"Recent Cases." *Rutgers Law Review* 13 (1959).
Rice, William Gorham, and W. Ellison Chalmers. "Improvement of Labor Conditions on Ships by International Action." *Monthly Labor Review* 42 (May 1936): 1181–1203.
Schoen, Brian. "Calculating the Price of Union: Republican Economic Nationalism and the Origins of Southern Sectionalism, 1790–1828." *Journal of the Early Republic* 23 (Summer 2003): 173–206.
Silverman, Gillian. "Sympathy and Its Vicissitudes." *American Studies* 43 (Fall 2002): 5–28.
Stanley, Amy Dru. "Beggars Can't Be Choosers: Compulsion and Contract in Postbellum America." *Journal of American History* 78 (Mar. 1992): 1265–93.
Stumberg, George W. "The Jones Act, Remedies of Seamen." *Ohio State Law Journal* 17 (Autumn 1956): 484–93.
Thompson, Walter C., Jr. "Notes." *Tulane Law Review* 44 (Fall 1970): 347–54.
Trodd, Anthea. "Collaborating in Open Boats: Dickens, Collins, Franklin, and Bligh." *Victorian Studies* 42.2 (2000): 201–25. ⟨http://muse.jhu.edu/journals/victorian_studies/v042/42.2trodd.html⟩.
Turnbull, Peter J., and Victoria J. Wass. "Defending Dock Workers—Globalization and Labor Relations in the World's Ports." *Industrial Relations* 46.3 (2007): 582–612.
Williams, David M. "Mid-Victorian Attitudes to Seamen." *International Journal of Maritime History* 3 (1991): 101–26.

Unpublished Works

Amante, Maragtas S. V. "Philippine Global Seafarers: A Profile." Unpublished paper: Cardiff University Seafarers International Research Centre, Nov. 2003.
Balachandran, Gopalan. "Producing Coolies, (Un)making Workers: A (Post-)Colonial Parable for the Contemporary Present." Paper presented to "Workers, the Nation-State and Beyond: The Newberry Conference on Labor Across the Americas," Chicago, Sept. 18–20, 2008.
Brunsman, Denver Alexander. "The Evil Necessity: British Naval Impressment in the Eighteenth-Century Atlantic World." PhD diss., Princeton University, 2004.
———. "Subjects and Citizens: Impressment and Identity Formation in the Anglo-

American Atlantic." Newberry Fellows Seminar Paper, Newberry Library, Chicago, Oct. 29, 2007.

Dixon, Conrad Hepworth. "Seamen and the Law: An Examination of the Impact of Legislation on the British Seamen's Lot, 1588–1918." Ph.D. diss., University College, London, 1981.

Flanagan, John. "The Mid-Victorian Settlement? A Study of the Miners' and Seamen's United Association." Paper presented at 27th Annual North American Labor History Conference, Detroit, Oct. 20–22, 2005.

Moynihan, Daniel Patrick. "The United States and the International Labor Organization, 1889–1934." PhD diss., Fletcher School of Law and Diplomacy, 1960.

Pearson, Susan J. "'The Rights of the Defenseless': Animals, Children, and Sentimental Liberalism in Nineteenth-Century America." PhD diss., University of North Carolina at Chapel Hill, 2004.

Philbrick, Thomas. "Cooper and the Literary Discovery of the Sea." Paper presented at the 7th Cooper Seminar, "James Fenimore Cooper: His Country and His Art," State University of New York College of Oneonta, July 1989. James Fenimore Cooper Society Web site, ⟨http://www.oneonta.edu/external/cooper/articles⟩.

Rafferty, Matthew Taylor. "The Republic Afloat: Violence, Labor, Manhood, and the Law at Sea, 1789–1861." PhD diss., Columbia University, 2003.

Rao, Gautham. "Visible Hands: Customhouses, Law, Capitalism, and the Mercantile State of the Early Republic." PhD diss., University of Chicago, 2008.

Sampson, Helen. "Powerful Unions, Vulnerable Workers: The Representation of Seafarers in the Global Labour Market." Unpublished paper, courtesy of the author, 2003.

Seekings, Jeremy. "The ILO and Welfare Reform in South Africa, Latin America and the Caribbean, 1925–50." Paper presented at the conference "The Past and Present of the International Labour Organization," International Institute of Social History, Ghent, Belgium, Oct. 4–6, 2007.

Oral History Interviews

Susan Cueva
Sam Dawson
Edwin Dela Cruz
Enrico Esopa
Ray Familathe
Harold Lewis
Gunnar Lundeberg
Brian McWilliams
Captain Gregorio S. Oca
Abdulgani Serang
Mahendra Sharma

Acknowledgments

One of the greatest pleasures in the pursuit of this book involved the personal contacts that it necessitated. Those contacts divided into two categories: old friends and strangers, both of whom proved invaluable for their knowledge, advice, and criticisms. I first tip my hat to those who have long labored in the maritime field. Early on, Marcus Rediker welcomed me on board, and subsequently, Harold Langley, Denver Brunsman, Nathan Lillie, Helen Sampson, Paul Craven, Tony Lane, and Steven C. McKay all provided gracious and expert guidance. For nineteenth-century references, I leaned on old friends James Epstein, Jeffrey Sklansky, Scott Nelson, Laura Edwards, Neville Kirk, Richard John, Susan Pearson, Peter Coclanis, Joshua Brown, and Carl Smith, but also benefited greatly from the counsel of Robert Steinfeld, Sam Truett, Ruth Paley, Christopher Tomlins, Anna-Lisa Cox, Sam Mitrani, Gerald Danzer, David Eltis, Thomas Heinrich, and Susan Donovan. Thanks to Newberry Library seminars, I also made some very useful literary friends in the form of Diana Robin, Jill Rappoport, Sarah Burns, Holly Pickett, Jennifer Hill, and Manushag Powell.

Similarly, for twentieth- and twenty-first-century research, I initially enjoyed substantive support from fellow historians and personal friends John French, Eric Arnesen, Julie Greene, Nelson Lichtenstein, Tobias Higbie, Mae Ngai, Dan Bender, Kerry Taylor, Howard Machtinger, and Philip and Mary Bowyer. I also benefited greatly from the advice and references of an excellent group of Indian historians, including Gopalan Balachandran, Ravi Ahuja, and Jo Sharma as well as the unfailing assistance of Sam Dawson from the International Transport Workers' Federation. Renee Berthon, Arnaud Dubois, and Ariel Golan proved most helpful at the ILO archives in Geneva. Similarly, Richard Temple at the Modern Records Centre, University of Warwick, saved me time and effort, even as the Interlibrary Loan desk at my own University of Illinois at Chicago rendered consistent and excellent service. I also benefited from the counsel and direct assistance of historian-activists around the International Longshore and Warehouse Union—in particular, Gene Vrana, Harvey Schwartz, and Don Watson. More formally, I drew on a group of varied but invariably accommodating and informative interviewees who are identified above in a separate listing. Among those not directly cited, Jessica Smith, Paul Krupa, Eric Mensing, Jeff Engels, Britt Richardson, and the late Archie Green favored me with valuable interview material on contemporary shipping and maritime labor issues.

My research was crucially facilitated by two fellowship years, one courtesy of UIC's

Institute for the Humanities, so ably directed by Mary Beth Rose, and the other thanks to the Guggenheim Foundation. My evolving chapters were much improved by trial runs at the Institute for the Humanities as well as the Tamiment Labor History Series (thanks to Michael Nash), the UCLA History Forum (Jan Reiff and Ruth Milkman), the Lockmiller Seminar at Emory University (Bianca Premo), the Penn Economic History Forum (Walter Licht), the Newberry Seminar in Early American History and Culture (Al Young, Sarah Pearsall, and Eric Slaughter), and the Newberry Fellows Seminar (Jim Grossman and Diane Dillon). As the dedication suggests, the Newberry Library proved my main research craft for this project, and I counted on Danny Greene, Diane Dillon, James Ackerman, Karen Christianson, John Aubrey, John Powell, Heather Radke, Rachel Rooney, Brodie Austin, Victor Benitez, and Jenny Schwartzberg for recurrent assistance. I was also aided by an extraordinary group of research assistants, all Ph.D. students at the time, in the concentration in Work, Race, and Gender in the Urban World at the University of Illinois at Chicago: Joshua Salzmann, Daniel Harper, Allison O'Mahen Malcom, and Thomas Dorrance.

Working with the University of North Carolina Press is like visiting an old friend. David Perry encouraged this project from its inception; Zachary Read proved an assiduous shepherd; and Julie Bush and Paul Betz lavished expert and caring attention on the manuscript itself. To them and the extended cast behind the publishing curtain, I am much obliged.

As always in my writing ventures, Susan Levine served as my first line of defense against gross abuses of language or logic. Finally, there are two people who must be singled out for service at once unanticipated and magnificent. Harold Lewis, who spent a lifetime in the cause of international unionism, took extraordinary pains with a distant researcher and lent me insights that I could have acquired no other way. Chris Daly, once a student and long a friend, did me more than a personal favor in passing the entire manuscript before his demanding but caring inspection. Though none of those mentioned above can be blamed for the shortcomings of this work, all of them are implicated in the spirit of critical inquiry that informs it.

Index

Note: *Italic* page numbers indicate illustrations.

AAA, 156, 157

"Able seamen": definition of, 94; on steamships, 145–46, 229 (n. 2); U.S. requirements for, 94, 145–46

Abolition of Slavery Act of 1833 (Britain), 25

Abuse of seamen, campaigns against, 45–50

Acheson, Dean, 224 (n. 92)

Ackroyd, Peter, 41

Adams, John Quincy, 25, 51–52

Adderley, Charles, 80

Admiralty law, 111–12, 223 (n. 89)

Advance notes, 57, 80, 82, 94, 111–12

AFL. *See* American Federation of Labor

AFL-CIO, 117, 191

African American seamen, 50–54; vs. Asian seamen, 131; in Navy, 211 (n. 51); number of, 51; restrictions on freedom of, 50–54; in Revolutionary Era, 11

Agricultural Adjustment Act (AAA) (U.S.), 156, 157

Ahuja, Ravi, *134*

Albert, Fred, 68

Alcohol, and flogging, 47, 48, 49

Ali, Aftab, 155, 231 (n. 33)

Alien Seamen's Bill of 1933 (U.S.), 162–63

All at Sea (film), 223 (n. 89)

Allotment system, 57, 94, 213 (n. 84)

American Federation of Labor (AFL): in ILO development, 149–50; on immigration restrictions, 162; La Follette Act supported by, 97; during World War II, 164

American Federation of Labor and Congress of Industrial Organizations, 117, 191

American Longshoremen's Union, 123, 226 (n. 25)

American Merchant Marine Memorial, *165*

American Revolution, impressment in, 11

American Seamen's Friend Society, 47

American Steamship Association, 98, 145

Amiens, Treaty of (1802), 13, 204 (n. 24)

Amoco Cadiz oil spill, 194

AMOSUP. *See* Associated Marine Officers' and Seamen's Union of the Philippines

Amsterdam, ITF headquarters in, 138

Amsterdam Congress (1904), 129

Antwerp, union organizing in, 123

Apprenticeship system, 30, 56

Arago case, 61–63, 97

Arango, Clemencia, 34

Arch, Joseph, 215 (n. 11)

"Asian articles," 90, 155, 166–67

Asian Maritime Conference, First (1953), 169

Asian seamen: in British shipping, 28, 133–34, 140, 227 (n. 69); in ILO conventions, 154–55, 166–67; in international unions, 131–32; ITF in conflict with unions of, 186–88; postwar rise in number of, 184–85; racism and xenophobia against, 106–9, 131–32, 163–64, 223 (n. 76), 224 (n. 95); as stewards, 163–64; U.S. citizenship ban on, 163, 164; in U.S. shipping, 106–9, 163–64; wages of, 101, 106, 140, 187, 189; after World War I, 140; in World War II, 168–69, 224 (n. 95), 233 (n. 71)

Asiatic Seamen's Union, 154

Asquith, Herbert, 87, 125

Associated Marine Officers' and Seamen's Union of the Philippines (AMOSUP), 186, 189, 190, 198, 199

Atlantic Coast Seamen's Union, 130, 220 (n. 6), 227 (n. 58)

Auerbach, Jerold S., 106
Austen, Jane, 41
Australia: in development of ILO conventions, 153–54, 159, 167; ITF in, 184

Bahamas: flags of convenience in, 179; Maritime Labour Convention ratified by, 195
Bainbridge, USS, 1
Balachandran, Gopalan, 169, 231 (n. 30)
Balkan Wars, 221 (n. 48)
Ball, Joseph H., 172, 202
"Ballad of the Seamy Side" (O'Neill), 229 (n. 7)
Bancroft, George, 208–9 (n. 117)
Banjo (McKay), 148
Banks, Hal, 177, 235 (n. 17)
Barbary Wars, 1, 11–12, 27
Barnacle Bill (film), 223 (n. 89)
Barnes, Leo, 187
Bass, M. T., 215 (n. 11)
Bates, Edward, 78
Belgium: in development of ILO conventions, 153, 159; union organizing in, 123
Benz v. Compania Naviera Hidalgo, 181–82, 183
Berghe, Henry, 67
Berrien, John Macpherson, 53
Bethel societies, 47
Bevan, David Gilroy, 176
Bevin, Ernest, 156
Bickel, Alexander M., 112, 224 (nn. 91–92)
Big Sea, The (Hughes), 229 (n. 12)
Blackleg workers, 121, 122, 125, 127
Black seamen: British, 51–52, 140; literary portrayals of, 148. *See also* African American seamen
Bland, S. O., 160–61
Blanqui, Jerome, 118
Blatchford, John, 14
Blue certificates, 184, 187, 188
Blum, Hester, 229 (n. 4)
Board of Trade (Britain): at ILO conferences, 152–53; Lloyd George as president of, 88–90; Plimsoll in conflict with, 76, 77, 80; shipwreck statistics of, 74; on unseaworthy ships, 79, 216 (n. 43)
Bodine, George, 130
Boer War, 129
Bolivia, flags of convenience in, 236 (n. 27)
Bolshevik revolution, 149
Boston Massacre (1770), 11
Bowles, Thomas Gibson, 87
Boyer, Richard O., 167, 168
Brandeis, Louis, 111, 112, 224 (n. 92)
Brandywine, USS, 50
Brassey, Thomas, 145
Brennan, William, 183
Bridges, Harry, 191
Bristol, strikes at, 121
Britain: in development of ILO conventions, 152–53, 156, 158, 159; establishment of free trade in, 25–31; liberal debate over government regulation in, 81–85; liberalism's rise in, 25–26; national identity of, 40, 210 (n. 15); population of, 203 (n. 10); regulation of foreign ships in, 88–90; slave trade abolition in, 24–25; U.S. trade agreements with, 27; in War of 1812, 10–23; in World War I, 135–41
British Bible Society, 47
British Board of Trade. *See* Board of Trade
British citizenship: inalienability of, 14; 19th-century vs. modern significance of, 18; and requirements for naturalization, 204 (n. 29)
British impressment. *See* Impressment
British maritime reform. *See* Maritime reform—British
British merchant navy: functions of, 10; name of, 2. *See also* British seamen; British shipping
British navy. *See* Royal Navy
British seamen: black, 51–52, 140; campaign against flogging of, 45–50; declining number of, 176; impact of free trade on, 27–31; job satisfaction of, 174–75; lascars in competition with, 90, 218 (n. 93); literary portrayals of, 40–42, 146, 148; number of, in 1800s, 11; political status of, 43–45; public perception of, 44; right to quit, 54–63; in U.S. shipping, 13, 14, 18, 204 (nn. 25, 27, 29); wages of, 101, 138–39; in World War I, 136, 138–39; in World War II, 165–66
British shipping: Asian seamen in, 28, 133, 140, 227 (n. 69); bilateral reciprocity agreements in, 27–28, 207 (n. 89); English language used in, 88, 89; flags of convenience and, 180; government subsidies for, 160, 162, 176; international competitiveness of, 87–92; international unionism in, 119–28; literary portrayals of, 40–42, 146, 148; 19th-century dominance of, 2, 32–34, 36, 88–89, 203 (n. 6); number of foreign nationals in, 88, 133, 218 (n. 86); opening to free trade, 25–31; protectionism in, 159–60; racism in, 140, 162; regulation of foreign nationals in, 27, 28, 30–31, 133, 162; technological advances in, 32–33; 20th-

century decline of, 168, 176; during World War II, 165–66. *See also* Navigation Acts
British unions. *See* Unions—British
Brown, Henry Billings, 61–62
Bruere, Robert W., 157, 158
Bryan, James Wesley, 104, 222 (n. 55)
Buck's Stove case, 97
Bullen, Frank T., 32–33
Burn, W. L., 25
Burnett, John, 108
Burns, John, 120, 125
Burton, Theodore, 98, 220 (n. 11)
Butler, Benjamin F., 60, 213–14 (n. 99)
Butler, Josephine, 67
Byron, Lord, 209 (n. 2)

Cabotage trade: British regulation of, 27–28; definition of, 33; U.S. regulation of, 33
Canadian Seamen's Union (CSU), 177, 235 (n. 17)
Canning, George, 16–17
Canning, Stratford, 52
Cardwell, Edward, 31
Cargo-handling, in contracts, 192, 239 (n. 73)
Cargo ships: foreign-built with U.S. flags, 100; growth in size of, 175–76, 235 (n. 11); technological advances in, 175–76, 235 (n. 11)
Casualty rates: in British shipping, 67, 74, 81; in World War II, 164, 165
Catholic Emancipation (1829), 25
Cavendish-Bentinck, George, 82
Chadwick, Edwin, 73
Chamberlain, Joseph, 79, 80–81, 83, 88, 218 (n. 72)
Chamberlain, Joseph Perkins, 157
Chesapeake, USS, 14–17, *15*, 19, 205 (n. 35)
China: Cultural Revolution in, 175; in development of ILO conventions, 155, 159; flags of convenience and, 239 (n. 65)
Chinese Exclusion Act of 1882 (U.S.), 106
Chinese seamen: in international unions, 132, 134; wages of, 101, 106, 140, 155; women as, 175; after World War I, 140; in World War II, 168–69; xenophobia against, 106–9, 132, 134, 223 (n. 76), 224 (n. 95)
CIO. *See* Congress of Industrial Organizations
Citizenship: of African American seamen, 52, 53; in impressment, 13–14, 17–23; 19th-century vs. modern significance of, 18. *See also* British citizenship; United States citizenship
Civil Rights Act of 1964 (U.S.), 212 (n. 56)
Civil War, American, 33, 40
Clay, Henry, 203 (n. 7), 206 (n. 51)
Cleanliness of seamen, 109–10
Clipper ships, 32, 33
Coastal trade: opening of British, 27–28; punishment for desertion in U.S., 61, 214 (n. 109)
Coast Guard, U.S., 239 (n. 82)
Coast Seamen's Journal, *96*, 106, 223 (n. 70)
Coast Seamen's Union, 95, 220 (n. 6)
Cobbett, William, 46, 48
Coffin ships, 72, *72*, 148, 229 (n. 8). *See also* Unseaworthy ships
Colchester, Lord, 30
Colden, Charles J., 157
Cold War, 177
Collins, Eugene, 82
Collins, Wilkie, 41
Coloured Alien Seamen's Order of 1925 (Britain), 140, 162
Commerce. *See* Trade
Commission on International Labour Legislation, 149–50, 230 (n. 15)
Communist Manifesto, The (Marx and Engels), 118
Competition. *See* International competition
Compromise of 1850, 48
Conference on Safety of Life at Sea (1913), 105
Confinement, as alternative to flogging, 49, 50, 211 (n. 50)
Conger, Omar, 56
Congress, U.S.: on cabotage trade, 33; on desertion, 43, 44, 55, 59–63; elections of 1912 for, 95; on flogging, 48–50, 212 (n. 54); Furuseth at debates in, 161, 233 (n. 60); on ILO conventions, 157; in ILO development, 149; "rule of the flag" and, 111; on state Negro Seamen's Acts, 52. *See also specific laws*
Congress of Industrial Organizations (CIO), 164
Connery, William P., 233 (n. 60)
Conrad, Joseph, 42, 146, 229 (n. 4)
Conscription, 207 (n. 73)
Constitution, U.S.: and African American seamen, 52, 53, 54; on citizenship, 20; Fourteenth Amendment to, 18; Tenth Amendment to, 53; Thirteenth Amendment to, 59, 61, 94
Contagious Diseases Acts (Britain), 55–56
Containerization, 175–76, 235 (n. 11)
Continuous-discharge books, 233 (n. 62)

Contracts: agricultural labor, 63; cargo-handling in, 192, 239 (n. 73); dockworker–seamen alliance in negotiations of, 190–94; elimination of public signing of, 175; entirety doctrine of, 211 (n. 32); free labor, 207 (n. 83); indenture, 24, 44; marriage vs. sailor's, 98; right to quit, 54–63. *See also* Desertion
Cooke, Thomas Potter, 42
Cooper, Anthony Ashley, 78, 216 (n. 34)
Cooper, James Fenimore, 37, 47, 209 (n. 2)
Copeland, Royal, 161
Corbould, Henry, *58*
Corn Laws (Britain), 25, 207 (n. 90)
Corporal punishment: decline of, 45; for desertion, 59; U.S. law on, 46, 94, 211 (n. 38). *See also* Flogging
Courts-martial, 50
Cowen, Joseph, 85
Cox, Archibald, 182, 236 (n. 36)
Cray, Robert E., Jr., 19
Crimean War, 23
Crimps: in desertion, 61; regulation of, 56–57, 80, 94; role of, 56, 213 (n. 83)
Croly, Herbert, 103, 104, 222 (n. 53)
Cromwell, Oliver, 12
CSU. *See* Canadian Seamen's Union
Cuba, in Spanish-American War, 34
Cuban blockade, 177
Cueva, Susan, 197, 198, 199–200, 240 (n. 94)
Cultural Revolution, 175
Curran, Joseph, 177
Cyprus, flags of convenience in, 179

Dana, Richard Henry, 37, 45–46, 201
Dana, Richard Henry, Jr., 60
Danish Seafarers' Union, 199
Dartmoor Prison, 11
Daud, Muhammed, 155, 231 (n. 32)
Davis, Jefferson, 49
Davis, Richard Harding, 34
Day, William R., 111–12
Deaths. *See* Casualty rates
Death Ship, The (Traven), 147–48
Dela Cruz, Edwin, 198, 240 (n. 95)
Democracy, union, 197–200
Dening, Greg, 4
Denmark, flags of convenience and, 185
Derby, Lord, 80
Desertion: motivations for, 60–61; rates of, 60–61; vs. right to quit, 54–63; unions on, 61, 63
—in Britain: abolition of category (1970), 59, 175; decriminalization of, 61, 81, 84; early law on, 55, 61; origins of law on, 43; Plimsoll's influence on, 80–81; punishment for, 43, 58–59; vs. right to quit, 58–59, 61
—in U.S.: decriminalization of, 94; early law on, 44, 55; La Follette Act on, 94, 97–101, 113, 162, 219–20 (n. 3); origins of law on, 43; punishment for, 43, 44, 59–60, 61, 63, 97, 214 (n. 109); vs. right to quit, 59–63; Supreme Court on, 61–63
Desha, Joseph, 20, 21
DeSombre, Elizabeth R., 193–94
Developing world: rise in number of seamen from, 184–85; voices of, in ILO, 154–55, 169; wages in, 186
Dickens, Charles, 41, 73
Dies, Martin, 163
Diesel fuel, 176
Dillingham Commission, 107, 108
Dillon, John, 112
Dingley Act of 1884 (U.S.), 57
Discipline: British law on, 58–59; U.S. law on, 59–60, 94. *See also* Flogging
Disraeli, Benjamin, 68, 78, 79–80
Diversity, in ITF, 129–35
Dixon, Conrad, 228 (n. 75)
Dockworkers, wages of, 173
Dockworker unions: in collaboration with seamen's unions, 120, 121, 190–94, 225 (n. 11); in strike of 1911, 124–27
Dodd, William, 216 (n. 34)
Dombey and Son (Dickens), 41
"Don't give up the ship!," 205 (n. 35)
Douglas, William O., 182, 183
Douglass, Frederick, 11, 50, 51
Doumbia-Henry, Cleopatra, 195
Dred Scott case, 54, 62, 97
Drift and Mastery (Lippmann), 103
Duff, Edwin H., 220 (n. 15)

Eastcote, in World War I, 136–37
East India Company, 27
Economic downturn of 2008, 195
Eight-factor test, 224 (n. 103)
Eight-hour day. *See* Working hours
Elcho, Lord, 82
Elderkin, Thomas J., 123
Elkison, Henry, 52
Ellenborough, Earl of, 28
"Emancipation day" for U.S. seamen, 93

Embargo Act of 1807 (U.S.), 16, 17
Emergency Railroad Transportation Act of 1933 (U.S.), 160
Employers and Workmen Act of 1875 (Britain), 59, 81
Employers' Liability Act of 1880 (Britain), 86, 87, 119
Employment Acts of 1980 and 1982 (Britain), 236 (n. 41), 238 (n. 60)
Engels, Friedrich, 118
Engineers, in transition from sail to steam, 145
English language: on British ships, 88, 89; global prevalence of, 191; Pidgin, 113; on U.S. ships, 94, 113
Entirety doctrine, 211 (n. 32)
Equiano, Olaudah, 11, 50–51
"Essential work" clause, 234 (n. 3)
Essex case (1805), 14
Established Service Scheme, 173
Ethnicity, in international unionism, 128–35
Evangelicals, in campaign against flogging, 46–48

Fair Labor Standards Act of 1936 (U.S.), 157
Familathe, Ray, 192, 193
Families of seamen, 57, 58, 120, 225 (n. 10)
Federalists, 15–16, 19–22
Fengtao (cargo ship), 175
Ferguson, Munro, 89
Fiction. *See* Literature
FILDAN, 199–200
Filipino seamen: entry into U.S. shipping, 164; government policies encouraging, 185–86; history of, 185; political power of, 198–200, *199*; rise in number of, 184, 185–86; unions of, 186, 189, 190, 198, 199–200, 240 (n. 95); wages of, 189; in World War II, 233 (n. 71)
Fimmen, Edo, 138
Fingard, Judith, 213 (n. 83)
"Fink" books, 233 (n. 62)
Firemen, in steamships, 145
Fishing rights, 193
Fitzhugh, George, 54
Five-Mile Vagabond Act (Britain), 156
"Flag, rule of the," 111, 112
Flags of convenience (FOCs): in cargo-sharing, 237 (n. 52); Chinese participation in, 239 (n. 65); conditions onboard and, 169; dockworkers and, 190–94; ITF inspection of, 187–94, *192*, 201; ITF Welfare Fund and, 188–90; original rationale for, 179; rise of, 6, 175, 178–86; union opposition to, 180–84, 186–87; U.S. Supreme Court on, 181, 182–83, 236 (n. 36)
Fleischacker, Samuel, 203 (n. 3)
Flogging: alternatives to, 49, 50, 211 (n. 50); campaigns against, 45–50; in literature, 37; public opinion on, 26, 45–50; U.S. law against, 46, 48–50, 94, 211 (n. 38), 212 (n. 54)
FOCs. *See* Flags of convenience
Food, regulation of, 55, 88, 98
Forced labor, decline of, 23–24, 26
Foreign nationals
—in British shipping: international organizing inspired by, 119; in National Union of Seamen, 128–29, 131; number of, 88, 133, 218 (n. 86); NUS levy on, 185, 237 (n. 45); regulation of, 27, 28, 30–31, 133, 162
—in international unions: resistance to, 131–35
—in U.S. shipping: number of, 204 (n. 25); regulation of, 19–22, 33, 161–64, 232 (n. 58), 233 (n. 62); xenophobia against, 106–9
Foreign ships: Britain's regulation of, 88–90; port state control of, 194–200; U.S. regulation of, 94, 100–103, 111–14, 219–20 (n. 3)
Forton Prison, 11
Foucault, Michel, 3–4
Fourteenth Amendment, 18
France: black seamen in, 51; desertion in, 113; in development of ILO conventions, 153, 155–56; flags of convenience and, 185
Franklin, Benjamin, 12
Freedom of seamen, 35–63; African American, 50–54; British vs. U.S., 36; flogging and, 45–50; in literature, 36–42; in political status, 43–45; to quit, 54–63; U.S. calls for, 35–36, 93; vs. welfare of seamen, 105
Free labor: in La Follette Act, 94, 97, 162; limits of, 206–7 (n. 73)
Free labor contracts, 207 (n. 83)
"Free seas" principle, 101
Free shipping: in Britain, 28; definition of, 28; in U.S., 33
Free trade: in national power, 26–27; opposition to, 28–31; origins of, 25; regulation of seamen in, 27, 28; retreat from, in 1930s, 159–64; rise of, in Britain, 25–31; Smith on allowable restrictions on, 9–10, 160, 203 (nn. 3–4); U.S.–British agreements on, 27
Friends of Andrew Furuseth Legislative Association, 114–15
Fugitive Slave Law of 1793 (U.S.), 44
Furuseth, Andrew: activism of, 94–95; Bran-

deis's friendship with, 224 (n. 92); at congressional debates, 161, 233 (n. 60); death of, 95; on foreign seamen, 106, 107–8, 131; on ILO, 105, 149; at ILO conference, 157; impact of, 94–95; on imprisonment for desertion, 97; on ITF, 105, 130; La Follette Act supported by, 5, 94–95, 97, 98, 102, 105; La Follette's friendship with, 95, 220 (n. 9); Maritime Labour Convention and, 196; nationalism in arguments of, 103; photo of, *99*; resistance to international unionism by, 105, 130; and right to quit, 61, 105, 214 (n. 109); on sanitation problems, 110; unmarried life of, 95, 220 (n. 7); on World War I, 136

Gallatin, Albert, 204 (n. 29)
Gardner, Augustus Peabody, 107–8
Garrison, James, 47–48
Garrison, William Lloyd, 47–48, 67, 97
Garvey, Marcus, 132
Gaskell, Elizabeth, 24, 41–42, 210 (n. 21)
Geneva, ILO conference in (1936), 155–58
Genoa, ILO conference in (1920), 151–53
German seamen: in ITF, 129; in World War I, 136–37, 138
Germany: ITF headquarters in, 124, 129; union organizing in, 122; in World War I, 135–38
Ghent, Treaty of, 23
Gildermeisen, Eugene, 135
Gilje, Paul A., 14, 16
Gilroy, Paul, 4
Giulietti, Giuseppe, 154
Gladstone, William, 71, 80, 81, 208 (nn. 90, 93)
Glascock, William N., 42
Glasgow, ISU in, 128
Glencairn series (O'Neill), 146
"Global economy," 118, 149
Globalization: flags of convenience in, 178; "global economy" as focus before, 118; ILO's attempt to address, 149; modern era of, 2, 178
Glover, John, 77
GM plant strike (1972), 235 (n. 7)
Goan seamen, 162
Goldsborough, Charles, 22
Gompers, Samuel: anti-injunction campaigns of, 103; Furuseth and, 105; in ILO development, 149–50, 230 (n. 15); in New York parade, 97
Goodrich, Carter, 158
Gorst, John Eldon, 84–85
Government subsidies: British, 160, 162, 176; U.S., 1–2, 161–64, 177
Granville, Earl of, 28
Great Britain. *See* Britain
Great Depression: and international unionism, 155–57, 231 (n. 34); protectionism during, 159–64
Great Dock Strike (1889), 120, 122
Green, Archie, 97
Griffiths, Anselm John, 23–24
Grundy, Felix, 19–20
Guest, J. C., 89
Guest, John, 69–70
Gulf War, 34
Guthrie, Robert Storrie, 153–54

Haarbleicher, André, 155–56
Hague Memorandum of Understanding (MOU) (1978), 194
Hairy Ape, The (O'Neill), 146–47, *147*
Hale, Edward Everett, 40
Hale, John Parker, 48–49, 211 (n. 51)
Half-wage provisions, 94, 113, 219 (n. 3)
Hall, James, 71–72, 73, 76, 215 (n. 13)
Haly, R. Standish, 206 (n. 72)
Hamburg: ITF headquarters in, 124, 129; union organizing in, 122
Hamlin, Hannibal, 49
Hand, Learned, 114
Harcourt, Sir William, 80, 217 (n. 48)
Hardy, Rufus, 101
Harlan, John, 62, 63
Harriman, W. Averell, 179
Haugen, Ingvald, 180
Helvering, Guy T., 105
HFW. *See* Holman, Fenwick and Willan
Hickey, Donald R., 205 (n. 44)
Hipwood, Charles, 152–53
Hiring halls, union, 172
Hobhouse, L. T., 81
Hobson, J. A., 81
Ho Chi Minh, 132
Hohman, Elmo Paul, 40, 102
Holman, Fenwick and Willan (HFW), 188–89
Home to Harlem (McKay), 148
Homosexuality, 220 (n. 7)
Honduras, flags of convenience in, 179, 180, 183
Hong Kong, 184
Hooper, Samuel, 56
Hospitals, marine, 43, 44

Hours of Work and Manning Convention, ILO (1936), 158–59
House of Representatives, U.S. *See* Congress
Howell, George, 78, 79, 85, 218 (n. 72)
Hughes, Langston, 229 (n. 12)
Hughes, Thomas, 78
Hull, strikes at, 121, 125
Hume, Joseph, 46
Humphrey, Hubert, 172
Humphrey, William E., 99
Hutchins, John G. B., 33, 210 (n. 12)

IBF. *See* International Bargaining Forum
ILA. *See* International Longshoremen's Association
Illingworth, Alfred, 215 (n. 11)
ILO. *See* International Labor Organization
ILWU. *See* International Longshoremen's and Warehousemen's Union
IMEC. *See* International Maritime Employers' Committee
Immigrant rights, U.S. debate over, 20–23
Immigration, U.S. restrictions on, 107–8, 162–64
IMO. *See* International Maritime Organization
Impressment, 10–25; in American Revolution, 11; citizenship issues in, 13–14, 17–23; decline of, 23–26; geopolitical motivations for, 14; history of, 12–14; in Napoleonic Wars, 12, 13; origins of, 12–13; scope of, 12, 13; selection criteria for, 13; vs. slavery, 13; slave trade abolition and, 24–25; treatment of seamen after, 13; U.S. certificates of citizenship and, 14, 22–23; U.S. legislative response to, 19–23; in War of 1812, 10–22
Impressment Bill of 1813 (U.S.), 19–23, 205 (n. 44, 47)
Impressment Fully Considered (Griffiths), 23–24
Imprisonment, for desertion, 44, 59, 61, 63, 80–81, 97
IMWU. *See* International Maritime Workers Union
Incres Steamship Co., Ltd. v. International Maritime Workers Union, 182–83
Indenture contracts, decline of, 24, 44
India, in development of ILO conventions, 154–55, 159
Indian seamen (lascars): clothing of, *134*; in competition with British seamen, 90, 218 (n. 93); flogging of, 48; ILO on working hours of, 152–55; in international unions, 133; in Navigation Acts, 27; 19th-century rise in number of, 88, 90; regulation of use of, 90, 133, 162, 218 (n. 93); in strike of 1911, 228 (n. 75); 20th-century rise in number of, 184–85; in U.S. shipping, 106–7; in World War II, 168–69; xenophobia against, 106–7, 219 (n. 94), 224 (n. 95)
Indian Seamen's Union, 155
Individualism, rise of, 24
Industrialization, in popular culture, 146–48
Industrial Workers of the World (IWW), 108–9
Injured seamen, U.S. law on, 113, 224 (n. 98)
Inspections: British law on, 72, 74, 79, 80; by ITF, 187–94, *192*, 201; under Maritime Labour Convention, 195–96; in port state control, 194–95; U.S. law on, 113
Insurance, maritime, 72, 74–75, 81
International agreements: goals of, 3; on load lines, 68. *See also specific agreements*
International Bargaining Forum (IBF), 188
International competition: British maritime reform and, 87–92; international labor standards and, 152–53; limits of union solidarity and, 167–68; national labor standards and, 118; U.S. maritime reform and, 93, 100–103
International Convention for the Safety of Life at Sea (SOLAS) (1914), 194
International Federation of Miners, 225 (n. 3)
International Federation of Ship, Dock and River Workers, 118, 122
International Labor Organization (ILO), 149–59; charter of, 149–50; conventions vs. recommendations of, 150; developing world's input in, 154–55, 169; development of maritime conventions of, 150–59, 166–67, 231 (n. 31); early challenges facing, 149–50; establishment of, 6, 149–50; fears of revolution motivating, 149, 150, 155–56, 229–30 (n. 13), 231 (n. 34); on flags of convenience, 180; Furuseth's opposition to, 105, 149; Geneva conference of (1936), 155–58; Genoa conference of (1920), 151–53; globalization addressed by, 149; goals of, 149, 150; on IMO standards, 195; inaugural conference of (1919), 150; International Seafarers' Federation and, 138; Maritime Labour Convention of, 195–97; membership in, 230 (n. 19); number of conventions of, 230–31 (n. 23); representational and juridical processes of, 150; Seattle conference of (1946), 166; U.S. role in, 149–50, 156–58, 159,

230 (n. 17); on wages, 155, 166, 186; on working hours, 152–59, 166; during World War II, 166–67; after World War II, 169
International Longshoremen's and Warehousemen's Union (ILWU), 173, 191–92
International Longshoremen's Association (ILA), 173, 226 (n. 25)
International Maritime Employers' Committee (IMEC), 188
International Maritime Organization (IMO): on flags of convenience, 179–80; SOLAS convention under, 194; training and certification standards of, 195
International Maritime Workers Union (IMWU), 182–83, 236 (n. 36)
International norms, vs. national norms, 87–88, 104–5, 222 (n. 60)
International Seafarers' Action Center (ISAC), 198–99
International Seafarers' Federation, 138, 151
International Seamen's Charter, 166
International Seamen's Code, ILO, 152
International Seamen's Union (ISU): establishment of, 61, 95, 220 (n. 6); at ILO conference, 157; on international norms, 105, 222 (n. 60); and ITF, 123, 130; and La Follette Act, 94, 96, *96*, 101; in NMU's origins, 234 (n. 79); resistance to international unionism in, 130, 149; World War I and, 113; xenophobia in, 106, 108–9, 223 (n. 70)
International Shipping Federation, 151
International Transport Workers' Federation (ITF), 122–41; Asian unions in conflict with, 186–88; British role in, 119, 122, 123, 129; on cargo-sharing, 237 (n. 52); communication problems in, 130; establishment of, 6, 122–23; flags of convenience opposed by, 180–84, 186–87; FOC inspection regime of, 187–94, *192*, 201; Furuseth on, 105, 130; as global union, 118, 188, 225 (n. 3); headquarters of, 124, 129, 138; at ILO conferences, 151; on IMO standards, 195; and ISU, 123, 130; longshoremen's alliance with, 191–92; in Maritime Labour Convention, 196–97; mission of, 6, 122; national and ethnic differences in, 129–35; organizing efforts of, 122–23; and political agency of seamen, 197; strikes supported by, 122–28; types of workers in, 124, 226 (n. 33); wages negotiated by, 186, 187–88; Welfare Fund of, 188–90, 238 (nn. 60–61); in World War I, 135–41; in World War II, 166; after World War II, 173–74
International unions. *See* Unions—international
International Workingmen's Association, 95, 225 (n. 3)
Inverclyde, Lord, 89–90
Involuntary servitude: impressment as, 24; U.S. prohibition of, 59, 62
Ionesco, Eugene, 171, 194
Iron ships, U.S. vs. British use of, 32–33
ISAC. *See* International Seafarers' Action Center
ISU. *See* International Seamen's Union
Italy, in development of ILO conventions, 154
ITF. *See* International Transport Workers' Federation
IWW. *See* Industrial Workers of the World

Jackson, Andrew, 53
Jackson, Howell E., 114, 224 (n. 103)
James, C. L. R., 38–39
Japan: on automated megaships, 176; in decline of British shipping, 176; in development of ILO conventions, 154
Japanese seamen, 131, 132
Jarman, Charles, 166
Jefferson, Thomas, 11, 15–16
Jerrold, Douglas, 42
Job satisfaction, after World War II, 174–75, 234–35 (n. 7)
Jochade, Herman, 124–25, 130, 136, 137
Johnson, Samuel, 97
Johnson, William, 52
Joint Negotiating Group, 188, 193–94
Jones, Andrieus, 113
Jones Act (Merchant Marine Act) of 1920 (U.S.), 33, 113–14, 224 (n. 98), 232 (n. 58)

Kalashi watch, 153, 219 (n. 2)
Kaplan, William, 235 (n. 17)
Kennedy, John F., 182, 236 (n. 36)
Kent, James, 53
King, William R., 20
Kingsley, Charles, 73
Kirkland, Lane, *165*
Knatchbull-Hugessen, Edward, 82
Knauth, Arnold W., 224 (n. 95)
Knight, Robert, 216 (n. 35)
Knowles anti-impressment riot (1747), 11

Korean War, 177
Korrespondenzblatt, 130
Kyles, MV, *69*

Labor force. *See* Seamen
Labor standards: international, ILO development of, 150–59; national, in international competition, 118
Labor unions. *See* Unions
Labouchere, Henry, 28, 30, 58, 208 (n. 94)
Labour Party (Britain), 216 (n. 37)
La Follette, Robert M.: Brandeis's friendship with, 111, 224 (n. 92); Furuseth's friendship with, 95, 220 (n. 9); ITF as heir to, 201; on passage of La Follette Act, 93; photo of, *99*; role in La Follette Act, 93, 94, 95–97, 101, 103; on Wilson (Woodrow), 98; xenophobia and, 107
La Follette Act (Seamen's Act) of 1915 (U.S.), 93–115; corporal punishment under, 94, 211 (n. 38); enforcement of, 110–15; foreign ships under, 94, 100–103, 111–14, 219–20 (n. 3); free labor provisions of, 94, 97, 162; Furuseth's role in, 5, 94–95; goals of, 5, 93, 94; impact on seamen, 99–100, 102, 222 (n. 58); international impact of, 100–103, 111–12; international influences on, 88, 104–5; introduction of bill, 95–97; La Follette's role in, 93, 94, 95–97, 101, 103; legacy of, 114–15; in Merchant Marine Act of 1936, 161, 233 (n. 61); opponents of, 98–100, 102–3, 220 (n. 15); passage of, 93, 103; racism and xenophobia in, 106–9; safety provisions of, 94, 96–97; scholarly interpretations of, 106, 222 (n. 66); Supreme Court on, 111–12, 114; unions encouraged by, 94; and U.S. competitiveness in world market, 93, 100–103
Lake Seamen's Union, 130, 220 (n. 6)
Lamport, W. J., 78–79
Land, Isaac, 210 (n. 15)
Lane, Calvin, 25
Langer, William, 182
Langley, Harold D., 49
Languages: on British ships, 88, 89; in ITF, 130; on U.S. ships, 94, 113; universality of English, 191
Lansdowne, Marquess de, 28
Lascars. *See* Indian seamen
Lauritzen v. Larsen, 114
Law, Andrew Bonar, 90, 218 (n. 90)
Lawrence, James, 205 (n. 35)
League of Nations, 149, 150
Lecointe, Georges, 153
Leggett, William, 45
Legislation. *See* Congress, U.S.; Parliament, British; State laws, U.S.; *specific laws*
Legrand, Daniel, 118
Lemisch, Jesse, 11
Lewis, Harold, 187, 236 (n. 39)
Liability, of shipowners, 104, 222 (n. 55)
Liberalism: and British maritime reform, 81–85; classical vs. new, 68, 81–85; end of impressment and, 25, 26; free labor contracts in, 207 (n. 83); neo-liberalism and, 178, 201; of Plimsoll, 71; rise of, 24–26
Liberal-Labour (Lib-Lab), 79, 216 (n. 37)
Liberal Party (Britain), 28, 79, 208 (nn. 90, 93)
Liberator, The, 48
Liberia: flags of convenience in, 176, 179, 182–83; freed slaves in, 25; Maritime Labour Convention ratified by, 195
Liddell, Henry Thomas, 31
Lillie, Nathan, 188, 201
Limitation of Shipowners' Liability Act of 1851 (U.S.), 222 (n. 55)
Lincoln, Abraham, 49
Lindley, Charles: on foreign seamen, 131; Furuseth's warning to, 130; in international unionism, 122, 123–24, 128; retirement of, 174
Linebaugh, Peter, 4, 13, 132
Lippmann, Walter, 103
Literature: American, 36–40, 146–48; British, 40–42, 146; and public opinion of flogging, 45–46
Little, Peter, 21–22
Liverpool, strike of 1911 in, 125, 127
Lloyd George, David: in Board of Trade, 88–90; on foreign nationals, 88, 218 (n. 86); on lascars, 219 (n. 94); liberalism of, 81; maritime reform efforts of, 88–90; and strike of 1911, 125
Lloyds of London, 72, 74
Load lines, 68, 69, 74, 79, 89
Lodge, Henry Cabot, 102–3
London: Conference on Safety of Life at Sea (1913) in, 105; Great Dock Strike of 1889 in, 120, 122; strike of 1911 in, 125
London Graphic, *91*
London Labour and the London Poor (Mayhew), 73

London Times, 79–80, 91–92
Longshoremen, 173. *See also* Dockworker unions
Lord Jim (Conrad), 146
Louisiana, African American seamen in, 51, 52–53
Lubin, Isador, 157
Lundeberg, Gunnar, 177
Lundeberg, Harry, 164
Lusitania, 136

Macarthur, William, 62, 131
MacIver, David, 81
Madison, James, 12, 16, 18
Maersk Alabama, 1, 2
Magna Carta, 13
Maguire, James G., 61, 95
Maguire Act of 1895 (U.S.), 61, 214 (n. 109)
Mahan, Alfred, 103
Malta, flags of convenience in, 179
Mann, Tom: on challenges of mobilization, 124; in Great Dock Strike, 120, 122; on mission of ITF, 122; as president of ITF, 122; on slowdowns, 124; in strike of 1911, 125–27; syndicalism of, 124, 125–27; union organizing by, 122–23
Manning requirements: British repeal of, 27, 28, 30–31; British "75 percent" rule of, 27, 119, 232 (n. 58), 233 (n. 62); U.S. "75 percent" rule of, 161–62, 232 (n. 58), 233 (n. 62). *See also* Foreign nationals
Mansfield Park (Austen), 41
Man Without a Country, The (Hale), 40
Marcos, Ferdinand, 185
Marine Cooks and Stewards union, 182, 236 (n. 35)
Marine Transport Workers Union, 108
Marisol, *165*
Maritime Commission, U.S., 161
Maritime Labour Convention of 2006 (MLC), 195–97
Maritime law, 111–12, 223 (n. 89)
Maritime reform
—British, 67–92; international competitiveness in, 87–92; La Follette Act influenced by, 88, 104–5; liberalism and, 81–85; Plimsoll's role in, 67–81; racism in, 140, 162; Wilson's role in, 85–87
—international: load lines in, 68, *69*, 74, 79, 89; U.S. resistance to, 105
—U.S., 93–115; enforcement of, 110–15; Furuseth's role in, 94–95; international competitiveness and, 93, 100–103; nationalism in, 100, 103–5; need for, 35–36, 93; Plimsoll's role in, 68; in Progressive Era, 93, 103–4, 106–9; racism and xenophobia in, 106–9, 162–64, 224 (n. 95); Supreme Court on, 111–12, 114; of working conditions, 94, 109–10. *See also* La Follette Act
Maritime Security Program (U.S.), 1–2
Marriage: contract of, vs. sailor's contract, 98; prevalence among seamen, 120, 225 (n. 10)
Marryat, Frederick, 209 (n. 2), 210 (n. 18)
Marshall, Thurgood, 183
Marshall Islands: flags of convenience in, 179; Maritime Labour Convention ratified by, 195
Marshall Plan, 115
Martin, Richard, 67
Marx, Karl, 118, 225 (n. 3)
Master and Servant Law (Britain), 24
Matthews, Edward W., 92
Mayhew, Henry, 73
Mazarello, A. M., 154, 231 (n. 30)
McCoy, Drew, 26, 207 (n. 86)
McCulloch v. Sociedad Nacional de Marineros de Honduras, 182–83
McFee, William, 168
McHugh, Edward, 123
McKay, Claude, 148
McKinley, William, 160
McLean, Malcolm, 235 (n. 11)
McPhee, John, 177
McReynolds, Samuel Davis, 156
Meany, George, 235 (n. 17)
Megaships, 175–76
Melville, Herman, 37–39; maritime experiences of, 37, 38; *Moby Dick*, 38–39, 209 (n. 8); portrayal of seamen by, 37–39; *Redburn*, 38, 45–46; *White-Jacket*, 46, *46*
Memorandum of Understanding (MOU): Hague, 194; Paris, 194–95
Mercantile Marine Act of 1850 (Britain), 56, 58
Mercantilism: definition of, 207 (n. 84); in War of 1812, 10, 26
Merchant marine. *See* Seamen; *specific countries*
Merchant Marine Academy, U.S., 162
Merchant Marine Act (U.S.): of 1920, 33, 113–14, 224 (n. 98), 232 (n. 58); of 1936, 160–64, 177, 233 (n. 61); of 1954, 177
Merchant navy, use of term, 2
Merchant Navy Reserve Pool, 165
Merchant Seaman Act of 1880 (Britain), 80–81

Merchant Shipping Acts (Britain): of 1850, 55; of 1854, 28, 55, 58–59; of 1867, 55; of 1871, 72; of 1876, 79, 83–84, 217 (n. 63); of 1894, 88; of 1906, 88, 104–5, 133, 134; of 1970, 175; of 1974, 175
Mexico: in development of ILO conventions, 159; return of immigrants from, 162
Meyerson, Harold, 117–18
Minimum wage: ILO standards for, 166, 186; U.S. Supreme Court on, 232 (n. 41)
MLC. *See* Maritime Labour Convention of 2006
Moby Dick (Melville), 38–39, 209 (n. 8)
Mohawk disaster, 160
Monroe, James, 12, 16–17, 18
Montgomery, David, 213 (n. 83)
Moore, Joseph, 99–100
Morley, Samuel, 215 (n. 11)
Morris, Richard B., 59
Morro Castle disaster, 160
Morse, Isaac E., 49
Motor Carrier Act of 1935 (U.S.), 160
MOU. *See* Memorandum of Understanding
Muckracking, 73
Muller, Paul, 129, 131–32
Mundella, A. J., 215 (n. 11)
Mutiny at the Nore, The (Jerrold), 42

"Nanny state," 84, 217 (n. 63)
Napoleonic Wars: end of, 22; impressment in, 12, 13; in literature, 41, 42; strikes during, 29
NASFU. *See* National Amalgamated Sailors' and Firemen's Union of Great Britain and Ireland
Nash, Gary, 11
National Amalgamated Sailors' and Firemen's Union of Great Britain and Ireland (NASFU): establishment of, 70, 85, 119; financial problems of, 121; internationalism of, 119, 122; name changes to, 119; Plimsoll in, 70, 85
National Defense Reserve Fleet, 177
National emergencies, 172, 173
National identity: British, 40, 210 (n. 15); U.S., 11, 40
National Industrial Recovery Act of 1933 (NIRA) (U.S.), 156, 157, 230 (n. 17)
Nationalism, in U.S. maritime reform, 100, 103–5
Nationalization, of U.S. shipping, 104
National Labor Relations Act (NLRA) (U.S.), 181, 182, 183, 232 (n. 41)
National Maritime Board (NMB) (Britain), 139–40
National Maritime Union (NMU): in Cold War, 177; on flags of convenience, 181; merger with SIU, 177, 235 (n. 16); origins of, 234 (n. 79); racial integration in, 167, 234 (n. 80); wages negotiated by, 173; in World War II, 164, 167
National norms, vs. international norms, 87–88, 104–5, 222 (n. 60)
National power: dominance in trade in, 9; free trade in, 26–27
National property, seamen as, 10, 27, 31
National Seamen's Union, 220 (n. 6). *See also* International Seamen's Union
National security, role of U.S. shipping in, 177, 235 (n. 17)
National sovereignty: regulation of foreign ships and, 90, 218 (n. 90); in War of 1812, 16–18
National Union of Seafarers of India (NUSI), 186–87, 189, 197–98
National Union of Seamen (NUS): on foreign nationals, 128–29, 131, 135; and International Transport Workers' Federation, 123; levy on foreign nationals by, 185, 237 (n. 45); New Unionism of, 120; origins of, 119; priorities of, 120; reform movement within, 173; in strike of 1911, 125; strikes by, 173; in World War I, 136–37, 138; in World War II, 165; after World War II, 173
Naval Discipline Acts of 1860–66 (Britain), 48
Navigation Acts (Britain): exceptions to, 27, 207 (n. 89); impact of, 27; legislation replacing, 55; provisions of, 9, 27; repeal of (1849), 10, 25, 27, 29, 30; "75 percent" rule in, 27, 119, 232 (n. 58), 233 (n. 62); Smith on, 9–10
Navy, U.S.: African Americans in, 211 (n. 51); end of flogging in, 48–50
Negro Seamen's Acts (U.S. states), 51–54, 212 (n. 62)
Nelson, Lord, 41
Neo-liberalism, 178, 201
Netherlands, in development of ILO conventions, 156, 159
New Deal, 156–57, 230 (n. 17), 232 (n. 41)
New Democracy, The (Weyl), 103
New Freedom, 103
New liberalism, 81–85
New Nationalism, 103
New Orleans, African American seamen in, 51
New Unionism, 120–22, 140
New York City: American Merchant Marine Memorial in, *165*; foreign nationals in, 204

(n. 25); 1909 parade in, 97; Triangle Fire in (1911), 96; union organizing in, 123, 226 (n. 25)
New Yorker, 167
New York Public Advertiser, 16
New York Times, 79, *126*, 127, 215 (n. 5)
Niles Register, 10
NIRA. *See* National Industrial Recovery Act of 1933
NLRA. *See* National Labor Relations Act
NMB. *See* National Maritime Board
NMU. *See* National Maritime Union
Noon, Faroz Khan, 155
Nore mutiny (1797), 29, 42
Norling, Lisa, 57
Norris-LaGuardia Act of 1932 (U.S.), 181, 182, 236 (n. 35)
North and South (Gaskell), 42
Norway: in development of ILO conventions, 156; flags of convenience and, 180, 185; Maritime Labour Convention ratified by, 195
Norwegian Seamen's Union, 190
Norwood, C. M., 82
NUS. *See* National Union of Seamen
NUSI. *See* National Union of Seafarers of India

Oca, Gregorio S., 186, 187, 190, 198
Oca, Roberto, 186
Officers: British regulation of, 28; vs. non-officers, working conditions for, 145, 174; in transition from sail to steam, 145; women, 175
Oil shock of 1970s, 176, 184
Oil spills, 194
Oil tankers, 175–76
Okasaki, Ken, 154
Olander, Victor, 104–5, 110
Oldenbroek, J. H., 174
O'Neill, Eugene, 146–47, 229 (n. 7)
OPEC, 176
Open manning, opposition to, 28, 30–31. *See also* Manning requirements
Orders in Council (1807), 14, 24, 205 (n. 33)
Organization of Petroleum Exporting Countries (OPEC), 176
Our Seamen (Plimsoll), 68, 72–79
Owen, Robert, 118
Owners. *See* Shipowners

Pacific Mail Steamship Company, 106, 109
Pacific Maritime Association, 172, 192
Panama: flags of convenience in, 179, 180, 181–82; Maritime Labour Convention ratified by, 195, 196
Panama Canal, 32
Paredes, Quintin, 164
Paris Memorandum of Understanding (MOU) (1982), 194–95
Paris Peace Conference, 149, 229–30 (n. 13)
Parker, Richard, 42
Parliament, British: on desertion, 43, 55, 58–59, 61, 80–81; Plimsoll in, 67, 71, 77–80, 217 (n. 48); rise of free trade and, 28–31; Wilson in, 85–87, 121, 133, 227 (n. 72). *See also specific laws*
Passenger Acts (U.S.), 218 (n. 90); of 1819 (U.S.), 206 (n. 60)
Passenger safety, U.S. law on, 94
Paternalism: codification of, 55–56; and political status, 43–44; vs. right to quit, 54–63
Payments to seamen: advance notes in, 57, 80, 82, 94, 111–12; allotment system for, 57, 94, 213 (n. 84); British regulation of, 56–57; U.S. regulation of, 56–57, 94, 111–12. *See also* Wages
PC5 system, 139
Pechell, Sir George, 31
Peck, John, 42, 210 (n. 15)
Peel, Sir Robert, 207 (n. 90)
Peelites, 27, 207 (n. 90), 208(n. 93)
Perkins, Frances, 157
Philbrick, Thomas, 36
Philippines: government policies on seafaring in, 185–86; IMO standards in, 195. *See also* Filipino seamen
Philippines Overseas Employment Administration (POEA), 185, 186
Pidgin English, 113
Pilot, The (Cooper), 37, 47, 209 (n. 2)
Piracy, 1–2
Pitkin, Timothy, 206 (n. 47)
Plimsoll, Samuel, 67–81; career of, 71, 80, 91; on coffin ships, 72, *72*, 229 (n. 8); death of, 91–92; development of views of, 71–73; family of, 71, 91; on foreign ships, 84; impact of, 5, 67–70, 91–92; ITF as heir to, 201; legacy of, 91–92; on load lines, 68, *69*, 74; opponents of, 77–80; *Our Seamen*, 68, 72–79; in Parliament, 67, 71, 77–80, 217 (n. 48); political views of, 71; portrait of, *91*; on safety inspections, 72, 74; on scurvy, 83; Wilson and, 85–86, 90–91
Plimsoll and Seamen's Fund Committee, 78
Plimsoll line. *See* Load lines

Plimsolls (sneakers), 70
Plimsoll Sensation, The (pamphlet), 77
POEA. *See* Philippines Overseas Employment Administration
Political parties in Britain, unions allied with, 79, 216 (n. 37). *See also specific parties*
Poor Law Amendment Act of 1834, 25
Poor Law Report (1834), 73
Pope, John, 17–18
Popular culture, seamen in: British, 40–42; 19th-century portrayals of, 36–42; 20th-century portrayals of, 146–48; U.S., 36–40
Ports of convenience, 192
Port state control, 194–200; administration of, 195, 239 (n. 82); definition of, 194; establishment of, 194–95; Maritime Labour Convention and, 195–97
Press gangs, 13, 24, 25. *See also* Impressment
Progressive Era: La Follette Act in, 93, 104, 111; maritime reform in, 93, 103–4, 106–9; nationalism in, 103; protectionism in, 106–9
Promise of American Life (Croly), 103, 222 (n. 53)
Protectionism: in Britain, 159–60; in international unions, 133; limits of solidarity and, 167–68; in U.S., in 1930s, 159–64; in U.S., in Progressive Era, 106–9

Quarterly Review, 28–29, 77
Quincy, Josiah, III, 21, 22
Quit, right to, 54–63; in Britain, 58–59, 61; in ILO, 149–50; union support for, 61, 63, 105; in U.S., 59–63. *See also* Desertion

Racial integration, in NMU, 167, 234 (n. 80)
Racism: in British maritime reform, 140, 162; in development of ILO conventions, 152–55; in international unionism, 131–35; literary portrayals of, 148; among seamen, 167, 234 (n. 80); in U.S. maritime reform, 106–9, 162–64
Radicals (Britain), 28, 208 (n. 93)
Rafferty, Matthew Taylor, 60
Raker, John Edward, 106–7
Randolph, John, 45
Rathbone, William, VI, 83–84
Ratzlaff, Carl J., 158
Rayner, Kenneth, 53
Reagan, Ronald, 177
Realism, in American literature, 37
Redburn (Melville), 38, 45–46
Rediker, Marcus, 4, 13, 60–61, 132
Rees, J. D., 219 (n. 94)
Reform. *See* Maritime reform
Reform Act of 1832 (Britain), 25, 208 (n. 93)
Registry books, 233 (n. 62)
Regulation. *See* Maritime reform; *specific countries and laws*
Rehnquist, William, 183
Reinalda, Bob, 151–52
Republicans (U.S.): on impressment, 17–18, 19–21; on trade, 26, 207 (n. 86)
Revolution, ILO motivated by fears of, 149, 150, 155–56, 229–30 (n. 13), 231 (n. 34)
Rhodes, 43, 62
Ridley, Sir Matthew White, 87
Riviera, SS, 181–82
Robertson v. Baldwin, 61–63, 97
Rogers, Nicholas, 13
Rolls of Oléron, 43
Roosevelt, Franklin D., 156, 157, 161
Roosevelt, Theodore, 103
Root, Elihu, 102, 103
Royal Commission on Labour, 86
Royal Commission on Unseaworthy Ships, 68, 77
Royal Navy (Britain): end of flogging in, 48, 211 (n. 50); history of impressment in, 12–13; literary portrayals of, 41
Ruef, Abe, 95
"Rule of the flag," 111, 112
Runciman, Sir Walter, 32, 139
Rusk, Dean, 235 (n. 17)
Ruskin, John, 40
Russell, John, 28
Rylands, Peter, 215 (n. 11)

Safety: British statistics on, 74; La Follette Act provisions for, 94, 96–97; of passengers, 94. *See also* Unseaworthy ships
Safety inspections. *See* Inspections
Safford, Jeffrey J., 232 (n. 56)
Sager, Eric, 60, 102, 228–29 (nn. 1–2)
Sailing vessels, decline of, 145, 228 (n. 1)
Sailors, use of term, 4. *See also* Seamen
Sailor's Magazine, 47
Sailors' Union of the Pacific (SUP): establishment and mergers of, 61, 95, 220 (n. 6); on flags of convenience, 181–82; growth during World War II, 164; headquarters of, 220 (n. 18); wages negotiated by, 173
Sandberg v. McDonald, 111–12

Sanitary Report (1842), 73
Scarman, Leslie, 189, 238 (n. 60)
Scharrenberg, Paul, 157
Schauer, Peter, 171
Schechter case, 157
Schetsky, John Christian, *15*
Schultz, Elizabeth, 51
Scientific rationalism, 73
Scobell, George, 30
Scotland, ISU in, 128
Scott, Sir Walter, 209 (n. 2)
Scott, William, 43–44
Scurvy, 83
Seafarers. *See* Seamen
Seafarers' International Union (SIU): in Canada, 177, 235 (n. 17); in Cold War, 177; on flags of convenience, 181; merger with NMU, 177, 235 (n. 16); in World War II, 164, 234 (n. 80)
Seamen: "able," 94, 145–46, 229 (n. 2); campaigns against abuse of, 45–50; class distinctions among, 145–46, 174; families of, 57, 58, 120, 225 (n. 10); impact of free trade on, 27–31; literary portrayals of, 36–42, 146–48; political power of, 84–85, 197–200; political status of, 43–45; as property of nations, 10, 27, 31; racism among, 167, 234 (n. 80); skilled vs. unskilled, 145–46; in transition from sail to steam, 145–46; women as, 175, 198. *See also specific countries and regions*
Seamen, freedom of. *See* Freedom of seamen
Seamen, impressment of. *See* Impressment
Seamen's Act of 1915 (U.S.). *See* La Follette Act
Seamen's Trust, 189
Seattle, ILO conference in (1946), 166
Senate, U.S. *See* Congress
Senior, Nassau William, 25–26
Serang, Abdulgani, 189, 197–98
Serang, A. K., 169
Serang, Mohamed, 169
Service Employees International Union, 117
Seven-factor test, 224 (n. 103)
"75 percent" rule, 27, 119, 161–62, 232 (n. 58), 233 (n. 62)
Seybert, Adam, 20–21
Ship(s): insurance on, 72, 74–75, 81. *See also specific types of ships*
Shipbuilders: British subsidies for, 176; on free-ships policy, 33; in late 20th century, 176; U.S. subsidies for, 161
Shipowners: cost-cutting pressures on, in late 20th century, 176; on free-ships policy, 33; free trade opposed by, 28; impact of free trade on, 28; insurance held by, 72, 74–75, 81; liability of, 104, 222 (n. 55); vs. public ownership of shipping, 104; U.S. subsidies for, 161
Shipping Act of 1916 (U.S.), 34
Shipping (Assistance) Act of 1935 (Britain), 160
Shipping Board, U.S., 179
Shipping commissioners, 56, 59
Shipping Commissioners' Act of 1872 (U.S.), 55, 56, 57, 59, 214 (n. 109)
Shipping Federation: in conflict with international unions, 119, 121, 124–27; establishment of, 121; strike of 1911 against, 124–27
Shipping Gazette, 77
"Ship shape," 41, 210 (n. 20)
Shipwrecks, British statistics on, 74
Shop stewards movement, 173
SIU. *See* Seafarers' International Union
Skentelbery, Charles, 109–10
Skilled seamen vs. unskilled seamen, in transition from sail to steam, 145–46
Slave(s): vs. African American seamen, 50–54; Barbary Wars and, 12; flogging of seamen and, 47–49; vs. impressed seamen, 13; U.S. Supreme Court on, 54, 62
Slave trade: British abolition of, 24–25; U.S. abolition of, 25
Slave Trade Act of 1819 (U.S.), 25
Slowdowns, worker, 124
Smith, Adam, *The Wealth of Nations*, 9–10, 160, 203 (nn. 3–4)
Smith, Hoke, 102
Smith, Sam, 70
Smith, T. E., 84
Smith, W. H., 215 (n. 11)
Socialist International, 225 (n. 3)
Social Security Act (U.S.), 232 (n. 41)
SOLAS, 194
Solidarity (newspaper), 108, 109
Somali pirates, 1
Somerset case (1772), 13
Southard, Samuel, 22
South Carolina, African American seamen in, 51–53
Sovereignty. *See* National sovereignty
Soviet Union: and Asian seamen, 155, 231 (n. 32); on ILO conventions, 159, 232 (n. 52); women as seafarers in, 175

Spain, Jonathan, 215 (n. 11)
Spanish-American War (1898), 34, 160–61
Spithead mutiny (1797), 29, 42
Stagg, J. C. A., 19, 205 (nn. 44–45)
Standards of Training, Certification and Watchkeeping for Seafarers (STCW), 195
Stanley, Amy Dru, 59
Stanley, Lord, 29
State laws, U.S.: on agricultural labor contracts, 63; on desertion, 43, 59
States Marine Lines, 172
STCW, 195
Stead, W. T., 67
Steamships: "able seamen" on, 145–46, 229 (n. 2); diesel ships replacing, 176; literary portrayals of, 146–47; rise of, 145, 228 (n. 1); U.S. vs. British use of, 32–33, 228 (n. 1)
Steffens, Lincoln, *99*
Steinfeld, Robert J., 24, 63, 207 (n. 83), 211 (n. 32), 214 (n. 101)
Steiwer, Frederick, 163
Stephen, James, 24
Stern, Andy, 117
Stewards: Asian seamen as, 163–64; in steamships, 145
Stockholm, union organizing in, 122–23
Stone, William, 103
Story, Joseph, 44
Stowe, Harriet Beecher, 37
Strathearn S.S. Co. v. Dillon, 112
Strike(s): by British unions, 29–30, 120, 121, 173; by Chinese seamen, 155; general (1926), 139, 173, 228 (n. 93); at GM plant (1972), 235 (n. 7); at Hull and Bristol (1892–93), 121; international (1897), 123; international (1911), 124–28, *126*, 130, 227 (n. 58), 228 (n. 75); international (1949), 177; ITF support for, 122–28; London Great Dock Strike (1889), 120, 122; during Napoleonic Wars, 29; slowdowns as alternative to, 124; after World War II, 173
Strikebreakers, 121, 122, 125, 127
Subsidies. *See* Government subsidies
Sudeley, Lord, 83
Suez Canal, 176, 177
Suffrage in Britain, male, 80, 86–87
SUP. *See* Sailors' Union of the Pacific
Supertankers, 175–76
Supreme Court, U.S.: on African American seamen, 52; on desertion, 61–63; on flags of convenience, 181, 182–83, 236 (n. 36); on La Follette Act, 111–12, 114; on New Deal, 157, 232 (n. 41); on political status of seamen, 44; on slaves, 54, 62
Swedish seamen: in ITF, 122, 129; job satisfaction of, 174; strikes by, 123; union organizing of, 122–24; wages of, 101; women as, 175
Sweeney, John, 117
Sylvia's Lovers (Gaskell), 24, 42
Syndicalism, 124, 125–27

Taft, Robert, 164
Taft, William Howard, 95
Taft-Hartley Act of 1947 (U.S.), 164, 172
Talbot, Earl of, 29
Taney, Roger B., 53–54
Tariffs, Adam Smith on, 203 (n. 4)
Tavistock Institute, 174–75, 234 (n. 5)
TCC. *See* Total crew cost
Technological advances: labor-saving, 175–76; U.S. vs. British, 32
Thatcher, Margaret, 217 (n. 63), 238 (n. 60)
Theater, portrayal of seamen in, 42, 146–47
Thirteenth Amendment, 59, 61, 94
Thomas, Albert, 150, *151*
Thompson, E. P., 46
Thompson, T. P., 26
Thorne, Will, 120
Three-watch system, 219 (n. 2)
Tillett, Ben: in Great Dock Strike, 120; ideology of, 225 (n. 16); on national and ethnic divisions, 128; role in ITF, 122, 128; in strike of 1911, 127; union organizing by, 122–23; Wilson's friendship with, 225 (n. 11); on World War I, 137–38
Tinig ng Marino (newspaper), 190
Tinkham, George H., 156
Titanic disaster, 95, 96, *96*, 194, 222 (n. 55)
Torrey Canyon oil spill, 194
Tory Party (Britain), 28–29
Total crew cost (TCC), 187–88, 189
Trade: British share of, 32, 176; dominance in, and national power, 9; FOCs as share of, 178–80, 184, 237 (n. 42); globalization of, 2; U.S. share of, 32, 99–100. *See also* Free trade
Trades Union Congress (TUC), 76, 138, 139, 228 (n. 93)
Trade unions. *See* Unions
Traven, B., 147–48, 168
Treasure of the Sierra Madre, The (Traven), 147
Triangle Fire (1911), 96

Tripartism, in ILO, 150
Trodd, Anthea, 41, 42
TUC. *See* Trades Union Congress
Two-watch system, 94, 219 (n. 2)
Two Years Before the Mast (Dana), 37, 45–46

UFS. *See* United Filipino Seafarers
Uncle Tom's Cabin (Stowe), 37
Union Network International, 117, 118
Unions: alliance of dockworkers and seamen in, 120, 121, 190–94, 225 (n. 11); critics of power of, 172; democracy in, 197–200; establishment of free trade and, 30; flags of convenience opposed by, 180–84, 186–87; hiring halls of, 172; renewal of, in late 20th century, 171, 188; on right to quit, 61, 63, 105; rise of, 2, 5–6; wages negotiated by, 172–73. *See also specific unions*
—Asian: Filipino, 186, 189, 190, 198, 199–200, 240 (n. 95); ITF in conflict with, 186–88
—British: "essential work" clause in, 234 (n. 3); and international competitiveness, 90, 167–68; in international unionism, 119–28; vs. laws, in protection of seamen, 85; limits of solidarity in, 167–68; New Unionism in, 120–22; political parties allied with, 79, 216 (n. 37); rise of, 85; strikes by, 29–30, 120, 121, 173; wages negotiated by, 173; in World War II, 165–66
—international, 117–41; British role in rise of, 119–28; developing world's input in, 154–55, 169; international competition in need for, 118; national and ethnic differences in, 128–35; origins of, 117–18; strike of 1911's role in development of, 124–28; U.S. resistance to, 129–30; in World War I, 135–41; in World War II, 166–67
—U.S.: on flags of convenience, 181–84; and international competitiveness, 167–68; La Follette Act on, 94; limits of solidarity in, 167–68; wages negotiated by, 172–73; in World War II, 164; xenophobia in, 106, 108–9
United Filipino Seafarers (UFS), 190
United Fruit Company, 179, 183
United Kingdom. *See* Britain
United Nations: on flags of convenience, 180; ILO and, 150
United Nations Conference on Trade and Development (1979–80), 237 (n. 52)
United States: in Civil War, 33, 40; in free trade agreements, 27; in ILO, 149–50, 156–58, 159, 230 (n. 17); immigration restrictions in, 107–8, 162–64; national identity of, 11, 40; national security of, 177, 235 (n. 17); population of, 203 (n. 10); regulation of foreign ships in, 94, 100–103, 111–14, 219–20 (n. 3); resistance to international unionism in, 129–30; slave trade abolition in, 25; in Spanish-American War, 34, 160–61; in War of 1812, 10–23; in World War I, 139; in World War II, 164
U.S. citizenship: Asians barred from, 163, 164; certificates of, 14, 22–23; in Impressment Bill, 19–23; 19th-century vs. modern significance of, 18; requirements for naturalization, 18, 19, 20, 23, 204 (n. 29); rights after naturalization, 20–23
U.S. maritime reform. *See* Maritime reform—U.S.
U.S. Navy. *See* Navy, U.S.
U.S. seamen: African American, 11, 50–54, 211 (n. 51); age of, 213 (n. 86); in American Revolution, 11; calls for freedom for, 35–36, 93; campaign against flogging of, 45–50; "emancipation day" for, 93; La Follette Act's impact on, 99–100, 102, 222 (n. 58); literary portrayals of, 36–40, 146–48; number of (1800s), 11; number of (1915), 99–100, 221 (n. 30); number of (1952–96), 177; political status of, 43–45; public perception of, 44; right to quit, 54–63; sanitary habits of, 109–10; "75 percent" requirement for, 161–62, 232 (n. 58), 233 (n. 62); wages of, 100–101; women as, 175; in World War II, 164. *See also* African American seamen; Impressment
U.S. shipping: British seamen in, 13, 14, 18, 204 (nn. 25, 27, 29); English language used in, 94, 113; flags of convenience and, 180; foreign-built ships in, 100; golden era of, 32; government subsidies for, 1–2, 161–64, 177; literary portrayals of, 36–40, 146–48; national security argument for, 177, 235 (n. 17); 19th-century decline of, 32–34, 36, 39; 19th-century dominance of, 2, 32; number of vessels in 1915, 99–100, 221 (n. 30); protectionism in, 106–9, 159–64; public ownership in, 104; racism and xenophobia in, 106–9, 162–64; regulation of foreign nationals in, 19–22, 33, 161–64, 232 (n. 58), 233 (n. 62); technological advances in, 32–33; 20th-century decline of, 168, 176–77; after World War I, 160–61, 232 (n. 56); during World War II, 164
U.S. unions. *See* Unions—U.S.

Universe Tankships v. ITF, 188–89, 238 (n. 60)
Unseaworthy ships: British commission on, 68, 77; British law on, 79; as coffin ships, 72, *72*, 148, 229 (n. 8); false reports of, 72, 215 (n. 12); Plimsoll on, 68, 72, *72*, 74–75; prevalence of, 67, 74, 79
Unseaworthy Ships Bill of 1875 (Britain), 79, 80

Vardaman, James K., 97–98
Venable, Abraham, 49
Versailles, Treaty of, 152, 230 (nn. 15, 18)
Vesey, Denmark, 51
Viceroy of India, SS, *134*
Vickers, Daniel, 39
Vietnam War, 34, 177
Vincent, Sir Howard, 90
Vines, D. F., 154
Voluntarism, rise of, 24, 26

Wages: on flags of convenience, 181; ILO standards for, 155, 166, 186; in Maritime Labour Convention, 196; minimum, 166, 186, 232 (n. 41); pattern of growth in, 172–73; total crew cost in, 187–88, 189; in transition from sail to steam, 145; U.S. Supreme Court on, 232 (n. 41); U.S. vs. foreign, 100–102, 106; vacation, 166, 232 (n. 50); during World War I, 138–39; after World War I, 139–40; during World War II, 164, 165, 173; after World War II, 173. *See also* Payments to seamen
Walcott, John Edward, 30
Walpole, Lord, 13
War Hawks, 20, 203 (n. 7), 206 (n. 51)
War of 1812, 10–22; buildup to, 14–16; causes of, 10–11, 203 (n. 7), 205 (n. 33); end of, 22, 23; flags of convenience in, 179; impressment in, 10–22; mercantilism in, 10, 26; national identity in, 11; sovereignty in, 16–18; start of, 16; U.S. Impressment Bill and, 19–22
War Shipping Administration (U.S.), 164
Washington Labor Conference (1919), 152
Watch systems: ILO conventions on, 157–58, 232 (n. 50); U.S. law on, 94, 113, 219 (n. 2)
Wealth of Nations, The (Smith), 9–10, 160, 203 (nn. 3–4)
Webster-Ashburton Treaty (1843), 207 (n. 78)
Weintraub, Hyman, 95
Welfare Fund of ITF, 188–90, 238 (nn. 60–61)
Welfare of seamen: in British reform efforts, 87–92; vs. freedom of seamen, 105; in impressment debate, 16, 19; in U.S. reform efforts, 103–5
Wellington, Duke of, 28
Westminster Review, 26, 77, 82, 85
Weyl, Walter, 103
WFTU. *See* World Federation of Trade Unions
Whig Party (Britain), 27, 28, 208 (nn. 90, 93)
White Act of 1898 (U.S.), 63, 97, 101
White-Jacket (Melville), 46, *46*
Whitlow, Jon, 240 (n. 86)
Wilberforce, Samuel, 28
Wilberforce, William, 67
Williams, David M., 55
Williams, Robert, 137
Williams, William Appleman, 207 (n. 84)
Wilson, Harold, 173
Wilson, John L., 53
Wilson, Joseph Havelock: autobiography of, 140–41; on foreign nationals, 128–29, 133–35, 228 (n. 75); and international competitiveness, 90; in international unionism, 5, 118, 119–25, 128–29, 140–41; La Follette Act supported by, 97; life of, 119; in Parliament, 85–87, 121, 133, 227 (n. 72); Plimsoll's influence on, 85–86, 90–91; pragmatism of, 128–29, 225–26 (n. 16); reputation of, 118; role in ITF, 122; strikes supported by, 121, 124–27; Tillett's friendship with, 225 (n. 11); union organizing by, 122–23; on World War I, 136–37, 138–41
Wilson, William B., 95, 97
Wilson, Woodrow: in La Follette Act debate, 98, 101; La Follette Act enforcement under, 112–13; La Follette Act signed by, 93; in League of Nations, 149; New Freedom of, 103
Winant, John, 157, 232 (n. 42)
Windward Shipping v. American Radio Assn., 183
Wirt, William, 53
Wobblies. *See* Industrial Workers of the World
Women seafarers, 175, 198
Wood, Fernando, 55, 213 (n. 95)
Wood ships, U.S. use of, 32
Worker discontent, postwar rise in, 174–75, 234–35 (n. 7)
Working class, in American literature, 38–39
Working conditions: for Asian seamen, ILO on, 154–55; flags of convenience and, 169; for officers vs. non-officers, 145, 174; sanitation in, 109–10; U.S. reform of, 94, 109–10
Working hours, ILO standards for, 152–59, 166

Workmen's Compensation Act of 1897 (Britain), 86
"Work-to-rule" tactics, 191
World Federation of Trade Unions (WFTU), 178, 181
World Trade Organization (WTO), 240 (n. 97)
World War I: buildup to, 221 (n. 48); decline of U.S. shipping and, 34; fears of revolution after, 149, 150, 229–30 (n. 13); impact on international unions, 135–41; and La Follette Act, 113; wages before and after, 138–40
World War II: Asian seamen in, 168–69, 224 (n. 95), 233 (n. 71); British seamen in, 165–66; decline of U.S. shipping and, 34; fall of postwar order after, 172–77; flags of convenience in, 179; Indian seamen in, 224 (n. 95); and La Follette Act, 113; unions in, 164–67; U.S. seamen in, 164
Wreck of the Golden Mary, The (Dickens and Collins), 41
Wright, James S., 205 (n. 35)
Wright, Robert, 205 (n. 47)
WTO. *See* World Trade Organization
Wu, Chau Chit, 155
Wyndham, George, 89

Xenophobia: in international unionism, 131–35; in U.S. maritime reform, 106–9, 162–64, 224 (n. 95)

Yom Kippur War (1973), 176
Yulee, David, 50

Zaalberg, C. J. P., 159
Zolberg, Aristide R., 18

Franklin Pierce University
00194534